D1604394

ANATOMY OF A ROBOT

Literature, Cinema, and the
Cultural Work of Artificial People

DESPINA KAKOUDAKI

RUTGERS UNIVERSITY PRESS
New Brunswick, New Jersey, and London

Library of Congress Cataloging-in-Publication Data
Kakoudaki, Despina.
    Anatomy of a robot : literature, cinema, and the cultural work of artificial people /
Despina Kakoudaki.
        pages   cm
    Includes bibliographical references and index.
        ISBN 978-0-8135-6216-2 (hardcover : alk. paper) — ISBN 978-0-8135-6215-5 (pbk. :
alk. paper) — ISBN 978-0-8135-6217-9 (e-book)
        1. Robots in literature. 2. Cyborgs in literature. 3. Robots in motion pictures. 4.
Cyborgs in motion pictures. I. Title.
    PN56.R56K35 2014
    809'.93356—dc23
    2013029877

A British Cataloging-in-Publication record for this book is available from the British
Library.

Visit our website: http://rutgerspress.rutgers.edu

Manufactured in the United States of America

For Linda

CONTENTS

ACKNOWLEDGMENTS

For a long while this book resembled an extensive and odd collection of stories, images, film references, and popular culture trivia that seemed to belong together, at least to me, but for no apparent reason and in no visible order. I have been incredibly fortunate in encountering people who saw potential in these alluring scraps and urged me to continue fitting things together. At the University of California at Berkeley, Linda Williams was an invaluable mentor and inspiring friend. Her thinking on race, melodrama, and American sentimental traditions informs my sense of how texts reflect but also affect culture, and I have found her advice and friendship indispensible over the years. Once I decided to approach contemporary films and stories through an emphasis on deep narrative and discursive structures, I recognized how formative reading archaic poetry with Leslie Kurke has been for me. Her strategies for the close reading of ancient texts and contexts course through my work in unexpected ways. Working with Nancy Ruttenburg, Carolyn Porter, and Charles Altieri was always exciting and illuminating, and I thank them for their generosity and support. It was an honor to work and teach with the late Barbara Johnson at Harvard University, whose fascination with perennial questions of vessels and contents matched my own, and to benefit there from the intellectual energy of Jan Ziolkowski, Eric Rentschler, Marjorie Garber, Robb Moss, Alfred Guzzetti, Ross McElwee, J. D. Connor, Brad Epps, and David Rodowick. My thanks to Steve Owen, Svetlana Boym, Tom Conley, and James Engell, who read early drafts of this book with patience and generosity when I was at Harvard. At American University, I am deeply grateful to Richard Sha, Jonathan Loesberg, David Pike, Erik Dussere, Jeff Middents, Deborah Payne, Fiona Brideoake, and Michael Wenthe for their thoughtful responses to recent versions. I am indebted to Marleen Barr for her support of this book when it was still in the ether, and to Sherryl Vint and Teresa Heffernan for helping me find its final form with their incisive comments and constructive criticism. My students at the University of California at Berkeley, at Harvard University, and at American University have challenged and enriched my approach to cinema, literature, and popular culture. This book would not have been possible without them.

I received research funding for this project from the University of California at Berkeley, research support from Harvard University, a fellowship from the National Endowment for the Humanities, and research leave from American University. I am grateful to Dean Kay Mussell and Dean Peter Starr at the College of Arts and Sciences at American University for their support of my work, and for facilitating the publication of images through a Mellon Fund Grant. My thanks go also to archivists and librarians at the New York Public Library for the Performing Arts, the Beinecke Rare Book and Manuscript Library at Yale University, the U.S. National Library of Medicine, Dover Press, Todd Ifft at Photofest, and Caroline Junier and Claude-Alain Künzi at the Musée d'Art et d'Histoire in Neuchâtel, Switzerland. My thanks go also to Jeremy Mayer, for allowing me to use his beautiful sculpture made of reassembled antique typewriter parts for the cover of the book.

Parts of this project were presented at the Southern California Colloquium in History of Science, Medicine, and Technology at UCLA, the Humanities Center at Harvard, the Croxton Lecture Series at Amherst College, the Harvard Graduate School of Design, the Maryland Institute of Technology Public Lectures Program, and the Maryland Colloquium on the History of Technology, Science, and Environment. I am deeply grateful to Leslie Mitchner, my editor at Rutgers University Press, for her invaluable advice and commitment to this project, and to Lisa Boyajian, Marilyn Campbell, and Pippa Letsky for their care in bringing the book to publication.

I thank my father, Ioannis Kakoudakis whose intellectual curiosity and enthusiasm for writing and research I have always admired, and my dear mother, Konstantina Kakoudaki, who died as I was completing this project and who is with me always. I am grateful to my sister, Georgina Kakoudaki, for her exuberant intelligence and her lively interest in this project over the years. John Chioles at the University of Athens, Greece, was a primary instigator for my critical work, as was the intellectual companionship of Costas Canakis, George Kyriazis, Andreas Karatsolis, Vicki Chatzopoulou, and Vassiliki Tsitsopoulou. My work would never have evolved as it has without long conversations and debates at Berkeley and after with Elliott Colla, Faith Barrett, Jeff Akeley, and Don Gilbert. I was fortunate to meet Christine Palmer during my very first months in the United States. Her friendship sustained me through long years of work, and her infinite capacity for analyzing the paradoxes of American culture informs many passages of this book. For their love and unfailing support my heartfelt thanks go also to my friends Rose Marie Mouzakis Richardson and Terry Richardson, Viola Voris, Delfina Voris, Janet and Bob Nicholas, Laura and Stephen Havlek, Kimberly Nicholas, Michael and Holly Wagner, Paul Fitzgerald, Michael McDermott, Paul Reinert, Katrine Bosley, Julie Des Jardins, Chris Bowley, Nancy Mitchnick, Sharon Harper, Dan DeGooyer, Carrie Lambert-Beatty, Colin Beatty, Rebecca McLennan, Rebecca Groves, Elena Maria, Becky Smith, Jeff Hopkins, Ginny and Randy Cohen, Jonathan Kahana, Jennifer Horne, Max Friedman, and Katharina Vester. Part of the research for this book was conducted in the beautiful town of Nafplion, Greece, where the staff at the Public Central

Library "Palamidis" and dear friends Sophia Dima, Christos Dimas, and Panagiotis and Sophia Katsigianni made all the difference. My sincere thanks to my colleagues and friends Charles Larson, Roberta Rubenstein, David Keplinger, Amanda Berry, John Hyman, Keith Leonard, Cynthia Bair Van Dam, Stephanie Grant, Madhavi Menon, Jonathan Gil Harris, Lindsey Green-Sims, Amy Green-Sims, Leah Johnson, Trisha Reichler, Anita Sherman, and Patrick Kelly Joyner.

This book is dedicated with love to Linda Voris, always the first and most eager to listen, and the most astute and demanding reader. Thank you.

ANATOMY OF A ROBOT

INTRODUCTION
Robot Anatomies

Stories and films featuring robots, cyborgs, androids, or automata often stage scenes that depict opening the artificial body: someone ejects a face plate, pulls back artificial skin, removes a skull covering, reveals a chest panel, lifts clothing, or pushes a button, thereby rendering visible the insides of the fascinating human-like machine. The interior space may include flashing computer lights, elaborate wiring, metal surfaces, old-fashioned cogs and wheels, or sophisticated electronic equipment. Sometimes the inside is stark in its clean modern efficiency, a gleaming metal box, but it can also be gooey, shocking, or opaque, display a minimalist emptiness, or reveal incongruous skeletal structures that seem unlikely as weight-bearing supports. In their technological interpretation of anatomical structures and process, such narrative moments enact a foundational gesture of revelation as well as of implicit seduction, suggesting that the act of opening will deliver new meanings, that the inside might explain the outside, or that in contrast to the fleshy mysteries of the organic body the robot's interior will be understandable, logical, or orderly.

Familiar though it may be, what does this impulse toward anatomy reveal? And what do we expect to find when we look inside a robot? The act of opening cannot help but promise clarity or understanding, even when it unveils a confusing interface behind the removable face, fascinating but misleading surfaces inside the body, and pseudo-scientific or fetishistic textures throughout. Anatomical gestures imply an expectation of equivalence between artificial and organic bodies, evident even in negative descriptions, such as "it had flashing lights instead of eyes" or "there was a speaker where its mouth should have been." Even when the robot's interior promises to have no secrets and no embarrassing fluids, or when its mechanical efficiency inspires the wish for replaceable body parts and the absence of pain, the transposition of the materiality of the human

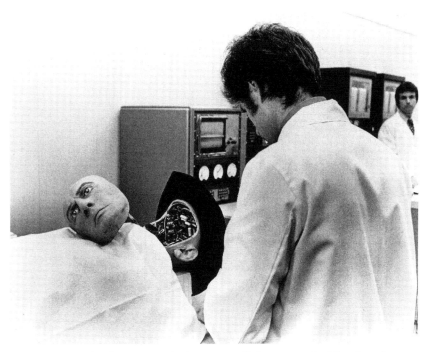

FIGURE 1 The cowboy hat stays on, the face comes off. Opening up the "Gunslinger" android (Yul Brynner) for repairs in *Westworld* (Michael Crichton, 1973). MGM/ Photofest. © MGM

body to these artificial analogues remains uncanny. Looking inside a mechanical body projects the desire for meaning onto a space designed to hold little insight. And looking inside the organic body is no simple matter, either: while anatomical investigation stages the analytical quests and fantasies of objectivity that characterize Western thought, it also brings these pursuits into confrontation with the enduring enigmas of the body, the limits of incision and evidence, and the limits of vision.[1] If in anatomies of the organic body we face the mysteries of blood, flesh, nerves and fluids, the prospect of health and disease, and more recently, microscopic ambiguity, genetic complexity, and protean adaptability, in imaginary anatomies of robots and cyborgs we reveal our attachment to the body's mysteries even in contexts that promise to dispel them.

Such complex fantasmatic relationships between real and artificial bodies, the fantasies associated with artificiality, and the conventions of representing mechanical or constructed people are the subject of this book. Enacting a metaphorical version of the anatomical impulse I have described, I also imagine that my project entails a gesture of opening up and looking inside—not inside a single robot or cyborg figure but inside the cultural discourse of the artificial person. And as with all anatomical gestures, this discursive analysis delivers new insights about the cultural and narrative tradition of the artificial person as well as new paradoxes. Immediately recognizable, culturally ubiquitous, emotionally evocative, and politically resonant, robots, androids, cyborgs, and automata need no introduction. Yet their very familiarity obscures their participation in culture. What accounts for our perennial fascination with such figures? And how do their stories work?

In the context of this study, an artificial person is an imaginary being who is partly or fully anthropomorphic, mechanical, or constructed from a variety of technological or natural materials and considered autonomous, animated, or capable of being animated. A brief listing of memorable fictional characters would include the monster in Mary Shelley's *Frankenstein* (1818), the beautiful automaton Olympia in E.T.A. Hoffmann's "The Sandman" (1816), the robotic Maria from Fritz Lang's *Metropolis* (1927), Isaac Asimov's many robots and androids in *I, Robot* (1950), Robby the Robot in *Forbidden Planet* (Fred M. Wilcox, 1956), the fantasy-fulfilling androids of *Westworld* (Michael Crichton, 1973), the artificial women of *The Stepford Wives* (Bryan Forbes, 1975), the thoughtful Replicants of *Blade Runner* (Ridley Scott, 1982), the relentless T-800 cyborg in *The Terminator* (James Cameron, 1984), the chrome Cylons of the original *Battlestar Galactica* (Glen A. Larson, 1978–1979), and the sexy human-looking Cylon models of the reimagined series (Ron Moore, 2003–2009). Artificial people may be mechanical, but they may also be engineered through chemical or biotechnological means, cloned, altered, or reconstructed. While such modes of production reference technological realities, actual artificial people are truly imaginary, creatures of fiction, the imagination, and the magic of representational media. And yet despite their unreality they seem to inform a host of cultural domains and debates, participating in a dense web of interactions between fiction and reality in contemporary culture. What is the relationship, for example, between twenty-first-century research in robotics and the fantasy of the ideal robot, as this fantasy was honed in fictions, plays, and films of the twentieth century? Why is it that new versions of the artificial person in science fiction literature and film cannot escape many of the representational patterns of older texts? Why do stories of artificial people return to the same arsenal of tropes and plotlines decade after decade? While a wide range of theoretical and cultural domains, popular fantasies, technological debates, and scientific research may refer to fictional artificial people, the literary and cinematic tradition that informs their cultural meanings has not been fully codified. Despite, or indeed because of, its cultural ubiquity, the discourse of the artificial person is often used to rehash stereotypes of these figures, a tendency to be examined in this book.

In order to investigate the meanings and cultural uses of the figure of the artificial person my project follows three fundamental insights. First, artificial people are not isolated instances of a modern literary or cinematic fascination but instead participate in a transhistorical discursive continuum that both informs the modern sensibility and predates it. Even in high-tech iterations, artificial people return to a literary and philosophical heritage that is centuries old, one that lends its apocryphal aura to new texts and figures. Second, in order to understand the operations of this discourse we need to address what seems most consistent or even stereotypical about the representation of artificial people. This morphology of the robot tale allows us to recognize the foundational logic deployed in their stories and to revise misconceptions about their meanings and impact. And third, the powerful aura of the artificial person does not depend, as current technoculture critics propose, on its relation to an impending reality but on its fundamental unreality. As imaginary beings, artificial people need not conform to current states of scientific knowledge, technological possibility, or ontological reality. But the unreal is both superbly dynamic and culturally reflective: when it is possible to imagine any type of being or type of body, then the beings and bodies imagined express a range of cultural expectations, projections, and desires. Artificial people are useful cultural fictions. One of the rewards of tracing the historical provenance and textual versatility of the artificial person is that it elucidates one of their chief cultural functions in modernity: their participation in a political and existential negotiation of what it means to be human.

Although often associated with technologies of the twentieth and twenty-first centuries, fantasies of constructed or mechanical people recur throughout the modern era since the Renaissance and feature prominently in both Enlightenment and post-Enlightenment worlds. In addition to fictional robots or cyborgs, historical examples include a range of figures that are both artificial and animated, from statues or paintings that come to life to ominous or uncannily active objects, machinery that seems purposeful, and puppets or dolls that move independently. The foundational element of these storylines is a fantasy of animation in which inanimate objects come to life, if only in the imagination, on the page, or on the screen. Intimately connected to the power of representation and language, the fantasy of animation is the oldest structural element of the discourse of the artificial person and conceptually aligns even the most technological artificial beings with an ancient representational vocabulary. The earliest origin stories of human civilization stage the beginning of life in terms of a fantasy of animation, whereby a divine presence or god creates people by animating inanimate matter. As one type of object we can imagine coming to life, mechanical entities such as robots, androids, and cyborgs are thus related to the proverbial oldest thing in the book.

I explore this fantasy of animation in chapter 1, using a discussion of Mary Shelley's *Frankenstein* to trace how versions of the artificial birth found in ancient myth and folklore connect to their counterparts in contemporary fiction and film. While ancient patterns persist to the present, there are also important differences between ancient and modern animating fantasies. In ancient contexts a divine presence breathes life into inanimate natural materials such as wood, clay, or stone, and this miracle proves the existence of the divine figure and explains the emergence of life. Modern depictions of animation revolve around technological animating agents and spectacular bodies. In place of a deity, it is a novel invention or process such as electricity that facilitates the transition, and since it is invisible to the eye, it is perceived expressly as it animates inanimate matter. No longer composed of natural elements, the animated body is a fetishistic collection of whatever materials seem remarkable at a particular time, from clockwork to trains, industrial machinery, computing networks, fiber optics, or isolated cells. The moment of animation changes as well, from a taboo or ritual scene that must remain secret to a transformation rendered spectacular through elaborate visual technologies and special effects.

In historical terms, the technological appropriation of the ancient fantasy of animation occurred gradually over the eighteenth and nineteenth centuries and resulted in an understanding of animation that seems self-evident or vernacular to us now. However, the fantasy of animation contains and expresses various kinds of thinking about technology. Animating scenes allow for the representation of technology as a life-giving force: since inanimate matter is transformed into live matter in such a context, the technological process that serves as the agent of animation acquires the supernatural patina of divine animations. Technological animations grant visibility and a certain level of coherence to complex scientific processes, giving material existence to animating agents that are as ineffable and unexplainable as the soul or the divine in ancient animating scenes. Without explaining what these entities are or how they work, the animating scene offers visible proof of their presence by staging their effect on an inanimate body. Animating scenes are thus perfectly suited for technological adaptations in the modern era, not because the technological processes used or implied in modern stories are any more real or powerful than ancient magic but because the animating scene proves the efficacy of the animating agent regardless of how invisible, ineffable, or imaginary that agent may be.

In its negation of conception, gestation, and growth, the animating scene transforms the processes of childbirth into a fantasy of the construction of adult bodies, replacing the vulnerability of childhood with a prefabricated or indestructible adulthood. As a result, the body of the artificial person contains excess meanings about bodies, machines, and materials. Fetishistic treatments of texture and composition in both ancient and modern stories attest to the enduring allure of metal surfaces and mechanicity. In chapter 2, I explore the ways in which recurrent fantasies of the mechanical body reflect long-standing conceptual alignments between bodies and machines, evident in the use of mechanical metaphors and analogies to model or explain the interior and the different functions of the human body. Since antiquity, the lungs have been described as bellows, the arm as a lever, the eye as a camera obscura, and so on. In anatomical drawings, the association of bones and muscles to simple machines creates analogies in the service of explanation, with the premise that we understand the body as we understand simple machines, and vice versa. Careful historical analysis reveals that far from regarding the human body and technological entities as antithetical, fantasies of the artificial body involve complex analogical and allegorical interpretations of the body's processes and structures.

Following this focus on the ancient roots of the discourse of the artificial person, in the second half of the book I trace the modern appropriation and redefinition of these ancient conceptual patterns. In modern contexts, animating scenes enable existential and politically resonant narratives of awakening, emancipation, and the legal recognition of personhood. This interpretation of animation and mechanism is the focus of chapter 3, in which I explore the deployment of mechanization and animation as political registers. Responding to the focus on legal and social definitions of personhood and citizenship in the modern era, stories about the animation of objects alert us to the social contingency of categories of being by presenting elaborate allegories of political disenfranchisement and emancipation as scenes of de-animation and reanimation. Such tales highlight the instability in concepts of personhood and remind us of the conferral of

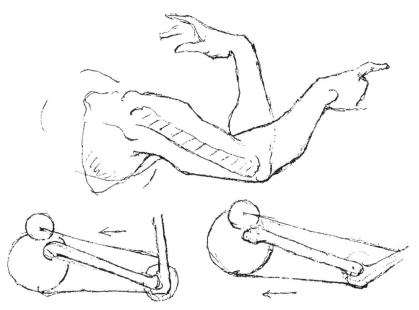

FIGURE 2 The human body through mechanical analogies: the shoulder and arm as a simple machine. George B. Bridgeman, "Arm and Forearm" in *The Human Machine: The Anatomical Structure and Mechanism of the Human Body* (New York: Dover, 1939), 42. © Dover

human status to slaves, serfs, workers, women, natives, immigrants, children, the disabled, and the disenfranchised among us. In depicting scenes of objectification and subjectification, the discourse of the artificial person combines political and existential questions. In these fictions the artificial person may be identified easily, particularly when its physical appearance marks it as nonhuman, but what can ensure that real people are, in fact, real?

This paranoid and existential dimension is my focus in chapter 4. In the twentieth and twenty-first centuries, the discourse of the artificial person is often deployed to demarcate the limits of the human, to distinguish between real and artificial people, and at the same time to interrogate these boundaries. The trope of artificiality offers a powerful existential register: we may describe ourselves as robots or androids when we feel dismayed by limited choices, dehumanized by repressive social and political institutions, oppressed by repetition or conformity, when we simply do not feel "real" to ourselves, or when we fail to recognize the reality and humanity of others.

In summary, then, this project examines what I consider as the earliest, most persistent, and most dispersed elements in the discourse of the artificial person: the fantasy of animation, and its narrative transformation into fantasies of an artificial birth; the fantasy of the mechanical body, and the use of bodies and machines as analogues of each other; the association of technology with slavery, which leads to the consistent depiction of artificial people as slaves and the political interpretation of the animating fantasy as a process of subjectification; and the interpretation of artificiality as an existential trope, which questions what it means to be human and critiques conformity and acquiescence. The trope of the artificial person reveals an intricate cultural deployment of allegory: animating fantasies stage ways to both establish and traverse sublime oppositions and facilitate the depiction of radical changes of status. We use artificial people in order to explore the difference between animate and inanimate matter, to embody in our representational media the linguistic and imaginative processes of bringing objects to life, to model and explain the mechanicity of the body, and to express our sense of the meanings of selfhood and political inclusion. In this book I explore the dynamic ways in which artificial people participate in ontological, political, and existential debates stemming from their unique relationship to embodiment, their complex position between animate and inanimate matter, between life and death, or between person and object.

BEFORE AND AFTER THE CYBORG

By treating the tradition of the artificial person as a discourse that is ancient, allegorical, politically invested, and not necessarily technological, I depart from certain contemporary theoretical trends. Stated axiomatically, my claim is that we do not grasp the full impact of the discourse of the artificial person we use so fluidly in contemporary culture, partly because we take this literary and cinematic tradition for granted. Although fictions of artificial people figure in a range of theories, informing Donna Haraway's concept of the cyborg or N. Katherine Hayles's analysis of the posthuman, these philosophical interpretations tend to reference literary and cinematic texts but quickly move on. Contemporary cultural uses of artificial people follow a migratory interdisciplinary trajectory that oscillates between fiction and reality, between actual experiments and speculative fictions, and between theoretical concepts and their presumed impending reality in technoculture. We are in the twenty-first century, after all, and robots are about to become real, as they have been for decades. But while advanced research projects in universities and companies as well as cultural theories and popular science texts herald the imminent arrival of pervasive robotics, this promise limits the potential and varied meanings of the robotic paradigm and conflates the relationship between real and imagined technologies and cultural conditions.

This confusion is most visible in the implicit presence of robotic characters within critical theories of technoculture.[2] Inspired by Donna Haraway's groundbreaking essay "A Manifesto for Cyborgs," at least in part, these approaches aim to explain the intensification of our relationship to information technology after World War II.[3] Using the cyborg concept to counter the patriarchal tenets of heroic science, Haraway describes the cyborg as an articulation of new possibilities for identity based on three premises: that it exceeds the boundaries between human and machine, it resists the hegemonic premises of "organistic" science, and it lacks a gender, a genealogy, and thus an investment in master narratives and myths of origin. Whereas in 1985 Haraway defined the cyborg as "a creature of social reality as well as a creature of fiction," ten years later, and in obvious reaction to the cultural explosion of the term, she implied a more historical and realistic origin for the cyborg as "a fusion of the organic and the technical forged in particular, historical, cultural practices."[4] For Haraway, the cyborg articulates a new social reality of interactivity with technology, but in the expansion and simplification of her approach that followed, cyborgs also become a shortcut for utopian or apocalyptic visions of gender, technology, and the body, with increasingly virtual technologies serving as a metaphysical site for extending or exploding the limits of the embodied self. The cultural vernacular of cyborg theory depicts cyborgs as actual contemporary historical entities, with most residents of the Western world qualifying as cyborgs insofar as we are inoculated against diseases, eat genetically modified food, and use computer systems connected through wireless devices.[5]

Similarly, N. Katherine Hayles discusses the posthuman as both the precondition of human embodiment, with the body identified as "the original prosthesis," and as the precondition of our seamless merger with computer networks and virtual technologies. In the posthuman, Hayles proposes, "there are no essential differences or absolute demarcations between bodily existence and computer simulation, cybernetic mechanism and biological organism, robot teleology and human goals."[6] The concept of the posthuman refers to contemporary modes of subjectivity, highlighting the constructed and embedded nature of the self within technological, social, and political contexts, but, as with the cyborg concept, may also express vague, apocalyptic, and transcendentalist aspirations for moving beyond the limits of the body or beyond matter altogether. In both Haraway and Hayles, the relationship between people and technology is articulated in terms of a redefined and appropriated figure or the artificial person, the cyborg/the posthuman, removed from fiction and solidly recontextualized in technological reality. In a sense this is a form of analogical thinking that capitalizes on what artificial people are supremely able to embody: hybridity and a kind of betweenness in terms of ontological and political status.

Following this trend, there are some commonalities in how technoculture critics analyze the post–World War II landscape, combining the analysis of advanced research projects with publicity stunts, science fiction literature and film, as well as texts from other disciplines and presenting the resulting storyline as an explanatory account of real technological conditions. Both Haraway and Hayles offer such trajectories, and I will too here, if only as an example of the limits of this method. My own version of such a storyline begins in 1939, when, among other engineering wonders, visitors to the 1939 New York World's Fair were treated to Elektro, a robotic man created by Westinghouse engineers that answered audience questions and performed, or pretended to perform, the advertised role of the robot of the future, a helper for household chores. Elektro was so popular that Westinghouse soon added Sparko, a robot dog, to the display, a modern pet for the modern family. The word "robot" was only nineteen years old. Coined in 1920 by Karel Čapek for his play *R.U.R.* (*Rossum's Universal Robots*), "robot" is derived from the Czech word *robota* (labor), linking robots forever to servitude, enslavement, and revolt.[7] The internationally successful play features human-like artificial people, created by the scientist Rossum to replace human workers and reduce labor costs. But while they are programmed to be compliant, by the end of the play the Robots revolt, kill the factory scientists, and make plans to take over the world.[8] By contrast, the Westinghouse robot was designed as a gentle giant and promoted a positive and nonthreatening relationship to technology. Photos of the World's Fair show the mechanical wonder standing on a raised platform, in the company of a human engineer who poses questions and listens to Elektro's stilted responses.

If he visited the Fair, Isaac Asimov—who, as it happens, was also nineteen years old in 1939 and living in New York—most likely found this display of

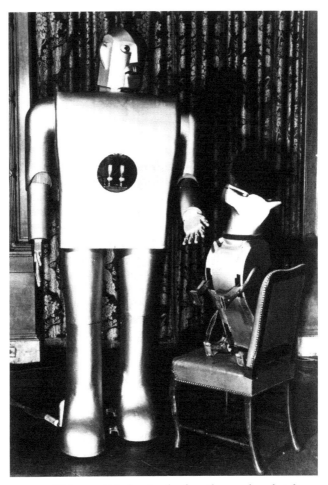

FIGURE 3 Elektro and his dog, Sparko, from the popular robot display by Westinghouse at the New York World's Fair, 1939 and 1940. Photofest

mechanical action irresistible. The robot stories he wrote in the 1940s, later collected with the provocative title *I, Robot*, develop a long evolutionary horizon for robotic humanity. Asimov's robots begin as gentle mechanical giants, become indistinguishable from humans (a robot is elected mayor of New York), and eventually take over the world through a vast network of computer-controlled automated factories. Asimov's stories carry echoes of the actual technological developments of the era in developing fields such as feedback and control systems, communication, information, and computer technologies. While earlier machine age representations of automation depicted vast, surgically clean environments controlled by powerful remote users, human-machine interaction emerges as a key research focus in the post–World War II era. The hierarchical model in which the engineer decides or pushes a button and the machine performs gives way to a new interactive model of feedback loops, adjusted calculations over time, and complex processes inconceivable without the aid of flexible information systems. Summarized by Norbert Wiener in the late 1940s, this new science of information, control, feedback, and human-machine coordination is named cybernetics, after the Greek word *kubernētēs* (governor/helmsman).[9]

The relationship between users and machines becomes more intimate still with the emergence of complex electronic applications in the 1960s, and is theorized and partly mythologized in the figure of the Cyborg (short for cybernetic organism), a term coined in 1960 by Manfred E. Clynes and Nathan S. Kline.[10] Initially a reference to astronauts whose very survival depends on the technology that envelops them, the Cyborg posits a human body permeated by technologies that enhance its abilities and change its perception of the world. After Haraway revisits and appropriates the cyborg concept in the 1980s and 1990s, cyborgs become shorthand for a variety of human-machine relationships and are now frequently associated with apocalyptic visions of technological humanity. By the end of the 1990s, innovations in robotics and computer technologies seem to deliver on the promise of the automated factories of science fiction, and of the wired world glimpsed in the World's Fair and ardently described in cyberpunk novels. Sparko reemerges in the form of AIBO, a mechanical dog developed by Sony.[11] Honda engineers present a remarkable mechanical prototype for modeling bipedal walking techniques, in a research project titled Advanced Step in Innovative Mobility.[12] Launched officially in 2000, the human-form robot embodying this research travels to "meet" politicians in the United Nations and schoolchildren around the world and is known by a symbolic nickname that resonates beyond the acronym of its research project: ASIMO.

In this account, I trace the interaction between a play from the 1920s, a mechanical performance in a real event (the 1939 World's Fair), its presumed imaginative representation in science fiction, all against the backdrop of developments in actual research. The technologies of the war years and their cultural ramifications are quickly subsumed under a conceptual reorganization that promises a new science, cybernetics, and produces the cyborg as its symbolic form, while a robot, ASIMO, appears as the culmination of a process that combines reality and fiction. In the contemporary critical landscape, accounts such as this are familiar and admittedly satisfying. And yet, this tale is not only inconsistent but also renders its inconsistencies invisible. For example, with his Robots, Čapek exposes the dehumanization of workers and soldiers through capitalist corporate and state practices in the mechanized factories and battlefields of the 1910s. Allegorical representatives of the industrial working class, Čapek's Robots stage a thinly veiled proletarian revolution. By contrast, the 1939 World's Fair

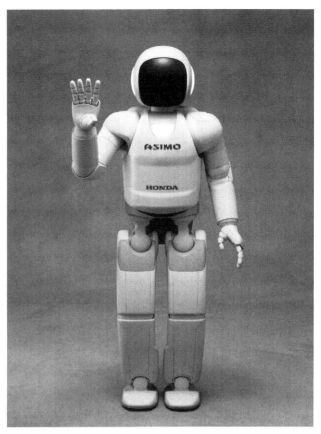

FIGURE 4 ASIMO, the Honda Humanoid Robot, has been a consistent presence in the company's advertising campaigns. Credit: http://www.world.honda.com/ASIMO/

commemorates the success of just those corporate practices that lead to the automation of industrial processes and war theaters. Defined by its allegiance to corporate platforms and products, the World's Fair is not an exotic international showcase but a vehicle of consumerist propaganda. Elektro may promise a vision of the future, but in fact the robotic man is not a technological marvel. Whatever its cultural meanings, his introduction at the Fair coincides both with the bloodiest and most mechanized war the world had yet witnessed and with a technological moment in which both government and commercial interests in the United States initiate secret proprietary research practices that will revolutionize the future far faster than any of the futuristic spectacles at the Fair.

What I hope to have exposed is the ways in which this sort of storyline, commonplace in the discourse of the artificial person, oscillates perniciously between reality and fiction without sufficient regard to historical context or textual provenance. Despite the historical and ideological divergence of these texts and events, we can trace a lineage among them because of the structuring presence of the discourse of the artificial, mechanical, or constructed person. Both the mechanical constructs (Elektro and ASIMO, for example) and the imaginary concepts, fictional robots, and theoretical cyborgs appear here as versions of a long-standing imaginary companion to human civilization: an artificial person that seems to come to life and, in its awakening, transcends the boundaries between inanimate and animate matter, embodying both technological and social innovation. As my quick tracing of a trajectory from Elektro to ASIMO suggests, the mere presence of mechanical people in a narrative delivers a technological promise, while their public performances display the successful harnessing of (and coexistence with) advanced technology.

Even though their technological aura is unmistakable, however, the relationship of constructed people to actual technologies is less clear. I focus on Elektro because, despite his advertised usefulness, he is not technologically avant-garde. Not only does Elektro not deliver on a future horizon of being-with-technology, but his clunky motions and limited actions were already antique in 1939, when scientists were splitting the atom and automating missiles and anti-aircraft weapons. Instead of embodying innovation, the star of Westinghouse's "Hall of Electrical Living" celebrates home appliances and electricity, old technologies by this time. To see the future in action, visitors to the Fair should have preferred the no-frills RCA exhibit, featuring UF radios and the first television sets—but these displays were not as popular as the Westinghouse gimmicks. What then is the attraction of Elektro as a figure? If the audience is not actually witnessing a technological feat, what is it that enthralls them?

To better understand the attraction of this event and the continued appeal of artificial people, we need to amend some assumptions about them and their cultural presence. Despite its campy simplicity, Elektro's routine is rooted in long-standing traditions of representation and performance, which it reactivates in the present and from which it draws allegorical power. To fully explain the ramifications of such performances we need to explore the attraction of anthropomorphic figures in general, the special allure of mechanical complexity, the resonance of gestures of explanation and revelation, the pleasure of witnessing nonhuman autonomous action, the oracular power of the engineer's invitation to have inanimate matter move and speak, and the echo of much older performative styles in the display of mechanical wonders for an audience. Taken together, such diverse cultural contexts inform the discursive continuum of artificial people, a network of philosophical and historical meanings that exist beyond the limits of a specific event. Put simply, figures such as Elektro and ASIMO are attractive not because of their "newness" per se but because they resonate with the gestures of older mechanical performances and, in turn, participate in the

evolution of what such performances mean. They also provide a safe setting for
the projection of an array of beliefs about technology, sentience, aliveness, animation, objecthood, personhood, and so on.

We certainly need histories of science and technology that can elucidate
the emergence of contemporary technologies in the laboratories and military
research projects of the war years, the evolution of informational models since
the 1950s, and the impact of these transformations on contemporary culture. But
why are figurations of fictional artificial people needed in such contexts? Why
is a science-fictional allegory of artificiality relevant to such investigations? In
their limited historical perspective and apocalyptic tendencies, theories that
announce the end of the human, the transcendence of the body, or the absolute merger between people and technologies often use fiction in order to make
reality claims. What I propose in this book is that we need to revise this tendency and begin by accepting that artificial people as figures owe much of their
aura and cultural presence to a textual and cultural tradition that has little to do
with technological actuality. As fields of study, cybernetics and robotics inform
but do not limit the imaginary presence of the cyborg or robot and have little
to do with the popular depiction of such figures in fiction, film, advertisement,
journalism, and other media. Even though it is heightened by symbolic connection with actual technologies, the appeal of artificial people is independent of
such technologies and their deployment in the real world. And it remains the
case that the special effects used in cinematic portrayals of robots and cyborgs
may be the only future-looking aspect of these retrogressive and apocalyptic
representations. Clearly, sensationalist approaches to an encroaching roboticism respond to the cultural upheavals of the last decades and the uncertainty
caused by rapid computer-related innovation.[13] The idea that cyborg bodies
are somehow beyond gender registers an existentialist wistfulness, as does the
desire for an exit from the limits of the self and its historical liabilities. Finally,
the tendency to merge realities and fictions leads to anachronistic methodolo-
gies in which concepts such as the cyborg and the posthuman are transferred
whole cloth to the study of older traditions, bringing along the dangers of evolutionary determinism (everything leads to the cyborg) and obscuring historical perspectives that may challenge contemporary assumptions.

As my critique of the technocultural appropriations of fictional artificial people implies, I propose reexamining how to include the metaphor of the artificial
or mechanical person in technological discussions. We might seek to avoid or
at least be self-reflexive about the tendency to use fantasmatic figures to fuel a
pervasive desire for neologism, apocalyptic proclamations, and facile historical
links. Instead, we can engage such critical challenges through attention to the
most important aspects of the discourse of the artificial person: its transhistorical presence, its interdisciplinary expansiveness, and its fundamental unreality.

STORIES AND OBJECTS

Artificial people may not have "legitimate" parents, but they have a rather large extended family. Once we set out on a historical trail for the provenance and ancestry of modern artificial people, we encounter an overwhelming array of relevant figures. The discourse of the mechanical or constructed person is admittedly pervasive, but contemporary critics and readers are also somewhat accumulative in their habits, more interested in collecting examples than making distinctions among them. Scientific and pseudo-scientific publications, ancient texts on occult magic, and aesthetic treatises on the ability of statues to express emotion in stillness all include elements of the discourse. How do we distinguish between an anachronistic impulse to fold such examples into a single historical narrative and the need to recognize relationships across time?

If the distribution and proliferation of figures and contexts is the first problem of a historical account, the second is the self-obviousness of the enterprise. A historian need not look far to find ancestors of artificial people. On the contrary, unmotivated and largely unchallenged listings presented as genealogies are easily available in books and online. What used to be the short list of such figures comprised of important robot, android, cyborg, computer, or virtual characters in science fiction and film may now include mythological figures from antiquity and various technological contraptions both real and imaginary. Stories of animation seem to relate seamlessly to each other, revisiting tropes and scenes in virtual independence from temporal and cultural limitations. Perhaps because anthropomorphic constructions share a common referent in the human body, human-form entities also inspire evolutionary narratives in which all manner of figures can be precursors to robots.[14]

What has been characteristic of these explorations in recent years is their aura of technological realism, with ancient myths described as dreams of future technology. Contemporary critics sometimes see automata everywhere. Scenes at Hephaistos's workshop in book 18 of the *Iliad* deliver self-moving tripods and golden handmaidens—both potentially automatic in recent accounts.[15] Stories of Talos, the mythical metal man who guarded the island of Crete, present him as a man made of bronze and constructed by Hephaistos or, alternatively, as the last of the men of the Bronze Age. Now he also appears as an automaton.[16] Ancient philosophical anecdotes about statues made by Daidalos, another legendary craftsman, mention binding these artifacts lest they run away. Were they self-moving automata too? Statues, mechanical experiments, political allegories, and philosophical jokes are fused into an account of the ever-present desire to create artificial humanity or the ever-present desire to create modern automated tools. Scholars seek to complicate these popular tendencies. Sylvia Berryman, for example, challenges the inclusion of ancient figures from myth into scientific narratives, while William Newman's work on medieval and Renaissance alchemy elucidates premodern definitions of nature and artifice.[17] In an effort to link older philosophical models with contemporary technoculture, Allison Muri uses the cyborg concept to explore notions of man-machine merger in the Enlightenment.[18]

Yet despite such critical interventions, the relationship of past to present fantasies remains open to anachronistic modern assumptions. In addition to the realist trends of cyborg and posthuman discourse mentioned above, the historical mapping of artificial people is affected by another important feature of the contemporary critical landscape. This is the shift—away from traditional literary styles of analysis that prioritize texts and philosophical traditions and mobilize modes of explanation that are attuned to metaphor, allegory, and double meanings—to a style of analysis that prioritizes objects, technologies, and scientific processes. Studies in material culture, "thing criticism," and histories of mediation and technology elucidate the past by focusing on our complex relationship to objects.[19] But when it comes to robots and automata, especially in popular science approaches, research in the history of objects is plagued by a "time-line" approach, in which contemporary models of thought are provided with premodern equivalents. This is not the application of a historical methodology per se, partly because it sometimes ignores contextual information and the complications that accompany actual sources, but a voracious ahistoricism. When the first abacus appears on such a time line as the primordial ancestor of computer technologies, it's as if an almost visible silvery thread is cast across time—making the past come alive but also rendering contemporary developments inevitable and preordained. To be fair, the impulse reveals the need to create connections with the past, which I agree is vital. Yet when such lists and time lines traffic in superficial alignments among mechanical concepts without reference to cultural and textual constraints, they undermine precisely those elements of the past that could challenge the modern worldview.

Before looking at the past, in other words, we must become acutely aware of our assumptions and impulses, especially those that are foundational and thus largely invisible. Because my own analysis traces the cumulative discursive effect of interactions between literary and philosophical stories and real and imaginary objects, I am vigilant about the effects produced by literary texts and those more characteristic of other entities. In fact, it is a challenge to clarify what provides meaning and power to what: an artifact such as Elektro holds little cultural sway without the literary and cultural context that would make its performance meaningful or attractive, as the actual performance fades from the cultural memory while the appeal of such performances persists. Similarly, a contemporary research project in robotics becomes evocative or fascinating in part because it deploys the meanings and aura of "the robot," without which it may not be that interesting. The meaning of constructs such as Elektro and ASIMO depends partly on their successful negotiation of the preexisting fictional and cultural tradition. One can even argue that, in their stylization, still images from the Fair help Elektro enter this tradition, whereas filmed footage of his stilted and campy performance merely reveals his distance from the robot ideal.[20] In the mysterious workings of culture, real experiences of robotic constructs, however complex, may disappoint, betraying our implicit expectations about what such experiences should entail.

In this discourse, then, stories and objects lend reinforcing elements to each other while inspiring different personal and cultural responses. Stories give expression to forceful animating fantasies only possible in the imagination. The linguistic and psychological predispositions that allow us to imagine an object coming to life are evoked and enhanced in representational spaces. Indeed, representation depends on the ability to sustain animating fantasies, since they make it possible to believe in characters that are nothing but words on a page, shadows on a wall, or images on a screen. The fantasy of animation is multiplied and restaged as a narrative and diegetic feature in animating stories. All fictional characters come to life in some way in our minds; but in some texts, certain characters are designed to represent objects that are then "literally" animated for the purposes of the fiction. In the specialized discourse of the artificial person, the narrative treatment of this diegetic fantasy of animation is honed in the gothic experiments of the eighteenth and nineteenth centuries and continues to channel the era's political and racial anxieties. In the Romantic/gothic paradigm, the animation of objects emphasizes dangerous verisimilitude, the sense that objects come to life to exact revenge or undermine important boundaries between authentic and inauthentic personhood. I refer to this model as the scale of imitation, because it links the threat that accompanies the potential animation of objects to their relationship with anthropomorphism and visual and behavioral approximation.

In contrast to stories, whose operations in language, in the imagination, and in representational spaces and media enjoy a sort of freedom from physical constraint, objects are precisely constrained by their materiality and the rules of the physical world. But this very materiality may trigger powerful personal experiences of presence and evocative mobility. The philosophical rubric that describes the animation of objects by starting from this everyday tactile and sensory relationship uses motion, not imitation, as its primary category. I refer to this model for the animation of objects as the scale of motion because it associates aliveness with mobility, and we need to consider it because mobility, defined as a much richer quality in other eras than our mere locomotion, functioned as a distinguishing characteristic of animate status for most of history up to the seventeenth century. This motion-based recognition of status is still with us, displaced though it may appear by the dominant philosophical emphasis on more abstract categories of being. According to Aristotle whose definitions of motion and life provide the philosophical basis for medieval and Renaissance models, as a property of live matter motion includes mobility in space but also mobility in terms of quantity and quality, growth and decrease in size, augmentation, propagation and reproduction, decline and decay.[21] Other philosophers focus on the natural mobility of matter and its observable capacity to transform itself, as when food is transformed into blood in digestion or plant and animal bodies turn into soil in decay. Life is a kind of motion. The difference between animate and inanimate matter, clearly pivotal in the discourse of the artificial person, is also articulated in terms of motion, in a definition again derived from Aristotle. He famously proposes that animate beings carry the ability for motion in themselves, while inanimate beings must be moved from the outside by another agent. This simple distinction, often misunderstood (as I will explain in chapter 2), has a complicated afterlife in modernity.

Long before gothic fictions stage the threatening animation of objects, then, such scenes follow older philosophical parameters, using the mobility of objects to define states of matter. Discussions of animation shift away from mobility and from Aristotle's philosophical legacies in the seventeenth and eighteenth centuries—at least this is when the transition to new models of thought appears in culture and philosophy. Galileo's theories disconnect the motion of the earth and stars from enlivening motion, while Newtonian physics treat motion as a mathematical not an experiential concept and certainly not as an embodied and enlivening quality. In his attempt to revise Aristotle's legacy, René Descartes separates consciousness from motion and materiality as well. For Descartes, while reason and consciousness cannot be materially defined, the body in its material presence is akin to a machine or automaton: it acts and performs, like a clockwork mechanism, but possesses no reason and no thought. Among their other effects, Descartes's propositions attack the centrality of motion in recognizing an entity's status. Things may move by themselves, but this is not what matters. Further insisting that our senses cannot assure us as to whether the figures we see are real people or automata, Descartes ties the modern philosophical definitions of consciousness and personhood to questions of imitation and verisimilitude. Without a bodily referent for understanding the difference between real and artificial people, without a sense of the fundamental cohesion of body and soul, we are on our way to the dangers of verisimilitude and to the scale of imitation that dominates the modern era.

Modern approaches to anthropomorphic designs revolve obsessively around imitation—a surprising trend given the emphasis on creativity and power we find in the discourse and the anti-representational tendencies of modern aesthetic theories that value constructedness and discursivity.[22] Nowhere is the idea of pure imitation more at home than in the discourse of the artificial or constructed person, replete with all Platonic skepticism of copying and Neoplatonic echoes of occult transgression.[23] Not only does imitation inform the dominant understanding as to why we would want to imagine artificial people (in order to imitate nature), it is also used to explain how they would look physically (in imitation of the human form), what we could imagine doing with them (construct them to imitate people closely in order to replace real people in one social venue or other), and why they would succeed or fail (they imitate too well or not well enough). It is a vicious circle: the construction of artificial people stems from an imitative urge, which is only satisfied when the imitation is equivalent to the original, which then undermines the status of the original, and so on. Presented as the fuel of human artistic pursuits, verisimilitude in these approaches is associated not only with transgression but also with a necessary failure. The idealized difference between a powerful creator and a subjugated created being echoes primordial stories of divine creation as well as dialectical conflict between masters and slaves, with both poles subsequently devalued when seen against the "original" moment of creation. As we see in myriads of stories of overreaching scientists and their constructions, the two players fail to reach the status they desire: the aspiring human does not become a god and the artificial person does not really become a person.

But is imitation unavoidable? The contemporary tendency to discuss the artificial person by highlighting imitation, verisimilitude, and simulation makes a different kind of sense when seen as conditioned by the fact that imitation provides the rubric for modern definitions of *the person*, not just the artificial person. It seems that modern philosophy somehow demands and produces these familiar accounts, featuring sovereign selves momentarily endangered by their own advanced creations. As a formal pair, the imitative constructed person and the "original" person join other such mirrored couples—the co-constitutive unit of the Hegelian master/slave dialectic, and the self-other/self-as-other of the Lacanian mirror stage—that continue to prevail in contemporary theoretical approaches. Despite their critical dissimilarities, all three pairs seem connected to the same Romantic epistemologies of competition and transgression. Why we may need constantly changing versions of this very story of doubleness and threat remains to be discussed in subsequent chapters. But we must at least begin by analyzing these self-perpetuating paradigms and their constant replay in literary and critical accounts. Far from being eternal human aims, simulation, imitation, verisimilitude, threat, and transgression structure modern versions of the artificial person—and our critical perspectives as well. Though powerful, these notions constitute a specifically modern filter that is rarely challenged or critiqued and that inhibits alternative analyses. We must put aside the scale of imitation and transgression if we are to see anything beyond our own proverbial noses.

As versions of accounting for animation, the two scales I identify here, the premodern scale of motion and the Romantic/gothic scale of imitation, are not mutually exclusive. The modern model that prioritizes imitation does little to dispel ancient modes that understood independent mobility as enlivening. In the discourse of the artificial person, the two scales combine with powerful consequences. The scale of imitation does not actually produce animation as its effect; it produces a desire for visual approximation that results in fictions of mirroring or doubleness and their inevitably threatening potential. On the other hand, the scale of motion evokes direct animating effects not only because it was once a parameter for determining animate status but also because the motion of an object is experiential and can create the impression of personality, intention, and purpose. We share the world with other bodies and objects and we are attuned to their patterns of mobility and change. Our sensory experience is also partly autonomic, independent from will and philosophical definitions, and designed to make categorical decisions without mental interference. To resort to a sort of cliché here, as readers of motion we are psychologically "wired" to notice the motion of predators and the motion of leaves on a tree and to distinguish between them instantly. When we imagine anthropomorphic constructions or mechanical bodies coming to life we combine the respective strengths of stories and objects. Objects may leap into life in our minds because representational processes enact enlivening events in the imagination and also because centuries of gothic and fantastic fictions train us to expect and supply animating interpretations. But the first condition for such animating events is the presence of the objects themselves: their materiality activates a sensory response while their motion suggests a certain aliveness, especially if such motion seems partly independent or mysterious. It is this object-related dimension of the animating fantasy that inspires my exploration of enlivening motion in premodern sources.

Our mental realities and everyday experiences are formed through relationships and interactions with objects that are more fluid in their distribution of activity and meaning than we generally admit. We should therefore consider the performative contexts of our experiences with mechanical structures. While reading about an automaton may activate an evocative nexus of meanings, seeing an automaton perform (on the piano, for example) produces pleasures unrelated to animistic and gothic representations of automata in literary texts. Its performance may trigger an interest in processes and explanations or inspire gestures that satisfy the desire for mechanical spectacle, as when the clothes or outer coverings of the automaton are removed to display internal processes. Or the automaton's visual and textural design may involve unforeseen emotional registers, with the texture and color of its clothing and hair or the audible or inaudible mechanical or pneumatic sounds of its workings informing the emotion one associates with the scene.

Recent scholarship takes on these questions of performance and meaning. Jessica Riskin and M. Norton Wise discuss the dynamics of automaton performances both in their original eighteenth century settings and long after, while in his long study of automata in the European imagination, Minsoo Kang traces the complex ways in which philosophical texts use experiences of the automatic in order to constitute modes of explanation of the world and the self.[24] Automaton performances involve both explicit and implicit markers of cultural value as well as political and social meanings. The gentility of the design of an eighteenth-century musical lady automaton has a different emotional effect than the presence of Elektro, whom audiences photographed in ways that enhance his metallic sheen and overall stature. Yet both utilize a gendered vocabulary despite their distance in time and place, with the figures acting a part for their respective audiences: the sweet aristocratic girl of court performances, the threatening metal hulk of 1930s science fiction pulp covers. Even the most mechanical spectacle deploys a grammar of class, gender difference, and sex appeal, while gestures and textures provoke both conscious and unconscious audience responses.

Mechanical performances thus exploit the co-presence of construct and audience and use multiple cultural registers in order to construct meaning. But to recognize the multivalence of such performances, we must hold off on the impulse to read them solely within the Romantic/gothic modes and their focus on the notion of the uncanny. The problem here is that few theoretical models consider the presence of objects without infusing them with the animistic aura that characterizes the gothic. Recent critical analyses of things tend to focus on objects that are somehow special: they belong to an aesthetic, artistic, or technological setting or come from distant historical contexts and exotic places. Objects that participate in the discourse of the artificial person combine these registers—as with statues and talismanic objects from antiquity, puppets and performing objects from different cultures, obsolete machines, and technological or pseudo-technological contraptions with enduring visual appeal. Most of these objects are overdetermined: their anthropomorphic designs inspire theories of simulation and imitation, they star in gothic fantasies, and they become famous examples in psychoanalytic analyses of the uncanny. But this effect is historically and culturally specific, as in the case of statues, for example. While the lifelikeness and immobility of statues becomes a privileged site for the uncanny in eighteenth- and nineteenth-century art and poetry, ancient statues had different effects within their historical era.[25] The meanings of the uncanny, the anthropomorphic, or the inanimate cannot be considered independently from cultural context.

It seems to me that despite many overdone readings of their meaning, we sometimes ignore the performative capabilities and material presence of objects. While it is difficult to imagine the impact of a particular texture on audiences, we

FIGURE 5 "The Lady Musician," a famous musical automaton by Henry-Louis Jaquet-Droz, made in 1774. Inv. No AA1. © Musée d'art et d'histoire, Neuchâtel, Switzerland. Photo S. Iori

should avoid resorting to stereotypes, about the whiteness and coldness of marble, for instance. Ancient statues were often painted in vibrant colors and even "inert" materials interact with their environment in evocative ways as when, depending on their placement in sun or shade, marble statues and stones can be pleasantly cool, warm to the touch (to the point of reaching the temperature of live beings), or inhumanly hot. To approach the figure of the artificial person as a transhistorical entity we need non-gothic and non-apocalyptic approaches to objects and textures. Things we wear and handle, things we see far away or up close, things made of reflective materials, things that feel solid or liquid—all involve sensual interactions that may be unconscious and under-theorized but that are also very familiar. We make rapid analogical and emotional connections when we relate to objects and may find this perspective reflected implicitly in the discourse of the artificial person, as in the preference for certain materials or events. To state this axiomatically, if the literary animation of objects occurs primarily in the imagination, our sense of the presence and meaning of objects structures everyday life. The sense of thrill, excitement, or fascination that accompanies the imaginary animation of an object cannot be elucidated without this experiential and sensual dimension.

I use the distinction between objects and stories as shorthand for reaching the epistemological distinction between the scale of motion and the scale of imitation, necessary for understanding my analysis of animation and life in pre-modern texts in this book. A historical approach must account for this impor-tant transition, from a worldview in which motion constitutes a quality of live beings or is itself enlivening to a worldview in which motion becomes a quality of mechanical objects that are not alive but merely active. Our current relation-ship to the mobility of objects can illuminate the complexity of this process. Now surrounded by independently moving objects and machinery, we assign the animating interpretation of things that move by themselves to innocent others—children, "natives," "primitive people"—as if we are beyond its powerful impact. Motion as a distinguishing characteristic of animate status, however, is only suppressed. Although we are in the habit of describing older cultural prac-tices as animist, it is in modernity that animism is most pervasive. While insist-ing that we are comfortable with the independent motion of objects, we are, on a fundamental level, just as impressed with its effects, and arguably more sus-ceptible than ever to its power because we spend so much psychic energy per-suading ourselves that it means nothing. Persistent patterns of storytelling and cultural production that imagine the technological animation of objects attest to just such a psychic investment. The textural and sensual impact of the presence of objects in our lives cannot be dismissed that easily.

Taking a somewhat estranged stance towards imitation and the vernacular definition of the person in the contemporary landscape may lead to surprising results. The selections and transformations of the artificial person in the twenty-first century signal the return or reinvention of premodern epistemologies, which seem poised to surpass or undermine the Romantic/gothic continuum of imitation and transgression.[26] Our philosophical analyses may be constantly questioning whether computers can think, but, to paraphrase Descartes's solu-tion to the age-old problem of motion, thinking may not be what matters any more. And while mainstream definitions of animation and humanity insist on dualist patterns of mirroring and responsivity, in the Cartesian, Hegelian, psy-choanalytic, and existential definitions of personhood that characterize the scale of imitation and prioritize mutual recognition, we find ourselves in a transitional phase similar to that of the seventeenth century which reorganized the status of motion. Just as the mobility of objects was removed from an overt relationship to animate status, with such objects defined as active but not alive, new technological objects that are responsive and reactive, even superficially emotive, now trigger an adjustment to definitions of animation and personhood. We are in the process of changing what aliveness and humanity will mean in the future, away from the nexus of imitation and responsivity, qualities easily within the performance scope of "smart" objects, and toward a new set of enlivening qualities. I can only speculate, but if fictions of artificial humanity are a sign for the transition, I suspect that old-fashioned characteristics of live matter such as motion, generation, and corruption, processes such as growth and decline, and deeply embodied experiences of emotion and sexuality will be crucial once again.

Is the discourse of the artificial person pointing to the return or reinvention of embodied motion as a key element in understanding aliveness and personhood? This question will come up again in this project, partly because the historical range of my materials rearranges the impact of the old and the new, with old concepts suddenly seeming rather fresh, and recent approaches feeling outdated. While seemingly as apparent and powerful as ever, the Romantic/gothic rubric of imitation is less pervasive when considered within an extended historical span. The conceptual landscape of the beginning of the twenty-first century seems misrepresented by the lingering tendency to read objects through an animist lens. Our theories do not reflect this change yet, but we are less obsessed by simulation and more fascinated with materiality, less paranoid about our coexistence with objects and more interested in the embodied forms of knowledge such coexistence produces. Active and potentially animate objects are not as ominous as they used to be, yet few critical styles express this feeling. In my view this is because the stereotypical and repetitive tendencies of the discourse are exacerbated by the critical habit of looking for answers in historical models that reinforce modern stereotypes. We need a different agenda. We need to exit the realm of the scale of imitation and consider it as an epistemological model whose power is fast diminishing.

The conceptual travel kit we need in this transhistorical exploration contains a number of warnings and suggestions. Consider the importance of motion in premodern descriptions of aliveness. Consider the structuring presence of objects without necessarily resorting to readings of gothic and uncanny effects. Consider the possibility that the Romantic/gothic model is currently under much needed revision, partly inspired by the return of pre-nineteenth-century interests in materiality, presence, complexity, texture, and allegory. Avoid positing imitation or simulation as a consistent aim in the discourse. Avoid explaining the presence of objects through anthropomorphic projections. Avoid imagining that physical constructs are more real than imaginary constructs, or that the two are at all separable. And most of all, allow actual sources and contexts to reveal their own weird meanings and conclusions, looking out especially for those that may challenge modern assumptions.

MORPHOLOGY OF THE ROBOT TALE

Partly because of the epistemological assumptions of current critical methods, the historical span and disciplinary lens one chooses in order to explore the figure of the artificial person tend to determine the outcomes of the investigation. Cultural and technoculture scholars privilege the rise of cybernetics and systems research from the 1930s and 1940s to the present;[27] film critics trace the cinematic appeal of artificiality through the twentieth and twenty-first centuries;[28] literary critics focus on the gothic continuum that connects recent texts to their precursors in the eighteenth and nineteenth centuries; and historians of science pursue associations to the Renaissance and the seventeenth century, and the early stages of the scientific revolution. Each of these time frames offers valuable perspectives on the realms of knowledge that affect our relationships with machines, metaphors, and the fantasy of the mechanical or artificial body. Part of my own approach involves extending the time frame to include ancient sources and philosophical contexts. But even an extreme temporal extension cannot account for the versatility of the trope of the artificial person. What allows these figures to resonate within such radically different worldviews? And what kind of methodology might one use to do justice to both the historical specificity of versions of the artificial person and their ability to remain abstract, evocative, and relevant across time?

Seeking an approach that takes modern choices and texts into consideration without enforcing a modern point of view, in this study I accept as a given the primary problem in approaching artificial people: their current incarnations—robots, cyborgs, and androids—are so familiar to a contemporary audience they almost need no description or explanation. Indeed a first attempt at theorizing such figures reaches an invisible boundary that protects ambient cultural knowledge, much of it stereotypical, from revision or challenge. Yet cultural ubiquity is meaningful, an eloquent sign of the relevance of artificial people, while the familiarity of a general audience with the patterns and stereotypes of their narratives should alert us to the structural integrity of this discourse. The cultural insistence on formula and repetition implies that something is at stake, that the narrative patterns of animating stories enact long-standing debates, fantasies, or desires.

As a theorist of popular culture, I find this mix of familiarity, proliferation, semantic stability, and cultural versatility intriguing. The diverse manifestations of artificial people offer a perfect example of what Michel Foucault describes as a discursive formation, "a system of dispersion," in which "objects, types of statements, concepts, or thematic choices" are characterized by a certain "regularity" that includes order, correlation, transformation, and multiple functions.[29] Consideration of the tropes that accumulate around the figure of the artificial person as components of a discourse allows us to balance, for example, the antiquity of certain patterns with their performance of newness or explain how the stereotypical forms of these stories might facilitate their cultural dynamism. My approach in this project borrows from structuralist analyses of popular culture, writings by Foucault but also Roland Barthes, Tzvetan Todorov's work on the fantastic, and structural analyses of science fiction literature and film by Vivian Sobchack, Christine Brooke-Rose, and Darko Suvin, as well as theories of genre and cultural studies.[30] Although I do not go as far as to describe the discourse of the artificial person as a kind of folklore, I have had Vladimir Propp's *Morphology of the Folktale* and Claude Lévi-Strauss's approach to structural anthropology in mind while writing certain parts of this book.[31] As with folktales, fairy tales, and myths, stories that feature artificial people seem to return to certain patterns across time, reiterating stereotypical kernels of meaning and repeating important storylines. This book seeks to elucidate the structural logic of such repetitions, to identify the semiotic relationships that emerge when we place the stereotypical patterns of popular culture under critical pressure.

Using a roughly structuralist methodology and taking both narrative and historical issues into consideration, in each of the chapters I focus on a core feature, a basic or fundamental ingredient of the discourse of the artificial person. I selected four such networks of meaning: the fantasy of the artificial birth, the fantasy of the mechanical body, the tendency to represent artificial people as slaves, and the interpretation of artificiality as an existential trope. Selected because they are typologically pervasive, these conceptual elements exceed the limits of a strictly contemporary worldview, while they also remain foundational for modern versions of the artificial person, inflecting audience expectations and informing the patterns of future texts. To explore their meanings I follow a backward trail for their provenance, historical and textual antecedents, and conceptual heritage. This hybrid mode aims to elucidate the discourse as it stands in the present by shedding historical light to its foundations, even when—or as I explained above precisely because—these foundations belong to very different worldviews. Symbolically speaking, we arrive at other historical eras as if armed with our ingrained sense of the contemporary typology, against which past models appear different but also occasionally all too familiar. If undertaken as a self-conscious enterprise, our overdetermined contact with the past may alert us to alternative conceptual models that challenge our assumptions.

Reflecting this insight, each chapter begins with an overview of familiar contemporary texts and films before undertaking a philosophical and historical investigation of the questions at stake. Since I assume that much of this discourse is already generally familiar to a contemporary audience, I use quick readings of well-known texts in order to ground complex philosophical or transhistorical questions. My assumption throughout is that fictional and philosophical traditions constitute the cultural archive that provides artificial people with their aura and power, but dealing with this archive requires considerable selection. My own abilities limit this book to mostly Western European and American contexts, and I am painfully aware of omitting relevant examples from other traditions. I trust that the encyclopedic reach of contemporary research tools can supply infinite additional textual examples, while the task of this book is to provide a rigorous investigative framework and to challenge the assumptions of our fantasmatic investment in artificial people in popular culture.

Common fantasies associated with artificial people—such as playing chess with a robot, owning a mechanical dog, having sex with a robot, deploying artificial soldiers, using robotic servants, and so on—present fetishistic responses to questions of animation, mechanical order, and technological materiality. But some of these fantasies also engage all the imagined luxury of action purportedly beyond ethical stipulations, the kind of action we call inhuman and that is morally permissible only with and against the inanimate. Interrogating the constant circulation of such investments can lead to chilling insights. Despite the claims of companies engaged in military research development, artificial soldiers will always be more expensive, more sensitive to the environment, and power-source dependent than human soldiers. For example ASIMO is not a true robot: currently, it is remote-controlled through portable computer units by one or two human operators, one for the upper and one for the lower body. And despite company claims that ASIMO is designed to operate as a worker in a human environment, its current work potential is only one hour, after which its battery must be recharged for three hours. With this work/rest ratio, why would we imagine that human-form robots like ASIMO could replace human workforces? Successful robotic applications in our everyday life from washing machines to automated factories, heavy industrial processes, or Roomba the robotic vacuum cleaner are function-specific and *not* anthropomorphic. Whether or not it is physically possible to design a mechanical form as versatile as the human body, the discourse of the artificial person offers other reasons as to why effective workplace robotic applications avoid the human form. In contrast to fictional robotic servants, whose design fetishizes the human body while negating its frailty, the human form is a liability for actual mechanical applications, not because these figures will be experienced as too frightening or uncanny but because they may be experienced as too familiar and sympathetic or too aesthetic and sculptural. The pleasure of the analogy between real and mechanical people depends partly on the disjuncture between the two states and the different ethical stipulations they entail; if robotic servants were to resemble actual human servants too closely, this pleasure would dissolve. And narratives that posit such situations usually retain important differences between real and artificial people despite their invitation to merge the two states into one.

Similarly, science fiction texts and films may include passionate pleas for the ethical treatment of mechanical slaves, artificial soldiers, or artificial people in general. What is the impact of this focus for the everyday treatment of real soldiers and real people? The exalted language and resident fantasies of the discourse of the artificial person conceal the fact that it has always been possible, and rather cheap, to produce people the old-fashioned way and treat them as expendable, all the while upholding noble notions of personal sovereignty, individuality, agency, and personal rights. In what are clearly projections of the feelings of real people about the vagaries of social and legal status, our fictions give artificial people the role of co-conspirators in this conflict. Since artificial people are often represented as desiring to become real people, in a process that first questions and eventually endorses reigning definitions of humanity and personhood, their quests allow us to idealize human identity and life in fiction, regardless of how devalued these may actually be on the battlefield or in the marketplace. At the same time, however, by posing questions about the ethical treatment of persons, artificial people do more than fetishize an ideal, if inaccessible, personhood. Existential fictions of animation reflect processes that real people describe as de-animating or objectifying and even allow us to see these as reversible. It is probably no coincidence that the philosophers who articulated the political discourse of individuality and human rights also theorized the possibility of artificial humanity. Surely it is no coincidence that the most intense cultural deployments of artificial people occur in periods that radically change the meanings of the categories of person and object in political, technological, and philosophical contexts.

The convoluted history of our imaginative lives with artificial people thus revolves around intimate philosophical questions: What does it mean to be alive? What does it mean to be a person? What responsibilities does personhood entail? And how can we regard and treat one another without the prospect or threat of objectification? As I hope to demonstrate, we seem to have invented and continually refined the figure of the artificial person in order to navigate these poignant human questions.

1 · THE ARTIFICIAL BIRTH

Perhaps the best-known story about a constructed or artificial person in modern literature, Mary Shelley's *Frankenstein; or, The Modern Prometheus* (1818) offers an evocative depiction of the animation of Victor Frankenstein's monster.[1] The creature is formed as a man about eight feet in height, assembled in Victor's workshop from body parts stolen from cadavers, and animated through a process that is both scientific and mysterious, potentially combining alchemical and electrical means. In contrast to its treatment in film, where it has acquired dials, vials, bubbling liquids, strange machinery, hunched assistants, and the power of lightning, in the novel the description of the monster's animation is evasive and remarkably brief. Victor recounts: "It was on a dreary night of November, that I beheld the accomplishment of my toils. With an anxiety that almost amounted to agony, I collected the instruments of life around me, that I might infuse a spark of being into the lifeless thing that lay at my feet. It was already one in the morning; the rain pattered dismally against the panes, and my candle was nearly burnt out, when, by the glimmer of the half-extinguished light, I saw the dull yellow eye of the creature open; it breathed hard, and a convulsive motion agitated its limbs" (37).

The novel's version of animation contains many of the elements that we find again and again in stories of artificial people: they are born adult, through processes that do not require sexuality, in contexts that often do not include women or family. The moment of animation includes at least one visible event that marks the radical change of status for spectators, in this case the opening of the eye and the convulsion that alerts Victor of the monster's aliveness. These visible markers structure the scene's before/after format and render it supremely suited for later spectacular treatments in cinema.[2] Everything that usually takes place inside the body is externalized: processes of conception and gestation are transformed into visible and instantaneous events, and the pain and mystery of childbirth are replaced by technological promises of clarity and control—promises betrayed rather quickly in *Frankenstein* but still operative in other texts of the discourse.

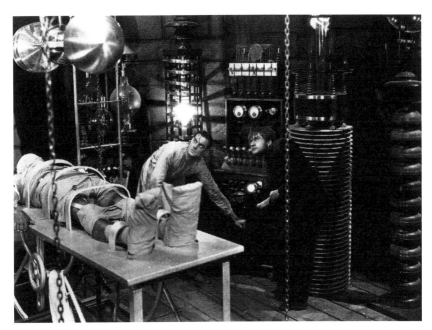

FIGURE 6 Prepare for lightning! Henry Frankenstein (Colin Clive) and Fritz (Dwight Frye) orchestrate the animation of the monster (Boris Karloff), in *Frankenstein* (James Whale, 1931). © Universal Pictures

While it may seem inevitable that a historical account of artificial people should begin with *Frankenstein*, the text functions as both origin and limit. Although *Frankenstein* is justifiably heralded as foundational for modern science fiction, the conceptual patterns of the monster's animation are not unique to *Frankenstein*.[3] Despite its technological trappings, the representation of the artificial birth is in fact rooted in a transhistorical conceptual vocabulary: Shelley's depiction of animation is consistent with an array of premodern animating scenes found in origin stories and cosmological myths, in literary texts that reference ancient ritual patterns, and in medieval and early Renaissance scientific and pseudo-scientific fantasies. Even elements we take for granted or experience as thoroughly modern, such as the focus on visibility, emerge in animating tales of great antiquity. This paradoxical dimension of the discourse of the artificial person is my topic in this chapter, which focuses on the multiple ways in which issues of origin structure stories of artificial people. Far from inspiring questions of influence or imitation, the transhistorical consistency of animating scenes becomes the basis for a more theoretical understanding of the stakes of the animating story, in premodern and modern contexts.

Taking the iconography of the artificial birth as a point of departure, this chapter proposes that to understand the origins of the discourse of the artificial person, to see "where artificial people come from," we might focus on how they are born. Indeed to say they are born is itself provocative or paradoxical: the fact that artificial people are usually not born is one of the most fascinating things about them. Yet even as their mode of construction couldn't be further from childbirth, this sense of conceptual distance—of two scenes that couldn't be further from each other—also signals a formal relationship. Stories of artificial people traffic in the reversal, negation, or transformation of bodily states, and primary among them is the negation of childhood. Although they are often depicted as proverbial children, new to the world, artificial people almost never appear as babies, and very rarely inhabit a child's body. From ancient tales of the creation of Pandora and Galatea to the ritualistic animation of the Golem in the Jewish Kabbalah, to the sexy physicality of the Replicants in *Blade Runner* (Ridley Scott, 1982), and the striking technological birth scenes of *Ghost in the Shell* (Mamoru Oshii, 1995), part of the appeal of artificial people seems to depend on the attractions of their adult bodies, bodies usually gendered and rendered in culturally specific ways in terms of race, ethnicity, age, and physical appearance.

Artificial bodies are also compartmentalized, either because they are made of stitched-together body parts (as with Victor's creature), or because they have no body fluids (as is the case with robots in later stories), or because their construction involves radically different interior and exterior materials, as with the metal skeleton and artificial skin of the cybernetic beings in *The Terminator* (James Cameron, 1984). Even the distinction made in Victor's workshop between the material body, the "lifeless thing" awaiting its animation, and the "spark of being" that will infuse it with life speaks to this compartmentalizing tendency and registers the discursive importance of dualist notions of body and soul, body and mind, or matter and spark for this story type. Yet despite these negations, artificial people cannot escape the burden of their embodiment: their appearance and physicality function deterministically, since it is often these features that mark artificial people as other, with tragic consequences in the creature's case. And while the artificial birth is often described as a cerebral process, as a construction or fabrication, it is in fact intimately related to processes of human generation.

The structural consistency of artificial birth fantasies offers an eloquent identification of what matters in the discourse of the artificial person. My contention is that when we ask "where do artificial people come from?" we are, and perhaps unconsciously, exactly at the crux, the linchpin of the issue. Artificial people emerge from the contexts that evolve around a similar question, asked since the beginning of human civilization: "where do people come from?" Origin stories, or stories that attempt to answer or radically expand this question, can be our guide to the relationship between real and artificial people before the modern era, when the boundary between them operates within different conceptual rubrics. My analysis begins from the middle of things, from a closer look at *Frankenstein* and the novel's inclusion of both premodern and modern conceptualizations of matter and animation, before moving on to ancient, medieval, and early modern versions of the artificial birth. Although the styles and means, visual effects, and scientific explanations may vary, the question of the beginning of life is never uncomplicated. Recognizing the transcendental roots of the artificial birth can help us explain why the narrative of animation later becomes so pervasive in technological, political, and existential contexts.

ON BIRTH AND DEATH: REREADING *FRANKENSTEIN*

No other text in the discourse of the artificial person enjoys the cultural position of Mary Shelley's *Frankenstein*. The novel's inspiration and writing are the stuff of legend, its impact dispersed and immeasurable. And it is perhaps both fitting and profound that a story about a being born fully formed, without parents, without peers, and without descendants, would be so concerned with questions of origin and progeny, that it would exert so much influence on later literary, scientific, and cinematic culture, and that it would inspire such speculation about its origins as a text.

Contemporary scholars generally agree that the two main versions of *Frankenstein* present two distinct approaches to science and ethics, and this bifurcation affects how we understand the artificial birth in the novel.[4] The original 1818 novel presents Victor's work as an unconventional but rational scientific project and does not judge or interpret his actions for readers. Although, as Marilyn Butler has argued, Shelley intends a subtle critique of Victor's loosely vitalist ideas, the novel's ambivalence masks its irreverence, allowing audiences to understand Victor as naïve, misguided, or obsessed, without rendering him or his pursuits particularly impious.[5] We owe the more stereotypical approach to the novel as a cautionary tale against hubristic overreaching scientists to Shelley's revisions for the 1831 edition. Some of her changes aimed to reframe the representation of science: while references to magnetism, electricity, and polar exploration were not controversial in 1818, by 1831 a series of public debates about radical science, vitalism, evolution, and genetics inflected the public's view of Victor's scientific aspirations.[6] Eager to legitimize the novel and keenly aware of the public's interest in her own tumultuous life, Shelley adds a moralistic tone in the 1831 edition, as Victor expresses regret, alludes to uncontrollable evil forces taking over his work and life, and frames his research as a form of hubris. In Shelley's new preface, Victor's work in natural philosophy becomes an engagement with the "unhallowed arts" (190), while her textual revisions target Victor's motivations and reactions, both in constructing the creature and in rejecting him. Indeed in the most clearly preemptive gesture of the 1831 preface, Shelley explains away the fundamental mystery of her novel, presenting Victor's panicked recoil from his creation as a moral and religious given. "Frightful must it be," she explains, "for supremely frightful would be the effect of any human endeavour to mock the stupendous mechanism of the Creator of the world" (190). By thus reestablishing divine and moral order, Shelley attempts to dispel the emotional and psychological chaos of the animating scene, instead presenting the novel as an expression of the desire for and failure of imitation. And Victor's symptom finds a name: hubris, pride, overreaching, solipsism, scientific obsession, moral blindness, the desire to become godlike, the unholy aspiration to understand or control what only the divine controls.

Returning to the 1818 version of the novel without such preconceptions, one finds a more dynamic range of meanings. The text does not actually explain why Victor panics when the monster comes to life, and it certainly does not interpret his revulsion as a sudden return to Christian piety. Instead, Victor's shock transforms the monster's animation into a traumatic parent/child scene, unparalleled in modern literature for the intensity with which it depicts the drama of narcissistic projection, and the trauma of withdrawal, rejection, and alienation. The monster, initially addressed as "it" during the animation scene and as "he" by the next paragraph, is curiously not recognizable as a human form, even though we are told that all his body parts were deemed beautiful when selected. Challenging essentialist notions of identity and disrupting both aesthetic and ontological chains of being, the monster embodies the unreadable, the unspeakable.[7] Far from feeling victorious, Victor experiences revulsion, a reaction that is all the more powerful for being so immediate and irrevocable. "How can I describe my emotions at this catastrophe, or how delineate the wretch whom with such infinite pains and care I had endeavoured to form?" he asks (37). Victor recoils, collapses, and then flees. As the novel unfolds, the former skeptic and scientist who had claimed early in the novel that he was immune to supernatural terrors will soon become a man terrified of shadows and sounds.

Despite its scientific trappings, the animating scene in fact performs a substitution of mysteries: while the creature's animation promises to reveal the order of nature, in the transformation of inanimate matter into a living being, his rejection evokes mysteries that are closer to home. Instead of presenting a unique sublime event, *Frankenstein* doubles the animating scene, creating a sequence in which the monster's body comes to life literally through Victor's technological processes, only to be de-animated symbolically and socially by his rejection. Combining the explanatory power of an origin story and the traumatic power of a primal scene, this treatment of animation also switches focus from science to emotion, and from the outside to the inside, and allows for multiple emotional perspectives. Readers may inhabit the position of the scientist faced with the ineffable, the parent faced with a child's wondrous or threatening otherness, the abandoned or rejected child, and the fascinated observer whose eavesdropping on the family drama is anticipated in the novel in the character of Robert Walton, the polar explorer listening to Victor's story. In the dynamic melodrama of identity facilitated in the scene, the reader may be defending or policing the human but also seeking to be included in the human fold or feeling unjustly excluded. And while Victor's motivation remains unclear, the monster's pathos is all too familiar. Despite the violence the monster unleashes in the course of the novel, his perspective is thereafter understandable, informed not so much by how he is *made* but by how he is *unmade* by processes of familial, social, and political rejection.

While the novel displays a philosophical pastiche of poetic, scientific, and social thought, much as the monster presents a collection of disparate body parts, there is a multivalent coherence of form in this unusual book. As if in narrative emulation of the questions of the inside and outside that motivate this story type, the novel's formal structure presents a series of framed narratives: in letters to his sister, North Pole explorer Robert Walton writes of his meeting with Victor, reporting Victor's narration of his tragedies, embedded in which we find the monster's own story and experiences, which include the narratives of the De Lacey family and Safie's tale.[8] This box structure itself deploys a symbolic

FIGURE 7 Confrontation, negotiation, rejection: the new mysteries of *Frankenstein* (James Whale, 1931). Henry Frankenstein (Colin Clive) finally comes face-to-face with the creature (Boris Karloff). © Universal Pictures

register in which the problems of exteriority and interiority, of material form and "spark of being," play out in the novel's composition, tempting us to look for an ever more interior story within the framed narratives or instructing us to notice the intra-frame connections. The novel offers numerous motifs that intersect within these nested narratives: orphans, idealized women, angelic but dead mothers, difficult or cruel parents, sailing, the North, ice, mountains, the desire for a friend, the desire for open travel to the ends of the earth, the desire for a quiet hearth amid the cold. A focus on passages and transitions can be found in the amniotic calm of Victor's many reveries sailing on various lakes, Walton's failed search for the fabled North Passage, and the novel's final chase scenes on a sea of ice. The novel in effect teaches us to read for both matter and spark: if the framed narratives offer the body parts, the materials, the matter of our encounter with the book, we find a different trajectory in the through-lines, repetitions, and serial returns among the frames. This dynamic trajectory moves across or through the framed narratives and engages readers in a significatory quest that animates the story beyond its basic content.

One of these through-lines affects how we understand the animating process in the book as a whole. Adding to the dispersed emphasis on passages, the novel does not treat the body as inert matter that comes to life with the addition of a soul—indeed the soul is not an animating agent but a record of experience for the creature and is used in relation to his character only twice in the 1818 edition. The first mention occurs when the creature entreats Victor to listen to his story: "Believe me, Frankenstein, I was benevolent; my soul glowed with love and humanity" (73). Later, when Victor reaches the end of his own narrative, he warns Walton about the monster's character: "His soul is as hellish as his form, full of treachery and fiend-like malice" (165). It is only after the monster's many murders that his soul, once pure and loving, matches his already hideous form. In the 1831 edition Shelley adds a trap, a misdirection that again enables a more Christian and classically dualist reading of the text. In this version, after the death of Clerval, when Victor returns to Geneva with his father in order to kill the creature he asserts: "I might, with unfailing aim, put an end to the existence of the monstrous Image which I had endued with the mockery of a soul still more monstrous" (207). In this doubly retroactive move, Victor misremembers the animating process, where a "soul" did not pertain as either concept or scientific entity, and Shelley misrepresents the novel, destabilizing the material relationship between body and spark that motivates the book.

In contrast to the top-down structure implied by the soul-added-to-body rubric (a conventional description for such scenes), the animations of the novel in the 1818 version do not depict a controlling soul or a single localized life source, instead favoring dispersed or pervasive animating agents, life forces that may be added and subtracted, or that fluctuate radically, but that exist throughout the body. This subtly materialist treatment of animation—and also of inspiration, vitality, and liveliness—infuses the text with a series of animations and de-animations, enacting a tendency toward circularity that adds an alchemical element to the novel's otherwise modern depictions. The animating language that permeates the novel reveals Shelley's skillful manipulation of linguistic referent, with words first appearing in their everyday or metaphorical sense and then reappearing as technical terms or as potentially scientific literalizations of a gothic reality. Victor, for example, is close to death when he first appears in the novel, "nearly frozen, and his body dreadfully emaciated by fatigue and suffering." After bringing him onboard their ship, Walton and the sailors "restored him to animation" by rubbing him with brandy until he "shewed signs of life" (13).[9] Walton more than once refers to Victor as a "creature" and thinks he is "wretched," the very terms that Victor will use to describe the monster (13, 14, 15). Walton describes himself "glowing with enthusiasm" as he begins his quest (6, 8), a term used later to describe Victor's research.

Animating and de-animating language shifts between Victor and the monster numerous times. In recounting his life to Walton, Victor is born and raised in the narrative, until he is de-animated again immediately before the monster's awakening: after two years of work, he becomes so obsessed with the mystery of life that he begins to lose his own liveliness. As if already embodying the relationship of matter and spark that the book will stage, Victor is "animated by an almost supernatural enthusiasm" (32): his cheeks grow "pale with study" and his body "emaciated with confinement" as he pursues "nature to her hiding places" with "unrelaxed and breathless eagerness" (35). He feels that he has "lost all soul or sensation but for this one pursuit," yet he finds himself propelled by "a listless, and almost frantic impulse," an "unnatural stimulus" (35). He becomes "insensible to the charms of nature" and remains silent and distant from his friends (35). The words used to describe Victor's body evoke the insensibility of the inanimate (pale, emaciated, rigid, unfeeling, silent, insensible), while those that describe his motivation present double meanings, from terms that combine the alchemical and religious echoes of "enthusiasm" to the potentially electrical and galvanic connotations of "impulse" and "stimulus."[10] The overall effect of Shelley's representation of life thus combines alchemical circularity and modern notions of circulation, the circulation of blood, nervous energy, or electrical energy through the body, as well as a materialist emphasis on energy dispersal rather than a purely dualist emphasis on centralized body controllers. Walton is propelled by ardent desire and enthusiasm, Victor's unfeeling body seems animated by scientific obsession, and the monster is literally brought to life by a similarly pervasive power coursing through his limbs. By the end of the book, it is as if the explorer, the scientist, and the artificial man are all bodies "galvanized" by invisible powers, some more metaphorical than others.

With everyday language infected by increasingly ominous meanings, the cycle of animation and de-animation continues with each rise into and fall from liveliness. Victor's tragedies sink him further into comatose and catatonic states from which he is roused by nature, the love of his family, and the assistance of Clerval, Elizabeth, his father, and various strangers, including at some point the monster and finally Walton. "I was lifeless," Victor says of his breakdown after the monster's animation (41), while after Justine's execution he finds his only consolation in "deep, dark, death-like solitude" (65). Victor's language and behavior shift from the compartmentalized body/spirit split he exhibits in the early chapters to a series of escalating hysterical fits and psychosomatic reactions that reunite body and mind, albeit in sorrow or grief, while the novel punctuates these transitions with scenes of sailing or floating. As if in evocation of a womb-like calm, Victor's sailing on lakes is often contemplative and restorative, with lakes allegorically treated as enclosed bodies of water that do not pose the threats of the open sea. He often has thoughts of suicide as he lies on the bottom of various boats but decides to live, and he is figuratively reborn into turmoil, responsibility, and sorrow with every arrival at the shore. By the end of the book the cycles of death and rebirth accelerate manically. Walton notes that the exhausted Victor can be "suddenly roused into any exertion [but then] he speedily sinks again into apparent lifelessness." Walton watches "the wan countenance of my friend—his eyes half-closed, and his limbs hanging listlessly" (169), which clearly resemble the monster's yellow skin and lifeless body before his animation, as well as murdered Elizabeth's languid "bloodless arms" (154).

As with her treatment of other opposing pairs in the novel, Shelley delves into the relationship between life and death, in the monster's creation from dead body parts, in Victor's dream the night of the monster's animation in which Elizabeth "in the bloom of health" turns into the corpse of his mother crawling with grave worms (37), in the monster's many murders, and the death wish that gradually takes over the grief-stricken characters. Victor longs for reversibility, especially when he wishes to undo things that have already occurred. He wishes he could undo his mother's death by researching the mysteries of life, undo the monster if only that would restore life to his murdered victims, and most of all he wishes he could undo himself after the monster's violence has made life unbearable. Indeed, despite his research in the principles of life, Victor only learns what life is through negation, as the monster's actions force him to understand life not as spark but as endurance, as an unwelcome resilience. "Why did I not die?" Victor asks after the death of Clerval. "Of what materials was I made, that I could thus resist so many shocks, which, like the turning of the wheel, continually renewed the torture" (139). After Elizabeth's murder, the question returns: "Great God! why did I not then expire! Why am I here to relate the destruction of the best hope, and the purest creature of earth" (154).

Victor's escalating dramatization of the fact of life in the face of death is a far cry from the pious resignation that Caroline Frankenstein expresses before dying calmly: "I will endeavour to resign myself cheerfully to death" (26); or Victor's early acquiescence and fortitude after her death: "we must continue our course with the rest, and learn to think ourselves fortunate" (26); and Clerval's clichés after William's murder: "he now sleeps with his angel mother" (50). The novel contrasts two formulaic responses to death, a pious and religious resignation and the melodramatic rage of gothic and sentimental writing. It is Elizabeth who brings this second tone into the story, when she more than once wishes for death after Justine's execution: "I never can survive so horrible a misfortune" (62), and "I wish . . . that I were to die with you; I cannot live in this world of misery" (64). The monster picks up the same attitude and exacerbates its existential implications after his confrontation with the DeLaceys: "Cursed, cursed creator! Why did I live? Why, in that instant, did I not extinguish the spark of existence which you had so wantonly bestowed?" (103). Victor seems to have sparked life without awareness of life's preciousness, but the novel resists treating the undoing of life as easily. "You purpose to kill me. How dare you sport thus with life?" the monster confronts him. "Life, although it may only be an accumulation of anguish, is dear to me, and I will defend it" (72–73).

Obviously, *Frankenstein* is deeply invested in questions of procreation and childbirth, but the novel's imagery also connects the desire for generation with death throughout.[11] While Victor tries to understand the mystery of life through his experiments in animation, he experiences this mystery most intensely when life continues past the limits of endurable pain, past grief, and past the desire to live. Hearing Elizabeth's dying scream, Victor is stunned into awareness of his own aliveness: "I could feel the blood trickling in my veins, and tingling in the extremities of my limbs" (154); while gazing at her dead body accentuates the paradox of life's resilience in the face of life's fragility: "Could I behold this, and live? Alas! life is obstinate, and clings closest where it is most hated" (154). Shelley literalizes the possibility of life-in-death and death-in-life, binding procreation to death and suicide.[12]

If this structural and diegetic emphasis in the merger of opposites marks a premodern, cyclical, alchemical heritage for the novel's treatment of animation, the monster enacts a modern violence that combines negation and drive, metaphorically breaking the circles of life and death in the novel and enforcing an arrow-like trajectory, a linear sense of temporality that leads from birth to death. This is the monster's vengeful instruction for Victor: as a force in the novel, the monster undermines the palliative effect of religious belief and the hope for death's reversal through science, imposing an awareness of death-as-such and life-as-such onto the stunned characters. While the monster embodies death in his very body, preserves Victor's life in order to prolong their battle for death, and even laughs at Victor's decision to live in order to avenge the deaths of his friends (159–60), he simultaneously occupies a very lively position and is defined by struggle and constant engagement with nature, action, and survival. Always aware of his existence as a live being, the creature displays a state of consciousness that Clerval alone experiences at one point in the novel, when he expresses the feeling of life as presence and pleasure: "This is what it is to live," Clerval cries as they embark on a trip down the Rhine, "now I enjoy existence!" (119). In what becomes an expression of pure existential self-awareness, the monster cannot be complacent about the fact of life and the fact of social rejection, as the two mysteries, one ontological and the other social or political, are irrevocably intertwined for him. Importantly, while the monster cannot help but constantly feel both the miracle and the tragedy of his existence, human characters must be transported out of their everyday lives through travel, reverie, or grief in order to have this intense experience of experience. In contrast to Victor's solipsistic tendencies and his recurring death wishes, the creature is always fully alive, and his struggles for recognition and community present a different allegorical referent for the elusive mystery of life—life not as it relates to beginning and ending, origin and purpose but as it relates to everything in-between, life as living, and as living with others.

If the modern questions that structure *Frankenstein* revolve around interiority, trauma, psychological motivation, and social rejection, there is an equally foundational set of primordial elements at work in the book, in its engagement with life and death, birth and corruption, the outside and the inside, the desire to live and the desire to die. These confrontations with the ineffable mark the novel's originary aspirations and also align the story with ancient narratives of origin and their visual and conceptual grammar. Similarly, the story's focus on circularity suggests a premodern approach to matter and animation. In Victor's disruptions of the natural order, what should be dead is alive, while life and death constantly exchange meanings and places. We find the scientific and epistemological roots of this palindromic treatment of life and death in late medieval and early Renaissance scientific and religious treatises that depict artificial birth scenes. A more focused historical exploration into ancient and early modern sources can provide a prehistory of the artificial birth that alters how we understand the fantasy of the artificial person in modernity.

ORIGIN STORIES: THE BIRTH OF PANDORA

Ancient cosmologies and myths of origin offer a variety of tales that explain the formation of the world, the beginning of life, and the emergence of humanity. As early forays of human culture into allegory, origin stories transmute observed events into mythical processes and then cast these imaginings into narrative and ritual form.[13] Recording the feelings of ancient people and their interpretations of what can be experienced but also what cannot be explained in the world, origin stories abound with miraculous births and outrageous bodies, and this iconography provides the basis for fantasies of artificial or constructed people.

Explaining the emergence of people in originary tales involves oblique or allegorized references to events of the natural world such as earthquakes and weather systems; body processes such as digestion and elimination; generative processes such as plant generation and growth; processes of decline, deterioration, and decay; and human emotions, conflicts, and relationships. Thinly veiled in origin narratives, these events fuel powerfully imaginative scenes. Gods and goddesses may create the natural world through sexual union, sibling rivalry, or battle, or they may dismember each other to form heavenly and terrestrial bodies out of their blood, body fluids, or torn body parts. Or, instead of embodied gods, abstractions such as the principle of destruction or of regeneration engage in similar acts of world-formation. Stories of spontaneous creation posit a primordial chaos that splinters to bring forward the earth and sky. Divine beings eat and vomit people or have offspring from body parts not biologically associated with gestation, as when Athena emerges full-grown from Zeus's head or when Dionysus is born from his thigh. There are few ordinary birth scenes in origin stories, in other words. People emerge after stones, bones, or teeth are sown onto fields, people sprout up from the earth fully grown, people are born out of the casting about of divine tears, blood, semen, menstrual blood, excrement, and so on. Darkness and light, observable heavenly bodies, and natural elements (water, fire, earth, and air, but also ice, salt, milk, smoke, and mist) feature in these tales as generative principles, as do various primordial trees, eggs, stones, birds, serpents, and other animals. In addition to cosmic, animal, and body processes, human tasks and crafts also inflect cosmogonies and origin narratives with the vocabulary of cultivation, food preparation techniques, ceramics, textile weaving, and metalwork. Gods may weave the world into existence, carve or mold people out of natural materials, forge the natural world, and so on.

The grand narratives of ancient origin traditions explain how the world came into being, and they may also be used to account for other events, from plant, animal, and human generation to national or regional histories of conflict, colonization, and succession. "Where do people come from?" can easily translate into "Where do *my* people come from?" or "How did we settle here?" and be used to explain why a particular social organization or stratification works the way it does. By allowing a present regime or epistemology to legitimize itself by seeding its necessity into the past, origin tales combine both macroscopic and microscopic perspectives, mapping the social order through reference to cosmological or divine events. Such tales also display a procedural and explanatory drive, as even stories that do not explain anything nevertheless promise divine or foundational explanations. Origin stories are displaced explanations, or displacements of explanation. They answer questions like "Where do people come from?" by not answering directly or by offering marvelous tales whose success depends on sufficient displacement. And perhaps because human generation has been experienced as uncontrollable or mysterious, origin stories often avoid what we assume to be the natural facts, instead diverging broadly from the iconography and order of processes like conception, gestation, and birth. In yet another form of explanatory displacement, this distance between the natural birth scenes experienced and witnessed by ancient people and the originary birth scenes they invented affects the representation of an imaginary artificial birth most directly.

Consider, for example, the story of the creation of Adam in the Bible solely as an origin story, divested for our purposes of its role in religious dogma and its cultural implications. After God creates light and dark, heaven and earth, plants and animals, he molds a form out of earth and water and breathes life into it. This becomes the first man and goes on to inhabit the already formed world. The basic structure of this scene provides a clear originary displacement for human generation. As the reverse of a natural birth scene, the creation of Adam does away with time, presenting an adult body that emerges fully formed into consciousness. It also dispenses with women, sex, gestation, body fluids, pain, food, need, crying, cold, helplessness, vulnerability, and so on. But if in order to explain the processes or mysteries of birth a story resorts to sublimating these mysteries, if it presents images of radically "other" types of birth to avoid describing conditions that resemble a real birth too closely, then the origin story contains both a narrative reversal of natural birth and the foundational story elements of an artificial birth. Adam's creation is a Judeo-Christian origin story that explains where people come from, but it also constitutes one important textual origin for tales of the creation of artificial people. From the Golems of kabbalistic traditions, which also have connections to ancient initiation rituals designed to commemorate the story's originary power, to the animation of Frankenstein's creature, to contemporary science fiction, myriads of artificial births replicate Adam's creation and depict beings formed through some combination of materials and then animated through a special agent, divine breath, the soul, the spark of life, electricity, and so on.

Origin stories and stories of artificial birth are in this sense isomorphic: they may contain precisely the same structures or elements and differ only in their arrangements or social uses, their strategies for avoiding or displacing the vocabulary of human generation. This constitutes yet another answer to the question of this chapter, "Where do artificial people come from?" Evidently, they come from the same place that real people "come from." The originary mythology a culture creates to explain its own emergence usually contains the basics for whatever entity, creature, or being it imagines as the other of real people. This is a complex triangulated relationship, between experiences or observations of childbirth, imaginative origin stories that reverse these observations and translate childbirth into explanatory allegory, and tales of an artificial birth that also reverse the structures of childbirth but to a different end. Stories of the origin of real and artificial people have their origin in the same displacements. And this relationship is sometimes so convoluted that in order to explain where real people come from, one may resort to stories about artificial people.

In view of this structural isomorphism, what would constitute a specifically *artificial* birth in ancient contexts? Despite their exuberance, the processes featured in origin stories ostensibly result in the natural order of things, and indeed their express purpose is to strengthen what a particular culture considers this order to be. Origin stories never present the creation of people as an unnatural event except insofar as cosmogonic or divine actions are always beyond the limits of human understanding. The more incredible the transformation (Athena and Dionysus born adult from unrelated body parts, Adam created from clay, people sprouting from stones), the better the story is in depicting the raw power of the divine principles at work.

Nor do these tales imply that first people are anything but authentic. Despite transcendental leaps, ancient lore connects the origin of people to the origin and the materials of the world, without alienation or skepticism that people made out of clay or stone may represent a suspicious other type of person. It is later re-readings that posit such problems: when readers in Late Antiquity and the Hellenistic era, for example, re-read origin stories in the context of the ambient mysticism of their own time, they interpret them in ways that fuel the mystical practices of Neo-Platonic, Hermetic, Mithraic, Kabbalistic, and other sects that engage in theurgic rituals. Victoria Nelson proposes that such rituals give rise to stories of animation after the dissemination of Neo-Platonic and Hermetic treatises, and paraphrasing Moshe Idel she describes the process as "*imitatio dei* by *generatio anime*," or "the attempt of man to know God by the art He uses in order to create men."[14] Similarly, insofar as modern epistemologies classify the natural world into categories of being, stories of creation seem strange or uncanny. The material continuity among people, animals, plants, and minerals that ancient peoples would have found reassuring may strike modern readers as an inappropriate merger of categories, an exercise in the undifferentiated and the mystical.

In order to find examples of a birth or animation that ancient stories treat as aberrant or artificial, we must consider the literary codifications of ancient cultural traditions. Some of the earliest examples of artificial creation, of the creation of beings that are somehow deemed different or inauthentic (although they emerge in much the same ways in which actual people are said to have emerged), are recorded in ancient tales of adding people into an already populated world.

Typically these are not just ordinary people but specific individuals whose creation is associated with divine purpose or instrumentality. Such tales retain the iconography and patterns of originary creation stories but reorganize them to produce a different effect. Tales of the creation of Golems in the Jewish Kabbalah, for example, are clearly modeled on the story of the creation of Adam in Genesis, and indeed Adam is called a golem in his in-between state before he is fully animated by God. In Hesiod's *Works and Days* and *Theogony*, Pandora is created by the gods as a snare, a "beautiful evil" that will entrap humans.[15] The statue Pygmalion calls "my ivory girl" in Ovid's *Metamorphoses* (named Galatea only after the eighteenth century) is animated by Venus to become a beautiful woman.[16] All three stories involve the paradox I am tracing to some degree. The story of the Golem's creation is similar to the story of the creation of Adam, Pandora's animation is somewhat mundane compared to the fabulous scenes of monstrous and divine generation that fill Hesiod's poems, and the animation of Pygmalion's statue is simpler than the transformations of people into animals, flowers, trees, and celestial bodies that otherwise characterize Ovid's text. While for a modern audience the magical manner of their formation renders these beings somehow special or different, in their original contexts it is their structural position vis-à-vis the human and the divine that differentiates them. The artificial person is specifically designed to fulfill a purpose, that is, to mediate between already established human and divine realms. As with the miraculous births of heroes or semidivine figures whose difference from the human norm reveals a special pedigree and an association with divine purposes, stories of an artificial birth include an overt social dimension and aim to materialize a space between the human and the divine.

One of the earliest literary tales of a specifically artificial birth revolves around the birth of Pandora, recounted in Hesiod's *Works and Days* and *Theogony*, dating roughly from the eighth century BCE but modeled on older sources and oral versions.[17] In both poems, Pandora's creation is part of the larger story of Prometheus's transgressions: he has tricked the gods into accepting the bones of sacrificed animals (thus ensuring that people would be able to eat the meat and thrive) and has stolen fire from the gods (thus inaugurating the rise of human arts, crafts, and technologies). In retaliation, Zeus orders the gods to construct a human-form effigy that will then become a living woman, according to the poet the first woman. The craft god Hephaistos uses a mix of earth and water to construct a young girl's form, with a beautiful face "like the immortal goddesses" and a human voice and vigor. Athena teaches her how to weave, and Aphrodite grants her beauty but also longing and desire. Finally, Zeus orders Hermes "to put in her the mind of a hussy / and a treacherous nature."[18] Dressed in silvery robes and wearing an intricately wrought veil and a crown with lively depictions of animals of the land and sea, the first woman is finally revealed. At her sight, "wonder seized both immortals and mortals," her beauty and power clearly "more than mortals can deal with."[19] Hermes names this first woman Pandora, which with great craftiness he explains as "the one who has received all the gifts," rather than "the giver of gifts." Pandora's double name is only one of the deceptions involved in her creation, and she is delivered as a gift that gives gifts to absent-minded Epimetheus, who forgets his brother Prometheus's warning to avoid any such bequests from the gods. Pandora carries with her a large *pithos*, or jar, that houses troubles for mortals. Only Hope remains within after Pandora opens the jar, later translated as the proverbial "Pandora's box," unleashing evils of the earth and the sea, diseases, and silent sorrows onto humankind.[20]

As with the creation of Adam and the animation of the monster in *Frankenstein*, Pandora is born adult, without natural processes of gestation. Qualities such as speech or beauty are granted or bequeathed to her individually rather than emerging or evolving from the generation process itself. Staging the problem as to how individual body parts cohere to make a complete being, this compartmentalization evokes numerous philosophical debates, from Aristotle's quest to locate the seat of motion and the soul in the body to the visual logic that emerges after the advent of modern anatomy, in which the body appears in concentric layers that expand outward from the bones to the skin. In the seventeenth and eighteenth centuries, the relationship of the parts to the whole would generate a long-standing philosophical debate on the function of the senses: the idea of the mind as a tabula rasa or the self as an inanimate statue that acquires human senses one at a time was a favorite philosophical topos as it allowed philosophers to debate the nature of human perception and consciousness and to express both dualist and anti-dualist approaches to mind, body, and self.[21] But while, in modernity, compartmentalization accentuates the epistemological differences between materialist, dualist, and transcendental philosophies, in its ancient context the process of granting individual abilities or qualities to Pandora emphasizes the specializations that already characterize the divine realm. Ancient gods and goddesses grant the qualities they allegorically embody, traits they have been assigned in myth. Rather than enforcing a separation between the person and his or her own qualities, ancient compartmentalization forges and affirms the relationship between the human and the divine, one trait at a time.

Nested within the story of Prometheus's disruption of divine order, the Hesiodic story of Pandora functions as a metaphorical conclusion to the Titan's actions.[22] Prometheus's devotion to human well-being is explained as a form of parenting: in versions that possibly predate Hesiod but which come to us from Pausanias and the Roman traditions, Prometheus himself created mortals out of clay. His transgressions are technological, resulting in a new diet and new knowledge and crafts for mortals, and in response the gods' revenge can be seen as technological too. Both Hephaistos and Athena are associated with metalwork and craft, while Aphrodite, the goddess most connected to sexual procreation, is absent in one version of the event, replaced by minor divinities. But when the gods are in charge there is little difference between art and nature, between *technē* and *phusis*. Pandora's liveliness and allure are precisely the effect of Hephaistos's art, while animation is described as an enclothing in *charis*. A collection of enlivening qualities such as charm, loveliness, vitality, beauty, radiance, and youthfulness, charis is granted from the outside, from the gods, and affects both the outside and the inside, one's visible presence and one's meaning or essence.[23] While much of the description focuses on external beauties and marvels, the verb used for the animation process—*entithēmi* (to place inside), rather than just *tithēmi* (to place)—signals affinities between Pandora's animation and the dedication of ritual objects, in which a special message is placed inside a vessel or statue to give the object its secret or final meaning. Charis is a complex gift that can enliven even already live beings: the gods can pour charis onto their favorite mortals, who emerge more glorious, more beautiful, and more "like themselves."[24] Pandora also becomes more like herself in this animating process. As Jean-Pierre Vernant has proposed, as the first woman Pandora is not an imitation or replacement of an already existing model but a new and unique entity, one that combines the divine, in her grace, beauty, and divine gifts, and the beastly or animal, in her "canine" disposition.[25] While patently misogynist, Hesiod's warning does not revolve around imitation. In contrast to modern readings of artificial creation that presuppose a mimetic purpose for the work of art, Pandora may be an artifact but she is not a copy or imitation of anything else.[26]

Instead, as Deborah Tarn Steiner notes, "the treacherous character of the image" depends on "the object's capacity to host a split between a surface appearance and inner reality, to assume an exterior that belies what exists below."[27] The poet has worked to ensure that the circulation of story elements balances transgression and revenge: Prometheus molds people out of clay / the gods mold Pandora out of earth and water; he hides the bare bones of the sacrificial animal under beautiful fat / they hide a treacherous nature inside the form of a beautiful girl; he smuggles fire inside a fennel stalk to bring progress to the human world / they ensure that the contents of Pandora's jar will unleash calamities and disease, natural impediments to human progress. In Vernant's formulation, the exchanges between Prometheus and Zeus define human life as a mix of evils under beautiful exteriors and virtues under ugly ones.[28] Both myth logic and poetic choice thus showcase problems of interior and exterior meaning. Pandora and the jar are containers, beautiful and innocent on the outside yet hiding something important and dangerous within.

According to Froma Zeitlin, the creation of Pandora functions as an etiological account of the existence of women and the advent of sexual reproduction, a process necessary for mortal beings that lack the gods' generative powers.[29] Marina Warner has also noted the similarities between the Hesiodic myth of a first woman with the Judeo-Christian account of the creation of Eve, another being whose addition to the world comes late, after things have been formed and named, and entails the onset of sexual reproduction but also toil and pain.[30] A metonymic counterpart of the jar she carries, Pandora's body is a proverbial vessel: the virginal seal that characterizes her state as the *parthenos*, the maiden, would be broken in marriage so that the vessel could then be filled with a future child, in Zeitlin's reading the element of Hope that remains in the jar after everything else escapes. Defined by her sexual presence, Pandora does not have a childhood, she does not exist before being created as a bride, nor does she ever enjoy a choice about her sexual identity or her partners. As with later figures of the artificial woman, she is designed to incite desire. The craft involved in her manufacture, the beauty and complexity of the materials used to adorn her, and the overall impact of her form are depicted as sexualizing at the same time that they are enlivening.

Pandora's story exhibits a surprising continuity with later artificial people, whose utilitarian depiction and sexualized presence also follow from the paradoxical fact that they are born adult. While they already possess language, strength, or adult sexuality, artificial beings are newborns and thus lack the kinds of power and social recognition usually granted to adult beings in a society. Their very adulthood thus becomes a liability. Why would one wish to imagine ready-made adult bodies? Why would one want to withhold the protections and nurture needed by or owed to new beings in a society? The narrative stereotypes of later stories that feature artificial people are already apparent in these questions: artificial people would be born adult in order to immediately enter social circumstances that infants and children cannot enter, they would be born with a purpose or a job, ready to step into the contexts intended for them. And these contexts utilize a stereotypical and exaggeratedly gendered vocabulary: artificial men are designed to be laborers, as evinced in myriads of tales about mechanical slaves, artificial soldiers, automated industrial workers, supersized robots, and enslaved cyborgs, while artificial women are sexualized, depicted as glamorous but inaccessible statue goddesses, as sex workers or slaves, or as idealized "perfect" wives. In addition to showcasing their artificiality, the depiction of artificial people as tools or instruments reveals a deep discursive investment in purposefulness. Even the ancient story answers not only how Pandora came into being but also why—to become the instrument for Zeus's revenge. The circulation of the concept of purpose is instructive, if paradoxical: existential wonder about the aim of human life inspires stories about people whose purpose is clear. But such explicit purposefulness also marks these figures as nonhuman, and human life remains associated with mystery and purposelessness. In the modern tradition, stories that begin with tool-like artificial people such as robots and androids may complicate or challenge the premise of instrumentality; or a story may evade the issue of purpose, as in the case of Frankenstein's monster, thus confusing the distinction between real and artificial people and thwarting the discursive desire for explanation.

Being born adult is thus a liability in the modern discourse of the artificial person, since it launches the new being into preassigned social function and purpose and into already circumscribed gender and sexual identities. Yet we find an alternative and illuminating understanding of the adult birth when we consider its premodern cultural origin in puberty rites. These ancient cultural practices focus on the ritual birth of specifically adult bodies and, indeed, revolve around navigating one's entry into social and sexual roles. In puberty rites, a young person departs from childhood and through ritual processes enters another state, that of the initiate or young adult, and becomes eligible for marriage, citizenship, or entry into a particular social order. While such rites differ among cultures, anthropologists propose that the transformation includes the symbolic death or annihilation of the person in the "before" state (usually childhood) and their rebirth as a new person with access to the privileges and responsibilities of their new peer group.[31]

Pandora's animation is marked as both an initiation and a marriage ritual, a common connection in the case of girls' puberty rites, in which the gifts she receives, beautiful clothing, flower garlands, jewelry, and access to adult crafts such as weaving, mark the girl's entrance into the state of the eligible maiden or bride. In a modern setting, the story's emphasis on the sexual allure of the animated woman evokes pervasive structures of misogyny and objectification. But in the context of puberty rites, the arrival into sexuality is a personal and communal victory, an event to celebrate. Allegorizing the emergence of adult abilities and desires, the ritual commemorates an additional achievement: initiates die as children to be reborn as adults precisely because they did not die as children.

Puberty rites and rituals of passage thus share with animating scenes their emphasis on rebirth as well as the focus on adulthood, marriage, and sexuality, states that the animating scene abstracts in presenting an adult, already gendered or sexualized artificial person who never inhabits a "before" state. Yet modern animating scenes are also failed rituals, unable to deliver the artificial person into the next social category, instead tending toward stasis or immobility. In *Frankenstein* we see the monster in limbo, perennially rejected and isolated, while, by refusing to create a female monster, Victor also withholds from the creature the possibility of sexual identity and sexual experience. Indeed, modern science fiction texts display a bifurcated approach to the arrival of the artificial person into adult sexuality, usually withholding it from artificial men and overemphasizing it for artificial women. Instances of sexually active artificial men such as the robotic

Gigolo Joe in *A.I. Artificial Intelligence* (Steven Spielberg, 2001), Jael's artificial lover in Joanna Russ's *The Female Man*, or Silver in Tanith Lee's *The Silver Metal Lover*, are rare or self-conscious revisions of established narrative parameters.[32] And while artificial women are often depicted as sexualized and sexually available, the discourse withholds a different "arrival" by undermining their ability to procreate. Despite the fact that artificial people embody the possibility of radical methods of generation, they are often unable to procreate by any means, natural or technological, and remain wistfully outside forms of human family life.

Perennially stuck in an unfinished rite of passage, artificial people thus alert us to the definitional power but also the limits of social and cultural classifications. While the classifications themselves may vary, the transhistorical investment in just such a myth of beings that represent the unmarked, the undifferentiated, or the untranslatable reveals a sustained interest in liminal states. The artificial person represents the existence of a realm between states, a permanent between, whether these states are imagined as absolute or sublime binary oppositions (life and death), categories of being (person and object), gender classifications (female and male), or social positions (citizen and noncitizen). Since this liminal space has important social and political ramifications, scenes of animation acquire much of their representational power in modernity precisely from their ability to stage sustained investigations of what happens between realms. They allow us to express our investment in changing or protesting the limits of these states, revealing them as culturally negotiable or arbitrary.

Finally, later stories of artificial people also tend to return to the two moments that anchor Pandora's story, her animation and the opening of the box. Mapping onto the biblical account of the creation of Adam and Eve and their expulsion from Paradise, this two-act structure provides an interesting precedent for the narrative treatment of animating scenes, which are often followed by scenes of disruption, danger, or upheaval. In the case of Pandora, while both narrative moments allegorically present the problem of what may be inside a vessel, ancient depictions of Pandora often prefer her animation scene, which allows for the representation of beauty, ritual, spectacle, and divine power. Since the Renaissance it is the opening of the box, with its potential for apocalyptic and moral readings, that has captured the Western artistic imagination. In allegorical paintings, the opening of the box warns of the dangers of curiosity and transgression, as artists depict the Seven Deadly Sins, the Vices, or even "The Phantom of Ignorance" emerging out of the box.[33]

Later stories present technological evils or modernity itself as a menace that allegorically emanates from the opened box/animated person, and it has become customary to treat animation and disruption as narrative counterparts. In texts such as *Metropolis* (Fritz Lang, 1927), for example, the first appearance of the artificial woman has a ritual tone, as Rotwang, the scientist who built her, shows off his construct to city leader Fredersen. The robotic being is on display, walking and turning minimally, and seems to be performing under the scientist's control. Although she already possesses properties of aliveness, such as formal coherence, motion, even a kind of attention and independence in the way she looks from one man to the other in this scene, the robot is a marvel to see but not yet an active agent in the story. Her scene of animation or, rather, her transformation into human form also feels ritualistic and has been one of the most iconic depictions of such a scene in modern times. Balancing these moments of ritual display are many proverbial openings of dangerous boxes. After the robot acquires the outward form of the beautiful labor organizer Maria, she unleashes herself as a sexually alluring and politically threatening force through the city. In contrast to the controlled and orderly style of her ritual scenes, in these later moments the robot/Maria is a destabilizing agent, a being whose transgressive sexual performances in the nightclub are followed by her instigation of even more destructive performances of mob violence.[34]

Reminiscent of the structure of Pandora's tale, the balance between ritual animation and dangerous action in *Metropolis* hints at the adaptability of the animating story. Taboo and secret in some ancient ritual traditions, the moment of animation becomes fascinating and spectacular in modernity, and

FIGURE 8 The animation of the robot Maria (Brigitte Helm) by Rotwang (Rudolf Klein-Rogge) in *Metropolis* (Fritz Lang, 1927). © UFA

this alters the energy of the narrative: the animation of inanimate matter no longer holds the mysterious and divine properties it once did, it is thrilling but visually available, all too successful in translating mystery into process, and too controllable, a display of linguistic or cinematic mastery. The sense of witnessing something sublime, uncontrollable, or truly powerful is instead transferred to what ensues, the unruly mob, the violent upheaval, the mysterious energy of terror or revenge that transforms the meek workers of Metropolis into frenzied pagans who flood their own houses and forget their own children. While the unruliness of this second act has become a stereotype, leading to an impulsive "They are out to get us!" pattern that speaks eloquently of modernity's nightmares of racially inflected war, the political deployment of animating stories hinges on this translation of the mystery of animation into a new spectacle. The scene's power moves from animation (or what goes into the box) to dangerous action (what comes out of the box).

Given the association of Pandora with sexuality and danger, artists turned to the story of Pygmalion's statue for an animating scene that would reverse the balance of power. Unlike Pandora, Galatea comes to life as a perfect beloved, a creature of male fantasy, an exemplar of a silent and demure femininity. For eighteenth- and nineteenth-century artists, both Pandora and Galatea could be depicted as beautiful female nudes in the animating moment, amid gods, goddesses, and allegorical figures. Or, as the tradition became more self-referential, Galatea could function as a metaphor for the power of art itself, as the scene of her animation increasingly involves only the artist and the statue, a private and secular event that evades the presence of Venus we find in Ovid's text. Indeed modern artists often misread the ancient story. Appearing in a series of supernatural love stories in the *Metamorphoses*, tales that pay tribute to the power of love but also lament the loss of a beloved, Galatea's animation is not a reward for Pygmalion's artistic merits but the last stage in Venus's revenge. After learning of the licentiousness of a group of women, the Propoetidae, who denied tribute to the goddess of love and were turned into stone for their shamelessness, Pygmalion swears to forsake women and sex. But while thus thinking himself immune to Venus's power, he soon falls in love with an impossible beloved, his statue, and eventually prays to Venus for a maiden like her. By granting life to the statue, the goddess affirms that Pygmalion has accepted her power, since even inanimate objects can be vessels of the deep passion she inspires.

Descriptions of Pygmalion's devotion resound with the iconography of ancient rituals, here overtly sexualized: he brings garlands, gifts, and clothes to the statue, and he touches and sleeps with it as if in marriage. But the centuries that separate the two tales have had their effect, and there is a palliative element in the Pygmalion/Galatea story, a desire for control over art, matter, and other people that comes in sharp contrast with the disruptive potential of the Pandora story. Instead of two entities, the woman and the jar or box, that present surprising combinations of surface beauty and interior content, Pygmalion's statue operates as pure surface. Galatea is both woman and box and seems to have no interiority as either entity but to function as a site onto which the fantasy of idealized femininity can be projected. Instead of staging a warning about mysterious, divine, or unruly powers as Pandora does and potentially facilitating the representation of femininity or sex appeal as a power, in its mainstream reading the Pygmalion/Galatea story translates the divine into a vision of male artistic accomplishment and reallocates the feminine as either a quality of the surface, in the statue's beauty, or as inert material, in the statue's inanimate stillness.

Despite its cultural currency, Galatea's animation revises the truly ancient patterns of the discourse preserved more faithfully in the story of Pandora. If we keep Pandora in mind, it is easier to recognize how consistent the patterns of the animating scene are over the centuries, motivated by the isomorphic tendencies described above and the rediscovery of the ritual iconography of origin stories in later eras. In the case of *Frankenstein*, it is not clear whether the reference to a "modern Prometheus" in the novel's title implies knowledge of Hesiod's poems.[35] Hesiod makes an appearance in Percy Shelley's reading lists for 1815, and both Mary and Percy read versions of the myth in Aeschylus's *Prometheus Bound* and Ovid's *Metamorphoses*, where Prometheus appears as the benefactor of mankind without reference to Pandora.[36]

While a direct intertextual connection is unlikely, there are remarkable similarities between the animating scenes in these texts. Like Pandora, Frankenstein's creature is born adult, his supersized body constructed from body parts collected from charnel houses, cemeteries, dissecting rooms, and slaughterhouses and thus perhaps by implication combining both human and animal remains just as Pandora combines the divine and the beastly.[37] His construction also showcases problems of appearance and content, although it is the monster's exterior that is ugly and uncanny while the interior holds kindness and gentleness.[38] The monster truly embodies the crisis of the unfinished rite as he is perennially stuck between states of being, rejected by Victor, attacked by people he meets, and existing in a pure state of otherness, expressed in moving passages of existential angst. "What was I?" he repeatedly asks in the novel. "Was I then a monster, a blot upon the earth, from which all men fled, and whom all men disowned?" (90–91). Structurally, the book can be said to follow the two-act format of Pandora's story, in which the focused, claustrophobic episodes of the creature's animation are followed by scenes of violence and disruption, but the novel depicts the monster's violence as surprisingly fitting, a reaction to the cruelties he has endured and the result of the social corruption of his innate goodness. In Shelley's version of social justice, resonating with the educational and political theories of her parents, the disruption that comes out of the box in this case is directly related to the violence that went into the box.

While the novel bequeaths these continuities to future texts that feature an artificial birth, it also includes elements that the later textual tradition resists or revises. In contrast to Pandora's story, the monster's animation in the novel is secular and antisocial with Victor toiling away alone in his workshop. Given its ability to render so much visible, the animating scene seems to demand the presence of spectators, and they appear in both theatrical and cinematic adaptations thereafter.[39] By resisting the pull of visuality, Shelley treats the animating scene as a representational void, a gothic space that enacts its own violence onto the rest of the novel. In addition to fueling the fascination of generations of readers (what does the monster really look like? how does the animation really work?), these elisions avoid ritualizing the animating scene, which remains frantic and uncharted. The physical description of the monster is similarly evasive and expressionistic, skewed by Victor's trauma that night, and consists of provocative and racialized clues, as in the creature's "dull yellow eye," the way "his yellow skin scarcely covered the work of muscles and arteries beneath," his "dun white sockets," and "shriveled complexion and straight black lips" (37).[40] Descriptions of the monster later in the novel tend to focus not on his face but on his stature, speed, and strength—not shocking attributes in themselves—and to linger on the reactions of Walton and other people. The novel thus deploys a contradictory approach to physicality and visuality: his appearance matters intensely and functions deterministically for the monster's fate in the book, yet it remains a matter of mystery. This stance toward description is countered in the later tradition of both films and literary texts, which treat animation as a spectacular if fetishistic display of technological order, with the artificial body, a fascinating conglomeration of materials and textures, as the main attraction.

We find a similar resistance to the foundational logic of the animating scene in Shelley's treatment of purpose. Perhaps the monster is necessary for Victor's research in the mysteries of life and death, but he never knows this, nor does Victor have a use for the creature once he is alive. The artificial birth in this case fails to provide the ready if insufficient purposefulness that artificial people often embody, when their social positions are assigned at birth by the establishment that creates them. Soon after his awakening, the monster has the same existential questions a real person would have about the beginning and meaning of his life, and these are compounded by social rejection. Sharing human existential indeterminacy while not sharing human community, the creature also quickly exposes Victor's own instrumentalized view of the encounters between them. Victor is unprepared to recognize that the being he forms would be another person, would demand reciprocity and recognition, would not be an object or a tool. In one of the novel's grim meditations on ambition and the goal-driven life,

Victor and the monster each gain a sense of purpose when they try to annihilate each other.

In other words, *Frankenstein* does not always conform to the narrative tendencies of the discourse of the artificial person and instead presents choices that are often reversed in later texts. Not only does Shelley's treatment of animation fail to resolve the grand mysteries the animating scene is designed to allegorically resolve or at least displace, but it also infects the story with new grand mysteries, from rejection and injustice to complex psychosexual subtexts that linger long after the resolution of the plotlines.[41] It should be no surprise that the story has inspired numerous psychoanalytic approaches, since it operates by evoking a new modern interior, an invisible space of contradictory desires, unconscious impulses, and unacknowledged motives. The novel also frustrates the ancient structural focus on a normative treatment of gender and sexuality, presenting the monster's desire for companionship and perhaps procreation as a shock, and depicting Victor and Elizabeth's phobic reaction to their constantly deferred marriage. Studying this dense web of psychosexual relations, critics read both Victor and the monster as ambivalent characters that combine male, female, androgynous, and homoerotic principles and both normative and transgressive identities.[42] Taken together, these deviations from the structural patterns of animating scenes alert us to the cultural role that artificial people play in modernity. Rather than stabilize the order of being, as Pandora does by reinstalling the difference between divine and human realms disrupted by Prometheus, characters such as Frankenstein's creature reveal that the boundary between worlds established by such texts may be unclear, porous, or arbitrary. By expressing pure existential angst, by embodying a space between the realms of human and nonhuman, male and female, person and object, these beings facilitate the conceptual and emotional investigation of the between, becoming useful figures in modern demands for political recognition and quests to imagine nonconforming bodies and identities.

THE GOLEM AND THE HOMUNCULUS: SCIENCE, MODERNITY, AND THE ARTIFICIAL BIRTH

As we have seen, in figuring an adult newborn body ancient origin stories and initiation rituals avoid both the iconography of birth and questions of life and death. Ancient animating rituals serve a social purpose, establishing the social order and presenting the processes that help integrate people into adult cultural, political, and social groups. But there is a third type of scene that informs the animating story, this one closer to the sublime vocabulary of life and death and of animate and inanimate matter. In their depiction of beings that traverse the gap between material and ontological states, animating scenes engage a fantasy of circularity and reversibility—indeed this focus on doing and undoing provides the basis for the technological appropriation of the animating scene in modernity. Perhaps not surprisingly, the fantasy of reversibility emerges from the iconographic transformation of death. Revolving around another set of adult bodies that experience a radical change of status, death scenes provide the experiential origin as well as the sense of narrative unfolding we recognize in animating stories. It is because death can be observed as a process, with stages that gradually de-animate the person and separate the body from its own liveliness, that in imaginary animating scenes life can be depicted as an opposite process of gradual animation, in which the qualities that death removes seem to be added on instead. If the animating story presents an imaginative reversal of the processes of childbirth, by flipping the inside and the outside and bringing conceptual visibility to interior body processes, it also reverses a death scene, which it flips in terms of directionality and time.

A memorably schematic version of this structural reversal of death can be found in *The Bicentennial Man* (Chris Columbus, 1999), the film adaptation of Isaac Asimov's story written in 1976. In this scene, a new house robot is delivered to the Martin family home. The company van pulls up, two deliverymen unload a big box and bring it into the house, and the box is opened to reveal the inert robot within. The family looks at its serene and unseeing form for a few seconds, and the robot is finally turned on. It moves its fingers, in evocation of the first motion of the animated monster in James Whale's classic cinematic *Frankenstein* (1931), then opens its eyes and moves its head from side to side. The film switches to the robot's point of view, which starts out in an exaggeratedly pixilated, black-and-white, out-of-focus view of the family and surroundings, then slowly comes into focus, and acquires definition and color as the startup process completes. The robot quickly focuses on the family, is named by them, and declares its mission among them. Through the course of the story after this point they will become his family too, and Andrew, as the robot is named, will become increasingly human. Now if one imagines playing this animation scene backward, its conceptual reversal of an abstracted death scene becomes clear: surrounded by family members, a person with a human name and identity begins losing his or her sense of belonging with them, loses focus, forgets his or her name, seems to turn away or turn off. The eyes close, the person stops moving, becomes unresponsive and inert, and (to put it bluntly) is then put in a box and taken out of the house.

Reading animating scenes backward allows us to recognize that they are based on death scenes, for narrative as well as psychological reasons. In the powerful imaginary spaces of representational media, animating scenes reverse the dissolution of human identity, thus providing an attractive if impossible palindromic view of human life. Such a symmetrical relationship, of death as an undoing of life and life as an undoing of death, is central to many religious systems, and it structures Christian belief. It occurs in God's expulsion of Adam and Eve from Paradise, where the text accentuates the reversibility of origin and ending: "In the sweat of thy face shalt thou eat bread, till thou return unto the ground; for out of it wast thou taken: for dust thou art, and unto dust shalt thou return" (Genesis 3:19). It echoes through burial services, in *The Book of Common Prayer* for example, when a body is committed to the ground with the phrase "Earth to earth, ashes to ashes, dust to dust." And orthodoxy abstracts the symmetrical and reversible relationship of death and life into an article of faith, affirming that the real life for believers begins after death.[43] Religious doctrine aside, one may readily imagine that ancient stories depict people made out of soil, mud, or clay because the dead decompose into what may look like these materials. Observation of what happens during and after death can indeed be examined as the foundation for all other reversals in this tradition and as the cognitive and experiential basis for imagining the invisible or incomprehensible events that the animating story allegorizes.

To understand this interpretation of animation, we should consider that, for most of human history, death was observable, intimate, and everyday: death was an unfolding event and had visual and experiential specificity, duration, suspense, and narrative heft. Conception, gestation, and birth, on the other hand, were mysterious and largely spontaneous processes, visually closed-off, and mostly immune to interference except by accidents, acts of Providence, or the affecting thoughts, fantasies, and desires of the mother.[44] Structured by these mysteries, animating scenes borrow the narrative unfolding of death scenes in order to provide visibility and narrative coherence to gestation and birth processes. Modern medical imaging technologies and the ability to respond more effectively to disease have reversed this balance. In contemporary culture, conception and birth are visually fascinating events, traced repeatedly in public discourse, medical documentaries, and visual media or in the private contemplation of ultrasound imagery. Our ability to see inside the body has added an element of narrative unfolding to childbirth, in which the birth itself is the culmination of a process, an end rather than a beginning. On the other hand, the same media treat death as taboo, as an unfortunate rather than inevitable turn of events or as a mystery that needs to be solved. Finding meaning in death, the primordial impetus of moral philosophy and religious dogma, may even be translated into obsessive technological quests, as seen in the forensic fascinations of crime television shows. We tend to avoid looking at death in popular culture unless we can technologize what we see, unless we can construct action-based narratives that "make sense" out of a fact of life that distinctly refuses to make sense. The finality of death, its moral and personal meanings, and the work of mourning are often barely present in our largely death-phobic public culture, while the materiality of the body after death, the processes of decay and decomposition, invite a fascination with order and control rather than chaos and the lack of control that humans experience in relation to death and dying.

Although it reflects a transhistorical desire to interpret death as reversible, as a structural element in the Western discourse of the artificial person the palindromic treatment of death coincides with a sixteenth-century reinvention of animating stories that bequeaths an alchemical and Kabbalistic iconography to later animating scenes, an iconography that also operates in *Frankenstein*. Victor's inspiration, research, and methods are thoroughly death-based. He frequently expresses the logical fallacy that motivates his work, and animating stories in general—the fallacy that presents the beginning of life as an inversion of death. We find the same desire for reversibility in two important animating scenes of the sixteenth century, one in golem stories from the Jewish Kabbalah and the other in recipes for the creation of a homunculus in alchemical writings. While they belong to different cultural and epistemological traditions, the golem and the homunculus function as important ancestors for modern artificial people, and their stories illuminate the conceptual threads that link ancient and modern patterns of animation.

In Jewish legend, a golem is a clay effigy that is animated though ritual, language, and incantation in order to protect the community and is later kept hidden in a secret location for the community's future needs. Recognizing their complex provenance, Gershom Scholem suggests that golem stories may have been used in mystical rituals of initiation that culminated in ecstasy.[45] In his medieval commentary, mystic Eleazar of Worms (c. 1200 CE) describes the staging of an allegorical process of formation and dissolution in such a context: two or three adepts take virginal mountain earth and mold it with water into an anthropomorphic shape. Over this shape they recite the 221 combinations of the alphabet proposed in the *Sefer Yezirah* (*Book of Formation/Creation*), an early mystical text written between the first or third and the sixth century CE. One ordering of combinations results in a male golem, a different order in a female golem, and reciting backward undoes the animating process and dissolves the golem back into earth. The creative process yields such power that it poses dangers for the aspiring creator, not because of any actions the golem itself will perform but because a mistake in the recitation of the letter combinations may undo the initiates themselves or unveil the impurities in their hearts and misdirect the process.[46] Such rituals for Scholem do not aspire actually to animate a golem but to represent the act of creation, enacting or commemorating in ritual the creativity and power of God.

In later legends, many from the late sixteenth and early seventeenth centuries, this mystical animation is reinterpreted as a literal act, with the dissemination of folklore about golem-making rabbis creating super-servants that are actual, powerful, mute, and potentially dangerous. These revisions also add new warnings: the story's emphasis on circularity, on making and unmaking the golem, takes on an urgent tone, as the golem becomes too strong or too tall for a rabbi to erase the name of God from its forehead and thus de-animate it. As a protective but also dangerous figure, the golem resembles ancient protective and apotropaic statues and the rituals that similarly animate, activate, or dedicate such effigies for the benefit of a community.[47] Just as Pandora's animation points to rituals of passage or initiation as well as statue worship, the golem story reveals complex echoes from ancient Mediterranean ritual culture where effigy-related animation rituals are widely attested in civilizations of the Bronze Age, in textual references and artifacts from Anatolia and North Syria, Assyrian and Hittite documents and clay tablets dating from the ninth and eighth centuries BCE as well as Greek and Etruscan ceremonies.[48] Animated statues in these rituals are activated as guardians by means of written incantations or inscriptions on clay tablets, some hidden within the statue or buried close to it, just as the name of God is spoken over or written on the clay forehead of the golem in order to animate it.[49] Just as the golem can be hidden in a secret location until it is needed by the community, in antiquity burying or hiding ritual objects enhances or extends their mysterious power. Nor are such important objects necessarily anthropomorphic. In addition to statues, the earliest Greek examples of protective or apotropaic talismans include unworked rocks, stones that "fell from the sky" (perhaps meteors), sealed jars filled with special herbs and grains, tripods and sacrificial knives, stone pillars, and wooden planks. The objects acquire or express protective powers after their ritual actualization when they are anointed with oil or wine, covered in wool, garlanded with flowers, and hidden, buried, or displayed at an important location.[50] Pandora's animation points to a ritual of display and similarly refers to everyday human customs of ornamentation and clothing, while the golem story revolves around hiding or burying the talismanic effigy and safeguarding the object's power by ensuring its obscurity. The inanimate object becomes culturally significant, in some cases even numinous or animated, in and through ritual.

Despite its antiquity, the golem story reemerges in the context of the Renaissance, and the era seems to be both formative and retroactively appealing for fantasies of the artificial person. Whether spuriously associated with Rabbi Judah Löw (c. 1520–1609) and Emperor Rudolf II in Prague or actually inspired by the first translations of the Jewish Kabbalah into Latin in the 1540s, later historical and artistic accounts locate the golem in the sixteenth century.[51] It was in the Renaissance that the ancient and medieval ritual echoes of golem stories were translated into what Scholem describes as the realm of "living legend," with stories of golem-making accruing around specific historical figures.[52] The general interest in mysticism that pervaded the fifteenth and sixteenth centuries along with the historical conditions of Jewish experience across Europe inspired both Jews and gentiles to study the Kabbalah for its mystical content and messianic possibilities. The writings of Rabbi Isaac Luria (1534–1572) and Rabbi Moses Cordovero (1522–1570) became the basis of the "Lurianic" Kabbalah, which shared with Christian and alchemical thinking an emphasis on reform and spiritual regeneration. Cordovero wrote commentaries on the *Sefer Yezirah* in 1548, while in the same period legends of golems circulated in the German Hasidim and Polish Jewish communities. Widespread intellectual interest in antiquity and natural magic inspired collections of stories about ancient and medieval rabbis who made their own servants, and about more recent figures such as Rabbi Elijah Baal Shem of Chelm (d. 1583), who was reputed to have animated a golem. Scholem argues that the golem became attached to the figure of Rabbi Löw when stories about Rabbi Elijah's golems moved from Chelm to Prague. Hillel J. Kieval proposes that it was Rudolf's patronage and support of occult arts and emerging science that inspired this association.[53]

In addition to respecting the historical dissemination of animating stories throughout Europe at this time, the critical tendency to locate the golem in the sixteenth century allows us to contrast the golem legend with the other famous animating story of the era and the figure of the homunculus. Taken together the two animating stories inform the modern approach to animation as a mystical but also potentially scientific process. The alchemical method for creating a homunculus originates not in ritual but in ancient approaches to matter and its transformability and, especially, in theories of spontaneous generation, or abiogenesis.[54] In the Middle Ages and the early Renaissance, animate matter and inanimate matter are not opposing elements in a binary opposition but could function as generative versions of each other, allowing for the possibility that under certain conditions living organisms could just emerge from nonliving matter. Attributed to Aristotle, who reserved it for explaining the origin of some lower types of animals and plants, the concept of spontaneous generation inspired experimental science and led to numerous symptomatic but satisfying observations of cause and effect. Recipes for the spontaneous generation of lice from sweat, maggots from putrefying meat, and mice from wheat husks or the mud of the Nile now strike us as ludicrous, but they provided an experimental way to prove material theories of the era and strengthened scientific interest in processes of chemical transformation such as digestion, fermentation, and especially, putrefaction.[55]

In its representation of matter on a continuum, alchemical science translates the palindromic desires that are a transhistorical characteristic of animating stories into scientific or pseudo-scientific principle. For alchemists, death and decay constitute a different kind of material beginning: from Galen's ancient physiological treatises to Paracelsus's writings, putrefaction in alchemical traditions is not an entropic process but a generative one. It proves the fundamental trans-formability of matter, its cyclical nature. For example, basing his work on models of fermentation and digestion, Paracelsus notes: "one could say that all things are born from the earth by means of putrefaction. . . . For just as the putrefac-tion in the stomach turns all food to dung and transmutes it, so also the putre-faction that occurs outside the stomach in a glass [a flask] transmutes all things from one form into another."[56] Recipes for the creation of a human-form entity, a homunculus, through the fermentation of blood, urine, menstrual blood, or sperm can be found in Arabic sources of the ninth and tenth centuries CE, as well as in alchemical treatises that regulated the proper uses of precious bodily fluids, especially sperm.[57] Attributed to Paracelsus, the Renaissance recipe for an artifi-cial human is also an exercise in the transmutation of matter: take human sperm and seal it in a gourd, he states, allowing it to putrefy in warm horse manure for forty days. After that time, it will be seen to move by itself and look "somewhat like a man, but transparent, without a body."[58] Partly because it is a product of art and partly because of its mode of generation, the homunculus has awareness of the marvels of matter and power. If it can be raised into adulthood, it will have apocryphal knowledge.

We recognize elements of both these Renaissance versions of artificial con-struction in modern texts that feature animating scenes. Some critics suggest that Mary Shelley had read a version of the golem story before working on *Franken-stein*, and although scholars have long defended the scientific vision of the novel by insisting on its distance from alchemical processes, the text shares important intertextual connections with William Godwin's novel *St. Leon* (1799) and Percy Shelley's readings and experiments with alchemy.[59] Of course the alchemists and natural philosophers that Victor studies (Cornelius Agrippa, Paracelsus, Alber-tus Magnus) offer far from a uniform curriculum, and their names function as mysterious intellectual markers that allow Victor to be both a scientist and a gothic protagonist.[60] But in addition to the novel's overall tendencies toward cir-cular and palindromic structures, Victor's fascinated research on decomposing bodies in his "workshop of filthy creation" (35) traces an alchemical approach to matter and animation, presenting a technologizing response to the fact of death while aiming for death's reversal. Although his axiomatic statement "To exam-ine the causes of life, we must first have recourse to death" references the inter-est in anatomy of the early nineteenth century, Victor's methods go far beyond anatomy and follow the alchemical interest in putrefaction, "the natural decay and corruption of the human body" (32).[61] Like the alchemists, Victor studies decomposition in detail, focusing his attention on "how the fine form of man was degraded and wasted," and his discovery of animation results directly from this study: "I paused, examining and analysing all the minutiae of causation, as exemplified in the change from life to death, and death to life, until from the midst of this darkness a sudden light broke in upon me" (32). The intellectual sleight of hand that enables the scientific turn of the novel, Victor's discovery of the principle of life, is revealed in this one phrase "from life to death, and death to life," whereby the paradox of biblical and alchemical circularity is extended into modern scientific possibility.

In addition to lending the book an aura of antique and potentially gruesome material knowledge, alchemy also structures the text's emotional landscape, as Victor often longs for the reversible, palindromic modes of the alchemists. Both modern and premodern modes of understanding matter and animation occur in the text, as the novel's focus on circularity, return, and the alchemical merger of opposites gradually give way to a linear trajectory that is as encompassing and much less reassuring than dreams of alchemical rebirth. If mystics and alchemists accepted the transformability of matter, its potential for corruption and generation, and corruption *as* generation, theirs is a view of matter difficult to uphold within modern epistemologies that organize the world according to an entity's animate or inanimate status. Rather than imagining matter as mobile, transformable, and transmutable, post-Enlightenment epistemologies install more rigid classifications that present material conditions as inherent or definitive. In this context, the monster's violence brings apocalyptic disruption because it unleashes an inappropriate kind of mobility, a mobility that blurs the categories of being.

In contrast to ancient origin stories, medieval rituals, and Renaissance alchemy, reversibility in modernity is not a comforting business, and paradoxically this partly motivates our investment in animating scenes. If matter is supposed to be either animate or inanimate, if a binary organization of the world insists on stable material categories, then the animating story fuels the fantasy that matter may be mobile—or indeed the story activates our implicit awareness that matter may be more mobile than our epistemologies propose. And by extension, if social and political structures present themselves as inevitable, necessary, or natural modes of social organization, the animating story offers a provocative dream for the reorganization of an all-too-logical and schematic world. As Chris Baldick has proposed, the monster in *Frankenstein* was quickly understood as a disruptive force, an allegorical embodiment of revolutionaries, downtrodden workers, and colonial subjects.[62] The epistemological dimension of the animating story thus also functions as the precondition for the story's disruptive potential as political allegory.

Because of their narrative stability, animating stories become records of the cultural resilience of old concepts even under conditions of radical historical change. They reveal an investment in exploring and even bridging both the divide between human and nonhuman and the divide between the modern and its historical and cultural others—divides that, as Bruno Latour proposes, also tend to be described in terms of irrevocable difference.[63] Readings of animation in *Frankenstein* may focus on the doubling of Victor and the monster, whose identities and subject positions expand into a series of sublime opposing pairs in the text: creator/created, person/nonperson, proper citizen/alienated outsider. But the modern propensity to focus on binary structures, the tendency to map other oppositions onto the seemingly unavoidable fundamental difference of self and other, tends to lead to exclusive, mutually defining, but hermetic relationships and obscures the fractal and palindromic tendencies I have been tracing in the novel. Almost any combination of characters in this uncontrollable book can be mapped as if on a grid of mutually defining oppositions—indeed the reader's construction of such oppositions has to be understood as a stabilizing gesture, one that organizes the dynamic fantasies and dispersed meanings of the novel into an orderly, and modern, dialectic. As with Latour's call to study "the production of humans and non-humans simultaneously," Judith Halberstam proposes that the creature's monstrosity both constructs Victor as the male, white, bourgeois subject and reveals humanity itself to be "a patchwork of morality, criminality, subterfuge, and domesticity, and one which barely holds together."[64] When we define the monster as the nonhuman or the most human, Halberstam proposes, we avoid the real challenge of the novel, which is that "the monster, in fact, is where we come to know ourselves as never-human, as always between humanness and monstrosity."[65] In its ability to highlight the processes of negotiation involved in defining the modern and the human, the animating scene brings to the foreground the continued relevance of the never-modern, the never-human.

Treating animating scenes transhistorically thus has the potential to elucidate both old and new structures of meaning, without lamenting the technologized modern world or attempting to supplement it with fantasies of premodern plenitude.[66] This approach can also amend our understanding of the technological appropriation of animating scenes in modernity. For example, the most overt difference between ancient origin and animating stories and their modern counterparts revolves around the presence of gods and the divine in antiquity and of scientists in modernity. But what is the meaning of this difference? One could easily propose that modern science transplants ancient magic, yet the continuities between ancient and modern stories should also alert us to the obviousness with which modernity identifies itself with technological innovation.[67] While the processes used to animate the monster's stitched-together body in *Frankenstein* posit a scientific and not a supernatural animation, it makes little structural difference for the scene itself whether the technologies used are real or not—the creature's animation itself stands in for the explanations we might have wished for regarding the technologies used by Victor. Despite the difference between ritual and secular modes of address and between ancient and modern cultural contexts, in this story type modern animating technologies are rather equivalent to ancient mystical processes. In its displacements of explanation, the animating scene stages a material transformation that proves the power of the gods, mystics, priests, scientists, or artists overseeing the event, as well as the presence and effectiveness of the animating agents involved, the divine breath, the name of a god, the soul, the power of love, art, and magic, or the powerful technologies replacing such entities in the modern era.[68] It is this ability of the artificial body to materialize and grant visibility to invisible, immaterial, or abstract entities that enables the technological interpretation of animation. From facilitating the depiction of electric and electronic processes, evoked in Shelley's galvanic metaphors in the novel and the electrical paraphernalia of cinematic versions of *Frankenstein*, to enabling the often alarmist presentation of the molecular and genetic explorations of recent decades, the animating scene allows technological processes to be rendered visible, efficacious, life-giving. In its spectacular presence, the animated body constitutes the sublime visualization of the invisible, in a narrative logic that includes the desire to see inside the body, the desire to understand conception and gestation, the desire to find purpose and meaning in life and death, and the desire to see the divine and the immaterial at work in the material world.

Because the materializing logic of animation coincides with the modern investment in modalities of externalization and explanation, it is difficult to recognize that the tenets of actual science are often undermined by the ancient structures of the story type. If we reconsider the sixteenth-century legacies of the animating scene, for example, we find that while they seem similar in their aspirations, Paracelsus's alchemical experiments and his homunculus recipe and the golem stories that were disseminated in the West in the same era produce different legacies for later animating stories. Although I doubt that a little transparent homunculus was ever generated through his work, Paracelsus uses what we can consider a realist animating approach: his mode of address promises that the creation of a homunculus is possible in the real world and can be achieved by human agents through the premises of physical and material science and without recourse to spiritual processes or divine interference. In contrast, golem stories present their animating scenes as metaphysical processes in which the power to animate belongs to a supreme entity channeled through human agents with special spiritual training. The dependence on a metaphysical animating process reveals the antiquity of the golem story, its affinity with origin stories and rituals that commemorate the divine creation or animation of the world through the use of effigies and mystical experiences. The modern tradition of animation displays a promiscuous borrowing from both narrative systems. The representational elements and visual treatment of the modern animating scene, as exemplified in *Frankenstein* and *Metropolis*, for example, are golem-based: they feature an adult or oversized inanimate body that appears fully formed before its animation; a melodramatic emphasis on "before" and "after" states; an often visually engaging process of awakening; and the absence of any sustained attention to body fluids, growth, or other physical body processes. Clearly continuous with even more ancient stories, such as the animation of Adam and the creation of Pandora, these structural choices revolve around the most basic and ancient ingredients of the animating scene. Of all the narrative elements available in the homunculus recipe, what it bequeaths to the modern discourse is a philosophical tone rather than representational particulars. Modern stories of animation share the secular setting and realist mode of address of Paracelsus's recipe, promising enhanced human power and privileged knowledge and eschewing supernatural elements and divine agents.

Given that the homunculus recipe is closer to modern science both in its mode of address and the biochemical processes it imagines, it is significant to note how thoroughly stories of animation avoid the visual logic of that scene, despite the consistency with which the homunculus is included in the historical ancestry of robots and cyborgs. In my view this is because alchemical transmutation as a process does not satisfy what seem to be major transhistorical desires of the discourse, such as clarity and visibility. The bubbling liquids and glass tubes that grace scientific laboratories in animating scenes may refer to the distillation processes, sublimations, flasks, and liquids of the alchemists, but they also refer to the desire for a visible and explainable process. Interestingly, it is precisely the desire for visual access to the process of animation that favors an ancient ritual structure for animating scenes, more reminiscent of the golem's awakening than the homunculus's creation. For all Paracelsus knew, his fermentation of sperm remained too close to the truth of generation according to the physical theories of his era: a fermenting process may be exactly what occurs in the womb during those mysterious months of gestation. In contrast, the majority of stories of artificial humanity display an abhorrence of body fluids, closed-off vessels, and invisible fermentations, instead using the representational space to provide an antidote to the invisibility and inaccessibility of natural conception and generation. As with ancient rituals, the modern animating scene exchanges the spontaneity of conception and the invisibility of gestation for willed, scheduled, and intentional processes, even when such depictions violate scientific knowledge. Although alchemical transmutation is based on the experimental science of the day, while kabbalistic animation harks back to metaphysical fiat and primordial origins, clearly it is at the symbolic and not the scientific level that explanation and visibility are necessary in the animating scene.

Despite its depictions of presumably scientific processes, then, the animating scene enacts an ancient structural logic that is hard to reconcile with actual science. This disjunction is palpable in texts that reference fields such as nanotechnology, genetics, and biotechnology. As Colin Milburn has proposed, processes of embodiment are fundamental to contemporary approaches to matter, since modern distinctions between animate and inanimate matter simply do not pertain at the nano-level.[69] One could imagine, therefore, that a contemporary conceptualization of the artificial birth would take advantage of this fluidity and present radically new modes of material emergence, becoming, or transformation. This has not been the case, and few animating scenes truly engage the grammar of the microscopic and the biochemical.

In the rare cases in which the artificial person is constructed through roughly alchemical or nanotechnological means, as in the film *Virtuosity* (Brett Leonard, 1995), the animating process is delivered in an implicitly derisive tone, as if the putrefactions and fermentations of the alchemists become a form of cooking up a person. In this film, a scientist places a gem-like computer module into a Petri dish that contains a colloidal medium full of nanomachines. The module holds the programmed personality of a virtual serial killer, SID 6.7 (Russell Crowe), and the nanomachines use the program as an "organizing principle" in order to create a material version of SID, silicon-based but fully animate and quite menacing. The process of creation takes place in a closed vessel, which at some point bubbles forth a giant organic-looking closed pod, as a noise similar to that of a microwave oven announces the end of the formation. Steam emerges from the opening pod, as if indeed what is metaphorically cooked here is an oversized bag of microwave popcorn, and SID emerges from the pod and continues to form in full view, with rough geometric shapes popping under the surface and quickly smoothing themselves into the appearance of skin. Even with its concessions to the microscopic aspects of matter that a modern biotechnological process would have to involve, the film can't resist the golem-based logic of visibility: because the nanotech process is invisible, the scientist first explains it visually using a snake that is cut in half, reformed, and de-animated in front of our eyes; then the process is rendered visible again through computer models that represent it on screens and in virtual reality goggles used by the characters; and finally SID emerges from the pod only halfway formed in order for the final construction moment and the revelation of his human-like exterior to be visually accessible yet again.

The same logic of visibility operates in *The Fifth Element* (Luc Besson, 1997), where a nanotechnological process reconstructs the alien being Leeloo (Milla Jovovich) from genetic code found in a few charred cells. In self-conscious evocation of the animating scene in *Metropolis*, the re-creation of Leeloo takes place in a glass enclosure, as her body is created by fast-moving machinery, molecule by visible molecule. Little pieces of bone matter are piled on like sliced-up Legos, muscles, tendons, and nerves are knitted onto the skeleton, a bright ultraviolet light forces the raw body to develop skin, thermal bandages cover

Leeloo's nakedness, and finally she is awakened abruptly by a bright camera flash and takes a sharp, shocked breath. While presumably the process is based on interpreting Leeloo's genetic code, the visual structure of the scene follows a Renaissance pattern of Vesalian anatomical explanation, in which the body is onion-like in its layering, made of concentric organ systems. The scene offers a prime example of the ancient logic of the adult birth, its focus on visibility and explanation, and its staging of an awakening into language, sexuality, and an apparently abrupt and traumatic integration into a new world. Leeloo emerges already able to speak her alien language and almost as immediately realizes she is in danger, breaks the glass coffin, and flees.

Similarly, in the television series *Battlestar Galactica* (2003–2009), the human-like Cylons are constructed beings that share the same genetic profile with others of their model and thus can be imagined as clones of each other.[70] But while Cylons are thus associated with biotechnology and genetics, their birth scenes follow the visual logic of the discourse and its insistence on visible births and adult bodies. When a Cylon dies, he or she is resurrected in a vat on a special spaceship, where the memories and individual experiences of the dead Cylon are downloaded into a new body of the same model, a body that is already constructed, already adult, and already gendered in exaggerated and often sexualized ways. Although their birth is depicted as a traumatic awakening into consciousness, language, and memory, the Cylons' beautiful adult bodies and their immediate assumption of prearranged roles and social positions follows the baseline requirements of the artificial birth since antiquity. Evidently, even in scientifically informed contemporary texts, the science has to conform to ancient narrative and structural patterns.

In retrospect, then, it becomes clear that while the animating story seems poised to take on the full force of technological mediation in the modern era, it displays a certain resistance to actual scientific applications when those do not subscribe to accepted iconography. In contemporary contexts, this transhistorical consistency of animating scenes indeed renders the discourse of the artificial person partly unfit to describe certain challenges we face today when defining the human and its limits in relation to technology. The problem becomes palpable, for example, in texts and public conversations about clones and cloning. In fiction and science fiction, clones may function as artificial people, in gothic fantasies that present them as doubles of an already existing person. When Ian Wilmut describes the research that led his team to the 1997 birth of Dolly, the first cloned sheep, he and his co-author, Roger Highfield, preface their book with a section titled "Drop the Doppelgänger," in order to warn against the public tendency to see cloning in these science-fictional terms. Of course, cloned embryos would have to be implanted in a womb, gestated, and born, the authors insist; of course, clones would have to grow and have individual experiences; of course, they would not be copies of anyone else. "Genetic identity," they write, "is not the same as personal identity, and selves, unlike cells, cannot be cloned."[71] Providing examples from the lives of natural clones, or twin siblings, the authors focus on the ways in which human identity encompasses more than just genetic individuality.

And yet, as I hope my discussion of artificial birth fantasies has made clear, the long-standing structural terms of the artificial birth prove so irresistible, they possess such transhistorical power, such cognitive clarity, such emotional draw, that it is not easy to revise or undermine them. Even at a time when the scientific facts of cloning and stem cell research are fast becoming common knowledge and are presented repeatedly in mainstream culture and public debates, the public imagination holds onto fantasmatic visions of adult births and body doubles; visions of decanting readymade children that have been grown in vats, as in Aldous Huxley's *Brave New World* (1932); or of activating adult bodies that are created precisely as replacements for dead people, as with the Cylons of *Battlestar Galactica*; or of the quick creation of adult bodies designed for organ harvesting, as with the captive clones of *The Island* (Michael Bay, 2005). What emerges in this intersection between the tenets of contemporary science and the structures of imaginative fiction is the limit of the discourse of the artificial person and its specific fantasies of the adult birth. Clones are formed adult in these imaginings because the default patterns by which we delegate the nonhuman in the discourse of the artificial person revolve around a body that is born or formed adult. Because the discourse depends on this difference in order to demarcate human from nonhuman, it is not easy for the label of the nonhuman to be assigned onto something that grows.

The result is an impasse, a conceptual paradox: in order to present the clone as a form of the nonhuman or as a threat to authentic humanity, a contemporary text needs to activate fictional traditions that predate current scientific knowledge and to depict adult bodies and adult births, engaging the whole slew of fantasies and iconographies of the artificial birth I have traced in this chapter. If a text instead attempts to respect contemporary science and depict clones in the microscopic vocabulary of manipulated cells, engineered DNA, or harvested stem cell components, if it presents clones as embryos that are implanted, gestated, and born as babies, then such a representation loses the structural certainties of the discourse of the artificial person and cannot depict the clone as nonhuman at all. The scientific processes and facts of cloning are at odds with the fictional tradition. According to the logic of this tradition, artificial people are born adult, they do not need to grow; if something is born as a baby and grows, it probably isn't all that artificial.

While fictional depictions of cloning often have little to do with actual science, there is an uncanny symmetry to the figure of the clone as a specific

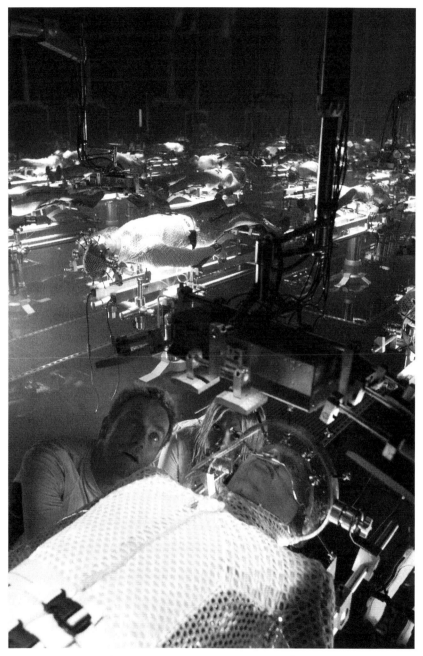

FIGURE 9 Two clones (Ewan McGregor and Scarlett Johansson) discover a reserve of cloned adult bodies grown for organ harvesting in *The Island* (Michael Bay, 2005). Warner Bros./Photofest. © Warner Bros. Photographer: Merrick Morton

contemporary example of the artificial person. As I proposed earlier in this chapter, artificial people "come from" wherever real people are imagined as "coming from" in a given historical and cultural context, and the discourse on clones and cloning respects this isomorphic tendency. In medical research and popular understanding alike, we seek the beginning of human life and the potential for artificial life in the same places, at the deepest levels of matter—when fertilization occurs, or when cells begin to divide, or when the divided cells are blastocysts and so on. Despite our medical and visual technologies, or indeed precisely because of our enhanced methods for accessing and experiencing the existence of interior body spaces, our technological environment pushes the question of the beginning of life to an ever-earlier moment of formation and similarly stages the threat to the human in the same originary moments and the same deep spaces.[72]

What emerges from this analysis is the sense that the animating story is intimately related to bodily experience, inspired by birth and death as liminal body states, and importantly related to understanding sexual identity and adulthood. But precisely because of the foundational function of the body in the discourse of the artificial person, bodily experience is also heavily contested in this story type. As I will discuss in the next chapter, generation, growth, and decline have acquired paramount importance for artificial people and often inform the existential requirements entailed in imagining under what circumstances a created being, a robot or android, could be considered a person. Along with the perennial question "Does it have a soul?" (which each era interprets in its own ways), there are recurrent questions concerning embodied identity in these fictions: "Was it born or made? Can it grow? Can it procreate? Can it die?" These are underhanded questions, of course, since the artificial body is a priori designed as the body that does not need to be born, does not grow, does not die. By safeguarding certain embodied experiences as the province of real people, the discourse of the artificial person provides a metaphysical security barrier that thwarts both the pleasures and threats of similarity. Enablers of a multiple transhistorical fantasy of reversal—the reversal of inside and outside and of birth and death—artificial people are fundamentally bound by their bodies. Artificial people and the narratives that feature them enact a logic of embodiment that is surprisingly consistent, a logic that confronts the modern constitution with its still active premodern desires.

2 · THE MECHANICAL BODY

At first glance, the tendency to imagine the artificial body as a mechanical, rather than organic, entity seems to be an extension of the animating story's focus on counteracting human vulnerability. Just as the ready-made, adult-born artificial people of ancient and modern tales usually bypass the frailty of childhood, so robot, android, and cyborg characters are imagined as impervious to need, disease, or even death, and their mechanical bodies present spectacular alternatives to flesh and skin. We see the desire for mechanical resilience in *The Iron Giant* (Brad Bird, 1999), for example. Based on a children's story by Ted Hughes, the film depicts a powerful robot that is not only incredible to behold in its enormous scale and technological complexity but also practically indestructible.[1] Even after the robot has been blown to bits, its body parts are so durable and independent that tiny rivets, wires, and scraps of metal find their way to a homing device and simply reconstitute the robot.

In such technological fantasies, the fictional artificial body promises to correct what the discourse depicts as body problems. Instead of skin, artificial people are covered in metal or synthetic textures that resist injury or can be repaired easily; their old or damaged body parts can be substituted or upgraded; they have no irreplaceable body fluids; and they experience few bodily needs that couldn't be satisfied with a new power source, updated materials, or better programming. In the process of presenting alternatives to organicity, fantasies of the mechanical body utilize an industrial age iconography, with its cog-and-wheel standardization, shiny metal obsessions, and dreams of assembly-line efficiency. They also evade or find alternatives to emotional vulnerability, both for the artificial people and for those who might become attached to them. Although some texts treat robotic beings as figures of pathos and sensitivity, they do so against a benchmark of stereotypes in which mechanical bodies are designed to be immune to emotional or psychological torment, unaffected by grief or pain, and resistant to suffering. Even when they are damaged, artificial people cannot

FIGURE 10 The indestructible robot protects the fragile boy, in *The Iron Giant* (Brad Bird, 1999). Warner Brothers/Photofest. © Warner Bros.

be hurt, and instead of dying, either they merely cease functioning or, as with the Iron Giant, they can be restarted or remade. A body that remains immune to pain does not need to be consoled, and since it can be reconstructed perhaps it need not be missed or mourned.

Yet, despite their cultural currency, such fantasies of invincible mechanical bodies allow us to suspend our awareness of the incredible resilience, versatility, and self-regulating strength of organic bodies, their ability to resist and fight infection, recognize pathogens, withstand and reverse damage, respond to stimuli, or regenerate. In comparison to basic, unconscious, everyday body processes, the robotic ideal of compartmentalization seems rudimentary. Fetishized in the discourse of the artificial person, the contrast between mechanical and organic bodies indeed obscures the fundamental logic that structures fantasies of embodied mechanicity, a logic that is fuelled by the allure of mechanical power but also reveals a deep emotional awareness of the organic body as a mechanical entity. In the process of tracing why stories of artificial people depict fascinating mechanical, robotic, cybernetic, or automatic bodies, we must confront the ways in which, at a fundamental level, something about the organic body includes an intimate register of automatism and mechanicity. Put simply, while they traffic in the presumed opposition between mechanical and organic embodiment, stories of artificial people allegorize the mechanical presence of the organic.

In order to be able to see how the discourse of the artificial person negotiates the concept of embodied mechanicity, we need to avoid treating the imaginary bodies of this tradition as imitations of the human form. Classic depictions of mechanical, constructed, and artificial bodies tend to align visual representation with narrative function, as an artificial person's actions in a story are circumscribed by its physicality, sometimes to a stereotypical degree. Robots are often metallic, oversized, strong, logical, and unemotional; androids are a little more human-looking but still awkward and baffled by human culture or humor; and cyborgs may be indistinguishable from real humans at least at first, but this also makes them dangerous or misunderstood and makes others paranoid about their intentions. It is tempting to interpret these patterns through concepts such as imitation or simulation, to focus on whether the artificial person looks sufficiently human-like, but this would be to misunderstand how body design affects the discourse of the artificial person and imply that all stories have the same character requirements. Any number of roughly anthropomorphic figures can be discussed as imitations of the human form, but this tells us little about the aims and effects of the representational particulars.

Instead of considering the mechanical body as an imitation of the organic body or as its symbolic negation, it is more helpful to see how mechanical body fantasies offer an allegorical or analogical translation of both bodies and machinery. As I propose in this chapter, such a treatment of the mechanical body connects the discourse of the artificial person to an expansive context of premodern and modern thought. While commonly associated with the industrial and technological innovations of the modern era, mechanical body fantasies have a much longer conceptual history and simple, but profound, origins. Fantasies of purely instrumental mechanical and robotic bodies, for example, seem to allegorize people's relationship to tools. This is a fundamental and dispersed mode for experiencing mechanicity through the body, since tools often become surrogates, enhancements, or extensions of body parts in the way they hold the imprint of the body both in their actual design (consider the tactile recognition of a well-made hammer handle), and in the way they negotiate between the body and natural forces (the weight of the hammer works with gravity and the length and anatomical structure of the arm to drive in nails more easily). As with everything we handle, tools are intimate objects and they structure human consciousness: they channel our will and desire, release energies of aggression or feelings of power, focus our attention and demand that focus, activate a sense of purpose or detail, and enforce coordination among the senses and different parts of the body and brain. Tools not only expand the limits and alter the abilities of the body, they also facilitate a certain way of thinking about the world and our ways of dealing with it, as they change the effectiveness and magnitude of human action. On a symbolic level, most everyday tools inspire a double gesture of conceptual modeling, in which we redefine objects and their properties but also body parts and abilities, through their respective relationships with tools.

In a complementary conceptual thread, imaginary mechanical bodies stem from a mechanical understanding of the body itself and from observations of bodily processes that are independent from conscious control. Since antiquity, philosophers, anatomists, and physicians turn to mechanical models in order to explain these autonomic or automatic functions, such as breathing and the beating of the heart, falling asleep, waking up, digestion, blinking, and various nervous reflexes. Special body events such as conception, gestation, and childbirth are also notoriously mysterious and unwilled, while the apparent but enigmatic connection between images and sexual arousal was for many philosophers a paramount example for how abstract things have material effects independently of any control mechanism of the self. This set of conceptual interactions reveals an alternative to the sense of mastery we might experience with tools: if tool use implies conscious control, the body's own mechanicity enacts a different kind of control over the self, "bottom up," as it were, instead of "top down."

As a transhistorical concept, the fantasy of the mechanical body stems from the contrast between these two main experiences of embodied mechanicity, between conscious actions and autonomic processes. Recognizing that questions about the autonomy of the body structure the discourse of the artificial person helps elucidate why issues of control are so prevalent in stories of artificial people, and in technological discourse in general. Countless texts investigate whether we control our technologies or whether they control us, whether imaginary robots would be ideal servants or out-of-control enemies. While the next chapter will focus on historical legacies of enslaved labor, and the depiction of artificial people as slaves that are both fully controllable and always on the verge of rebellion, this chapter presents a more structural perspective: fictions of mechanical bodies focus on issues of control because there is something in our experience of the body that presents questions of control and presents them in ways that are somehow understandable through mechanical explanations or metaphors.

In visual terms, mechanical body fantasies express the anatomical desires of the discourse of the artificial person most directly, as they seem to flow from the representation of the body as a concentric structure proposed by artists and anatomists since the Renaissance. To the ancient focus on explaining the function of major organs and dissecting the cavities of the body, which follow Galen's modes of explanation and aim at aiding physicians rather than theorists or visual artists, Renaissance anatomists such as Andreas Vesalius add a new fascination with the "similar parts," the bones, muscles, nerves, and arteries. The uncanny illustrations that accompany Vesalius's *De humani corporis fabrica* (*On the Fabric of the Human Body*) (1543) show a body rendered in this systemic way, in independent layers made of just bones, or just nerves, arteries, or muscles. Not only are these depictions offering a compartmentalized narrative of body systems that can be imagined as being independent of each other, they also create a good foundation for depicting a technological body: all one needs to do is extrapolate replacing one of these body systems with an inorganic equivalent, with a metal skeleton, synthetic fluids, plastic skin, or electronic interiors. The mechanical body of the

Iron Giant shares with Vesalius's skeletons the ability to stand and move without internal organs, without tendons, muscles, nerves, or any secondary supports. Such a denuded skeletal structure, spectacularly empty in the areas that the human body is usually full of organs and liquids, also presents the impact of industrial technologies in the eighteenth and nineteenth centuries, when steam-operated pistons offer a new mode of interior mobilization for mechanical structures, as if the motion could come from inside the bone, as it were, rather than from outside it.

Renaissance art and anatomy provide interesting legacies for the representation of artificial bodies. In depictions of artificial people, a concentric approach—in which the body is made of onion-like layers of body systems, as in anatomical studies—is combined with a part-based compartmentalization as seen in artists' manuals, in which the body is put together by attaching independent body parts, ears, eyes, arms, legs, as if putting together a doll, a manikin, or a mechanical contraption. Both modalities engage fantasies of constructing and deconstructing the body and provide a narrative of visual order to counter the body's complex reality. Stories of artificial people often use a combination of the two modes, as when a body that has been put together in parts, out of disparate elements, is then revealed to us in layers, as a body that follows a concentric and systemic logic. Alternatively, a human body can be amended or enhanced with the addition of technological body parts (an arm, a foot, an eye, or a heart) and remain human, while a figure that has a technological body layer (plastic skin or synthetic blood) becomes aligned with artificiality. In their use of either or both modalities, stories of artificial people involve a promise of logical or at least visually satisfying orderliness, while still engaging the paradox of how these spectacularly understandable constructs (this is how this body was put together) still retain much of their mystery (how does this body work anyway?). The question of what may be inside the gleaming metal exteriors or the latex artificial skin coverings of robots and androids thus evokes the larger issues of interiority that inflect this discourse and inscribes questions of function, control, and agency as problems of the interior.

Mechanical interpretations of the body emerge through history, in dense philosophical texts but also in commonplace analogies that align body parts with simple machines: the arms can be imagined as levers, the knees as hinges, the lungs as bellows, the eye as a camera obscura, and whole body systems can be mapped onto technological processes as when the bones, muscles, and tendons are likened to lifting mechanisms of pulleys, ropes, and springs. "Examine attentively the physical economy of man," Giorgio Baglivi wrote in 1696. "What do you find? The jaws armed with teeth: what are these but pincers? The stomach is nothing but a retort; veins, arteries, the whole system of vessels, are hydraulic tubes; the heart is a spring; the viscera are nothing but filters and sieves; and

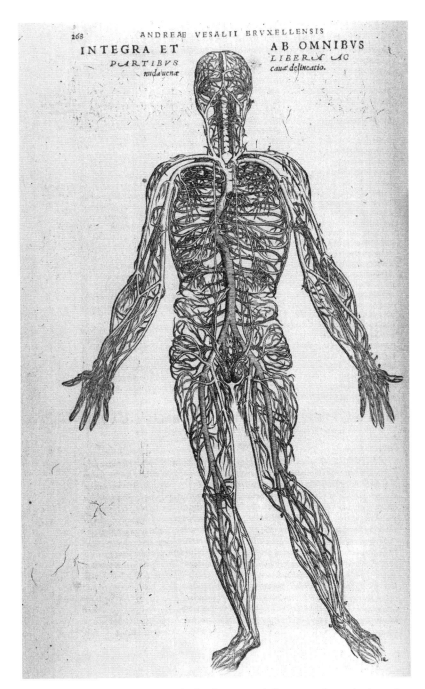

FIGURE 11 The uncanny and systemic body of anatomical illustration: here a body made solely of veins and arteries. Andreas Vesalius, *De humani corporis fabrica* (1543). Image scan courtesy of The National Library of Medicine.

what are the muscles if not ropes?"[2] Likening body parts to mechanical contraptions is a familiar philosophical and rhetorical modality in the West and often informs specific practices of organization, abstraction, and explanation. The question for this study is how these conceptual and philosophical tendencies inform the fantasies of mechanical bodies we see in science fiction literature and film, bodies that really feature lever-like arms and camera-like eyes. By depicting bodies that look like machines, the discourse of the artificial person channels a range of concerns about the occasions when the human body looks, feels, or acts like a machine. And because they retain conceptual connections to transhistorical concerns about embodiment, the patterns of popular culture archive and reconcile seemingly incompatible approaches to the body and its mechanical autonomy.

ROBOTS, CYBORGS, AND IRON MEN: THE MECHANICAL BODY IN SCIENCE FICTION

Even if we begin from well-worn stereotypes, imagining robots involves a range of fantasies. One may want to imagine being a robot, which J. P. Telotte describes as a way to control death and to experience an "ecstatic possession by the spirit of objecthood and emptiness."[3] Or one might imagine inventing a robot, having a robot dog, playing chess with a robot, dissecting a robot, being persecuted by a robot, having sex with a robot, living in a universe where robots exist, or occupying a social position that can afford robots.[4] All these fantasies pivot on the robot's mechanicity, but the mechanical may be associated with loyalty in one fantasy and with intelligence in another, with impenetrability and then also sexual availability, and so on. Fantasies are both dynamic and projective. The notion that one might enjoy the labor of robotic slaves without feeling guilty also contains the kernels of a fantasy of emancipation and social justice and the desire to experience an absolute awakening from one's own object status into a condition of enhanced aliveness. Fetishism affects this rubric too, since robotic fantasies may involve projections about metal surfaces, electronic circuitry, the absence of body fluids, or indeed skin, again differently visible in the context of metal attractions. Fictions of unemotional robots may express the need to avoid affect, to respond to affect with logic, to represent affect as logic. Even material design is not unambiguous, as metal exteriors may channel the desire to be cold as metal, strong as metal, shiny as metal, or to see oneself reflected onto metal surfaces.

The range of possibilities alerts us to the complexity of our fantasmatic investments with artificial people and their mechanicity. Although the distinction between conscious actions and autonomic processes is foundational for the fantasy of the mechanical body, it often remains implicit or disavowed. Stories of artificial people show an insistent discursive investment in highlighting aspects of mastery and control, over tools, bodies, and other beings, at the same time eliding those aspects of embodied experience that are more associated with the autonomic. Legacies of dualist thought also complicate this analysis, since dualism literalizes "top-down" control structures, presenting the possibility that the body could be purely instrumental, a tool that responds to the desires of a controlling ego. In contrast to the abundant representation of spectacles of mastery in the discourse, autonomic body states and functions are heavily contested. Artificial bodies are designed to remain immune to many of the needs and processes of organicity, to sleeping, eating, breathing, and other such functions. In *The Bicentennial Man* (Chris Columbus, 1999), the robot Andrew decides that in order to appear more human-like he has to blink—but since autonomic processes are by definition invisible and impossible to control or stop, deciding to blink means that blinking is conscious for Andrew, not autonomic at all. As a result of their paradoxical relationship to embodiment, artificial bodies can be seen as purely autonomic, because all their body processes are unwilled, programmed, and deterministic, or they can be seen as having no autonomic functions at all, since all their processes are designed, known, and indeed, preprogrammed or open to reprogramming.

What often goes unnoticed in the cybernetic theories of the mid-twentieth century is that they also begin from theorizing autonomic functions. When Manfred Clynes and Nathan Kline propose the concept of the "Cyborg," in a 1960 paper titled "Cyborgs and Space," their ideal of a human/machine hybrid depends on making "biochemical, physiological, and electronic modifications" to the body in order to expand its functionality in alien environments.[5] Short for "cybernetic organism," the "Cyborg" (which the authors capitalize) removes certain physical constraints, like the dependence on breathing or sleep, and bypasses natural chemical and hormonal states, thus allowing the explorer or astronaut to avoid stress or panic, to withstand different levels of fatigue, and to regulate intake of nutrients or pharmaceuticals. Most important, all these functional changes occur through the body's homeostatic controls and without the subject's control, thus allowing the conscious mind to engage in its primary activities—exploration, problem solving, and scientific experimentation. The cybernetic proposition partly facilitates a classic Cartesian dream, of eliminating the body as a physical limit in order to free the sovereign ego and facilitate the actions of a pure unfettered consciousness.[6] Nevertheless, cyborg theory has used the concept of the cybernetic body/machine merger in order to question lingering conceptual attachments to binary thinking and has sought to complicate the opposition between body and mind in contemporary philosophy.[7] What we must also underscore is that this ideal, self-regulating, hybrid body combines organic and mechanical function at the autonomic level and without noting any difference between the two registers. Clynes and Kline imagine retooling the parts of the body that already feel somewhat mechanical, and in this process the theorists of the new merger between machines and bodies join a long historical line of philosophical thinkers who have also questioned the relationship between willed and unwilled action and between conscious and unconscious body processes.

In the discourse of the artificial person, the two main modalities of embodied mechanicity are associated with distinct narrative depictions. Conscious actions and "top down" command structures are associated with tool use, and since science fiction literature and film delight in the presentation of spectacular technologies and gadgets, this is a most expansive dimension of the mechanical body fantasy. The spectrum of representational possibilities includes human characters using tools that are exterior to the body and wholly controlled by the user, as with the exoskeletons that enhance human abilities featured in *Aliens* (James Cameron, 1986) and *District 9* (Neill Blomkamp, 2009); figures that internalize the tool or incorporate it into the physical and decision-making processes of the self, as with the techno-utopian vision and bionic body parts of *The Six Million Dollar Man*,[8] and the more complex cybernetic merger between robotic and human components in *RoboCop* (Paul Verhoeven, 1987); and artificial people whose bodies are so mechanical and instrumental that the distinction between body and tool does not pertain any more, as with the powerful T-800 cyborg in *The Terminator* (James Cameron, 1984). When the technology is merely enabling, the user's sovereignty is not threatened or undermined, and despite enveloping the user, the tool is removable and distinct. In *District 9*, for example, a powerful exoskeleton invented by aliens acts in ways that seem independent, but its actions are always instigated by a user—who can be human or alien, may be located inside the robotic-looking structure or operate it remotely, or preprogram a series of actions that the suit undertakes later. The suit looks animate or independent, but it does not act on its own. Similarly, when Tony Stark wears one of his super-suits in *Iron Man* (Jon Favreau, 2008), he becomes so powerful he can fire-blast through buildings, fly through space, and withstand almost any attack.[9] Stark may look like a mechanical or robotic being at these moments, but his humanity and his control of the technology are never in doubt. Even the software agent that manages the super-suit's programming disappears at some point, to display Stark's face (Robert Downey Jr.) directing the suit as if by thought alone. In a classic treatment of the ego-enhancing use of advanced gadgetry, when Stark flies through space he both inhabits his body and leaves it behind, as the enveloping machine facilitates a dream of transcendence, allowing pure will and desire to interact with the material world. While the experience must entail a supreme adrenaline rush, and the film aims to produce a similarly visceral sensation for the audience, the flying fantasy works by partly abstracting the body's material presence.

FIGURE 12 Tony Stark (Robert Downey Jr.) as the man inside the machine in a scene from *Iron Man 2* (Jon Favreau, 2010). Paramount Pictures/Photofest. © Paramount Pictures

In the simplified choreography of control and agency the discourse of the artificial person sets up, if the tool, apparatus, mechanical implement, or mechanical person is properly under an operator's control, then the story offers a reinforced version of techno-supremacy, and the magnificent capabilities of the machine, robot, or cyborg can be absorbed narcissistically into the ego of the operator. But if the tool, apparatus, or artificial person acts independently, then the fantasy changes, and the animate machine appears more complex or ominous. For example, while *Iron Man* posits that there is a man inside the machine, we see the opposite possibility in *The Terminator*, where there is a machine inside what looks like a man. While the T-800 model (Arnold Schwarzenegger) is designed to be human-like, it is also a perfect tool, programmed to be efficient, task-oriented, and focused. Its actions invite paranoia rather than thrill, and this is partly because its body does not conform to the dualist configuration of will and action. There is no controlling ego external to the body of the T-800. The whole unit is so instrumental and so programmed that deciding is acting, acting is deciding, body and will are one. In stories of artificial people, what we perceive as the independence of mechanism infuses the narrative with questions about who or what controls such a unit and occasions paranoid scenarios, in which either the machine acts out its inhumanity or the whole unit is so empty of agency that it can be taken over by anyone and for any purpose. Such is the implicit investment in dualist principles that when the cyborg begins to separate deciding and acting, under the tutoring of young John Connor, not only does it seem that the cyborg is learning, evolving, choosing, and changing its programming but also that it is finally doing some proper thinking.

As with many robots and cyborgs in science fiction, the T-800 as a mechanical man constitutes an ideal industrial/capitalist subject, undistracted by needs and second thoughts, purely instrumental, perfectly efficient. But combating a figure as mechanical as the Terminator conveys both the pleasures and the limits of these values, as the story reinstates binary oppositions at the level of narrative after removing them somewhat at the level of body design. In addition to

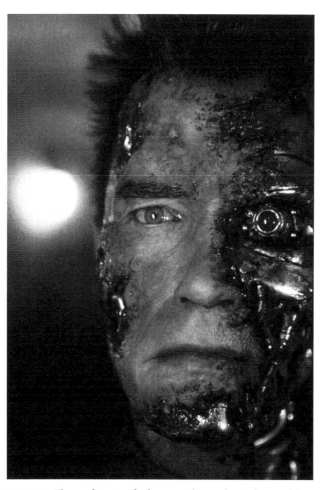

FIGURE 13 The machine inside the man. The mechanical core of the familiar T-800 model (Arnold Schwarzenegger) in *Terminator 3: Rise of the Machines* (Jonathan Mostow, 2003). Photofest

expressing the fetishism of exaggerated muscularity, machine-like efficiency, and a permanent emotional and bodily rigidity, the story also articulates the unspoken values of human frailty, messiness, inefficiency, and emotional vulnerability. Since the film posits the mechanical and the human as opposites, as viewers we can oscillate between admiring the pure expression of purpose and focus and eventually dismissing these attributes for the human qualities of care, attachment, and dogged resilience. The mechanical body functions as a foil that first negates and then valorizes body qualities that are all too human and that might go unappreciated without this contrast, precisely because they are at odds with the prioritization of focus, specialization, and productivity that characterizes the modern industrial world.

By focusing on mastery and control, the dominant paradigms for depicting tool use do not represent how we might relate to actual tools and technologies. At stake here is not the state of a specific technology but how we understand the embodied aspect of our experience with technology. Even the simplest tool is not merely operated, it interacts with the user and even creates rudimentary feedback loops. Similarly, everyday life is far from an experience of continuous and conscious mastery and instead includes important experiences of mechanicity and automatism, whether from habit, training, repetition, or muscle memory. For example, in one of his interviews, Bruce Lee describes a desire familiar to athletes, dancers, and other body performers, the desire to not think about acting, to remove will and conscious control from bodily movements and actions. Lee's lithe martial arts style and dancerly versatility couldn't be more expressive or unmechanical, but he describes the ideal responsiveness of a martial artist as a lack of consciousness, in which his hand, fist, or leg acts on its own: "I don't hit. It hits all by itself," Lee explains. In contrast, when technique is somehow experienced as external to the self, it is mechanical and robotic, despite the fact that it is the same arm that acts, perhaps even performing the same action. Lee describes thinking of himself as a robot when he first started in Hollywood, because he was looking for external affirmation instead of deep and embodied expression.[10] The distinction is important somehow without being clear: the body is trained in mindfulness so that it can act without thinking; the arm moves by itself but in the service of an expressing self; the self is most honestly expressed when it is not altogether present as an acting self in the action; and the same action can be robotic or also perfectly human. What at first looks like a contrast between expressive action and mechanical action, or between the body as a self and the body as a tool, turns out to be a less stable distinction between two kinds of mechanicity, the first deeply embodied and ingrained into the self, the second also deeply embodied but somehow experienced as exterior and mindless, technical and empty of meaning.

The paradoxes of the way mechanical embodiment is presented in the discourse of the artificial person resemble similar paradoxes in modern conceptualizations of the self. Although in mainstream culture and proverbial everyday expressions the mechanical is empty, meaningless, mindless, simply repetitive, we also associate the purest expressions of the self with states that include implicit types of mechanicity. We may not describe these types of action as mechanical but perhaps as unconscious, ingrained, spontaneous, or even authentic, and we may ascribe their efficacy to training or practice or to pure impulse, pure action. Unconscious or mechanical actions may be most personal because they bypass cultural conventions, self-censorship, or learned behaviors and instead express the self at its most intimate. Despite the overt valorization of both conscious rationality and expressive spontaneity in modern culture, we also understand the authentic self as partly automatic.

If tool use allows us to see the fantasmatic investment in mastery, control, and "top-down" command structures in the discourse of the artificial person, depictions of emotion, sexuality, and sexual experience provide examples for "bottom-up" experiences of embodied mechanicity. Despite the absence of adult sexuality from much of the archive of stories of artificial people, the elisions and typological selections of the discourse are quite eloquent about its importance. The fantasy of the mechanical body includes not only the desire to enhance the body or find an antidote to its vulnerabilities but also the desire to avoid feeling altogether. The imaginary being that cannot feel pain expresses something that is other to the human but also expresses what may be a very human desire, the desire to be a little more immune to emotion, a little more mechanical, more distant from feeling and from pain. Mechanicity may be something we sometimes crave. In the character of Commander Data (Brent Spiner), for example, the android officer on *Star Trek: The Next Generation*, feeling is both desired and inaccessible. Data confronts difficult or potentially hurtful situations with indifference or bemused detachment, and when asked by his concerned shipmates if something hurts his feelings he eagerly responds with "I am incapable of experiencing pain," or "I am unable to feel this emotion." Yet despite these limits, viewers do not merely dismiss such characters. Rather than considering them irrelevant to human issues, we become attached to their symptom, their inability to feel. The design of such characters expresses both an appreciation of what it means to have an emotion and the desire to avoid emotion sometimes, to be a little more immune to pain.

Perhaps it is this desire for emotional immunity that aligns robots, androids, and cyborgs with occulted versions of a stereotypically unemotional and super-strong masculinity. While ostensibly beyond or outside gender categories because of their inorganic status, mechanical bodies nevertheless refer to a visual and narrative vocabulary that is exaggerated in its depictions of gendered humanity. The presence of technological or mechanical imagery indeed accentuates the stereotypical gendering of artificial bodies, with artificial men presented as strong silent types and artificial women as oversexualized, idealized depictions of a perfect woman, perfect wife, or perfect sexual slave or, alternatively, as phallic and dangerous, mechanical pinups that fuel new types of fetishism. Again here the presence of mechanicity in these bodies alters the sexualized aspect of the fantasy. Despite their often asexual depiction, artificial men embody allegorical elements of male sexuality in their hardness, rigidity, and even the sense of mechanical rhythm, relentlessness, or pure drive. With artificial women the same sexualized mechanical vocabulary pertains and is actually more expressible as a sexual vocabulary, in ways that are not visible in stories of artificial men. There are very rare occasions when artificial or mechanical men participate in sexual experience, but somehow sexual availability is a fundamental fantasy in imaginary artificial women, and this despite the textural or body design problems such imaginings include. The fantasy of the sexually available female mechanical body seems unconcerned with the fact that such a body might lack the very body parts that facilitate sexual contact. And while artificial men are visibly aligned with a kind of masculine hardness, they are consistently devoid of sexuality as characters.

We find some helpful insights if we reflect on fantasies of the mechanical body against the backdrop of their origin in embodied experience. The artificial female body is sexy and sexually seductive and more sexually available somehow not despite its mechanicity but precisely *because* it is mechanical. At first, mechanical

FIGURE 14 Technology, militarism, and sex appeal at the moment of animation. The artificial female body in *Ghost in the Shell* (Mamoru Oshii, 1995). Photofest

women seem to engage the representation of a controllable and subservient artificial woman, a mechanized Galatea. But even though the overall story structures
of such depictions follow the tenets of Pygmalion's story, again the textures and
body designs make a difference. A statue that comes to life may be related to
silence and coldness, to inactivity, mystery, opacity, and stillness. The statue is
partly imagined as a blank, as a surface that facilitates male projections and male
desires, and its animation seems to flow from a desire for a woman that is perfectly controllable, perfectly defined by her lover's desires. A mechanical woman,
however, does not exactly follow this pattern, and in recent versions of artificial
women the difference is palpable. Because their bodies present a mechanical
mobility rather than a marmoreal stillness and because mechanicity is intimately
related to sexuality, mechanical women are sex, they are embodied abstractions
of the mechanical workings of sexuality in ways that can be seen, in their visual
depiction and narrative range, rather than in ways that have to remain allegorical,
as with the sublimations that occur in the representation of artificial men.

In addition to presenting artificial women as beautiful, sexy, and often
defined by their sexuality, recent figures of the artificial woman, in *Battlestar
Galactica* for example, align many of these figures with a voracious or dangerous sexual identity. The sexy and sexually aggressive female Cylons embody
the same qualities of mechanicity we would recognize in the depiction of artificial workers or slaves, repetition, relentlessness, inevitability, or single-minded
focus, but in the context of sexual behavior these qualities become a list of the
conceptual associations of mechanicity with sex appeal or sexual behavior.
The association reveals that in a deeply embodied way, sex is a mechanical
process or, at least, an experience that shares certain important qualities with
mechanical processes. This conceptual alignment of mechanicity and sexuality
accounts for the ways in which stories of artificial men usually withhold sexuality from these characters. In the discourse of the artificial person, robotic
bodies serve as allegorical displacements of a sexual imaginary: their rigidity
and hardness function as a thinly veiled register of an idealized state of arousal,
while the focus on relentlessness, insistence, repetition, or mechanical tempo
refer conceptually to the driving rhythms of sexual experience. The artificial
female body expresses this mechanical sexual logic, while the artificial male
body has to sublimate it, as if the mechanical body that stands for an allegorical mechanical penis cannot also possess a mechanical penis. Artificial men are
thus often asexual for two reasons: in order to retain the robotic focus on negating the body's limits and vulnerabilities (the body's potential for emotion and
sensation) and in order to avoid a conceptual collapse of sexuality and mechanism into a form of tautology.

Narratives of mechanical embodiment thus debate the limits of the body
not just by presenting the body in terms of frailty and enhancement but most

FIGURE 15 Human-looking, and just as dangerous, the Cylon known as Number 6 (Tricia Helfer) embodies the fantasy of the sexy artificial woman in *Battlestar Galactica*. Sci-Fi/Photofest © Sci-Fi. Photographer: Frank Okenfels

importantly by questioning the meanings of what is inherent in the body and what is exterior to it. In this articulation of the perennial problem of the inside and the outside, will, agency, initiative, and the potential for change are all qualities of the interior. But in a classic psychoanalytic modality, we may be most honestly ourselves when we don't know why we say or do something, when such actions seem to bubble up unbidden, when their source seems to be beyond or outside the knowable self. The unwilled, impulsive, spontaneous action may be an authentic expression of the self precisely because it is already somehow secretly determined, the effect of submerged or unconscious experiences, complex psychic structures that may never be fully known or revealed, sexual urges, and disavowed desires. As with autonomic body processes that occur without our control, urges, drives, and impulses operate independently of consciousness and will, they compel or drive us, they enact their own order and meaning. A modern psychoanalytic sense of the self preserves or reinterprets certain elements of mechanicity, automatism, and autonomy, within the overt rationalism of the modern subject.

The mechanical body fantasy, then, stems from and expresses an intimate sense of embodied experience, whether this has to do with feelings of vulnerability, emotion, or sexuality. What artificial people often lack at the level of body design, they embody at the level of narrative action or fantasmatic projection. To explain the provenance of these deeply rooted mechanical conceptualizations of the body, I now turn to a more historical and philosophical perspective, which elucidates certain consistent narrative patterns we find in stories of mechanical and artificial people as well as the main philosophical models that affect the representation of mechanical bodies. In the premodern mythical and philosophical tradition, in ancient stories about mechanical people and ancient philosophical analyses and debates about motion, the soul, and the explanatory power of mechanism, we find the latent conceptual content of modern artificial and mechanical bodies.

METAL ATTRACTIONS: MECHANICAL BODIES IN ANTIQUITY

From a contemporary standpoint, the main waves of cultural interest in mechanical and artificial people coincide with the advent of modernity and its technological innovations. During the golden age of automata and anthropomorphic mechanical contraptions in the seventeenth and eighteenth centuries, notions of mechanical action and mechanical humanity were associated with new styles of work, new types of government, and new relationships to the material world, although mechanical fantasies usually conformed to the depiction of clockwork as orderly or understandable, as a desirable register through which to conceptualize social and bodily structures.[11] In the late nineteenth and early twentieth century, mechanical men function as embodiments of processes of industrialization, and their full-on emergence in fictional figures such as robots and androids in the 1920s and 1930s coincides with the massive militarization of technology that occurred in World War I and the mechanization of workers and soldiers in the increasingly dominant military/industrial complex.[12] In *The Human Motor*, Anson Rabinbach describes the historical and social conditions that transform tropes aligning machines with the human body into a new conceptualization of a relentless motorized and electrified body that is both more productive and more prone to fatigue.[13] Embodied mechanicity in this period emerges everywhere, in the theater, in artistic manifestos, in new avant-garde movements, and in social theory.[14] During the same period, in popular culture and the emerging genre contexts of science fiction literature and film, the constructed or mechanical body allegorizes our relationships to technology and codifies, sometimes in paradoxical ways, our responses to an increasingly mechanized world.

In more cultural or conceptual terms, the genealogy of mechanical body fantasies reaches much further back in time, far predating the advent of complex mechanical contraptions and industrial contexts. In addition to recognizing the structuring effects of embodied experience, a more transhistorical view also requires a self-conscious engagement with the paradoxical workings of popular culture. Just as every story about vampires has a fundamental connection to blood, a connection it can negotiate and manipulate in new ways but never avoid completely, every story about robots involves a fundamental connection not just to simple or complex machines but also to metal, weapons, knights, and armor. Each new depiction of a robot or mechanical man reactivates and negotiates this structural vocabulary and, self-consciously or not, allows a certain fascination with metal surfaces and simple mechanicity to return to contemporary contexts, regardless of how antique and old-fashioned it may be.

We discover some of the conceptual ancestry of robots, androids, and cyborgs in the origin myths discussed in the previous chapter. In the process of presenting the creation or construction of people, origin stories displace the iconography of childbirth by borrowing from other registers of human experience. People can be imagined as emerging out of processes of cultivation, cooking, or fermentation, as in alchemical depictions, but may also be molded, made, constructed, put together in some way. In the subset of ancient origin stories that utilizes the imagery of human crafts, the presentation of constructed or mechanical bodies is often linked to art, artifice, and technology, to the presentation of craft-gods (such as Hephaistos in ancient Greek mythology or God as a craftsman in Christian theology), and to human skills that involve the transformation of natural materials through active and purposeful processes, as in weaving, ceramics, or metalwork. For the figures that will be traced here, the mechanical or metallic supermen of popular culture, the operative vocabulary revolves around working with machinery and metals.

Although complex wooden machines and contraptions existed in antiquity, the conceptual association of mechanical bodies with metal and metal with masculinity seems to select for a nexus of meanings that involve metallurgy, war, and processes for the construction of weapons and armor. In medieval alchemy this connection was beautifully codified in the alchemical symbol for "man," a circle with an arrow pointing up, which was also the symbol for iron and for the planet Mars, named after the god of war. In addition to its implicit reference to sexual arousal, the symbol also presents a graphic depiction of armor, a shield and spear, thus again linking men, metal, and war. Perhaps there is room for speculation that there is a historical context that informs the emergence of such connections in ancient mythology: while showcasing a textural contrast between flesh and the natural materials that feel most different from it or that hurt flesh horribly, such stories also allegorize the experience of advances in metallurgical processes, registering a sense of pride in the expert handling of metals and celebrating master-craftsmen melting and forming metals. Metallurgical processes themselves evoke war-like themes, like striking, firing, quenching, or hammering and involve intense material transformations through smelting and the creation of alloys. In archeological and anthropological terms, such metallurgical advances have specific moments of emergence and considerable impact, and they help date the prehistoric evolutions of a community. The transition from softer precious metals such as silver and gold to more durable metals such as tin, copper, bronze, iron, and their alloys also marks the history of migrations, trade practices, and conquests, the transition of a community into more complex metallurgical techniques such as casting and forging, the development of hotter burning furnaces, and new practical applications for new metals. The men of gold, silver, bronze, and iron glorified in the proverbial "Ages of Man" of ancient poetry also refer implicitly to the numerous cultural transitions of metalwork from precious to workaday metals and processes for the construction of weapons, tools, metal objects, and statues.

In order to see the relevance of such historical events for later narrative patterns, we need to notice the ways in which technological or social processes enter into culture and myth and are allegorized in stories of metal or mechanical people. In variations on the story of Talos, for example, the legendary bronze man who served as the guardian of Crete appears as an embodiment of protective technology, patrolling the island and throwing rocks at incoming ships; as a weapon, when he heats himself up in the fire before embracing and killing his enemies; as a mythological memory of the legendary men of the "Bronze Age"; and as an allegorical interpretation of the casting of bronze statues through a "lost wax" process.[15] Talos has one vein that goes through his whole body, and when that vein is unplugged by Medea's tricks all his "blood" runs out.[16] The technological process, in which molten metal takes the place of the flowing or evaporating wax shape inside the cast during firing in order to form the statue, has here been imaginatively replaced by a story of de-animation, in which the bronze man Talos dies or becomes inert, like a statue, when his blood runs out, like wax flowing out of the cast. Since human blood has a slightly metallic smell and taste, there is something in the story that also contains other embodied registers of how metal may function in the imagination, and these are the kinds of analogies that we should look out for when we re-read ancient myths. As with other fantasies of mechanicity that seem to emerge out of bodily experience, imagining the blood of a metal man could be inspired by experiencing the metallic smell and taste of human blood. That a person can become metal is similarly imaginable in this affective logic, since handling iron tools leaves a lingering metallic smell on the skin.[17]

If we consider that mythical constructions may be responding to actual historical events, stories of metal men may also be recording an experience of seeing metal-clad men for the first time, of seeing an army in unknown forms of armor, of seeing men who seem encased in metal or look like they are made of metal parts. Contact or combat with people who know how to use different metals can account for the advent of such stories, and this association with metal and war is hard to shake for artificial people, even in the present. The imagery of ancient myths about metal men often returns to their depiction as warriors, protectors, or guardians, and the connection persists to the depiction of automatic medieval knight figures in mechanical clock towers, to fantasies of animated armors, to the depiction of robots as super-guardians or super-soldiers, and even to *Iron Man's* high-tech super-suits. Full body armor itself is an irresistible topic for mechanical body fantasies: because it holds an imprint of the physical body it was designed to encase, armor projects a sense of presence, a sense that there is still something in the armor itself that may act or move without the body. Or, alternatively, the armor covers the body so completely that one may not be able to ascertain whether there is anyone inside, or whether it is just the armor itself moving and acting. Visual puns and gags about inanimate armor that suddenly comes to life abound in both pre-modern and modern texts, alerting us to another form of the familiar problem of the inside and the outside that all artificial people embody: something that looks animate may not be, something that is animate may not seem so at first, and so on.[18]

In addition to metal texture and the evocative presence of armor, the conceptual framework of the constructed person includes the vocabulary of the foreign, the marvelous, and the animate. In her analysis of ancient lore about Daidalos, another legendary craftsman, Sarah P. Morris observes that he represents a vision of Eastern technologies, of marvels at the ends of the earth, and such traditions in the depiction of wonders pertain throughout Western history.[19] The supremely technological and the marvelous often coincide, with one easily presented in the garb of the other, and marvelous objects or machinery are often described in the language of animation: a *daidalon* in ancient Greece describes an object so finely wrought and so intricate and complex that it possesses a certain power of autonomy, of animation, of life. Ancient texts offer numerous examples of such wonders, constructed by Daidalos and by various gods: golden handmaids in Hephaistos's workshop, a mobile wooden statue of Aphrodite designed to move through the use of mercury, or statues so mobile and lively that they would have to be tied down so as not to run away. But even ancient texts show awareness of the exaggeration implied in these turns of phrase, and stories of Daidalos's mobile and talkative statues functioned as comic moments on stage.[20] Although the trope of the animate statue harks back to older talismanic uses of effigies, in which a mystical or ritual context could facilitate the potential of an object to be experienced as animated, by the classical era we are better off understanding such references not as actual descriptions of technologically facilitated animation but as metaphors of a certain state of wonder, mobility, or presence. In contrast to Western eighteenth- and nineteenth-century idealizations of verisimilitude in sculpture, when the language of animation was associated with lifelikeness in terms of surface and appearance, in antiquity the most talismanic or animate-able effigies were often quite roughly made. By the time anthropomorphic designs with aspirations to verisimilitude emerge in the West, active ritual contexts of animation are already obsolete, while mystical enactments of ancient rites continue to revolve more around roughly hewn effigies, not lifelike statues.[21] Although the figures of speech have continued literary power and appeal, they reflect a secular, not a ritual context.

But what is also important to notice here is that, when mechanical contraptions are described as animate or almost alive, the assignation does not refer to visual verisimilitude, to looking human or animate in some representational sense, as it would if we imagined a painting or statue that was described as almost coming to life. It refers to motion, to the experience of active functionality we have with mechanical objects, and the sense that things that move by themselves may be alive. This understanding of motion is inspired by a basic human reflex to notice motion and quickly evaluate it for its potentially animate origin, as when our attention is immediately captured when we see something moving out of the corner of our eye. In this situation, it does not matter whether the moving object looks lifelike at all, because the momentary impression of animation is the result of mobility, not verisimilitude, and until the question of the object's actual status is resolved through better observation, it is its motion that we instinctively respond to. Expanded to include the mobility of live beings, the "quickening" of a fetus in the womb when its first motions are evident, and the transformability of organic matter in general, this basic understanding of motion evolved into many premodern philosophical and physiological approaches. The sense that "things that move by themselves are alive" continues in less ancient contexts and, I would argue, persists even to the modern era as a descriptor of potentially animate status, with important adaptations.

The conceptual and philosophical association of mobility with aliveness is paramount for understanding the attraction of mechanical body fantasies as well as for tracing the continued relevance of philosophical debates on motion, animation, and independent mobility. We are used to considering objects that move by themselves as everyday in modernity and have dissociated motion from animate status. But premodern models for making these assignations persist and are surprisingly visible in narratives of the artificial or mechanical body. Here, the important philosophical ancestor is Aristotle, whose theories of motion and its operations in the body set a certain philosophical agenda for later debates on mobility, animation, agency, and the soul. For Aristotle, motion is a complex quality of live beings and includes mobility in terms of space but also in terms of quality or composition, as in processes of generation, growth, change, decline, and decomposition. Even in this summary description, and despite the radical epistemological and historical differences, it is clear that narratives of artificial people reflect these qualities, presenting us with figures that display an exaggerated version of independent mechanical mobility but also with figures that do not grow, do not procreate, do not change, and do not die. The bifurcation of motion is important: in the Aristotelian canon and many premodern philosophies, motion in space was just one aspect of possibly enlivening mobility, while, after the advent of modern physics, complex clockwork machinery, and self-moving mechanisms, this is precisely the type of mobility that is dissociated from animate status. Qualitative or embodied forms of mobility—biological forms of mobility such as growth and decline—were at the same time clearly immune from similar reorganization. Artificial people preserve this distinction and give it narrative form, in a way continuing to embody the problem of motion long past its cultural emergence. And in a secondary effect of the transformation of motion from a quality of live beings to a quality of beings that may be merely active but not alive, the role of mechanicity in understanding life changes too. Metaphors and analogies of mechanical function, favorite tropes in philosophical, physiological, anatomical, and religious treatises for centuries, have to be monitored or policed differently once mobility in space is associated with mechanical mobility and radically dissociated from proof of animate status. This is a modern anxiety formation of sorts. In older philosophical models there is a level of comfort in the operations of analogy that could sustain describing the workings of natural or bodily processes through mechanical analogies, even finding the same types of motion in both organic and mechanical constructs. Indeed (as I will explain below), organic functions are precisely the kinds of processes that benefit from mechanical explanation. An implicit assurance that mechanism does not devalue or alter the body evaporates at some point, after modern interpretations of motion, to be replaced by an anxiety over just how mechanical the body may indeed be.

Fundamentally, to study the constructed, mechanical, or artificial body is to contemplate the power of analogical thinking. Ancient philosophers often resort to favorite analogies between machines and bodies or between tools and body parts, as though such associations are a natural expression of the already connected nature of the world, and I made my own analogical links in the pre-vious section, discussing the origins of mechanical body fantasies in relation to tools, the autonomic processes of the body, and the mechanical rhythms of sexu-ality. Despite modern descriptions and contemporary science-fictional exam-ples, these aspects of mechanical embodiment schematize very old analogical associations. But the body does not just offer meanings: as a cultural object, an entity structured by social, political, and cultural concerns and interpretations, the body is itself discursive. So this investigation does not focus on the body but on the mechanical analogy, the tendency to explain or understand the body through recourse to mechanisms, machines, puppets, tools, process narratives, and so on. While the explanations and syllogisms may vary across time, both the impulse to explain the body through mechanical analogies and the resulting connections made between bodies and mechanisms matter for our understanding of artificial people. The discourse of the artificial body in effect reveals the persistence, or perhaps the return, of premodern concerns and worldviews that are otherwise invisible in the modern world.

In this process of moving across time in order to create a rough outline of the mechanical analogy, I start from ancient philosophies, focusing on Aristo-tle's mechanical metaphors and explanations of body function. Aristotle is a fascinating figure in this context because his theories of motion, mechanism, and the soul are both sophisticated and commonsensical, articulating certain things about embodiment that seem experientially apt despite their philosophi-cal intricacies. Most importantly for my purposes here, Aristotle is not a dualist: following his hylomorphic understanding of the relationship between body and soul challenges many of the conceptual tenets of the discourse of the artificial person and the critical approaches commonly used to interpret it.[22] Artificial people seem irrevocably structured by a popular version of dualism, in which body and soul are radically and materially different from each other, with the soul functioning as an independent immaterial substance and the body a mere mechanism, alive but not necessarily sentient. In their embodiment artificial people are also often radically split, with their bodies depicted as purely mechan-ical, perfectly functional but not really ensouled, and lacking something immate-rial and transcendental despite their functionality (and even their rationality).

There are interesting reversals here as well. In Cartesian thinking the body has action and performance but no reason. But in myriads of stories and films, artificial people are separated from the human because they have too much rea-son and no soul, or not the right kind of soul, because they are reasonable in their mental processes, and active in their mechanical presence, but not prop-erly alive and not properly soulful. Is the discourse of the artificial person then presenting a desire for a non-reasonable soul, a reaction against modern sche-mas of rationality and abstraction? The artificial person similarly challenges easy oppositions. Since in dualist thinking the body can be understood as a tool, an instrument, under the command of the rational soul, the artificial body is doubly suspect and dangerous as it is indeed designed to be a perfect tool and is not under the command of a "proper" soul. Again the problem of motion complicates this and reveals that the issues that plague artificial people affect the definition of body and soul for real people too: if mechanical mobility is disconnected from animate status in modernity, and if the body in popular Cartesian summaries is somewhat mechanical in its mere living, then the body is somehow both too alive and not truly alive, and the soul is both essential and completely irrelevant to life.

In contrast, Aristotle's theories present the soul as an emergent property of matter itself, as the final purpose and forming quality of all entities. In the intimate connection between matter (*hulē*) and form (*morphē*) that is proposed with hylomorphism, objects and beings are emergent as themselves, their essences and qualities flowing from their presence and material constitution.[23] In hylomorphic worldviews we find little of the modern dualist tradition that presents matter as inert, the body as machine- or puppet-like, and the soul as an animating but also detachable entity. Yet Aristotle also constantly uses puppet and mechanical analogies to explain the workings of the body and the meanings of the soul and seems fascinated by intimate kinds of mechanicity that are more involved and more directly embodied than the classic "body as tool, soul as controller" narrative. Aristotle's mechanical examples structure both the logic of philosophical analogy and many premodern relationships of matter and motion, in formulations that make provocative connections between mechanical and live beings.

THE MECHANICAL ANALOGY, FROM ARISTOTLE TO DESCARTES

Aristotle typically chooses mechanical examples that are conducive to the visualization of sequence, cause and effect, and dependent mobility, that is, mobility that has verifiable or easily posited sources. Machines, statues, puppets, tools, and mechanical automata work well for analogical explanations because they depict or represent sequential and visible motion and the unfolding of processes over time. Most importantly for our explorations of embodied mechanicity, Aristotle turns to such examples especially in his treatises on the natural world—on the motion of animals, the generation and corruption of live beings, the motivating functions of the soul, and the basic processes of life. In these contexts, explanations involving complex correspondences between tools, mechanisms, scientific processes, and the body are used to explain invisible or complex body functions, specifically interior and autonomic functions. In mutually reinforcing associations, mechanical processes, or at least processes that *look* mechanical, are put into service to explain processes that *feel* mechanical: mechanical analogies elucidate the mystery of interior body functions, functions that seem to inspire and demand mechanical explanation because they are experienced as being somewhat mechanical already. In order to be able to integrate these ancient philosophical tenets with the later history of artificial people, we should remember that, despite all the other disparate uses they have had over time, since antiquity mechanical analogies and metaphors have been associated with the mysteries of process and response posed by the autonomic body.

This is the case with Aristotle's explanation of breathing in *De Respiratione* (*On Breathing*), a short treatise in the *Parva Naturalia*, in which he associates the lungs with bellows in a smith's forge—one of the most common mechanical analogies in philosophical and physiological writings and one that has been used to explain a variety of disparate theories from antiquity to the eighteenth century. Aristotle proposes that respiration facilitates the necessary cooling and heating processes of the body: breathing is necessary to life because it is related to heat, which is essential to the nutritive soul, the most fundamental part of the soul for animate beings.[24] The nutritive soul, located in or somewhere close to the heart, heats up and expands (as all things exposed to heat must), and rises. As it rises, the cavity in which it resides must also rise, allowing cool air to enter the lungs from the outside, just as a blacksmith's bellows expand to invite air into them. Incoming air quenches and cools excessive heat in a process that facilitates and maintains the internal balance of the body's temperature necessary for health. Incidentally, this process explains why the breath is hot: exhaled air takes heat out of the heart, the hottest part of the body. And, according to Aristotle, this explains the breathing of fish as well: the motion of their gills moving up and down, expanding and contracting, allows water to cool the heat of the heart.[25] So important is this process of heating and cooling that most animals inhale and exhale continuously throughout their lives. Life depends on breathing.[26]

Aristotle's account of breathing as a kind of air-conditioning is rather typical of physiological approaches of his era. Philosophers may not have agreed about the process of breathing, but the relationship of life to heat, of heat to the heart, and of breath to both soul and cooling were common premises for such descriptions. The bellows-as-lungs example was probably in existence before its appearance in *De Respiratione*, and it certainly survives it, continuing well into the modern era. The two entities reveal more than mere surface similarity; for Aristotle's students, the connection between lungs and bellows would have seemed self-obvious since breathing and blowing are etymologically as well as functionally related. The word *phusai* (bellows) comes from the word *phusao* (to blow, exhale), and both are related to *phusis* (nature, the way things naturally work) because of their common association to *phuo* (to grow). The bellows both expand/grow and exhale. *Pneuma* (breath, and also spirit) stems from *pneo* (to breathe or blow, and to draw breath, i.e., to live), and so does *pneumōn* (lung).[27] Life depends on breathing, since to draw breath literally means to be alive. Linguistic affinity demonstrates that an analogy based on observation is expressed in the words themselves: the bellows are named *phusai* because they blow air out in the same way that people exhale. Aristotle makes this explicit when he asserts that etymologies are often functional, and that the lungs are named after their function: *pneumōn* is a receptacle for *pneuma*.[28]

By making these inherent etymological relationships literal, Aristotle's philosophical argument also offers his students a mnemonic device in the bellows. If they forget the nuances of Aristotle's heating and cooling system, the bellows would bring to mind his account of breath as a life force in the linguistic and associational universe of breath, life, nature, spirit, and lungs.[29] Aristotle's syllogism not only refers to a mechanical tool, it is also fundamentally mechanical in style, that is, in its specific focus on sequential explanation (first this, then this), and in its use of material properties and well-known scientific facts (heat causes expansion) to explain the process of respiration. The obvious paradox, that bellows in a forge make the fire or coals hotter instead of cooling them down, has no place in Aristotle's argument: he specifically refutes that breath nourishes internal heat insisting on his cooling explanation instead.[30] Aristotle also avoids reminding readers that, as a tool, bellows are already modeled on and perhaps named after the act of exhaling, since the object was probably invented in order to expand the effect of blowing on coals or fire. Clearly, he needs the etymology to shed light on the body part of this syllogism (lungs work like bellows), not the technological or etiological part (bellows work like lungs). Although it seems simple, his analogy is actually very specific: while he utilizes the etymological affinity between bellows and blowing, the bellows illustrate the expansion of the chest rather than any other part of the process, and indeed reference an advanced scientific principle: the possibility of a vacuum created in the lungs that air cannot help but rush to fill.[31]

In his account of breathing Aristotle brings natural and linguistic observations together in order to propose an explanation of breathing as a process. The tool in this example is not merely symbolic but actually functional, and its workings structure the kinds of mechanical processes Aristotle imagines to be taking place in the body. This explanation, therefore, is not purely mechanical or analogical but more properly mechanistic: in philosophical terms, while a mechanical explanation proposes that the way something nonmechanical works is equivalent or analogous to the way a mechanism works, a mechanistic explanation proposes that such mechanical analogies are sufficient, that is, that in principle they are not merely symbolic representations of function but *actually describe* how something functions.[32] With his account of breathing, Aristotle aspires to mechanistic explanation, and his care in observing technological processes informs what might otherwise have been a fanciful or linguistic demonstration of a superficially analogical argument.[33]

We see a less mechanistic and more analogical use of mechanical connections in Aristotle's explanations of the relationship between motion and the soul, where he frequently brings up mechanical puppets and automata in order to explain how bodies and beings are alive, and how the soul moves the body. In descriptions that confused later scribes and scholiasts, who had no experience of the constructs he refers to, Aristotle mentions a variety of figures, from *neurospasta* (meaning "string-pulled" or "string-jointed"), a type of articulated figure moved by internal strings, to puppets that may be moved by external strings, and groups of puppets hanging from visible strings and moved in tandem. He also frequently refers to complex mechanisms with many parts that represent human and animal figures or entire scenes and that move through the use of hanging strings, wound-up strings, axles, pegs, and pulleys as well as "automata" that utilize cranks, cogs and wheels, and screws and levers.[34] He uses such constructions in order to explain how the world works, how the universe has been put into motion, and how one element affects another in a sequence of actions that unites and animates the world. Aristotle's interest in sequential motion suggests that some of his mechanical examples refer to articulated flat or relief constructions, something like moving paintings or sculptural scenes, in which many figures could move at different intervals or in different directions one after the other. Such constructions are not difficult to create out of basic materials like wood and metal, and in fact, articulated and mobile effigies in the round exist in many folk art traditions even in contexts that show no other mechanical sophistication. Cords looped around screws, threaded through pulleys or attached to slowly descending weights could provide the necessary mobility, while some automata may also have included visible motion transfer effects, such as pegs hitting or pushing each other.[35]

Overall, Aristotle distinguishes three kinds of motion in the human and animal body, and they are surprisingly consistent with the mechanical body fantasies of contemporary popular culture. For Aristotle, voluntary motions (*ekousios*), mostly understood in terms of spatial change, are inspired by desire, judgment, and imagination (*phantasia*) and propel the being to move toward food or away from danger. Such motions are properly explained through the interaction between different aspects of the self, and since they are conscious and willed they require no mechanical illustrations for Aristotle. In the schema proposed earlier in this chapter, these are the kinds of motions that provide the baseline for tool/user interaction, in which the body acts out the desires of the self through conscious thought, will, or desire.

For Aristotle, as for other ancient philosophers, it is the other types of motion that need the explanatory power of mechanical analogies, and these are presented in two categories. Involuntary motions (*akousios*) characterize the heart and the penis, "for often those are moved when something appears, but without the command of thought."[36] The heart skips a beat confronted with danger or surprise, and when aroused, the penis acts as an independent entity in the body. Both respond to stimuli, impressions, and imaginary situations with or without conscious thought and also have the capacity not to respond to the same stimuli on a different day.[37] The third type of motion, which he describes as nonvoluntary (*ouch ekousios*), encompasses processes such as sleep, waking, and respiration which are truly automatic, controlled by neither *phantasia* nor desire but possessing their own regularity and order. To explain the latter two types of motion, Aristotle claims that there is a hierarchical organization of motion within the body, a centralized control system, more or less, that resembles the motion of the universe and that of puppets and that features an "unmoved mover," in this case the heart or the penis as initiators of motion.

In a passage of *De Motu Animalium* (*On the Motion of Animals*) that offers the most direct identification of animals with automata, Aristotle begins by saying that the motion of animals is like the motion of automatic puppets, insofar as one motion in one location can cause many related motions. But also in this section the organs of animals are said to correspond to the mechanical parts of automata: the bones and skeletal structure of the animals are the equivalent of the puppets' wood and iron armature, and animal tendons and nerves the equivalent of puppet strings.[38] Even though he uses the word *neuron* to describe strings in other puppet examples (*neuron* refers to both "tendon" and "string" at the time and will mean "nerve" only later), in this passage Aristotle uses *neuron* for animal tendons and the word *strebla* for puppet strings (a word that refers to the state of being wound, twisted, crooked, or curved). Perhaps the automata he has in mind here operate by means of helix- or screw-shaped pulleys, or perhaps the strings are strung so that they can wind and unwind. In any case, it is clear that Aristotle shies away from the equation of animal tendons and puppet strings when the analogy between the two becomes too close. The word *neuron* could have been used to describe both animal and mechanical parts in this section.

Yet, the next section of the text is haunted by the proximity of the barely avoided alliance between animal *neura* and mechanical *neura* or *strebla*. Aiming to prove that the motivator of animal locomotion cannot be in the extremities of the body, Aristotle radically disconnects and mechanizes the limbs. When we hold a stick, he claims, it becomes an extension of our body, and its motion depends on and seems to start at the wrist. The relationship of stick to wrist is equivalent to the relationship of the forearm to the elbow, and consequently of the whole arm to the shoulder. Therefore, the beginning of motion in the body cannot really be located in these body parts, which can be removed much as we can throw away the stick.[39] The seat of motion is thus clearly in the central part of the body. But now the disconnected body parts become intriguing: maybe each body part is separate and alive in itself.[40] Indeed, how do we account for involuntary and nonvoluntary (unconscious and automatic) processes and motions such as breathing, sleeping, waking, our heartbeat, and the motions of genitals? The ability of the penis to move on its own accord and to generate sperm (which itself seems independently generative and alive to Aristotle) may mean that the penis is alive as a separate animal within the animal body.[41] To avoid giving each organ its own soul, Aristotle returns to his focus on hylomorphic interpretations: each organ in the body is constituted for its particular uses or functions by nature and thus has no need for a special other kind of soul. In addition, body parts are guided in their motions by association with the two locations of involuntary motion, the heart and the penis. As the source of vital heat, the heart acts as a central puppeteer orchestrating the motions of the limbs and imparting life into them, while the penis is a potentially independent animal, set into motion in more metaphorical ways through the generative association of sperm with potentiality and mobility.[42]

In other treatises Aristotle (or one of his successors) explains this generative power through a different mechanical example: when we look at any part of an automatic display, he notes, we can see motion at that location but may not be able to discern the origins of that motion, because the "circles," disks, or cogs that instigate the motion and determine its direction are no longer in view. In order to explain whether the internal organs of the body are already contained in the sperm or whether they develop in sequence one from the other (an early articulation of what would come to be known as the debate between preformation and epigeneticism), Aristotle uses a combination of the notion of potentiality with the sequential mechanisms he observes in automata. Both in nature and in art, he states, things begin in potentiality and then become what they will be in actuality. While the sperm, or that which created the sperm and endowed it with life-giving abilities, does not seem to be present at the moment of the creation of the organs, it is there, "just as in automata the external force in a way moves the parts without touching them at that moment, but having touched one earlier."[43] As in the case of circles (perhaps cog-like structures) that put other circles into motion, animal body parts exist potentially in generative matter. The sequence of motion has already begun or, rather, the principle of motion has already been provided (in and by the semen), and so one thing follows another without interruption just as motion flows sequentially from prior motion in the wondrous automata.[44]

For Aristotle, as for many thinkers since, mechanical motion explains the autonomic, involuntary, mysterious body by capitalizing on the visibility of motion effects and the sheer attraction and explanatory power of sequence and causality. The attraction of artificial bodies and mechanical constructs thus seems to revolve around the power of analogy itself: when posing difficult questions about the nature of body and soul, analogical relationships between real and mechanical or imaginary bodies facilitate understanding because they promise representational and explanatory clarity, make processes and causes visible, and engage the pleasures of sequence. By means of his automata examples, Aristotle can extend the system of causes to include prior or inaccessible actions without undermining his insistence on processes of actualization and potentiality. For Aristotle, the effect of these sequential motions is that the whole universe can be understood in terms of continued mobility once somehow set into motion by an entity he extrapolates and names "the unmoved mover."[45] In a simple way, the concept of an "unmoved mover" allows Aristotle to solve the problems that emerge when the soul is defined in relation to mobility, problems he summarizes in the beginning of *De Anima* (*On the Soul*): if the soul itself is kinetic, does it move, or does it simply cause movement? If it causes movement, is it like a magnet that attracts iron, as other philosophers proposed?[46] Can it move sometimes and other times not? If it moved constantly it would be in danger of going in and out of the body, thus making dead things come alive again.[47] Yet, if the soul doesn't move all the time, how does it start moving? In his explanations, Aristotle traces the motions of natural bodies to the "unmoved mover," a cosmic principle that started the motion of the world. Not anthropomorphic for Aristotle, this entity was revised by his later Christian and Muslim commentators who used his mechanical explanations within a religious worldview and imagined God as a "first mover" who kick-starts the world and thereafter pulls all the important strings.

This interpretation of motion can explain the attraction of early clockwork automata for Christian and Scholastic science in later centuries, when both the church and the scientific community were steeped in Aristotelian notions. Independently moving clockwork objects—such as the marvelous tabletop automata designed for the delight of courts in the 1560s by mechanical prodigies like Hans Bullmann, Hans Schlottheim, and Juanelo Turriano—were politically and theologically conservative.[48] Evoking both religious and secular imagery, such wonders depicted musical ladies, little clockwork soldiers, and saints or monks who could walk and turn, seem to mouth prayers, and occasionally kiss a miniature rosary.[49] Considered in light of the Christian interpretation of Aristotelian motion, such designs are pious not just in their iconography (monks and saints) but especially in their mechanism. Although they would appear to "move by themselves," these small scale automata enacted the type of movement most desirable for Catholic orthodoxy: they showed a first mover putting the machine in motion, and a clear mechanical/causal sequence for the transfer of mobility from one segment of the machine to the next. The gestures of revelation we see in stories of robots and androids occur here too, both literally, as when the clothes and exterior coverings of the clockwork automaton are lifted to show the interior mechanism, and figuratively, as when philosophical explanations and doctrines interpret and set the meanings of the performance. If we also consider that there was a delay, as such designs often allow, between the moment of winding up the automaton and the moment it begins to move, the wonder of its independent motion would lead seamlessly into a pious subsequent explanation of the powers of God as the first mover, just as Aristotle explained the mobility found in body processes and human generation through a primordial mobilization.

The fate of what I like to think of as Aristotle's favorite "machinations," honoring the way "machine" in ancient Greek means both a mechanical construct and a rhetorical syllogism, has interesting ramifications for our history of artificial and mechanical bodies and for their appropriation by dualist philosophies. As with the changing interpretations of clockwork motion, Aristotle's careful uses of mechanical mobility were later discarded in favor of simpler readings of mechanism in which theatrical puppets or *neurospasta* are used as the metaphorical opposite of conscious and relevant action—someone literally pulls the strings, or the strings set limits to possible motion.[50] Two narratives coexist in puppet analogies. A Platonist or Neo-Platonist reading describes puppet motion as a top-down structure in which one part of the self (the intellect or will) provides intention and directs the mobility of the rest. The analogical connection posited is simple: body is to soul as the puppet is to the puppet-master, with the strings conveying the puppet-master's will and intention to the several body parts. This reading is the precursor to later Cartesian distinctions between a body that is independently alive and a rational soul that is ethereal and immaterial but determines the body's motion and action. The more Aristotelian, later materialist reading treats the action of the strings in just the opposite way, in a bottom-up puppet analogy, which accepts that will and mobility start from the body. In this analogy, soul is to body as the strings are to the whole puppet: there is no motion without the strings as there is no life without soul. In philosophical treatises and science fiction stories alike, we often see these two models in contrast or in conflict, as narrative patterns stage the problem of where will and intention reside in the body or where to find the origin of motion and the source of agency.

Although materialist readings are more in keeping with Aristotle's original formulations, even they capitalize on the primacy of one entity over the other (the physical over the mental), and in the process they miss Aristotle's insistence on the material basis of the body/soul unit. In Aristotle's hylomorphic and emergentist formulations, the ideal Aristotelian description of natural bodies would sound tautological, even mystical: soul and body are not doing something to or for each other, they are each other. Even at his most mechanistic, Aristotle does not propose that soul and body can be separated, and again here his favorite examples utilize inanimate objects because they embody qualities and purposes more clearly than animate beings and people would. If an axe were an animal, Aristotle proposes, its soul would be cutting or chopping; if an eye were an animal, its soul would be seeing. Since the soul is the first entelechy (culmination or actualization) of a natural body, "there is no reason to wonder whether the soul and the body are one, just as we don't question whether the wax and its shape are one."[51] Again here we see Aristotle's classic explanatory style: it is much easier to describe the soul as a final achievement of the design of an object, to make design and its final expression as inseparable as the wax and its shape, or the axe and its entelechic capacity for chopping. It would be much more complex to imagine presenting the purpose, or final cause, of people and animals in this way, and indeed Aristotle reserves such questions for his political and ethical treatises, texts like the *Nicomachean Ethics*, where the problem of human purpose is elucidated through an analysis of political and social contexts, personal aims, social behaviors, and the impact of actions. Instead of such dense political and ethical investigations of the meanings of the human, in the physiological treatises he focuses on purposes derived from designs and processes and on explanations based on technical examples that attempt to model what is usually elusive and unexplainable.

Aristotle's mechanical analogies respond to the impulse to define purpose by redirecting it toward the inanimate. Indeed this would be the most useful way we can orient our study of the attraction of artificial people in defining the human: as with the axe, the puppet, the bellows, and the automatic mechanical display of figures in motion, the inanimate offers direct experiences of process and purpose, in ways that live beings, animals, and people never do. It seems that we turn to such figures when we crave a kind of certainty or order, an instrumentalist, mechanical, teleological, or causal understanding of life and purpose.

The tendency to read clockwork mechanisms in conservative Aristotelian ways, in relation to teleology and first movers, is all but invisible to us now but would have been a standard feature of interpreting mechanical performance in earlier centuries.[52] It is against these concepts that we have to contextualize the transformation of the mechanical analogy in the modern era, when, instead of presenting a sense of embodied power and will, the mechanicity of the body becomes a liability, a sign of the body's irrelevance in important action. This is the transformation effected by Cartesian notions of embodied mechanical motion, according to which the body may be mobile and alive and even have its own sense of purpose, but this purpose is just a matter of performance, the course and effects of which have been predetermined by the design and disposition of the mechanism, the body parts and their functions. Just as a clock cannot help but tick and keep time, so the body cannot help but be alive and continue to live and move without thought, as animals move. The two types of matter Descartes proposes—*res extensa* and *res cogitans*, or matter that has material presence and matter that thinks—offer a variation on the ancient problem of motion: "I now came to realize," Descartes writes in a 1649 letter to Henry More, "that there are two different principles causing our motions: one is purely mechanical and corporeal . . . the other is the incorporeal mind, the soul which I have defined as a thinking substance."[53] While in earlier epistemologies the functions shared between people and animals and the functions taking place in the body without thought proved the motivating and enlivening presence of the embodied soul, for Descartes these same autonomous or unconscious functions prove the independence of the thinking soul from the living body.[54]

Much has been written about Descartes's mechanistic epistemological and philosophical proposals, and the broader implications of his philosophy fall beyond the scope of this study. His work participates in the larger transformational processes of modernity, the conceptual revisions of the meanings of motion, soul, and the body, as well as new technological and scientific interpretations of the meanings of mechanism. Indeed we would be hard-pressed to find cultural domains in the seventeenth century that are immune to analogical and allegorical analyses of machines and people. Rampant anthropomorphism dominates the arts; new studies explain the state, the city, and the body itself as a machine; and a taste for unusual *naturalia* and *artificialia* stretches the limits of what could be found or produced in the natural world. The pleasures of mechanical analogy and mechanistic explanation also enjoy an intensification partly due to the rise of the new sciences. For example, Johann Kepler describes the eye as a camera obscura in 1604 and claims that the eye *is* a camera obscura, not merely equivalent or analogous to one.[55] Even the meaning of "machine" varies in Descartes's formulations, referring sometimes to clockwork objects and at other times to large-scale hydraulic applications, the kinds of automata in vogue at the time in spectacular water gardens and grottoes.[56] As Dennis Des Chene explains, even though Descartes frequently mentions "the machine of the body," he means this machine to run by liquids, as "a statue moved by flows of water, an organ whose pipes are filled with air," or indeed, in Des Chene's articulation, as "a petroleum distillery."[57] The workings of such machinery would depend less on the visibility of motion and its transfer from one part of the structure to another and more on theoretical understandings of programmatic action, the kind of action that follows by necessity from the disposition and design of the parts. Descartes does not inaugurate the use of mechanical metaphors for understanding body process, but he does change their meaning for his philosophy, moving from a teleological understanding of sequence to an epistemological focus on the self-sufficiency of mechanical action.

It is partly the need to revise the Aristotelian hylomorphic unit of matter and soul that inspires Descartes to turn to a familiar and old-fashioned animating scene in order to establish a differently compartmentalized relationship between the soul and the body. His approach separates aliveness from reason and presents a double animating scene: "I contented myself," Descartes states, "with supposing that God made the body of man entirely similar to one of ours, as much in the outward shape of the members as in the interior conformation of the organs." In a variation of classic animating scenes, Descartes adds an alchemical element in the formation of the body and its independent animation: this God-formed body contains no rational or any other kind of soul but is animated in some alchemical fashion by "one of those fires without light" that God places within it, a fire akin to "that which heats hay when it has been stacked before it is dry, or which makes new wine ferment, when it is left to ferment on the lees." This vital heat, a mere chemical reaction like the spontaneous generations of the alchemists, accounts for the functions of the body, which can all proceed perfectly well without reason, "without our thinking of them, and, therefore, without our soul." He finds no thinking in the living body, and the similarity of this kind of living for people and for animals proves that it is independent from what must be God's own additional bequest to people, the rational soul. Thus, the soul is not necessary for living but it is certainly necessary for thinking and for being a person, and he describes it as "that part distinct from the body, about which it has been said above that its nature is only to think." Finding no other aspect that pertains to men alone, he sees the presence of the rational soul as what separates people from everything else and concludes "that God created a rational soul, and joined it to this body in a particular way which I described."[58]

Not one but two animating events are thus arranged by God in this scene: the moment of man's coming to life by receiving the fire without light and the moment of man's becoming human by receiving the rational soul, the process that for Descartes distinguishes humans from other live beings. And here in a nutshell is the fantasy of animation as it inflects the modern world, a double scene that features animation as life and as intellectual or spiritual awakening. This double animation is indeed specifically crafted to reflect the independence of the soul from the body in dualist thought. The body is reduced to its most autonomic aspects, it can't help but live, and the soul's controlling presence can then be aligned with will, agency, and intellect, all the registers of mastery that we find amply exemplified in stories of artificial people and in Western cultural tendencies for supremacist rationalism.

Des Chene argues that after Descartes's interventions, the types of soul associated with living—sensation, procreation, and growth (the Aristotelian vegetative and sensitive souls)—leave the philosophical tradition, and the category of the mental increasingly takes the place of vitality as a register of animate status.[59] Much of philosophy and much of the discourse of the artificial person would hereafter have to negotiate with this paradoxical modern soul, crucial but immaterial, animating but non-vital (at least according to Descartes). Putting it simply, by making the soul immaterial this strand of philosophies dislocates the soul from its appropriate containers, in contrast to Aristotelian understandings that may have used mechanical analogies, but in the service of unified forms of explanation. If the eye were an animal, Aristotle claimed, then its soul would be seeing. There you have it, form, matter, substance, soul, first cause and final purpose, all entelechically meshed. Descartes's new immaterial soul is hardly connected to the world or to the body's mobility or vitality. Struggling to absorb this paradoxical soul, not an embodied property but an agent of animation, modern culture has been ever more consistently prone to animism, as ancient questions about the mobility of the soul reemerge with a vengeance: if it does not absolutely have to inhabit its appropriate body, does the soul wander? Would it inhabit other things? If the link between *this* body and *this* soul is not of necessity exclusive, what is to say that a different soul does not occupy this body, or that without its unique link to the soul the body does not wander aimlessly—or, more threateningly, with a purpose of its own? The narrative patterns of myriads of stories of artificial humanity should ring in our ears, loud and clear from the future.

Considered in the context of dualist animism, narratives of artificial people play with the legitimacy of the constitutive parts of the animating scene. Maybe a legitimate animating entity (a soul) acts onto an illegitimate or nontraditional vessel (a body made of strange materials); maybe an illegitimate animating entity (demonic agency, or electricity later) is used to animate a legitimate vessel (a human body), control it from a distance, or reanimate it. Maybe some other dysfunction or alteration of the "normal" process is taking place, for example when someone else, not a god, mediates the process. Narrative developments follow the typological permutations concerning what kinds of bodies may be infused by what kinds of entities, by whom, under what conditions, and to what uses or effects. Animating scenes add visibility to a cohort of invisible animating agents, and "coming to life" or "awakening" become powerful tropes of arrival into human status, consciousness, sexuality, and political presence. Later narrative treatments of the animating scene will reuse Descartes's division between vitality or life and thought or personhood and will focus on a narrative of mental and political awakening: the modern double scene of animation will become increasingly important as a metaphor of arriving into human status for people who are indeed already alive.

In addition to staging complex animating scenes, modern narratives of the artificial person also seem to counteract the focus of modern philosophy and modern life on rationality, reason, and order. In contrast to Descartes's notions of the modern soul as a primarily rational entity, in modern stories, artificial people are often excluded from the human because they are depicted as being too rational, too clearly bound by the primacy of mind over matter. We can thus see the fantasy of the artificial or mechanical person as a complex response to the dualist treatment of body and soul, and as a register of the continued relevance of an older version of the embodied soul, nostalgically, intuitively, or allegorically reframed in modernity in figures that are purely mechanical in their embodiment. What narratives of artificial people can teach us about popular interpretations of dualist dilemmas is that when the soul is disconnected from the mobility and the liveliness of the body, its departure does not render the body more compliant, more understandable, or more controllable. On the contrary, despite the desire for a certain kind of transcendence and the attending narrative and philosophical patterns of disregarding the body as a locus of meaning or knowledge in dualist thought, the body remains quite lively in its independence. Without the necessary link to the soul for its vitality (a link that premodern philosophies held on to), the body can express what it could always express, another source of motion, another motivating will, another kind of soul. The aspects of bodily mobility that had since antiquity been associated with autonomy are in modernity more autonomous than ever, and their potential as an alternate source of power or motivation is captured in a proliferation of narratives of pure mechanical being, as with robots and cyborgs, but also narratives of possession and psychosomatic interaction, of being driven or moved against our will, of being made to feel puppet-like or under someone else's control.

Again here, we see that stories of artificial people express fears and questions that may affect everyone, by highlighting the inherent liabilities in the ways in which our philosophies define the person or the self. Cartesian and dualist approaches to the body create a new mystery out of the already long-standing mysteries of ancient bodily agency and bodily independence. From classic androids with their single-minded focus, to the brainwashed ruthlessness of the poor preprogrammed Raymond Shaw in *The Manchurian Candidate* (John Frankenheimer, 1962), trained to become a lethal assassin against his will and without his knowledge, there is no scarcity of popular culture examples of the disconnect between conscious and unconscious actions, willed and unwilled motions, and the parts of the body we control versus the parts we sometimes experience as controlling us. What exacerbates the long-standing problem of top-down and bottom-up control structures and gives it new impetus in modernity is the emergence of new forms of mechanical presence, new approaches to the understanding of conscious or willful action, the advent of disembodied technologies, and the new modern experience of electricity.

MECHANISM, ELECTRICITY, AND
MODERN ARTIFICIAL PEOPLE

In order to appreciate the importance of the mechanical analogy for the discourse of the artificial person, we need to understand how the function of analogy itself has changed over the centuries. I already mentioned some of the conceptual and intellectual changes that have made a difference in the ways in which mechanisms and bodies could be discussed together: the transformation of motion into a quality that may still be associated with animation, implicitly, but is also an aspect of inanimate or clockwork mechanisms in modernity; and the prioritization of rationality and reason in Cartesian thought and in the Enlightenment, especially as these mental qualities transform the meanings of embodied motion. For most of the seventeenth and eighteenth centuries, a love of analogies, a fascination with mechanical automata, and an interest in the rise of new scientific approaches to social, cultural, and political processes ensure that mechanical analogies would proliferate, with elaborate discursive links created between machines, bodies, and other entities. But in general, and despite many interrogations of mechanical presence and mobility, clockwork mechanisms could still be folded into a narrative of orderliness and understandability, the cornerstones of the mechanical analogy as a philosophical device.[60] Despite the lifelikeness of their performances, the famous automata of the age are small or life-size in stature; and even when their workings are designed to model organic processes such as breathing, digestion, or speech, their mechanisms could still be associated with process and order and could still offer the promise of understandability, much as puppets and simple mechanical contraptions did in Aristotle's day.

But as new forms of knowledge emerged, in medical science, for example, with its new emphasis on the circulation of the blood and new approaches to the body's interior landscape, the explanatory moves facilitated by mechanical analogies were replaced by a more aggressively mechanistic style. In proposing explanations, a researcher did not have to depend on superficial similarities or flights of fancy but could make scientific assertions with a new claim to authority or truth, to the way things really worked rather than the way in which they could be imagined as working. If this conceptual change signals the new preeminence of mechanistic thinking, it also heralds the demise of the old comfortable mechanical analogies, with their assumptions of universal connectivity and penchant for visual and intuitive associations. As the art historian Barbara Maria Stafford proposes, after the late eighteenth century an eruption of romantic individualism and an epistemological fragmentation of discourse ensured the demise of analogy. Today, she warns, "we possess no language for talking about resemblance, only an exaggerated awareness of difference."[61] As we see with the often uncanny treatment of machinery and animation in modernity, what may have been intriguing, satisfying, or even revelatory in an older context becomes oppressive or tautological in modernity, as old associations between bodies and machines now carry the prospect of an improper merger of categories.

In addition to the onslaught of new technologies and scientific insights in the modern world, it is this change in the function of analogy that affects the depiction of artificial people: they emerge as new types of modern, embodied, fictionalized analogies, characters that combine both the old fascination with similarity and the new fear for the total loss of difference that analogy may enact. The imaginary being whose arms are levers, whose eyes are cameras, and whose nerves are electric clearly evokes and reinterprets a range of philosophical associations, cultural theories, and analogical connections that had accrued around mechanical embodiment through the centuries. And in the process, this new artificial being deflects or redirects the modern discomfort with the intimate similarities between bodies and machines, similarities that other centuries may have found appealing but that now feel just too close to the truth. In fact this redirecting or deflecting impulse may account for the recurrent desire of stories of artificial people to enact and strengthen a sense of absolute difference between real and artificial people, a difference that may evaporate without proper vigilance.

In addition to the changing meanings of analogy itself and the successive political, historical, social, and scientific transformations of the eighteenth, nineteenth, and early twentieth centuries, two major technological innovations alter the status and meanings of the mechanical analogy for understanding the body. The first is the rise of the modern industrial factory, with its radical scale and inhuman work rhythm, its ability to absorb and diminish the individual and operate beyond the physical limits of the human body and without consideration of the circadian rhythms of the natural world. In contrast to the small size or human scale of most seventeenth- and early eighteenth-century popular automata, factories present mechanical spectacles that are not only gigantic in their proportions but also oppressive or demanding in the way they determine the order, pace, and duration of work processes. The mechanical characteristics that robots, androids, and cyborgs absorb from industrial machines—such as insensitivity, relentlessness, inhuman scale, and a disregard for bodily limits—emerge first as human responses to the scale and rhythm of factories. Because they are associated with slavery and the metaphor of being a cog in a big machine, I will return to these allegorical translations of mechanical embodiment in the next chapter.

The second similarly transforming technological innovation emerges in the last decades of the nineteenth century, and it revolves around the new practical uses of electricity. Electrical applications have a paradoxical relationship to embodiment. On the one hand, they facilitate the rise of thoroughly disembodied modern technologies, from telegraphy and the telephone to incandescent light and electric pulses that can traverse long distances, to modern electronic and wireless devices, computer applications, remote networks, and virtual spaces. On the other hand, however, electricity is so invisible that it can only be experienced through its effects on material bodies. Electrical experiments and parlor tricks, in vogue since the eighteenth century, relish the effects of electricity on the body, as when, in one documented amusement, a young lady wearing insulated shoes is charged with static electricity and gives a little shock to the gentlemen who try to kiss her.[62] But after Luigi Galvani's famous experiments with the frog's leg in 1791, the representational distance I described above, a distance that safeguards the pleasures of analogy, begins to close: electrical charges in nature or the laboratory seem to function exactly as nerves do in the body. The frog's leg twitches and moves in response to stimuli that seem to be more than just analogical equivalents to animal motion, instead revealing that the nerves may have always been electric. As evinced in gory public demonstrations of the early 1800s and in myriads of gothic and later science fiction stories, nonliving bodies infused with electric energy could be made artificially mobile, *galvanized* into lifelike activity, compelled to move by a force external to them that acts in all respects as if it is internal. In fact, with the advent of electrical applications there may even be a problem distinguishing between external and internal motivations. The independent mobility of the body thus becomes ever more gothic and uncanny, as the purportedly non-ensouled modern body offers an emptiness that anything, including new and mysterious technologies, rushes to fill. The idea that technology can be life-giving is mirrored in science-fictional texts that implicitly or explicitly refer to electricity as the source of animation, as well as in marketplace applications that present themselves as enlivening or liberating. In the course of the nineteenth and twentieth centuries new technologies are often described as animating, and inventors and companies use the animating fantasy to represent their inventions as willful and responsive, with innovation being the agent that can "bring good things to life."[63]

But the advent of electricity also changes the meanings of the mechanical in radical ways. In contrast to electric bodies, mechanical bodies now seem to have a form of solidity and to be explainable and understandable visually in ways that electric bodies are not. If the mechanical body is inspired by the primordial intimacy of tools and simple machines in human culture, and by the explanatory power of mechanical analogies as old as Aristotle's examples, the electric body is associated with the immaterial fascinations of the eighteenth and nineteenth centuries, the interest in auras, emissions, possessions, and atmospheres. Instead of presenting order, progression, and the material transfer of motion from one part of a structure to another the way machines do, electric applications enable simultaneity and enforce new relationships with space and time. And again, in their immateriality, electrical processes have a radical effect on other material bodies. An electric current makes live bodies or body parts twitch and convulse, it makes certain metals heat up and glow, it creates magnetic force fields around metal constructions (the principle behind the dynamo), and so on. The association of electricity with animation is intuitive and increasingly a matter of direct experience for people at the beginning of the twentieth century.

In a fundamental way, the experience of electricity also challenges the sense of objects as inert and inanimate. When Thomas Edison was laying the first underground electric cables in New York in 1882, he had to spend days and often nights supervising his workers because "the Irish laborers of the day were afraid of the devils in the wires."[64] Touching a conducting material and being shocked by the contact gives the uncanny feeling that one has touched something that intended to sting, or hurt, or repel. Live wires indeed. And given the new conceptual equation of body processes with electrical processes, to say that an object can move by itself now evokes very different meanings from those characterizing clockwork and mechanical motion. The independent mobility of objects is more acceptable conceptually when its sources are mechanical and the transfer points of the motion are visible. When the origin of motion and its workings are not comprehensible, the motion of objects evokes magic or possession, the sense that something is *in* the object itself, that the object is alive or coming to life. Even as mechanical mobility is commonplace by the turn of the twentieth century and steam applications quite familiar, electricity revises the existing levels of public comfort with independent mobility, infusing the modern world with new uncanny possibilities. The ability of some electromagnetic applications to create action from a distance also has both a threatening and an exciting effect. Considered as emissions and attractions, electric and electromagnetic rays seem to penetrate within the self and threaten will and autonomy. As forces, electricity and electromagnetism join other invisible, ineffable, and permeating forces such as faith, sexual attraction, inspiration, the imagination, and the will.[65]

The contrast between the two modes of experiencing technological embodiment, in relation to mechanical and electrical registers, thus accounts for the clunky appeal of robots and other mechanical people and their emergence at a time when their mechanical embodiment was far from contemporary, far from cutting edge. Their nostalgic mechanicity retains—or returns to—the pleasures and promises of explanation and understandability of older machinery and older mechanical analogies. Indeed the split between two allegories of technological embodiment, one through the familiar and old-fashioned forms of mechanical embodiment and the other in the new and less stable electrical vocabulary, also inflects the gendered versions of artificial people that emerge in this period, versions that align artificial male bodies with mechanicity and artificial female bodies with the new electric and magnetic sublime. The distinctly gendered versions of artificial people we see throughout the twentieth and twenty-first centuries have their origins in the structural contrast between these two modes of technological embodiment. Associated with electricity and invisible technologies, artificial women provide representational visibility and a certain sexual allure to the invisible electrical realm, and artificial men remain connected to mechanical motion, machine constructs, cog-and-wheel applications, metal surfaces, and industrial processes. While artificial women dominate the technological and representational landscape of the turn of the century, artificial men emerge in the 1920s to negotiate ideas about bodies, labor, and mechanism that intensify after the First World War.

We see the artificial woman as a technological vamp in texts such as *Metropolis* (Fritz Lang, 1927), but the film summarizes the literary, cultural, and cinematic trends of a much longer period, from the 1870s to the 1920s.[66] The vocabulary used to describe the allure of the artificial female body combines sexual and technological references, electric charges and magnetic attractions, and a type of sexual allure that pivots not on visible action but on magnetic stillness, the ability to stir others into action. As we see with the robotic Maria in the film, the vamp's overwhelming attractive effect depends on an importantly intense mysterious gaze and a body comportment that occults power and femininity. The genealogy of this association reveals an already active landscape of allegorizations of feminized electricity and sexualized magnetism. Leopold von Sacher-Masoch in *Venus in Furs* (1870) describes beautiful and cruel women in fur coats as charged electric batteries. His mélange of sensual metaphors combines marble coldness and electric heat: Wanda's body resembles a marble statue, her heavy hair is electric, the effect she has on Severin pure magnetism.[67] In Villiers de l'Isle-Adam's *L'Eve future* (1880–1886), Thomas Alva Edison himself constructs and animates a perfect artificial woman for a friend who wants to remove the frivolous soul of his beloved from her noble body. The vamp-like power of the real woman to attract the men around her provides the basis for the technological interpretation of sexual attraction in the creation of an artificial woman.[68]

Metaphors of sexual allure and intense body presence of the era routinely involve overt or covert references to electrical energy, sometimes veiled under allusions to amber (the mineral that produces static electricity), abundant red hair (always associated with fire, and increasingly with electric emanations), lightning, and various body emissions. Majestic or domineering femininity becomes the metonymic locus for much of this network of meanings. Walt Whitman's poem "I Sing the Body Electric," first added to *Leaves of Grass* in the 1881–1882 edition, encodes sexual masculinity in terms of a rugged and earthly solidity and sexual femininity in terms of flows and emissions. Even while making seemingly exhaustive lists of body parts and insisting that the body *is* the soul in this poem, Whitman reserves a certain mystical and magnetic quality for the female form: "It attracts with fierce undeniable attraction!"[69] In "The Dynamo and the Virgin" (1900), Henry Adams comments that ancient goddesses were not worshipped for their beauty but for their force: "She was goddess because of her force; she was the animated dynamo; she was reproduction—the greatest and most mysterious of all energies."[70] Absorbing such cultural responses to femininity from the 1870s to the New Woman of the 1910s, the artificial woman enables a retrogressive vocabulary of idealized and occult femininity, while incorporating promises of sexual liberation and electromagnetic sexual attraction.

The contrast between mechanical and electric technologies informs the depiction of artificial people throughout the twentieth and twenty-first centuries and can be discerned even today, as with the robots that inhabit the post-apocalyptic future of *WALL-E* (Andrew Stanton, 2008). The design of WALL-E evokes the metal surfaces, replaceable parts, rivets, and cogs and wheels of classic robotic fantasies and industrial technologies, while the luminescent plastic exterior and subtle blue lights of EVE, the other robot, display the seamless, unified design of contemporary electronics and a not too subtle version of mysterious, electronic, occult femininity. The distinction between old and new forms of mechanicity in the film restages the public frustration with the invisibility of electricity in earlier eras. In contrast to the hands-on construction of WALL-E, a robot you can tinker with, EVE has no clear panels or input locations, no visible rivets or articulated machine parts. It is as self-contained and opaque as an egg, designed to respond or glow, to be intuitive in its function in its original cultural context and truly mysterious outside it. The dream of the perfectly seamless future machine—responsive, intuitive, versatile, self-sufficient—coexists easily with the nostalgia for an old-fashioned understandable machine, one that performs according to classic notions of mechanicity, of replaceable parts, visible functions, and rustic, working-class good looks.

In the algorithm I am putting together here, not only are artificial people channeling both old and new, mechanical and electric, forms of technological embodiment since the beginning of the twentieth century, they also absorb the mechanical metaphors about consciousness and will that proliferate in that era. Keeping in mind that mechanical metaphors have had a long life in human culture, we can see the ways in which new theories and definitions of the person complicate the very position of the mechanical or the automatic in understanding humanity and personality. For example, in William James and Sigmund Freud alike, a certain kind of automatism is described as a sign for the existence of subjective reality. For both, the classic Cartesian divisions obscure the multivalent interactions between body and mind, and the pervasive importance of emotion, sexuality, drive, and consciousness not as purely mental or purely bodily functions but as mind/body interactions.[71] Actions that used to be merely physiological and associated with mechanism (at least since Descartes and La Mettrie), such as impulse or reflex, now seem to be soulful and revealing and exactly the opposite of mechanism in its current meaning as prescribed and proper learned behavior. Rather than being mere expressions of the body in its most mechanical and animalistic modes, sexuality and sexual experience become paramount sites for personal expression. Similarly, in their experiments with automatic writing, modernist authors try to overcome the limits of culture, propriety, and habit in order to reveal unconscious processes and unknown feelings. To find the truth about the self also requires trying to induce psychosomatic reactions that bypass consciousness and self-control. The intense focus of popular culture in this era on hysteria and mediumistic automatism, as well as new brands of spiritualist possession and electric medicine, point to important processes of the embodiment or incorporation of mechanical thinking and technological entities. Rather than being the effect of inherent design or programming as in Descartes's reading of mechanism, unwilled action now reveals emotional truth. And lifting new obscuring layers, psychoanalytic researches reveal the unwilled and the automatic to be at the core of personality and personal identity.

Despite its domination of scientific discourse and social and political taxonomic processes, in the early twentieth century reason is a suspicious entity in popular culture, associated with the determinism, inevitability, and prescribed order of mechanisms. Impulse, on the other hand, while related to automatism and the electric energy of the nerves seems to be powered by unconscious will and body knowledge and thus resonates with Romantic notions of the imagination and the self as partly unpredictable. Long before Freud's theories of the unconscious, artists of the nineteenth century had valued the non-Cartesian qualities of irrationality, impulsiveness, and excess, and the advent of psychoanalysis strengthens the tendency to associate authenticity with the nonrational, the nonconscious. The design of new kinds of artificial people, especially robots, reflects these new priorities. Robots have reason but no impulse. They are not real people because they lack a "soul," and soul here is precisely the opposite of Cartesian rationality. Everybody can behave in prescribed or rational ways, but only artists (and "real" people) can bypass this inculcated behavior to reach authentic or spontaneous emotion. That these spontaneous experiences are considered most intimate and that they are associated with the automatic or autonomic aspects of the self should alert us to just how much has changed since Descartes wrote about mechanism, impulse, and sensation.

Let me again point out here that at the turn of the twentieth century this is not a debate between nature and culture, even though this language is endlessly deployed in the period, but between two versions of the technological imaginary: mechanical, clockwork, or visibly orderly processes and electric, magnetic, or invisible and fundamentally mysterious processes. Considered in this light, the mechanical metaphors that abound in politics, public culture, and the visual arts in the 1910s and 1920s—and the rise of mechanical people themselves in the literary and visual texts that will soon be identified as science fiction—point to the widespread cultural use of mechanism precisely as an explanatory trope. The mechanical analogy, in other words, is deployed in this era partly in the service of nostalgia, as it refers to an understandable balance between machines and bodies and has an explanatory aim. It is as if the mechanical body is deployed in an effort to understand the electric body, and since the two systems of metaphor are at conceptual odds with each other, their friction delivers the kinds of problems visible in the narrative patterns of stories that feature artificial people: bodies that seem to be designed so as to be perfectly orderly and perfectly understandable but yet behave, or are always on the verge of behaving, in unpredictable and violent ways, and minds that on one level work according to the most desirable standards of logic and reason yet in the process miss most of the meanings of the language they use, and most of the payoffs that possessing a rational soul should entail.

There is no denying that artificial people are creatures of modernity. But as I hope this long historical view has shown, the actual conceptual work they perform is not necessarily clear when they are considered solely through the lenses of the modern worldview. A more digressive and historically more expansive exploration of mechanical bodies and analogies reveals how artificial people mediate between two worldviews, always channeling the attractions of a premodern sensibility about the body and the self into the modern world. Although modern artificial people seem inspired by dualist thought and would certainly not be understandable in its absence, they also signal the persistence, or the return, of an understanding of body and mechanism that has its roots in transhistorical tendencies and ancient philosophical debates.

What becomes clear, for example, when we consider the consistent conceptual emphases of the discourse of the artificial body, is that what seems to be a purely external register of action—of using tools and treating tools, objects, and the body itself as purely instrumental in order to produce an old-fashioned sense of mastery—is based on an understanding of the self that depends solidly on non-mastery, on body experiences that are outside our control. Are artificial or mechanical bodies expressions of the autonomic body? Or are they precisely bodies that have no autonomic functions, no unknowable core? If these bodies start as paragons of a knowable, programmable, understandable body, then we can see why stories of the artificial person return so insistently to the breakdown of control structures, and why they pivot on the unexpected, the act that violates programming or breaks the rules. In light of the way I have theorized the artificial body in this chapter, these necessary "malfunctions" establish a new kind of autonomic interior within bodies designed to have no such space. In the human body, the autonomic reveals the mechanism deep inside us. In an imaginary artificial body, in which all the processes are known and designed, the autonomic reveals itself in the malfunction, the release of violence, anger, or emotions that should never have been there, the desire for humanity, the breakdown of safeguards, the impulsive or artistic act, the emotional impulse, the moment of kindness, the existential interrogation, the outpouring of desire. Despite their thematic reversals, what we see in the patterns of stories that feature artificial or mechanical bodies is the emergence of a necessary unknowable, a core of embodied nonconscious willfulness that can be approached through different philosophical models but that is fundamentally unexplainable, and unavoidable.

This is an important dimension to note especially in the context of contemporary technoculture. Although cybernetic and posthuman theories have proposed hybrid forms of embodiment that aim to counter Cartesian modalities, other contemporary theories exacerbate the popular association of technological embodiment with a pervasive break between body and mind. We find these echoes in desires to upload human consciousness on virtual or networked computer spaces after death, for example, as if thought, experience, emotion, or memory could really exist solely as information, without the body and without the world. As efforts to locate, explain, and equate body processes with mechanical or electronic processes, such theories imagine new forms of equivalence between mechanical and human bodies and experiences.[72] Here is another misreading of categories, in which a conceptual association, a shortcut, a classic mechanical analogy, is recognized or misrecognized as a tautology. Indeed, medical research shows that human memory is partly electrochemical, although this piece of news does not even begin to explain how memory works or what kinds of "storage" we are talking about in the brain. The fact that we may be using the same vocabulary for embodied processes and for electronic processes provides the impetus for aligning everything that is organic with the potentially electronic, the disembodied, the digital. How different is this very high-tech and eagerly debated line of thought from the explanatory mechanical analogies of other centuries? The craving to collapse the analogy, to make the mechanical and the organic into one, is actually itself a response to the continued mysteries of the organic, a desire for explanation, for total understanding, even for control. As an exaggerated version of certain symptoms of the dualist tradition, this tendency is also complicated by the technophilic dynamics of contemporary culture, and the desire implicit or explicit to overcome the limits of the body yet again. Aristotle would have understood the impulse, but he would have been a little more honest about its fundamental inspiration, about the structuring confrontation with the mysteries of the interior, and about the need to understand, to capture, to explain, how the body works and what it means to be a self.

3 · THE MECHANICAL SLAVE

It takes Andrew Martin two hundred years to be declared human. Over the course of these two centuries, the robot protagonist of Isaac Asimov's story "The Bicentennial Man" (1976) faces human prejudices, anti-robot sentiments, questions about his legal, civic, and social status, and endless judicial debates, slowly acquiring the right to make and keep his own money, the right to wear clothes, the right to be free, the right to make decisions.[1] Yet although he exchanges his original metal robot body for a fully organic one, while human beings in his world alter their bodies through the artificial organs and prosthetic limbs he invents, Andrew remains nonhuman under the law. His final legal victory arrives only after he insists on undergoing an operation that would ensure his deterioration and death. It is on the basis of this pathos, and after the indestructible, immortal robot submits to the fate of living things, that Andrew attains his goal. The "World President" delivers the news in person to a weakened wheelchair-bound Andrew: "Fifty years ago, you were declared a Sesquicentennial Robot, Andrew," the president says. "Today we declare you a Bicentennial Man, Mr. Martin" (172).

Andrew's humanization is carefully orchestrated so as to be both legalistic and melodramatic. Asimov's minimalist narrative style renders the transition from robot to man and from "Andrew" to "Mr. Martin" a textual event, and this despite the nerdy dissonance of the clunky "Sesquicentennial," the honorary title given to Andrew on the 150th anniversary of his construction. While the story seems to emerge out of a logical series, an algorithm of parceling out human rights, its dry focus on argumentation is animated by the robot's sense of continued, insistent, and finally undeserved exclusion. In the drama of identity that ensues, the story's implicit and explicit references to the historical conditions of chattel slavery add the emotional layer otherwise missing from logical propositions: Andrew Martin is designed to be a perennial slave, permanently shut out of human status, and his quest for full humanity refers self-consciously to the

FIGURE 16 The robot as slave in *The Bicentennial Man* (Chris Columbus, 1999). The "Three Laws of Robotics" separate the Martin family from their new robotic servant, Andrew (Robin Williams). Buena Vista/Photofest. © Buena Vista Pictures.

political and legal battles that grant civic standing to disenfranchised persons. Under the imaginative license of the science fiction mode and the unsentimental logic of the robot's own arguments and desires, we find echoes of historical processes of enslavement and emancipation, the loss and restoration of rights, and the modern philosophical tendency to prioritize legal definitions of personhood over an intuitive, embodied, or private sense of self.[2]

In their depictions of enslavement, robot stories reveal a commitment to address issues of cultural memory, to make provocative interventions to the historical record, or to revisit the traumatic impact of historical events. Asimov's focus on legal processes is eloquent in this respect. Written so that its publication would coincide with the Bicentennial of the Declaration of Independence in 1976, "The Bicentennial Man" allegorizes the nation's historical experiences in its chronological symmetry: the time it takes Andrew Martin to be declared human can be seen to refer to the time it takes the United States to live up to its Declaration of Independence, by ratifying and upholding in court the rights of its African American citizens after the civil rights movement.

Such legal and historical connections are both intimate and illuminating. Robot stories showcase the longevity of repressive structures and separatist or racist epistemologies and the authority of legal institutions, their ability to confer or ascertain different definitions of personhood. Despite the pathos of figures like Andrew, the foundational premise of the robot-as-slave story revolves around the unemotional logic of law and the real-world effects of legal and political small print—especially the kinds of small print used in order to enact spurious or self-serving social distinctions. When connected to the discourse of rights and social justice, robots embody our penchant for technicalities.

The legacies of chattel slavery resonate throughout the discourse of the artificial person, in relation to manual and industrial labor but also to questions of human purpose. The fantasy of the robotic servant, worker, or slave promises that if the enslavement of real people can no longer be tolerated in the modern world then mechanical people may be designed to take their place, and their labor will deliver the comforts of a laborless world for the rest of us. Such is the role of the Robots of Karel Čapek's play *R.U.R. (Rossum's Universal Robots),* which introduced the word "robot" in 1920 to describe artificial workers.[3] Derived from the Czech word *robota,* which refers to serf labor but also generally to drudgery and hard work, the concept unites old and new types of oppression and obliquely connects serfs and chattel slaves to the modern and newly awakened proletariat classes of the twentieth century, which the artificial people in the play embody more directly. Both as workers and as slaves, artificial people are designed with an explicit purpose, and this relationship to instrumentality distances them from certain aspects of the human condition. In contrast to real people, whose lives are not prearranged and whose purpose as beings is indeterminate or unknowable, artificial people are designed to do something specific and usually (or ostensibly) productive or useful. This coded interpretation of enslavement safeguards the difference between real and artificial people, implying that, ideally, human life is purposeless, while the lives of those constructed or enslaved have been given explicit limits and overt purposes by their oppressors. When stories that feature artificial people do not offer clear statements of their purpose, as with the monster in Mary Shelley's *Frankenstein,* or when the beings themselves claim open-endedness as their right, as with the Replicants of *Blade Runner,* their difference from the human evaporates as they come to experience and express very human existential dilemmas.

Recent critical approaches arrive at the question of enslavement by recognizing the encoding of race and ethnicity, but also persecution and racism, in stories and films that feature artificial people. While theoretical discussions of the cyborg focus on the hybrid organic/mechanical status of cyborg bodies as a reference to ethnic and racial hybridity, in popular culture it is not the technological origin but the cyborg's human appearance, its human-like skin, that brings this vocabulary to the foreground.[4] Viewers and critics note the specifically Aryan beauty of the human-like Replicants in *Blade Runner,* their social position as workers designed for specific occupations in other planets and barred from Earth on penalty of death, their status as runaways to be hunted and killed by the corporation that owns them, as well as the use of derogatory terms to describe them, as in the term "skinjobs." Similarly, in *Battlestar Galactica*, the Cylons are referred to as "toasters" by hostile humans in this version of the anti-mechanical slur, while their human-like appearance and their ability to pass for human provide the basis for numerous paranoid scenarios of infiltration and species impurity, as even those who think of themselves as human may have been Cylons all along. Narratives of miscegenation emerge as well, as the Cylons' propensity to fall in love with humans results in hybrid human/Cylon children, both respected and feared for their potential to evacuate the differences between the two civilizations.[5] Race, gender, ethnicity, age, national origin, all are the kinds of human characteristics that in the discourse of the artificial person function as skin effects and that alter what becomes recognizable or literally visible in the story.

But given that stories of artificial people often function as allegories of otherness, we do not need to see racially marked human-like figures in a story or a film in order to recognize the encoding of racial categories and concerns. Indeed in the robot-as-slave story, it is the otherness, the inhumanness, or the very metalness of robots that aligns science-fictional narratives with the historical legacies of slavery and their cultural memory. In critical ways, robots have the potential to materialize what Toni Morrison has called an "Africanist" presence, a figuration of otherness that captures complex feelings about mastery and enslavement, sovereignty and its vulnerabilities, the social death of the slave and the desire for awakening and political participation.[6]

Robots embody ethnic and racial otherness despite their nonhumanity, an effect that I am describing here as metalface: the metal exterior of the robot functions as a site for projecting numerous kinds of difference, and in this fundamentally ambiguous space metalness can stand in for a type of blackness or, indeed, for other states of abjection that the position of the African slave embodies in Western modernity. The robot's potential for racial or ethnic representation comes from its objecthood: the robot is a priori designed as a being whose ontological state maps perfectly with a political state. Robots are designed to be servants, workers, or slaves. They occupy that social and political position by default and carry its requirements and limits on their very bodies. The more self-evident this is, as in the case of metal-looking robots who would never be mistaken for human, the more obvious the alignment of the discourse with racist epistemologies, in which again one may be able to tell where a person fits in a social hierarchy just by looking at them.

The representation of artificial people as slaves alters the meaning of the other structural elements of the discourse. The fact that artificial people are born adult becomes the necessary precondition for their immediate entry into preordained social or workplace functions. And the depiction of their mechanical bodies in the context of labor renders them purely instrumental, instead of fascinating or potentially revelatory—the conceptual intimacy between bodies and machines here providing the grounds for treating people as functional objects. Whatever else these structural elements may have meant in premodern contexts, in modernity they are involved with the problematic social and conceptual organizations of slavery, and this is no coincidence. Studying robots as slaves reveals that both real and artificial people in modernity are defined and structured through their relationship to that "peculiar institution."

METALFACE: THE ROBOT AS SLAVE

By referencing the iconography and popular memory of slavery, robot stories infect the technological promises of the future with the legacies of oppression and injustice of the past. This is inevitable, of course. Any context in which one character can say "Yes, Master" to another *must* be considered in relation to actual histories of oppression, no matter how fictional or imaginary the settings for such utterances may be. In addition, the presence of robots alters the techno-utopian vision because robots are actually very personal, very human. In contrast to automated solutions, robots perform direct and personified actions that retain a connection to how humans might perform the same labor. The desire for impersonality, for automatic solutions, invisible laborers, or the total abolition of labor is thus complicated by the way robotic fantasies continue both to embody the laborer and to present historical and cultural memories of conflict and oppression. Understanding this allows us to refrain from the stereotypical reading of anthropomorphism in these stories. Instead of proposing that anything that has a human-like body is competing with the human (a classic master/slave dialectic move that is both pervasive and problematic in this discourse), we should consider that anything that has a human-like body is related to the experiences, desires, and aspirations of the human.

In Isaac Asimov's "The Bicentennial Man," for example, historical memory is both self-conscious and essential. Although not the last of Asimov's robot stories, "The Bicentennial Man" is a culminating moment in Asimov's robot explorations, launched in 1940 when he was only twenty years old. One of the most anthologized of his tales and his personal favorite, the story also marks a comeback for Asimov. By the late 1970s, the infusion of the science fiction field with new voices and experimental writing styles that emphasize complex social and political topics and the critical and theoretical revolutions of the New Wave render the story type Asimov had perfected in the 1940s and 1950s a little more old-fashioned, stylistically bare, and rudimentary in terms of characterization and depth.[7] As if in response to this context, with "The Bicentennial Man" Asimov pushes his robot stories to a new level by making overt references to historical slavery, thus externalizing a racial subtext that is implicit if prevalent in Asimov's earlier robot tales. Andrew refers to Mr. Martin consistently as "Sir," and to the young members of the Martin family as "Miss" and "Little Miss," while his devotion to Little Miss resembles other versions of friendship between a trusted, gentle, older servant or slave and an angelic young girl. As versions of Uncle Tom and Little Eva from Harriet Beecher Stowe's *Uncle Tom's Cabin*, Andrew and Little Miss play out a classic scenario of devoted servitude and well-meaning liberalism. Little Miss provides Andrew with his name, derived from the initials of his serial number, NDR, a classic robot naming convention for Asimov and other authors. The family's reaction to Andrew's request to buy his freedom, once he saves enough money from the artifacts he makes and sells on his own time, similarly echoes familiar plotlines. While Little Miss supports this aim, Sir is insulted and sulky, expressing in his reaction the paradoxes of the slaveholder's point of view that Asimov renders palpable without addressing. Hasn't Andrew felt free while he has been with them? They have done nothing but respect and support him. Why would he abandon them like this? As Wanda Raiford has noted, Andrew's depiction in the story is a veritable checklist of elements we can connect to the African American experience of slavery in the United States, from the name he does not choose to his relationship to the master's children and the process by which he has to split his earnings with his owners and only keep half.[8] Working on political readings on this story, both Raiford and Sue Short discuss the ways in which the legal process of Andrew's emancipation provides an imaginary happy ending to the Dred Scott case, which in 1857 proclaimed that people of African descent, enslaved or free, were not citizens and, as property, also had no standing in court.[9] In its legal focus "The Bicentennial Man" replays these legal premises but gives different final answers, as does the *Star Trek* episode inspired by the Asimov story, titled "Measure of a Man" (aired February 13, 1989). Andrew is eventually recognized as a human, and in *Star Trek*, after humans and aliens speak in Commander Data's support, the court eventually declares that he is not the property of Star Fleet.[10]

Asimov's assumptions about the connection between robots and slaves extend to other storylines as well. Andrew's steadfast devotion to the Martin family and the total obedience desired of robots resemble a kind of preprogrammed Tommism, while even Asimov's insistence on the ethical safeguards of the famous "Three Laws of Robotics" can be considered as an enforced application onto robots of romantic racialist notions of the moral superiority of slaves (in abolitionist discourse of the nineteenth century) and later African Americans (in stereotypical portrayals in popular culture). The constant refrain of human suspicion of robots and even violence against them, a feature that permeates all of Asimov's robot stories, presents such anti-robot sentiments as versions of racism and racist violence. The consistent fear of the unenlightened public that robots are always on the verge of revolt is clearly a register of racial paranoia, treated in most robot stories as an unfortunate but largely unchangeable cultural trend. The dramatic subtext of the robot's story can thus be found in historical and literary references and real-life practices of oppression and political exclusion, while the legal focus of Andrew's battles for personhood mirrors the series of Supreme Court rulings that grant rights at times when public prejudice and established social structures might withhold them. Even the choice of the last name, Martin, for this unique family of people who fight to emancipate their robot perhaps pays homage to the work of Martin Luther King Jr. In a way the story interprets the historical bicentennial of the United States through a series of embodying acts, in which the country, its historical legacies, its disenfranchised citizens, and the battle for equality are all allegorically embodied in the figure of the finally emancipated robot.

If representing the robot as a slave seeking emancipation leads to questions about the legal standing of humans and the fragility of civil rights, a second line of questioning emerges when we consider the robot as a worker. In "The Bicentennial Man," Andrew's original position as a servant, "a valet, a butler, a lady's maid" (137) quickly changes when he becomes a playmate for the family's young children and then an artisan, crafting beautiful sculptures, cabinets, and desks out of wood. Andrew's specialness, his artistic sensibility, and his unique handiwork explain why he deserves different treatment and different rights than other robots do, and his relationship to work remains artisanal and nonindustrialized even when he later invents artificial organs and limbs. Andrew's emancipation is as unusual and unique as he is, and it remains politically irrelevant for other robots in his world, robots designed to be functional and limited in scope. Although the emancipation narrative rewards Andrew's individuality, his specialness isolates him economically and politically. The classic robot's association to industrial labor, mechanized factories, the military-industrial complex, and the modern processes of mass production could not be further from the kind of labor we see in this story. And when Andrew eventually designs systems that would allow a robot "to gain energy from the combustion of hydrocarbons, rather than from atomic cells," thus in effect enabling robots to eat and breathe (161), these innovations become useful for ailing humans but are never used to enable any other robot, except Andrew, to reach such embodied experience of life. In response, U.S. Robotics, the company that created him, designs central computers that can control thousands of robots "by microwave." A backlash to Andrew's innovative ways of being, this new tendency in robotics ensures that no robot will ever be as individualized and adaptable, as creative and potentially troublesome, or as alive as Andrew: "The robots themselves have no brains at all. They are the limbs of the gigantic brain and the two are separate" (160). In this neo-dualist robot order, a robot's subservience will be more securely designed, more total and unassailable. It may not be possible to reverse the political process underway for finalizing Andrew's humanization, the story implies, but

U.S. Robotics can make sure these options will never be available for any other robot. In effect, Andrew's artistic sensibility, his access to money, his family relationships, and even his finally acquired rights, all function as a series of insulating events, protective layers that instead of integrating him into the human world serve to shield him from a rapacious and uncaring capitalist world.

This political layering, in which a feel-good story of endurance or emancipation hides an undercurrent of continued and ever more totalizing oppression, is essential to the questions that structure this chapter. Enslaved robots may be earnest and well-meaning and may be articulating real social and political concerns. But in their battle for human rights do enslaved robots tell us anything new or important about these rights? If indeed Andrew's emancipation is at the same time a gesture of insulation, then his story includes a fantasy of safety for people rather than robots, a fantasy in which we are able to withstand or counteract the objectifying and dehumanizing processes of our world. The very descriptions we use for these processes ("objectifying," "dehumanizing") point to the power of a political fantasy of animation, in which disenfranchised objects are transformed into political subjects as if coming to life, presented here as civic existence, and the accompanying fear of de-animation, in which we become as powerless and politically invisible as the mindless robots that populate Andrew's world.

To add to these conundrums, we may notice how old-fashioned or rudimentary the emancipatory narrative of "The Bicentennial Man" is when seen in the light of race relations or the legacies of slavery as these might have been felt in 1976. Consider, for example, another text produced that year, Richard Pryor's "The Bicentennial N___," which also takes the milestone of the bicentennial as its basis and also wonders about what has changed during the first two centuries of the United States. In his characteristically incisive way, Pryor gives us the perspective of another "Bicentennial Man" who Pryor imagines will be paraded out for the celebration. "They will, they'll have some n___ 200 years old in blackface, with stars and stripes on his forehead, little eyes, lips just a' shinning. And he'll have that lovely white folks expression on his face, but he's happy! He's happy 'cause he been here 200 years." Pryor's voice and intonation change as he embodies an accented "Uncle Tom" persona for this character, who embarks on an understated but rather direct telling of the history of racial abuse in the United States, amid awkward chuckles and self-deprecating humor. The band begins to play "Glory, Glory Halleluiah," as Pryor's Bicentennial Man begins:

> I'm just so thrilled to be here . . . over here in America. I'm so glad y'all took me out of Dahomey. [chuckles] Yuk yuk yuk . . .
>
> I used to could live to be 150, now I dies of high blood pressure by the time I'm 52. And that thrills me to death. I'm just so pleased America is going to last. Yuk, yuk, yuk . . .

They brought me over here in a boat. There was 400 of us come here. Yuk
yuk yuk . . .
     360 of us died on the way over here. Yuk, yuk, yuk . . .
     But I love that. Yuk yuk yuk . . .
     That just thrills me so. Yuk yuk yuk . . .
     I don't know, you white folks are just so good to us. Yuk yuk yuk . . ."

As with the related piece, "Bicentennial Prayer," in which Pryor impersonates a
preacher leading his congregation in a prayer for the future of the United States
titled "How Long Will This Bullshit Go On?" the celebration of the bicentennial brings up complicated feelings about the past and the future. In contrast to
the palliative effect of Asimov's allegorical commemoration of a kind of progress, Pryor's view of the passage of time offers little solace. "I'm just so happy.
I don't know what to do. I don't know what to do if I don't get 200 more years
of this. Yuk, yuk, yuk, yuk . . . ," our speaker remarks. The history of suffering,
abuse, disease, separated families, and death escalates in intensity, and the punch
line of the piece comes in a rather chilling form as our speaker concludes: "Y'all
probably done forgot about it. Yuk, yuk, yuk . . . [voice turns serious and dry, music
stops] But I ain't gonna never forget it."
     For Pryor's Bicentennial N___, the future cannot be separated from the past,
and the memory of abuse persists despite all efforts to obliterate or beautify history. As Pryor's speaker drops the façade of the conciliatory and ever-forgiving
happy slave, he also subtly evokes the possibility that this history deserves a
response in the present, a response that may include what oppressors always fear,
the rightful rage, the violent retaliation, the revenge of the slave. What is striking
about Pryor's last line in this piece is how quickly he can conjure this new figure
of a former slave who is self-aware, critical, potentially vengeful, and even mili-
tant, a figure that embodies a guilty culture's fears.
     In contrast, Asimov's Bicentennial Man remembers Little Miss fondly on his
deathbed, the one human connection that holds for him through the centuries.
Andrew Martin is an ideal former slave in this respect: his quests are not motivated
by hard feelings, his memories do not focus much on traumatic experiences, and
his desire for equality is abstract, disembodied. We hardly have the sense that the
robot is aware of human abuses as abuses, and the story brushes the possibility
of emotional response aside, allowing nostalgia to be the main human emotion
Andrew expresses. There seems to be little in the past for Andrew to remember
with bitterness, little to mourn or avenge. As with other narrative patterns we find
in robot stories, the robot fantasy responds to loss by presenting a being that is
unaffected by it. The memory of Little Miss humanizes the robot and is related to
wistfulness, rather than grief, and never to rage or revenge.

Despite their differences, Asimov's and Pryor's versions of a Bicentennial Man engage a range of stereotypes: Andrew Martin embodies both a forgiving or assimilationist stance and a politically utopian promise of equality; Pryor's speaker is both a conciliatory and self-effacing "Uncle Tom" and a potentially explosive budding activist who will eventually hold his oppressors accountable; and in the background of both tales we have the implicit presence of the silent slaves, dead, abused, or lost, and of the brainless robots that cannot speak or act, not yet or not ever. Their potential for action, for revolution, uprising, revenge, or social transformation fuels both the paranoid scenario of the avenging slave and the palliative scenario of the emancipated one. In addition, the centrality of the law and of constant aggression, constant battle, in these stories cannot be underestimated. In "The Bicentennial Man" we see a series of legal proceedings that grant rights in partial, limited, and incremental ways, rather than a single definitive decision, and this long duration parallels a similarly extended civic process, the legal battles of the nineteenth and twentieth centuries that uphold the civil rights of African Americans against ever-lurking racist and segregationist practices. In Pryor's historical account we similarly see how expansive both the events and the effects of enslavement are, not a single act but a series of acts of violence and domination. By focusing on processes rather than on single events, these stories present complex mechanisms for subjugation as well as emancipation. And taken together, the two stories create an interesting circle, consisting first of a long process of divesting persons of their rights and then of a long process by which rights might be reinstated. If the robot emancipation story presents the tale of how an object becomes a subject, it evades the ways in which, in historical circumstances, a subject becomes an object, a process that is both legal and social. Similarly, in an essay that commemorates the bicentennial of the U.S. Constitution in 1987, Justice Thurgood Marshall underscores the defining role of legal principles in the lives of African Americans, for processes of enslavement as well as emancipation. "They were enslaved by law, emancipated by law, disenfranchised and segregated by law; and finally they have begun to win equality by law," Marshall wrote.[12]

This is where the historical and legal processes of disenfranchisement and emancipation share fundamental conceptual similarities with the discourse of the artificial human and the circularity of the animating story, its focus on traversing the boundaries from birth to death to rebirth. As I proposed in the first chapter, the fantasy of animation seems to be an investigation of birth, but it is both inspired and structured by the imagery and processes of death. Scenes of an artificial birth present a double reversal: they reverse birth by bringing everything that is inside outside, thus granting understandability and visibility to the mystery and interiority of birth, and they reverse death by switching the directionality of de-animation, imagining the gradual acquisition of sensation, cognition, and selfhood instead of their loss. The implicit desire of the artificial birth is for a palindromic or circular process, an alchemical process of infinite rebirth from death. Recast in the scenes of subjugation and emancipation we find in stories about the enslavement of real people and the liberation of robots, these fantasies take on a poignant political tone. As Justice Marshall notes, while we may be eager to celebrate the ways in which the law can confer rights, we would do well to remember the first half of this circle—in which sovereign persons are divested of their rights, and often through legal means. Indeed, considering the animating story in this political context may grant a new kind of visibility to these processes, refiguring in the allegorical context of science fiction the problems and debates with racist definitions and epistemologies that plague not just the historical record but the very definition of the person in modernity. And just as every story of artificial birth or reanimation contains the structuring memory of death and de-animation, in the political fantasy of animation every story of emancipation contains the history of disenfranchisement. This characteristic circularity provides a valuable perspective on the political potential of the fantasy of animation and its deployment.

REVOLUTION, EMANCIPATION, ABJECTION: ON BEING MECHANICAL

Implicit under the metal exterior of the robot we thus find versions of the enslaved human, representations rife with echoes of real historical conditions and collective cultural responses to the legal and social limits created by racist epistemologies. The figures of the violent slave, the emancipated slave, and the silent abject slave structure the science-fictional traditions for depicting imaginary robots in this story type, and the narrative scenarios that ensue are all intertwined with the preconceptions of what slavery may mean or entail. But as with other aspects of the discourse of the artificial person, the actual deployment of these patterns is dynamic. In any given story, we may inhabit both the position of the robot, frustrated by limits and regulations, tragic in its exclusion, and evocative in its embodiment of difference; and the position of the human community, driven by a desire for order or comfort or threatened by the onslaught of something that is inhuman, non-understandable, gothic.

The first narrative pattern revolves around violence, rebellion or war, with the enslaved robots rising up against their human masters, threatening to take over the world and annihilate humanity. This paradigm informs originary texts such as Čapek's *R.U.R.*, in which the rebelling Robots succeed so well that only one human engineer remains alive, but also modern revisions, as in the reimagined *Battlestar Galactica*, in which a quick credit sequence provides the story's premise

THE CYLONS WERE CREATED BY MAN.

THEY WERE CREATED TO
MAKE LIFE EASIER ON
THE TWELVE COLONIES.

AND THEN THE DAY CAME
WHEN THE CYLONS DECIDED
TO KILL THEIR MASTERS.

FIGURE 17 A history that needs no explanation, in the opening credits for *Battlestar Galactica*. Taking the plotline of enslavement and revolt as a given, the miniseries begins with a set of intertitles that provide the backstory of the Cylons. © Sky/Sci-Fi Channel

boiled down to the basics: "The Cylons Were Created by Man. They Evolved. They Rebelled. There Are Many Copies. And They Have a Plan." While the narrative repercussions of this plotline are complicated as the show progresses, both the grounds for creating the Cylons (to be slaves) and the main reasons for their rebellion (slaves rebel against their masters) can be taken for granted at the onset of the series. Although in some texts there are political and social reasons for the robots' uprising, sometimes the rebellion subplot is so rudimentary as to seem reactive, as if the main job of robots is to eventually be "out to get us" or "run amok." Here we have to remember that what robots present narratively and what they express emotionally may be two different things. The robots' rebellion may stand in for the kinds of frustrations we feel with a particular status quo (don't we wish that we could run amok sometimes?) but may also occasion a reactive human awakening. Human history provides numerous examples of such ostensibly retaliatory actions against imagined attacks—leading to various forms of mob violence against minorities, from pogroms to race riots, genocides, and ethnic cleansing campaigns. Or the human response may be uncharted and loose—as in *Metropolis*, for example, in which the unruly android Maria fuels a destructive human reaction that affects everything indiscriminately before turning against the instigator herself. Despite the fact that Maria is acting on Fredersen's ideas and so is not the full agent for this process, her actions unleash a deep need for the workers of Metropolis, a need for revolution and an almost pagan release.

When its grounds are not simply taken for granted, robotic rebellion may be related to insecurities about whether we control the range and scope of advanced technology. Robotic violence may also be the result of malfunctions, human mistakes, misunderstandings, and so on, in which case it is difficult to read rebellion as a political act. Or a story may be purposefully ambiguous about questions of agency, as in *2001* (Stanley Kubrick, 1968), for example, in which we do not know whether the murderous computer HAL is malfunctioning or killing the crew because it has been given a particular mission. In contrast, in *Alien* (Ridley Scott, 1979), the interfering android follows company policy in endangering the crew of the *Nostromo*. When the violence enacted by artificial beings ensues from their ability to obey orders, it presents a different aspect of their enslavement to their programming or to their human masters. How political this plotline will be thus depends on the narrative treatment of the robots' agency: the robots rebel because they know they have been oppressed, or they rebel for no reason at all as if they are mechanical maniacs, or it doesn't matter why they rebel as long as they allow us to rebel too. Alternatively, maybe the robots are not actually rebelling, they are violent because of malfunction or human mistakes, or they are violent because they *cannot* rebel against their orders. Whether or not the premise of robotic mayhem is legible politically, the spectacle of robotic violence itself carries echoes of social uprising, of slave rebellions and socialist revolutions that refer to historical realities and their aftermath in the cultural memory.

The second narrative pattern follows the robot through processes of emotional and cognitive development, which prioritize human connections and often result in the desire for acceptance and legal emancipation, as in Andrew Martin's case in "The Bicentennial Man." In these tales, a worthy and often misunderstood robot fights for rights or acceptance—in the process expressing what is most important and valuable about humanity. Asimov famously claimed that when he began writing robot stories he sought to counter the then dominant representation of dangerous rebel robots that followed *R.U.R.* and other texts of the 1920s and 1930s.[13] In sharp contrast to the depictions of rabid mindless attackers that he criticizes in early pulp science fiction, Asimov presents the robot as a figure of interest and occasional pathos, usually logical, functional, and indeed with an ethical demeanor. In fact both the safety and the moral content of Asimov's robots stem from his explicit reaction to the "robots running amok" subplot, which he often described as the "Frankenstein complex," a fear that our technological creations will rise up against us, destroy us, or be "out to get us," like the monstrous attackers of popular imagination.[14] But, Asimov insists, any tool could be dangerous, and if they were ever to be invented, robots would be treated as other technologies have been over the centuries, with a prioritization of usefulness, inbuilt safeguards, and a sense of limits. In his famous "Three Laws of Robotics," created in 1941, Asimov builds such a system for ensuring ethical, or at least safe, robot function. According to these laws robots may not injure humans or allow them to come to harm through inaction; robots must obey human orders, unless they conflict with the primary requirement of avoiding danger to humans; and robots must protect their own existence, but only after ensuring that such protection does not violate the other two laws.[15] Many of Asimov's robot stories from the 1940s to the 1980s emerge from the interaction between the tasks robots have to perform and the limits of the "Three Laws." But in terms of robot behavior, Asimov's system of safeguards also solidifies a particular worldview: robots start as a priori dangerous, and people start as a priori fearful of robots, for reasons that often remain undisclosed or resort to stereotypical notions of mastery and supremacy. The idea that robots would be universally feared and disliked presents a sense of anti-robot racism that Asimov and other writers take for granted, even in stories that do not otherwise involve an overt racial or ethnic premise for robot representation. This is one area in which historical echoes of slavery and racism are pervasive and structuring for the robot story.

In its various permutations, the story type of the gentle robot or android enjoys wide cultural relevance. In some stories and films the robots may request civic, political, or human rights, while in others they may substitute rights for love, acceptance, understanding, or just freedom from harm. The fundamental core of this storyline is related to pathos and the vagaries of social inclusion and exclusion, and it always seems to return implicitly to the portrayal of the monster in *Frankenstein*, to the intensity of the monster's desire to be accepted, and the finality and incomprehensibility of his exclusion. Family dramas and parental rejection also inform more recent stories, as with David, the artificial boy of *A.I. Artificial Intelligence* (Stephen Spielberg, 2001), who has been programmed to love his human family even after they reject him. David's loyalty and his craving for human acceptance are heartbreaking, while his parents' ability to withhold their affection challenges given certainties of who and what is inhuman. His acceptance by his colleagues is essential for Commander Data on *Star Trek*, as well, while true love emerges as the primary goal of many humanoid Cylons in *Battlestar Galactica*. Seeking rights, love, or inclusion in a family and social unit, the robots in these tales come quite close to intimate human desires for

social and familial acknowledgment. Dramatic treatments of the robot's acceptance can have a cathartic "feel-good" effect, but stories that focus on rejection or
abandonment can be just as powerful.

In fact, the desire to be loved, wanted, or included has such affective force
that, to a certain extent at least, it renders the robot's ontological status irrelevant. One of the most fascinating paradoxes in this discourse is that texts can
create powerful emotional situations for metal or mechanical beings that could
not even be considered alive by any organic standard. For example, David, the
boy android of *A. I.*, will always be a young boy, will never grow or develop; he
cannot eat, drink, or sleep, and his body remains mechanical and inhuman to
the end. Yet his desire to be loved by his human family and the cruelty of his
abandonment are just as powerful for the story as if he were organic—maybe
even more melodramatic than if he were real. "Why do you want to leave me?
Why?" David asks Monica, the woman who should act as his mother. "If you
let me, I'll be so real for you!" Ever the expert in creating dramatic poignancy,
Spielberg implies that biological makeup does not matter; it is our response that
matters, that has the capacity to humanize or objectify others. Swept into the
feeling of what it means to be abandoned by one's parents, we don't care about
the status of David's body. But other texts, less secure about how this would
work solely on the basis of empathy or dramatic treatment, make sure we have
a more secure hold on biological humanity. For example, in "The Bicentennial
Man" it is no accident that Andrew is accepted as human only after he has indeed
transformed his body to such an extent that he is biologically and functionally
indistinguishable from humans. Similarly in *Battlestar Galactica*, the humanoid
Cylons are so close to human biology as to be able to procreate with humans,
again dissolving any sense of their difference.

These stories align the biological, the emotional, and the civic or legal, making it easier to accept preemptively on emotional or intuitive grounds what
seems to be an intellectual, objective, unemotional, or legal judgment. Despite
the overt focus on politics, political coexistence, and civic acceptance, these
texts ensure that another underlying requirement is satisfied first, as if the two
types of recognition—intuitive and legal—would be at odds with each other.
And in legal terms the two definitions of humanity or personhood can indeed
be at odds. Chattel slavery provides one such example, in which people who are
clearly persons are treated as nonpersons under the law. The intuitive recognition
of their humanity has to be policed and "corrected" by supremacist self-interests,
legal precedents, and racist epistemologies in order to actively dehumanize and
objectify them.

We find an early and unusual treatment of the acquisition of rights without
biological transformation in Earl and Otto Binder's collection of Adam Link
stories. Published under the name "Eando Binder" (a penname formed by the

brothers' initials "E" and "O") but mostly written by Otto, these stories are unusual in the context of 1930s pulp science fiction, inaugurating the post-pulp depiction of robots as sympathetic human-like figures that sacrifice themselves for the common good.[16] In the first story, titled "I, Robot" (1939), the robot Adam Link not only faces human prejudice in ways that become standard for later robot tales but also presents these troubles through a first-person perspective that is itself rare in robot narratives.[17] Questions of racial difference and social injustice also emerge rather quickly, as when Adam Link describes his awakening as a new being: "My first recollection of consciousness was a feeling of being chained" (7). We later find out that this was for safety reasons, but the emotional connection between historical and figurative slavery has already been made. Adam recognizes Dr. Link, his creator, as his "master," while Dr. Link considers the robot his son and envisions helping Adam become a U.S. citizen before creating more robots. Dr. Link's dream is a classic articulation of robotic helpfulness: "Think of robot police! And robot firemen, robot scientists, robot lawyers, and so on down the line. The ultimate machine, with human intelligence, boosting civilization to greater heights" (14). Dr. Link plans to make more robots, "but not as slaves, or pieces of property," a reluctance that does not stem from a belief in the inherent equality between people and robots but that is instead inspired by his expectation that, if created as slaves, "one day the robots might revolt" (14). A similar expectation of the impending revolt of the robots propels the neighbors repeatedly to attempt to burn, lynch, and generally destroy Adam Link. Yet, instead of repaying hatred and isolation with violence, like the frequently mentioned monster in *Frankenstein*, Adam remains faithful, peaceful, and helpful.

Adam Link's quest for citizenship predates and anticipates Andrew Martin's later legal battles for emancipation. Like Andrew, Adam does not revolt or become violent, and he requests his rights only after he works hard to deserve them. He is kind, attentive, heroic, loyal, and supremely moral—indeed his decision to never harm humans, written before Asimov's stories and before the popularization of the "Three Laws of Robotics," is part of Adam's own ethical code and not a programmed response. But this idealization also silences him politically: Adam is often promised that if he could perform patriotic acts for his country he would be integrated into the community. While Andrew Martin focuses on legal action and financial security, Adam Link's route to citizenship is related to patriotism. Yet after he fights against crime, saving the girl, the town, and finally the whole world from alien attacks, his hope for equal citizenship is disappointed—and on the basis of arguments that start from his physical difference. While it never becomes clear to him that being an American citizen is out of the question because he is made of metal and is visibly "other," even a minor court clerk thinks that his exclusion is self-evident. When Adam's advocates claim that according to the law any "person" can apply for citizenship, "regardless of race, color, creed or nationality" and that Adam is a person, the official scoffs: "It's quite obvious that he's nothing more than a clever mechanical apparatus. . . . What you want is a *patent*" (112). In addition to the representation of patriotism as a gateway to full citizenship (a promise that was made to ethnic communities during both world wars and was quickly betrayed after the wars), this emphasis on physical difference and exteriority affirms the assumption that robots are racially marked—and subject to discrimination based on their metal "skin." By the end of the story, Adam receives a Congressional Medal of Honor and becomes a citizen of the United States through a special presidential act, but the conflict between intuitive/ biological and legal definitions of his status remains important.

Asimov's stories of the 1940s also present roboticism as an implicitly racial category of being. But because Asimov also insists that the robot is a functional, logical, helpful machine, these representational echoes operate implicitly, as if a racial subtext could be recognizable for readers without much expansion. For example, the Uncle Tom/Little Eva dynamic of the supersized but gentle robot and the diminutive but loyal mistress we see in "The Bicentennial Man" also structures Asimov's first robot story, "Robbie" (1940).[18] Even without a focus on humanization, in "Robbie" we see that little Gloria understands something about Robbie's gentleness and care that the adults cannot see, and the robot displays a sacrificial devotion that exceeds all parameters of mere programming. Gloria's parents decide to get rid of Robbie in response to public pressure: "There's bad feeling in the village" (9). They are only persuaded to value the unusual bond between the two when Gloria recognizes Robbie on a factory floor full of robots and Robbie saves her life from an oncoming tractor. Expanding the implications of the robot-as-slave premise, Asimov's next story "Runaround" (1942) features robots that have a "slave complex" built into them and are unable to move unless guided by a "master." When one of the more advanced robots in this story malfunctions, it behaves in the absurd ways of what one critic describes as the stereotype of "the plantation 'darkie.'"[19] As the robots in Asimov's stories become more sophisticated, the sense that their developmental horizon would eventually approximate the human results in storylines that involve passing. Again the very idea that passing for human would be a desirable aim for robots reveals a racially inflected understanding of the robot. Asimov's "Evidence" (1946) for example, features a paranoid political system in which accusations about being nonhuman could be used during elections. But Stephen Byerly, an intelligent and patient android, is finally elected mayor of New York after proving he is human: he hits a man in public, something the "Three Laws" would never allow for a robot. In the final lines of the story, robopsychologist Susan Calvin provides a counterpoint to this certainty: an android could hit a man if the man in question were another android. Public paranoia about passing thus continues unchallenged.

One of the best examples for the ways in which robots function for Asimov is in the linguistic strategies of a story titled "Reason" (1941). Working in a remote space station, two human engineers become increasingly frustrated with the rationality of the robot they have to train, nicknamed "Cutie" (inspired by its serial number, QT-1). Cutie is a strict rationalist, a "robot Descartes," and his relentless logic and sense of superiority frustrate the human engineers. In what becomes an escalating level of verbal abuse, the engineers invent more and more insulting phrases to describe Cutie, all revolving around the robot's metal surface and composition, in anger calling the robot a "walking junkyard," "metal maniac," "tin-plated screwball," "brass baboon," and "electrified scarecrow" (49–56). It is not unusual for Asimov to include cringe-worthy puns in his stories, as in "There's going to be trouble with that robot. He's pure nuts!" (53), but there is something more to the insult pattern here. We have complex anti-metal insults such as "you son of a hunk of iron ore"; elaborate threats such as "If that metal mess gives me any lip like that, I'll knock that chromium cranium right off its torso"; and the surprisingly overt "do-jigger" using the word "jigger," meaning doodad or gadget but also echoing racial slurs like "jigaboo" and all the words that "rhyme with trigger," as Ralph Ellison would say.[20] This multiple pun is insulting as both anti-mechanical (a gadget!) and racist. Although racial and other slurs usually have nothing to do with visual referents, the insistent return of these insults to the robot's metal skin and physical presence as well as its materiality and mechanical composition point to the implicit critique Asimov is engaging here. In a pattern that continues in later texts, the robot is insulted on the basis of its physical description, its metal exterior, its skin.

In their narrative containment of rejection and acceptance, these textual paradigms thus encode a subtle racial subtext and a historical reaction to the legacies of slavery, with the violent uprising of slaves motivating the imagery of one version and the legal emancipation of slaves inspiring the other. But as Asimov rightly sees, it is illogical to depict malfunctioning machines by alluding to fears of racial uprising; and the alternative depiction of noble machines that deserve human emancipation is no better. If one scenario is paranoid and racist, the other is idealistic and racialist, with the noble suffering of kindly robots presenting allegories of kindly slave figures that are just as stereotypical. To the question of why the history of slavery is cast onto robots at all, one could respond that, since our cultural contexts continue to be informed by the legacies of slavery, robot stories cannot help but reflect this influence. In terms of cultural memory and social relevance, the eighteenth and nineteenth centuries are but minutes ago, and American culture in the twentieth and twenty-first centuries is still reacting to the aftermath of the slave trade, chattel slavery, the abolition of both, the rise of segregationist practices and Jim Crow, the battles for civil rights, and our ongoing struggles with institutional racism and everyday discrimination today. But I think that a much deeper connection is also at stake here, a philosophical, experiential, and epistemological connection that emerges in unexpected ways within popular culture.

To understand this deeper conceptual legacy, we need to consider the third variant of the robot-as-slave story, which is not as easy to define, partly because it is always in the background of other robot plots, not at the center. This version presents an association between roboticism and slavery that renders both ambient and immanent and reveals that they are indeed the same condition. The silent remote-controlled robots of Andrew Martin's world, the silent abused slaves of Richard Pryor's story, these are the figures that operate in this plotline. We see them also in the obedient and expendable robotic armies of films such as *I, Robot* (Alex Proyas, 2004), a film inspired by Asimov's work but not based on any particular story, where the robots' computer-generated abundance creates evocative spectacles of a massive impersonality. When seen in the background of more glamorous stories, stories of individual robots who rebel or demand rights as the case may be (and individualism is partly what is at stake), this faceless, nameless mass of robots (and "mass" will also be an important term) seems to be there as mere atmosphere, a "before" state that should be rehabilitated, one way or another, or made invisible as soon as possible. Despite being on the narrative margins, these robots are at the conceptual core of the storyline, especially since they represent a perfectly successful roboticism. It would seem that these are ideal robots, working as designed, useful, expendable, and efficient, yet most texts quickly ignore them or undermine their appeal and textual relevance.

On the one hand, imagining masses of undifferentiated robots is related to the desire for abundant and impersonal robotic labor. The more faceless and brainless these figures are, the better the fantasy setup works, since their impersonality absolves us from the guilt of subjugating conscious individual beings to do our work for us. The ideal slave in this context is one who does not need to be seen or recognized, whose operations are seamless and invisible. In robotic storylines, there is a tension between the ideal of disembodied automation—something like a program that delivers certain types of news to your inbox, or the thermostat in a refrigerator, a perfectly efficient solution that does not need to be noticed unless it breaks—and the discursive desire to actually see the laborers in some form without acknowledging their presence. The fantasy of robotic masses expresses a complex desire, to embody and de-personate at the same time. Precisely because these masses are never a pure mass but instead masses of distinct bodies, they are recognizable as entities in a way that a program, a type of wiring, or a series of thermostats could not be. Their sheer number leads to an exaggerated paranoid reaction (what if they *are* out to get us?), while their absolute abjection triggers a melancholy response in which we recognize our own life conditions in their very facelessness. Robot masses embody a form of abjection that is total and absolute, a state of preconsciousness in which neither the gestures of emancipation nor those of revolt are available. The pathos of the inanimate—its silence and stillness, its inability to act—becomes evocative for unspoken forms of submission and helplessness in the human world.

On the other hand, the sense that a type of robotic labor could become ambient or pervasive inspires a dream for the perfectly automated world, ready to fulfill our needs without involving the spectacle of submission that even the most impersonal robots cannot help but evoke. Such a fantasy structures early science fiction stories such as E. M. Forster's "The Machine Stops" (1909), which features a society of such perfect mechanization that it renders direct experience of the world as well as face-to-face communication obsolete.[21] Yet despite their comforts, these automated environments evoke a nightmare of absolute enslavement. Engulfed by the all-encompassing care of "The Machine," the pampered, almost paralyzed people of this world live in underground hives of small isolated cells and yet retain the illusion of freedom, connectivity, luxury, and creativity. Similarly *The Matrix* (Andy and Lana Wachowski, 1999) presents a totally automated world where a massive technological apparatus has annihilated human needs by removing any sense of agency, mobility, and independence from people. The nightmarish quality of this scenario hinges not just on the absence of human identity and the shocking vision of endless pods of human bodies "plugged" into the massive machinery but also on the radically utilitarian use of human beings in that world, with their bodies used as biological batteries.

Within the realm of Asimov's robot stories, the advent of "The Machines" similarly automates the world, as expansive computer networks and their robotic appendages make humans irrelevant. In Asimov's "The Evitable Conflict" (1950), the combination of robotic labor and computer control by the networked Machines results in a "worldwide robot economy."[22] The state of the world "is stable, and will remain stable, because it is based on the decisions of calculating machines" (201), but this stability undermines the humans' sense of autonomy, however illusory that sense may be. By ensuring that humans cannot have another war the Machines materialize the power of grand forces and absolute limits. Under their control "all conflicts are finally evitable. Only the Machines, from now on, are inevitable," the story concludes (224). In "The Life and Times of Multivac" (1975) Asimov presents the difficulties of human resistance to such a robotic world: since the supercomputer Multivac controls information, travel, and communications, it is near impossible to mount a rebellion, or even a distraction that would allow someone to unplug the machine.[23] In the memorable last lines of the story, the unexpected revolutionary Bakst manages to turn Multivac off forever, but the human Congress receives the news with stunned silence. "You have talked of freedom. You have it!" Bakst says, "Isn't that what you want?" (124)

Visions of ambient and ubiquitous roboticism also stage questions of labor: since work partly shapes or makes sense of the world, the robots' expansive usefulness isolates humans and undermines their self-sufficiency and identity. Stories that posit automated worlds combine a utopian desire with the fear of totalitarianism and suggest that the two may be intricately related, as in stories that present a totalitarian state that also seems to deliver luxury, leisure, well-being. Along with agency and choice, humans stand to lose their relationship to their own bodies in such scenarios, as we see in the humorously passive, flaccid, overweight, and indecisive society of space-stranded humans in *WALL-E* (Andrew Stanton, 2008), where decision making has disappeared and so has muscle tone, while robotic helpers take care of everything. As in "The Machine Stops," in *WALL-E* self-sufficiency has been replaced by self-absorption, political community by luxurious isolation, and work by submission to an invisibly totalitarian leisure. This relationship between mechanical labor and the prospect of robotic and human abjection informs the first robotic fantasies of the 1920s, when the Robots on stage challenge us to see the implied abject robot in us all.

ROBOTS AND WORKERS: THE COMPLEXITIES OF *R.U.R.*

In terms of their actual provenance in the twentieth century, robots were first presented as allegorical interpretations not of chattel slaves but of workers, both blue- and white-collar, at a time when the ideological association of labor, enslavement, and revolt had found political expression in Marxist and Leninist ideologies and in the Russian Revolution of 1917. Karel Čapek's play *R.U.R.* (*Rossum's Universal Robots*) responds directly to this historical environment, making direct allusions to socialism, militarization, capitalism, and industrialization.[24] The Robots are artificial beings in human form (what we would now call androids, because of their human-like appearance) and are designed to perform specialized roles in industrial and military as well as corporate and business contexts. While they embody the promises and dangers of advanced technologies and political circumstances, the Robots remain evocative and mysterious. The super-logical, uncaring, expendable workers at the beginning of the play emerge at the end as complex sensitive beings that value love, loyalty, and self-sacrifice. In the context of work in a modern industrial setting, the play combines the fear of an encroaching dehumanization, effected by social and technological processes, and a victorious re-humanization, in which fundamental human values persist even within a mechanized world.

While, on the surface, the play depicts a classic dystopian scenario of overreaching scientists, avaricious capitalists, and murderous nonhumans, none of these figures is as simple as they may seem at first, and this complexity accounts for the play's freshness. Čapek is a gifted satirist with a keen sense of the philosophical contradictions of his era and an impatience for platitudes and slogans. As a result no position is safe in the play. In the story of the Robots' creation, for example, Čapek indicts materialism, science, capitalism, ambition, and modern ideals of productivity all by presenting a double tale of their origin: old Rossum who invents the first Robot prototypes is a materialist seeking "to prove that God is unnecessary" (7) and works for ten years to produce an amazingly detailed but short-lived person. His son, young Rossum, is an engineer who scoffs at this aspiration: "This is nonsense! Ten years to produce a human being?! If you can't do it faster than nature then what's the point?" (8). Young Rossum sets out to create "living and intelligent labor machines" by simplifying the design. As the current General Manager of the Rossum factory, Harry Domin, explains, certain things are just not necessary for a worker who needs to weave or add: "A human being. That's something that feels joy, plays the violin, wants to go for a walk, in general requires a lot of things that—that are superfluous." Doing away with all that, the Rossum Robot designers posit that "manufacturing artificial workers is exactly like manufacturing gasoline engines" (9). At the beginning of the play, this new labor force has become so successful that orders are in the hundreds of thousands, and while human workers are quickly displaced, the Robots' constant labor also makes things cheaper, more affordable, more abundant. A world of leisure, a new Eden, seems about to become reality.

Although the Robots are not addressed or described as slaves, from the beginning the text encodes a Marxist and socialist understanding of the worker as an oppressed or enslaved figure. In reference to recent historical events, communist slogans, and socialist activism, the play begins with the arrival of the young Helena Glory to the Rossum island factory. Helena has come with the express aim to sensitize, radicalize, and liberate the Robots, only to be told that this is impossible. The Robots may be the new proletariat, but they cannot "awaken" or "unite," and they remain immune to consciousness-raising. Helena is further confronted by Domin's cool logic.

"From a practical standpoint, what is the best kind of worker?" Domin asks, to which Helena attempts a humanist response: "Probably one who—who—who is honest—and dedicated."

"No," Domin responds with certainty, "it is the one that's the cheapest. The one with the fewest needs" (9).

It seems indeed that the Robots are designed as perfect workers, immune to both hardship and desire, an imaginary capitalist solution to the propensity of human workers to take breaks or get sick but also to rebel, go on strike, or unionize. Allegorizing the oppression and bondage of the working class, the Robots are the replaceable and uniform mechanical operators of a similarly streamlined assembly line of uniform machine parts.

This is an exaggerated, hyper-capitalist nightmare scenario, and as H. G. Wells complained in his scathing review of the similarly enslaved workers of *Metropolis*, one that discounts the power of the laboring classes as consumers, as producers of culture, as active participants in the cycles of production, demand, and technological innovation without which the capitalist edifice fails.[25] No modern financial system can sustain an underclass that does not desire, purchase, or consume anything.[26] The Robots present a worker in a state of false consciousness, that is, the state of a not-yet-awakened proletariat that does not see its position within the structures of class struggle. But they also embody a total immunity from false consciousness, since the Robots have no beliefs or fantasies about their social position. They do not have to be fooled into believing that their place in the grand scheme of things is inevitable, because they lack any sense of political reality and because, of course, their position is designed to be inevitable. Roboticism is both a form of absolute abjection and a form of

FIGURE 18 The Robots of *R.U.R.* in the first U.S. production of the Theatre Guild, New York, October 1922. As with the Prague production in 1921, the Robots wear regular clothing. Image courtesy of Yale Collection of American Literature, Beinecke Rare Book and Manuscript Library, Yale University. Francis Bruguiere/© Billy Rose Theatre Division, The New York Public Library for the Performing Arts

immunity from abjection although, as the narrative choices of these texts attest, we don't actually believe in the perfect object status of even the most perfectly designed obedient robots.

Predictably, things do not go as planned in the Rossum factory. Despite their foolproof design the Robots nevertheless become self-aware and declare war on humanity. In the world-scale violence that ensues, the Robots kill everyone (except the engineer Alquist, who gains the Robots' respect because he is the only human capable of building things with his own hands) and thus bring to harsh reality all the paranoid fears about rebellious human workers that fueled the invention of mechanical alternatives in the first place. And a strange side effect plagues the worldly Paradise that Robotic labor has brought about: humans are not having children anymore. In one of many references to biblical scripture in the play, Čapek here implies that the advent of the Robotic age destabilizes an older way of being, in which work and childbirth function as the gender-specific labor-related punishments of Adam and Eve on their expulsion from Paradise. Labor as work and labor as childbirth are both undermined by the Robots' efficiency and the suddenly attainable dream of a laborless future. No labor means no future.

R.U.R. proposes that the fantasy of abolishing labor results in new forms of human enslavement, for people and Robots alike. The moment some Robots acquire any self-consciousness, they display the same megalomaniac desire for supremacy as their human overseers. This is the case with Radius, who was redesigned by Helena and Dr. Gall to be smarter than other Robots in order to prove that Robots and people can be equals. Radius, of course, becomes violent for familiar-sounding reasons: "I don't want a master. I know everything," he proclaims, "I want to be the master of people" (37). As Kamila Kinyon notes, Čapek's philosophical training is visible in the depiction of the Robots' rebellions and their gradual rise to self-consciousness, some modeled on classic philosophical approaches to the master/slave dialectic and others on Kantian and pragmatist philosophies.[27] Radius's desire for mastery is revealed in his ability to enact violence on others and his willingness to risk his own life, although without a concept of life as a precious, valuable, and vulnerable entity such sacrifice does not result in the kind of self-consciousness Hegel describes. The desires for recognition and subjugation, however, circulate freely in the play, affecting humans and Robots in a presentation of mastery and enslavement that is both vernacular and philosophically sophisticated. The mutual definitional dependence between humans and Robots enacts a Hegelian syllogism in later robotic texts as well. Put very simply, in Hegel the masters are masters because at a categorical moment they decide to die in order to have their ego fully expressed. The slaves are slaves because they decide to live, and live in submission.[28] Although, for Hegel, this moment of competition is but the first stage in a quest for full consciousness for both master and slave, and is followed by the recognition that it is the slave that holds the master in thrall and partly because of the slave's continued relationship to the world through labor, these mirrored selves structure myriads of readings of competition between self and other, with their obsessions of threatening doubleness and dangerous similarity, and their emphasis on co-constitutive pairs unable to break from their locked gaze into the self/other narcissistic pool.

But while the society of *R.U.R.* seems focused on a battle for dominance between people and Robots, the demise of this world comes at the hands of Helena, who first inspires Dr. Gall to infuse Robots with a sense of self and then, later, burns the manuscript that describes the construction of Robots. In addition to Radius, Helena's interference inspires the creation of Damon, who institutes the first Robot unions at Le Havre, and other self-aware Robots who quickly learn to use violence against people. Having been militarized for vain human wars, the Robots eventually establish an unwittingly totalitarian regime, motivated by nothing but work and devoid of all ontological difference—a world of pure roboticism. Paragons of industrial design, in their efficiency they annihilate humanity before realizing their own dependence on human beings, so when Helena burns the manuscript that contains the secret for creating more Robots, the whole world is at a literal dead-end. Idealistic, if misguided, Helena destroys the possibility of survival for people, since the Directors of Rossum's factory now have nothing to barter in order to buy their escape, and also destroys the possibility of survival for Robots, who cannot construct any more of their kind without Rossum's old manuscript. Early reviews of the play indeed missed the importance of Helena's role—as blinded by the masculinist competitiveness of the play as are the Robots and human Directors of the Rossum factory. At least one London critic of the time complained that the play would have been much better if "the silly woman" had been "eliminated" from the action.[29] But the play offers a sustained negotiation of gender roles: from the ways it presents Robots, which are gendered because work is gendered in Domin's explanation, to the cruel insistence that the very lifelike Robot secretary Sulla should be "opened up" or cut open at the beginning of the play, just to persuade Helena that she is not a real woman, and to the quick inevitable way in which Helena is absorbed into the Rossum world by marrying Domin. Helena's grand gesture of burning the manuscript results from the fact that she has been kept in the dark during the escalating conflict, treated as a child, protected from complex knowledge of the political situation. Had she known the manuscript was the only way for anyone to survive perhaps she would have acted differently.

Despite the ostensible focus on the ontological and philosophical differences between people and Robots, the play thus also alerts us to a difference within the human world that was never negotiated successfully. Acting as another Eve, in this mirror image realm destroying a book of knowledge instead of seeking knowledge, Helena embodies the play's presentation of inequality beyond the masculinist focus of the master/slave competition. Helena is the invisible third rail of this dialectic. She has already experienced her exclusion from the human and acts implicitly against the men's dream of mindless efficiency and their solipsistic debates about supremacy. And her association with Rossum's manuscript offers a poignant parallelism: the woman and the book are at odds because the book presents the possibility that now there are two ways of creating people. Through Helena's actions, at the end of the play things are restored to a prelapsarian—that is, a post-lapsarian—order: two of the atypical Robots that Helena helped design fall in love, and their return to heterosexual procreative union restores what the play considers the order of being. The experiment of reversing the Fall and installing a new Eden is over, as the new Robotic Adam and Eve start off a new human life full of identity-forming labors.

Despite its quick happy ending (an ending that Čapek felt offered an inadequate sense of closure), the play was an international success, resonating with audiences for its warnings about both social and technological modernity. As the first visual depiction of a mechanical person on stage, the play also presents the paradoxes of robotic presence for later artificial people. We know that the Robots are played by human actors, who enact the gestures and demeanor of an imagined nonhuman, and the play dares viewers to oscillate between dehumanizing the actors on stage and re-humanizing them at particular moments. Staging decisions structure this effect. In the first productions, the Robots of *R.U.R.* were depicted as people, somewhat stilted perhaps in their "laconic" movements and speech and their "expressionless" faces and eyes, but human-looking nevertheless. According to the playwright's directions, the robots are dressed simply, with "linen shirts tightened at their waists with belts" and "brass numbers on their chests" (2). While the description of linen shirts suggests a peasant's tunic, appropriate perhaps for the linguistic echo of serfdom in the Czech *robota*, in images we have from the first production in Prague, the Robot outfits are faintly military, a light-colored uniform and cap with a dark belt and numbers on the chest. Importantly, Alquist also wears a simplified light-colored military uniform, in contrast to the dark business suits of the other human Directors of the Rossum factory, and this visual alignment confirms Alquist's structural affinities to the worker Robots. In a tableau, the light color outfits of the Robots and Alquist and the dark suits of the Directors would create a visible contrast, not just between humans and Robots but between labor and management. In the first U.S. production by the Theatre Guild in New York in 1922, the Robots' outfits are job-appropriate: suits and ties for the managerial models and uniforms that evoke both a modern military and an industrial outfit for the workers. The Robots' severe matching haircuts, expressionless faces, and stiff body language clearly distinguish them visually. But despite this uniformity, the Robots are not all that inhuman, a design feature that is accentuated at the end of act 2, when a swarm of violent Robots rush on stage into the Directors' headquarters and kill everyone. The attack scene contributes to the feeling that both the play and its first stagings aim to depict the Robots as a still recognizably human population in revolt against their oppressors.

It is important to note that neither the Prague nor the New York productions register any commitment to the emerging science fiction or modernist visual aesthetics, as we see for example in the constructivist costumes of *Aelita: Queen*

FIGURE 19 Helena (Sylvia Field) with the Robot Radius (Albert Van Dekker), whose bound arms evoke an enslaved worker struggling against his chains. From the 1928 production of *R.U.R.* by the Theatre Guild, directed by Rouben Mamoulian. Image courtesy of Yale Collection of American Literature, Beinecke Rare Book and Manuscript Library, Yale University. Vandamm Studio/© Billy Rose Theatre Division, The New York Public Library for the Performing Arts

of Mars (Yakov Protazanov, 1924) a few years later or in the clearly metallic exterior of the robot in *Metropolis* by 1927, and they also don't engage other avant-garde theatrical costume styles of the 1920s. Indeed, we can track how and when the *R.U.R.* Robots become metal: in the London production of 1923 the Robots wear full body outfits in a silvery metallic fabric, with distinctive belts and chest plates that refer visually to the front apron grill of a steam train, a car grille, or other mechanical apparatus. In images from the production, the Robots are tall, stiff, and have a severe angular haircut. By the time of the New York revival of *R.U.R.* by the Theatre Guild for the 1927–1928 season, a fuller symbolic mechanization of the Robots on stage has occurred. Their costumes seem to be made of a type of thick canvas or oilcloth with a metallic sheen, accented by metal rivets to suggest a manufactured origin, strange angular edges on their boots, shoulders, and elbows, and a riveted helmet. Faintly reminiscent of the Tin Woodman in L. Frank Baum's *Wizard of Oz* stories, these Robots are not just regular workers wearing a worker's outfit but some other type of being. The success of *R.U.R.* in the years between the first and second New York productions partly accounts for this effect, since both the word "robot" and the concept of an artificial worker have become vernacular by 1927 and the association of robots with metal made memorable in texts like *Metropolis.* And while the Robots' visual difference, their overt expression of otherness in their outfits, marks them as inhuman or as symbolic embodiments of racial or ethnic difference, it also has the unexpected effect of freeing them emotionally. With their whole exterior depiction bearing the brunt of the need to represent otherness, the bodies and faces of the Robots suddenly become much more expressive and their relationship to bondage more directly stated. The give-and-take between visual difference and emotional pathos is clear in images from the production. In the confrontation between Radius and Helena, he is tied with his hands behind his back, a creature of urgency and desire and not a megalomaniac supremacist as he appears to be in other productions. Similarly, when the Robots appear en masse on the stage, the staging and lighting enhance their visual presence as strange metallic or mechanical beings, not regular workers, but their faces have a lot of expression and they are visible, not just dark outlines. They are fascinating, visibly other, threatening, and metallic, but they are also expressive as a fighting group of humans might be.

Indeed neither type of staging can escape the association of Robots with the desires and demands of real people. If the Robots are dressed as people, as in the Prague and first New York productions, they may use stiff and mechanical body language and inflection to create alienating effects on stage, making a distinction between real and artificial people in the manner of modern-day androids. But at important moments, especially the kinds of frozen gestural tableaux that the play involves, they would also look like a group of people, of workers or soldiers or slaves, in the midst of a collective action or rebellion. If

FIGURE 20 Radius (Albert Van Dekker) leads the Robot attack against Dr. Gail (Harry Mestayer) in the 1928 production of *R.U.R.* The Robots' costumes emphasize metal surfaces, rivets, and helmets that imply their industrial origin and nonhuman status. Image courtesy of Yale Collection of American Literature, Beinecke Rare Book and Manuscript Library, Yale University. Vandamm Studio/© Billy Rose Theatre Division, The New York Public Library for the Performing Arts

the Robots are dressed to suggest they are made of metal, as in the London and especially the New York revival production, this visual alienation aligns the storyline with a science-fictional distance (these are clearly not people) but then also allows the story to become allegorical so that we still see the possibility of human otherness, racial difference, or ethnic specificity under the metal exterior of the Robot. There are many ways to render Robots as "other," but they can never be "other" enough. And this is how "metalface" works: the more metallic the Robots are, the more they allow the underlying debate about the human to remain free-floating and multivalent. The alienation of the human form on stage enacts a form of distance that makes the allegorical content of the play ever more adaptable for new audiences and new fears.

When *R.U.R.* was first performed in the United States, it was subtitled "A Fantastic Melodrama," and the phrase resonated with critics of the era, who also described the play as a "hair-raising melodrama," a "murderous social satire," and a "brilliant satire on our mechanized civilization."[30] Under the guise of their metallic exterior and technological origin, the Robots can stand for the dehumanizing effects of technological change and industrial capitalism but can also be used to remind audiences of the effects of large-scale militarization during World War I and to critique socialism, ideological totalitarianism, or the loss of humanist values in the modern marketplace. Partly because of the success of *R.U.R.*, by the end of the 1920s the figure of the robot is vernacular and can be used to poke fun at middle-class conformity and political passivity, as in the short satirical piece "The Iron Man and the Tin Woman," by Stephen Leacock (1929), in which a thoroughly modern couple lives by proxy through mechanical servants.[31] In this sarcastic commentary on modernity, even leisure activities such as playing golf and important emotional milestones such as a marriage proposal can be easily and efficiently dispatched by the helpful robots.

Although their forms and narrative deployments are by no means stable, robots emerge in various storylines in the 1930s. In the short animated film *The Robot* (Dave Fleischer, 1932), Betty Boop's friend Bimbo owns a helpful little car that turns itself into a robot boxer in order to help win a boxing match for its owner— becoming the first "transformer" perhaps and first in a long line of robot boxers.[32] In 1937 a short opera titled *The Romance of Robot* was staged in New York as part of the Federal Music Project of the WPA. The opera uses the figure of a "man of steel" to criticize mechanization and optimization in terms that follow from the debates of *R.U.R.*[33] Robots become household figures in the 1930s, convenient as friends as well as foes and found in both science fiction and mainstream modes. Popular spectacles, such as the New York World's Fair in 1939, sell the dream of future robotics without much critique, in the public performances of the Westinghouse Robotic Man Elektro and his dog, Sparko, as embodiments of the household luxuries of the future. Even Superman, a different man of steel, has to fight robots in a beautifully rendered cartoon (also directed by Dave Fleischer in 1941): Superman fights hordes of flying robots, whose burglaries of banks and jewelry stores are revealed as the work of a well-dressed mastermind inventor.[34]

But the serious questions posed by *R.U.R.* also resonate with a tradition of dystopian allegories both social and technological. Proud of their achievement in bringing *R.U.R.* to American audiences, the directors of the Theatre Guild sought new writing that would continue to address questions of technology and modernity.[35] In 1923, they followed the long run of *R.U.R.* with Elmer Rice's *The Adding Machine* (1923), in which clerk Mr. Zero is cruelly replaced by a simple adding machine, his supreme adding skills made irrelevant after twenty-five years of work at the same company.[36]

Similarly, after the revival run of *R.U.R.*, the Theatre Guild staged Eugene O'Neill's *Dynamo* (1929) in which a young man called Reuben, driven away from home by the conflict between his sexual awakening and the religious conservatism of his family, returns to work as an engineer at the local hydro-electric power plant and begins to worship the electricity-generating dynamo there.[37] Combining the modernist interest in primitivism with the overwhelming presence of both technology and sexuality in the play, O'Neill describes the process by which the dynamo becomes "a dark idol" for Reuben, "a great, dark mother" (871), its ability to electrify akin to generating life itself. Although didactic and heavy-handed, the play's final tragedies unfold in the realistic and modernist setting of the power plant, where Reuben kills his girlfriend and then is electrocuted while embracing the dynamo, his one final act of worship.

The political implications of an assembly-line world are taken up in Yevgeny Zamyatin's *We* (1924), in which people are literally just numbers in a society so afraid of imagination, desire, and revolt that it mandates lobotomies for all citizens. Influential for later critiques of totalitarianism, such as Aldous Huxley's *Brave New World* (1932) and George Orwell's *1984* (1949), Zamyatin's novel articulates the threat of robotic abjection in the terms of *R.U.R.* without positing the Robot as a separate entity. We are all potentially Robots in these texts, Robots are Us. In the storyline that emerges, the technological world is associated with abjection, as an encroaching roboticism removes human qualities in the service of an organized, placid, productive, totalitarian modernity. Robotic masses appear in dystopian texts of the Cold War, treated by both sides as insulting versions of the ideologically driven populations of the *other* side, who follow their political scripts without thinking. Though far apart in time, the numbered citizens of *We* resemble later versions of grand-scale abjection, as with the beings that constitute the Borg in *Star Trek: The Next Generation*, with their identical outfits, hive mind, and emotionless voices. "Resistance is futile," the Borg warns its enemies. "You will be assimilated."

Since its articulation in the 1920s, the fantasy of *having* mechanical workers contains the nightmare of *being* mechanical, an understandable dynamic reversal, but both of these options also contain the specter of a complete dissolution of identity. Robot stories refer implicitly to the paradox of modern subjectivity, considered here as a political and not a psychological entity, by embodying what threatens or undermines it. Tracing the provenance of this conceptual constellation brings us to foundational moments of modernity, to the modern definition of the individual, the articulation of what counts as an artificial body in political terms, and the structures of political and philosophical transformation that create the sovereign modern subject, on the one hand, and annihilate it, on the other.

A NETWORK OF FEARS: THE LEGACIES OF SLAVERY

Both in their likeness to the human form and in their distance from it, robots embody many threats to personhood, individuality, consciousness, and political presence. In the discourse of the artificial person, this diverse network of threats settles into a range of narrative patterns in which we imagine owning or using mechanical slaves (who might rebel), or becoming mechanical slaves ourselves (and desiring or demanding our freedom), or being absorbed into a mechanical apparatus (that enslaves us utterly). The fantasy of a laborless world and the desire for mechanical slaves who would never rebel or have needs are the flip side of a more personal nightmare, in which people become fully absorbed into an automatic world that does not permit desires or needs. The range of fears these patterns can encompass is thus quite extensive: in addition to the fear of becoming automatic or mechanical, we have the fear of being enslaved, the fear of being a tool, the fear of being an object, the fear of being inanimate, the fear of being rejected, the fear of being abandoned or isolated. All these fears operate on a trajectory of legal or political objectification and subjectification and of social acceptance or isolation. In terms of the narrative patterns of robot stories explored above, this set of threats maps onto the plotlines of both rebellion and emancipation, which are also social and political in this subject/object way.

The third plotline type that revolves around automation, abjection, and totalitarianism, in stories of fully automated worlds and paralyzed passive people, engages a different network of fears, and these do not sound as clearly robotic as the first set: we have the fear of absolute, silent, or unconscious abjection, the fear of being absorbed by an automated world, the fear of being mindless and vacant without knowing it, the fear of being unable to act, the fear of being used as mere material or as a power source, and so on. Instead of staging a confrontation between bodies or between a body and a legal or social context, the imagery of these scenarios alludes to being engulfed. This conceptual network is surprising in its logic and also much older, operating on a trajectory of ingestion and dissolution that involves the primordial fear of being eaten. In their most literal sense, some memorable formulations of these fears occur in texts that, perhaps not surprisingly, feature workers eaten or absorbed by machines. In *Metropolis*, for example, young Freder's feverish dream transforms the main machine room of the city into a vision of Moloch, a pagan god who is devouring the tired workers of Metropolis as if in never-ending sacrifice. In one of the most iconic sequences from Charlie Chaplin's *Modern Times* (1936), the Tramp as an overwhelmed worker is swallowed by the giant machinery of the factory and cheerfully travels through the mechanical innards. The mechanical nightmare in both films literalizes fears about uncaring social institutions and dangerous work, with the image of the machinery functioning as a metaphorical reference to capitalism, greed, or technology devouring the workers. And the almost infinite interior space of *The Matrix*, full of innumerable pods of human power cells, feels like an immense body cavity, a giant's high-tech stomach with uncanny appendages that ooze viscous liquids, or a giant uterus with millions of amniotic

FIGURE 21 Devouring the workers of *Metropolis* (Fritz Lang, 1927). © UFA

sacks and sticky umbilical cords. The people of this world are never born and yet they have already been ingested.

These two overlapping networks of meaning offer interesting perspectives on how the robot-as-slave story channels the fear of enslavement in modernity. Although they may coexist, the subjectification/objectification logic and the ingestion/dissolution logic present different aspects of threat to the individual or the person. The first focuses on individuality vis-à-vis the law or the social contract while the second presents fears where there is no assumption or presumption of individuality and no negotiation and may indeed contain an implicit or disavowed fantasy of nonindividuality, a fantasy of being so protected, coddled, or comforted by automated luxuries as to be in a state of suspension or animalistic pure being. In a way, the two fears form the end points of a conceptual gradient that tracks many stages of loss of sovereignty or autonomy, from imagining being a robot or other mechanical figure, still individual and embodied; to being a tool, with embodiment being about usefulness rather than about presence; to being a cog or a small mechanical part in a big machine, where there is mostly function and little individuality to speak of; to being a mere material or power source, a state of absolute absorption. Such a gradient restages the discursive emphasis on instrumentality, with implicit though coherent variations. The fear of being a tool is different from the fear of being treated as a power source, as if the tool retains an element of individuality that the human battery no longer possesses. In the most nightmarish scenarios envisioned by this discourse, the utmost level of abjection reduces the human body to its materiality and aligns the human with bodily functions, indeed autonomic functions, that are independent from skill, will, or consciousness.

For example, in another version of such a nightmare featured in the reimagined *Battlestar Galactica*, a Cylon research project keeps all-but-lobotomized human women alive to be used as "baby machines," incubators for various genetic experiments.[38] In addition to evoking contemporary concerns with reproductive technologies, the series presents a gendered version of the nightmare of abjection and absorption.[39] The women are reduced to a body function they have no control over, their will and consciousness undermined by the urgency and irrevocability of the quintessential bodily mysteries of conception and gestation. Perhaps a more literal analysis of this situation would align the relationship between the women and the apparatus as a type of penetration, and although such descriptions abound in modern technoculture they do not engage the deeper conceptual connections evoked by the images themselves.[40] In some primordial psychological algorithm, being penetrated by machines is a modernized, reversed, externalized version of the fear that we may be absorbed or eaten by them, and pregnancy itself also involves a similar conceptual slip in which the fetus may seem to have been absorbed into instead of produced by the mother's body. As I discussed in the previous chapter, in certain contexts the autonomic functions of the body figure a most immediate, earnest, intimate sense of presence. But in the context of labor, that irrevocable quality of autonomic body processes also flattens everything else into the realm of pure functionality, and since functionality is the issue in this aspect of the discourse of the artificial person, the autonomy of the body is at the core of what quickly becomes an existential problem: it is precisely here that a distinction between deterministic forces and personal will or agency would be staged.

Being eaten by machines, in other words, seems to have little to do with robots or with slavery, yet it is exactly the kind of image and fear that makes a link with the past, with the advent of modern slavery and its conceptual transformations in the last five centuries. The narrative patterns of stories of artificial people adjust our understanding of slavery in two ways: first by presenting slavery as a dynamic reversible condition, which is how the palindromic logic of enslavement and emancipation appears in stories of robots acquiring human rights; and second by alerting us to the structural presence in the discourse of the premodern, indeed primordial, fear of being eaten and its modern translation into political and technological contexts. Considered in a historical light, the logic of mechanicity as it relates both to objectification and to absorption allows us to see why it is impossible to separate robots from slavery: in the discourse of the artificial person, slavery affects individual bodies but also functions as an absorbing, assimilating, devouring institution. And far from being science-fictional, both conceptualizations of slavery have a solid historical and philosophical basis.

We find some of these historical connections in early descriptions of the slave trade, where the experience of slavery as a devouring institution is transposed into the consistent representation of the slaves' fear of being eaten, both in sailors' accounts and autobiographical slave narratives. In *A New Account of Some Parts of Guinea, and the Slave Trade* (1734), for example, here is how Captain William Snelgrave of Bristol informs his newly bought slaves of their status. "When we purchase grown People," he writes, "I acquaint them by the Interpreter, 'That, now they are become my Property, I think fit to let them know what they are bought for, that they may be easy in their Minds.' (For these poor People are generally under terrible Apprehensions upon their being bought by white Men, many being afraid that we design to eat them; which, I have been told, is a story much credited by the inland Negroes)."[41] John Barbot, who documented his travels to the West Coast of Africa in 1678 and 1682 for the French Royal African Company, also mentions the slaves' belief "that they are carried like sheep to the slaughter, and that the Europeans are fond of their flesh," which he decides is a major cause of mutinies, suicides, and the general unhappiness of the slaves.[42]

Similarly, Olaudah Equiano returns to the same fear numerous times in his autobiography, published in 1789. When he is first transported to the slave ship, he is so startled by the sight of a multitude of dejected black people and a large furnace boiling away that he faints, asking others later "if we were not to be eaten by those white men with horrible looks, red faces and long hair."[43] When the slave ship arrives at Bridge Town in Barbados, the fear occurs again: "We thought by this we should be eaten by these ugly men" (78). More experienced slaves are brought on deck to pacify the trembling and crying new arrivals: "They told us we were not to be eaten, but to work, and were soon to go on land, where we would see many of our country people" (78). Although the report eases the slaves' fears, these are reawakened again in the slave market, no doubt in response to the hungry eyes and hands of the over-eager buyers, rushing into the yard (79). The threat of being eaten seems ever present and manipulated by the slavers. When the ship transporting Equiano to England experiences food shortages he notes, "the captain and people told me in jest they would kill and eat me; but I thought them in earnest, and was depressed beyond measure, expecting every moment to be my last" (82).

In addition to expressing a personal or cultural response to the violence of enslavement, the metonymic alignment of the evils of slavery with the fear of being eaten is a multiple projection. It combines a popular historical account of the time that many Africans were sold to slavery (or according to slavers' accounts, sold themselves to other Africans) at times of famine, with the spurious idea that the Africans are cannibals and thus expect nothing less than to be eaten by their captors. As a rhetorical escalation of the real threats of slavery, the specter of cannibalism supplies a convenient extreme for Snelgrave and his readers, a classic example of the West constructing otherness in order to sublimate or deflect its own predatory actions.[44] And cannibalism is actually very much related to labor—which may be why it lurks in the background of stories of enslavement as well as stories of robotic workers. Notice the contrast implied in these narratives: compared to being eaten, going to work or becoming someone's property in slavers' accounts appears merely like a social reorganization or a change in status and should be less frightening and even welcome to slaves. Equiano mentions the supposedly calming effect of the contrast between being eaten and being forced to work, as if in reference to a similar distinction set up in Daniel Defoe's *Robinson Crusoe* (1719). Crusoe saves Friday from being eaten, and Friday becomes his willing slave and companion, as the novel presents the ideological contrast between "savage" slavery, which revolves around cannibalism, and European slavery as a rescue into contractual labor.[45] But of course the slaves *are* allegorically ingested—not just by entering the cavernous bellies of the ships that transport them across the oceans but by becoming small, non-sovereign body parts of a big capitalist body. The loss of personal sovereignty Equiano experiences is so extreme that it can only be described as being devoured.

The fear of being eaten predates many of the more recent figurations of threat to the person that emerge in robot stories, but it also functions partly as their conceptual basis, and so it pays to explore its permutations and its relationship to technology. The metaphor of being eaten is used by Irish and other peasants of the seventeenth and eighteenth centuries, by European and American citizens and colonists, by colonial subjects throughout the world, by indentured servants, and by African slaves, giving expression to the loss of body integrity in relation to materiality (as people become raw materials), functionality (in which people are given an express purpose), and scale (in which the human being disappears in structures of gigantic proportions). Jonathan Swift makes excellent use of the metaphor in his sarcastic indictment of social injustice in *A Modest Proposal* (1729), where he mischievously advocates the eating of the poor as a kind of humane social management, one that reduces people to useful raw materials.[46] The issue of purpose is clearly associated with slavery, a state that defines people according to their usefulness for another's gain. And the experience of scale is itself eloquent of the conceptual changes underway in the seventeenth and eighteenth centuries. Since the King, the State, the Commonwealth, and the Government had all been conceptually represented as either huge bodies with distinct body parts (the different government departments or functions) or huge aggregates of smaller bodies (the sovereign's innumerable subjects), the logic of ingestion is political, economic, and increasingly technological. During the Enlightenment, with the rise of new democratic ideologies, new political and economic analyses, and a new vocabulary of individualism, the aggregate collective bodies of earlier political philosophy—in the manner of the composite artificial body of Thomas Hobbes's *Leviathan* (1651), for example—no longer hold in the same way. Instead of presenting the ideal of harmonious multi-part coherence, such sublime sovereigns seem to have merely eaten their subjects.

I am focusing roughly on this historical period because the cultural meanings of ingestion, mechanicity, and scale change during the eighteenth century. If we were to look for what being mechanical or being an object implies in texts of the era, in Jonathan Swift's *Gulliver's Travels* (1726), for example, we would find that these particular threats to the self do not yet warrant a special conceptual or narrative treatment. Gulliver's body, repeatedly transformed and threatened by the norms of different social and material contexts, encounters a rather expansive network of fears. In Brobdingnag alone he almost suffers being stepped on, eaten by rats, torn to pieces, swallowed, devoured, picked up by birds, crushed by mistake, or drowned in cream; he is called an abortive birth or embryo and worries that he is equivalent to an insect, a toy, a dwarf, a mechanical doll, a manikin, and a homunculus. Uniting organic and mechanical associations in his descriptions, Gulliver conflates multiple types of body violation and disintegration, as his body and his perception of its structure, size, and emissions—especially body odor—change radically with every adventure. But in this baroque show of material pliability, being a mechanical toy, an object, or a miniature automaton are not fundamental fears for Gulliver, and among the many troublesome alternatives he faces, being considered mechanical is rather eclipsed by fears of being eaten, ingested, or crushed. In other words, in contrast to the primacy of the fear of being eaten, the mechanical or constructed body is not especially uncanny yet in this story, and it does not entail its own narrative and representational codes. This is about to change. By the beginning of the next century, what it means to imagine being a machine, an automaton, or an object will not be as easily equivalent to other types of body trouble.

In order to see how ingestion, objectification, and mechanicity evolve into the robotic fantasies of our era, we need to explore the relationship between capitalism, labor, slavery, and the definition of the sovereign subject. Indeed Gulliver's descriptions of endless eating in Lilliput and his fear of becoming food everywhere else express a capitalist logic of incorporation that resonates with early Enlightenment theories of property and labor. In John Locke's descriptions in *The Second Treatise of Government* (1690) both the body and its labor are the property of the self, a self that includes goods as these become transformed and thus acquired through labor. He states: "Every man has a property in his own person: this no body has any right to but himself. The labour of his body, and

the work of his hands, we may say, are properly his. Whatsoever then he removes
out of the state that nature hath provided, and left it in, he hath mixed his labour
with, and joined to it something that is his own, and thereby makes it his property."[47] Because labor expands the material limits and property lines of the self,
the opposite process can be registered as a metaphorical ingestion, in which
one is absorbed into another's bodily boundaries. In addition to expressing a
primordial fear of being eaten, threats of incorporation and absorption reflect
a response to an equally elemental capitalist hunger.

Locke's sovereign subject, whose interaction with nature through labor rede-
fines parts of the world as his property, is thus intimately related to the enslaved
man who has himself become property. As Paul Gilroy proposes, the philosophical foundations of the modern self include an important investment in
and interpretation of slavery.[48] In Locke, the free and the enslaved begin from
the same condition, and slavery comes about from the direct disenfranchisement of sovereign subjects—a process that was historically both dynamic and
reversible, at least for a while and for some. In contrast to the racist epistemologies of later eras, early Enlightenment philosophies describe slavery as an inci-
dental state, neither lifelong nor hereditary, but the result of accidents of fate or
difficult circumstances such as war, famine, debt, crime, or family legacies. Any
such circumstance could force someone into servitude, a state that covers white
indentured servants, debtors or criminals expelled from prisons into forced
labor abroad, and kidnapped Africans; and this servitude would be modeled
on historical precedents or on examples of enslaved geographic regions that are
required to pay taxes or supply workers and soldiers. These social positions are of
course complicated by historical and ethnic legacies and are never as impersonal
or circumstantial as such philosophical explanations would have it.[49] But what is
interesting to me, and helpful for our discussion of subjects and objects, is the
presumed reversibility of this kind of slavery, its circularity, its focus on sovereign subjects who lose their rights to become enslaved and who could regain
these rights when circumstances allow. For emerging democratic ideologies and
political theories, slavery is described as a forfeiture of natural rights: in Locke
a slave becomes a slave either willingly by indenturing himself to another man
(slavery is between men in this political philosophy) or through acts of war.[50]
Captain Snelgrave again almost quotes Locke directly when he justifies slavery as
a historical commonplace and an effect of war. Responding to the slaves' desire
to be free, Captain Snelgrave informs them, "they had forfeited their Freedom
before I bought them, either by Crimes or by being taken in War, according to
the Custom of their Country; and they being now my Property, I was resolved
to let them feel my Resentment, if they abused my Kindness." War-related
slavery is presented as more honorable than barter-based slavery, as in Aphra
Behn's *Oroonoko* (1688), in which the African prince of the title, now betrayed

into slavery and renamed Caesar, instigates a slave rebellion by contrasting the two ways of becoming a slave—the first, taken in battle, honorable and manly, and the second, bought and sold "to be the sport of women, fools, and cowards," detestable and disgraceful.[51]

In his analysis of slavery and social death, Orlando Patterson argues that while in the seventeenth century about 60 percent of exported slaves may have been really captured in war, in the eighteenth and nineteenth centuries the proportion changes radically, with as many as 70 percent kidnapped outright—in regional campaigns that were waged *in order to* capture slaves to be sold to European slavers—and often sold for guns and ammunition.[52] These "sordid kidnapping expeditions" make a never-ending business out of both war and enslavement, and in the 1750s, French minister of foreign affairs Étienne-François Choiseul describes this business as the "motor" of all commerce of the era.[53] So even though the rhetoric of divestment of rights obviously functions as a self-serving and legitimizing argument for slavery, it also alerts us to the process of making a subject into an object. The notion of "forfeiture" of natural rights functions as a euphemism for the violence of disenfranchisement of what were clearly sovereign subjects of sovereign nations, expressly targeted for and submitted to such a process.

In most cases, political philosophers resort to this reality when they want to minimize the impact and difference of chattel slavery, rendering enslavement more commonplace and other conditions more urgent. In Jean-Jacques Rousseau's explanations in *The Social Contract* (1762), for example, which provocatively begins with "Man is born free, and everywhere he is in chains," all persons forfeit some of their natural rights by virtue of their participation in society. Slavery is a metaphor here for Rousseau, a state of submission that explains political conditions in Europe while abstracting and ignoring the slave trade and chattel slavery. As Rousseau claims, whole nations seem to have sold themselves to kings in exchange for peace and prosperity, only to then be submitted to the whims and expenses of unfair governments.[54]

But the radical potential of the notion of forfeiture is that it renders all subjects immanently vulnerable to being enslaved. Keeping political slavery and chattel slavery distinct and separate requires the deployment of supremacist epistemologies that obscure the fundamental violence and arbitrariness of all enslavement. What seem like two diametrically opposed states, citizen and slave, subject and object, person and property, are fundamentally the same state: all persons are sovereign subjects with natural rights, but they always stand on the verge of being enslaved. As a practice that transforms a person into an article of property, enslavement can be considered as the dynamic process of the objectification of subjects—and thus a danger for all sovereign subjects regardless of race.

This conceptual rubric is at the heart of the historical coincidence that structures the West, in which the emergence of sublime notions of personal and political sovereignty is accompanied by sublime methods for undermining and violating the rights of persons. Patterson describes "the joint rise of slavery and cultivation of freedom" as no accident but a "sociohistorical necessity."[55] In the course of the eighteenth century, however, enslavement changes from being an accident of fortune to being a process of divestment of natural rights, then a reversible legal state, and finally, a racially defined and legally hereditary status or condition.[56] The natural rights of persons are suddenly debatable, and "alienable." This racial understanding of slavery, effected through laws that insist on the slaves' inherent inferior status, implies that persons are defined in legal terms, not according to ontological, religious, or physiological criteria and not according to circumstances. In the descriptive mode I have engaged here, such a definition of the person suggests that there are persons, and there are objects, and the latter are always and a priori objects without variation or change of status. The reversibility that accompanied earlier notions of slavery is replaced by a focus on a binary opposition that has become formative for the modern world, a world it continues to infect with the racist premise of the slave-as-object.

Both the notion of reversibility and the conceptualization of slavery as a hereditary condition are pivotal for understanding why robots can take on the role of slaves. Robots are designed as perfect objects whose social status is fixed a priori, beings that were never in possession of rights, and therefore slaves we can confront without guilt. Their absolute objecthood makes the second part of the cycle, the robots' rebellion or emancipation, ideologically satisfying, because such gestures express the value of individuating processes and validate active, intense, indeed sovereign forms of being. Yet if we consider the historical legacies of slavery, these narrative patterns may indeed accentuate processes of reanimation, but they also always carry the memory and imprint of the first part of the cycle, the disenfranchisement, violation, de-animation of sovereign subjects. Robot stories try to make us forget that indeed the difference between robots and people or between subjects and objects is arbitrary, not natural, not inherent, and not ontological.

This certainly sounds paradoxical, but again, although robots may depict an absolute difference in their physicality, they also express the sense that this difference is not inherent but imposed, and this is the reason that the notion I describe as metalface works so well in this discourse. The more robotic, nonhuman, and metallic the artificial people are, the clearer it is that they are nonpeople, and the more the discourse can both hide and hint at the underlying reality that who the "real people" are and how they are distinguished may be up for grabs. This is why there is such pathos and emotion in the robot's story: the robot's object status signifies the constant threat of objectification for everyone and the continued instability and arbitrariness of who counts as a person. In fact within this discourse we are so reluctant to show the first half cycle, the process of the objectification of sovereign subjects, that when we address such pervasive threats to the modern self we resort to a completely different register, and to images of ingestion, absorption, and cannibalism. Nothing evokes the state of abjection better than absorption, the loss of the body. Even becoming a machine is better, an option we see in stories that feature people gradually turned into mechanical or robotic beings, as with the body alterations of Roger Torraway in Frederick Pohl's *Man Plus* (1976), which allow him to survive on Mars; the replacement of human with artificial limbs and organs, in *The Six Million Dollar Man* (1974–1978) and *The Bionic Woman* (1976–1978); the increasingly cybernetic Darth Vader in *Star Wars* (George Lucas, 1977); and the complete transformation of wounded Alex Murphy, in *RoboCop* (Paul Verhoeven, 1997). While these hybridizations structure the emotional development of characters such as Darth Vader and RoboCop, they also provide new avenues for action and expression and are not therefore equivalent to a narrative of pure objectification. On the contrary, such transformations often replace grief, loss, and social death with fetishistic new powers and new types of sovereignty. And upholding the fantasy of the sovereign subject seems to be the basis of the emotional investment in fantasies of artificial people.

In a way, therefore, the Enlightenment did not just create the sovereign self in opposition and intimate relation to an enslaved self. The sovereign self instead is always on the threshold of being politically, economically, and technologically enslaved. If, as many have argued, the objectification of subjects is a frequent and immanent process within capitalism, obviously the insistence of racist epistemologies, national agendas, and political treatises on the objectification of certain bodies (marked by race, gender, ethnicity, class, national origin, and so on) attempts to dispel awareness of the same prospect and danger for all bodies. If subject/object positions can be understood as reversible, then not only can objects become subjects (emancipation), but subjects can also become objects (enslavement). Advocates of slavery and southern economists of the 1850s promote exactly this view when they argue that workers in industrial capitalist economies are the true slaves, "slaves without masters," and thus vulnerable to rampant exploitation by the state and by corporate interests. Such an account was proposed by George Fitzhugh in his books *Sociology of the South; or, The Failure of Free Society* (1854), and *Cannibals All! or, Slaves Without Masters* (1857).[57] Despite their inflammatory rhetoric, Fitzhugh's books provided Marx with some of his historical information on slavery, directly informing and influencing his theories of capitalist and industrial enslavement.[58]

But what slavery advocates disavow is that there is nothing inherent in either position. Instead, the distinction between subjects and objects is arbitrary, merely structured by law and convention and enforced by violence. For sovereign subjects lulled into ideas of racial supremacy, remembering that this is the fragile and threatened basis of all sovereignty can be traumatic and desta-bilizing.[59] I am paraphrasing a Marxist notion of "false consciousness" here, writ large to include not just the fantasies we may entertain in relation to our posi-tion within social forms of stratification but also our fantasies of subjectivity and action in general. In other words, it is because everybody can be potentially enslaved or *is already* enslaved (as Marxists would posit) that racist epistemolo-gies insist on the inherent increased vulnerability to enslavement of some bod-ies over others. And it is those who are already economically enslaved that such arguments most attempt to appease or soothe by promoting the view that such enslavement only happens *to* others. Indeed the more "other" they are the better, and again here we must read both racial difference and ontological difference (as it is posited in robot stories, for example) as welcome registers of this distance between who can be enslaved and who cannot. Both in its social limits and its physical difference, the robot in the room assures everyone else of their natural humanity and their natural access to rights. The metal exterior of the robot both conceals and reveals everybody else's invisible enslavement.

What emerges through this historical and conceptual journey is the way metaphors of the artificial body evolve, from describing the multi-part bodies of a feudal or monarchic order to becoming flexible and apt descriptions of new threats to subjectivity and political sovereignty. As Chris Baldick has proposed, after the French Revolution and despite democratic insistence on the poten-tial of collectivities, body metaphors of multi-part coherence in politics rap-idly evolve into nightmarish visions of monstrous bodies, hideous specters, or amorphous crowds.[60] In *Black Frankenstein*, Elizabeth Young discusses the ways in which the monstrous bodies of the Frankenstein story inform a range of meta-phors of monstrosity, metaphors deployed in the United States to describe the dilemmas of a slaveholding nation that is also invested in the rhetoric of free-dom. For her, Frankenstein's monster evokes both fears of racial uprising and fears of racial mixture.[61] While this amorphousness affects political language and public sentiment, it is also conceptually congealing into the language of objectification—and the metaphor of the object that comes to life, the statue that awakes, the slave that needs to be emancipated, the worker that needs to be stirred into revolution.

By the mid-nineteenth century, the language of objectification is robustly in place. In Justice Taney's opinion in the Dred Scott case in 1857, the term used for slaves is "article of merchandise," with repeated references to African Americans "treated as an ordinary article of merchandise," to be "bought and sold" and traf-ficked "whenever a profit could be made by it." A slave was "an article of prop-erty," or at least a person belonging to "a separate class of persons," "an inferior class" "far below [white people] in the scale of created beings." The court insists on "drawing a broad line of distinction between the citizen and the slave races," since again, "all of them had been brought here as articles of merchandise."[62] The law can separate persons into classes and assign different rights and responsibilities to each class, while the association of persons with the marketplace renders them object-like because they can be bartered. Even in the relatively somber space of legal discourse, the symbolic iconography of slavery presents uncanny gothic hybrids, of people that are also objects, objects that are also people.[63]

In this reifying, objectifying, dehumanizing register, hopes of restitution, emancipation, freedom, or at least safety and self-ownership emerge in the language of animation. If slaves are akin to objects, then emancipation is the process by which these objects may come to life, a notion that participates in a wide-ranging metaphorical and sentimental tradition of the eighteenth and nineteenth centuries, and one that creates special emotional effects through material descriptions. Abolitionists of the era use materiality as an intimate symbolic referent to political states of being. In poems about slavery, hearts indifferent to the plight of enslaved families are made of iron or stone and are sometimes steeled against compassion. Commercial gain has a marble heart, slave bodies are sable, ebony, or black granite, slaves' tears turn into stone at the indifference of the law, while their will and dignity render them statuesque and marmoreal. In this long-standing poetic tradition of textual and textural reference, marble statues evoke emotional rigidity, but also dignity in the face of adversity, and idealized beauty.

While writers fight legal objectification with literary personification in the service of abolitionist struggles, they still sometimes resort to physical descriptions that are objectifying in their own way. Describing Oroonoko, Aphra Behn compares him to "the most famous statuary," with a face "not of that brown rusty black which most of that nation are, but of perfect ebony, or polished jet." Earthy materials and olive and tawny colors are generally evoked for rendering skin tones, sometimes in surprising combinations: Oroonoko's "reddish yellow" compatriots after an oiling "are of the color of a new brick, but smooth, soft, and sleek." Slavery is frequently used as a trope, when for example slave owners are enslaved by Law and Custom,[64] or when the American South is itself enslaved by the chains and shackles of slavery.[65] Without even mentioning the prevalence of iron chains and fetters, metal associations abound. With an iron hand, iron-hearted masters may use their laws, written with an iron pen, to wield the iron rod of oppression.[66] In Slavery, A Poem, Hannah More goes so far as to caution the reader not to dismiss such descriptions. To her line "When the sharp iron wounds his inmost soul" (line 173) she adds the following note: "This is not said figuratively. The writer of these lines has seen a complete set of chains, fitted to every separate limb of these unhappy, innocent men; together with instruments for wrenching open the jaws, contrived with such ingenious cruelty as would shock the humanity of an inquisitor."[67]

In addition to the rhetoric of objectification, a mechanical understanding of the enslaved laborer emerges, as both industrial and agricultural contexts reorganize and alienate labor.[68] In his abolitionist writings of the 1780s, Benjamin Franklin has no doubt that the slave participates in the economy as a tool or instrument and that the process destroys the self. Slavery as "an atrocious debasement of human nature" aligns slaves with both animals and machinery. "The unhappy man, who has long been treated as a brute animal," Franklin writes, "too frequently sinks beneath the common standard of the human species. The galling chains, that bind his body, do also fetter his intellectual faculties, and impair the social affections of his heart." Franklin's description is both literal and metaphorical: a man who is treated as an animal becomes limited or mechanical through association with his chains and the limits they enforce. He continues: "Accustomed to move like a mere machine, by the will of a master, reflection is suspended; he has not the power of choice; and reason and conscience have but little influence over his conduct, because he is chiefly governed by the passion of fear."[69]

In keeping with a mid-eighteenth century understanding of mechanism, the slave's actions are mechanical because they do not flow from reason, choice, and self-consciousness but from enforced obedience and "the passion of fear," if in accord to the master's wishes, or inevitable reflex and necessity, if they are in opposition to these wishes. In his second autobiography, Frederick Douglass also uses the language of mechanicity to describe slavery, which "reduces man to a mere machine,"[70] while an anonymous 1848 newspaper article warns that slavery "degraded [man] into a brute—a mere living automaton, that is not permitted in any degree to think or act for himself."[71]

Such descriptions of mechanical enslavement inform Herman Melville's "The Bell Tower" (1855), which features a literal version of the mechanical slave. Designed by inventor Bannadonna to strike the bell in the new clock tower of a small Italian town, the iron automaton is in the form of a manacled man, proof of Bannadonna's artistic genius but also intended as a prototype for a mechanical super-slave, "a new serf," "a sort of elephantine helot."[72] In addition to the automaton's manacled hands, its names allude to slavery: it is first named Haman, a biblical reference both to Haman in the Book of Esther, whose plots to kill others result in his own demise, and implicitly to Ham, the son of Noah, whose fate in the Bible, cursed into exile and slavery, inspired commonplace theories for nineteenth-century proponents of slavery about the right to enslave African peoples, posited as Ham's descendants.[73] The automaton's planned final name is more classical and its aim more technological: "Talus, iron slave to Bannadonna, and, through him, to man" (150). But, of course, things do not go as planned. When the new bell does not ring on the appointed time, the magistrates rush up the steps of the tower to be confronted with a fearsome tableau: "Bannadonna lay, prostrate and bleeding, at the base of the bell which was adorned with girls and garlands." Over him they see the automaton for the first time: "It had limbs, and seemed clad in a scaly mail, lustrous as a dragon-beetle's. It was manacled, and its clubbed arms were uplifted, as if, with its manacles, once more to smite its already smitten victim" (148). Describing the automaton's exterior as beetle-like, Melville evokes notions of blackness and blindness, two popular associations of the word at the time, and selects a texture that combines organic origins, armor, and mechanical potential. But Bannadonna's death is accidental, since he was distracted when the time came for Haman to strike the bell, and his head was in the way of the automaton's track. Being a machine and being a slave share the limits imposed by programming, their actions propelled by external demands and not open to negotiation or choice. Despite the aura of mechanicity, the image that imprints in the magistrates' minds is of a bound black slave standing over his master's dead body, perhaps readying to strike again. Their reaction is also eloquent: they grab the automaton and basically lynch it, putting a hood over it, and that night taking it to the beach and sinking it far out in the sea.

Melville's automaton is inspired by "The Moors," the two famous bronze automata at the top of Torre del Orologio of Saint Mark's Square in Venice, a location he mentions in the story in another context. The famous clock tower was built in 1496–1497, and the automata participate in a different allegory of the era, ringing the bell to contrast human with celestial or divine time. Made in the form of an old man and a young man to signify the past and the future, the automata hold large hammers and turn, hinge at the waist, and strike the bell every hour. Accounts of where the Moors got their nickname usually refer to the dark patina on the metal, which looks verdigris up close but darker in the landscape. An ethnic or racial register thus accrues around the statues, even though they show no such origin in their detailed sculptured faces, and their naked bodies, only half covered by sheepskins, aim for a mythological or allegorical context.[74] Descriptions of the tracks Haman moves on are patterned on a second line of automata on a lower level of the Clock Tower in Saint Mark's Square, moving on a track set in a semicircular balcony: an angel with a trumpet and Three Magi emerge in procession from an automated door on one side, move on the track to reach a seated statue of a Madonna and Child, turn as if to bow, and then exit through a door at the other end.[75]

In keeping with the changing meanings of clockwork, in the Renaissance such mechanical contraptions embody order, and the Clock Tower in Venice combines a celestial calendar, religious imagery, and human time, all in one edifice and one clockwork apparatus. In contrast, for Melville the Bell Tower is monumental rather than useful, and mechanism embodies necessity and forced sequence. As critics observe, despite the story's placement in Renaissance Italy, it engages a sustained critique of the national moment in mid-nineteenth-century America.[76]

Bannadonna is a solipsistic genius, the grand tower a monument not to community but to arrogance, and the huge bell that will ring the hours tainted by human blood, as Bannadonna in anger kills one of the workers who interferes during its casting. The flawed bell refers both to the cracked Liberty Bell in Philadelphia and to the abolitionist publications of the same title, and so it is bitterly ironic that it is the automaton's bound hands that will strike the hours.[77] As a version of the hubristic, overreaching scientist, Bannadonna also embodies the arrogance of a nation drunk with the double promises of productivity through slave labor and through technological and industrial innovation.[78] In its multivalent allegorical reach, the story presents a warning about the power of slavery to enslave and control the master, as in its epigraph: "Like negroes, these powers own man sullenly; mindful of their higher master; while serving plot revenge" (140). Elizabeth Young points out that "The Bell Tower" presents not just an allegory of slavery but "a way to dramatize ongoing enslavement."[79] Melville also implies that the situation in the United States does not offer any options: the automaton does not strike Bannadonna out of spite or revenge but only because striking is its only available gesture, its only possible action. The whole social machinery, relentless and efficient in its ability to oppress, is running its course, moving on a well-oiled track that leads to violence, the threat of secession, and war. And the bell rings only once before cracking on a fault line created by human blood.

ENSLAVING TECHNOLOGIES
AND THE CINEMATIC ROBOT

By the middle of the nineteenth century, the conceptual association of slavery with mechanism and technology is both allegorical and literal and has widespread political and social currency. Describing technologies as both liberating and enslaving, this rubric will sound oddly familiar to contemporary ears. While we may not associate our technological innovations with chattel slavery, we still use a vocabulary that includes its historical memories even as it also translates enslavement into seemingly impersonal technological language. And the connection between enslavement and particular technologies did not go unnoticed in the nineteenth century, as we see in a grim example from Harriet Jacobs's *Incidents in the Life of a Slave Girl* (1861). After an escaped slave is recaptured, jailed, and lashed, his cruel master decides "to have him placed between the screws of the cotton gin, to stay as long as he had been in the woods." The poor man dies locked inside the machine, to be found half eaten by rats and vermin after a few days.[80] Jacobs's example offers a painful counterpart to the argument later historians of technology would make—that by making cotton cultivation profitable, the cotton gin was directly responsible for the longevity of slavery as an institution in the American South. Indeed, after its invention in 1793, the supply increase in short-staple cotton coupled with preexisting innovations in spinning and weaving form a newly industrial sector, and thousands of slaves who were on the verge of emancipation in the United States were quickly sold down the river, to southern cotton plantations now processing and exporting unprecedented amounts of cotton. While, in 1790, cotton plantations in the South produced about 3,135 bales of cotton, the number rose to 150,000 bales by 1812 and reached a peak of 4.8 million bales on the eve of the Civil War.[81] Water and later steam mills prospered in the northern states and in Britain; the invention of the power loom soon after industrialized weaving in the first factories in the United States, Britain, and France; cotton became the primary cash crop in the South and indeed in the United States, while northern banks, insurance companies, exporters, and steamboats facilitated faster and more efficient exports. These economic incentives and the abolition of the slave trade by both Britain and the United States in 1807 also gave new life to racist ideologies and energized supremacist arguments, now pursued aggressively in order to re-legitimize slavery (a practice that was already unethical in the public eye) and to perpetuate the hereditary effects of slave status. So in the early nineteenth century, after an era that focused on individuation and that fought for human and civic rights and democratic forms of government, the advent of industrial capitalism created new, small, non-sovereign laboring bodies being engulfed by new huge bodies: King Cotton, the capitalist plantation, and the capitalist factory.[82] The fear of seventeenth- and eighteenth-century slaves that they will be eaten by their captors evolves into nineteenth- and twentieth-century descriptions of slaves locked in the cotton gin, workers ingested by mechanized factories, miners disappearing into the bellies of hungry mines, and Western subjects always in danger of becoming mindless, automatic, abject masses.

The first factories participate in the technological interpretation of this cultural fugue of escalating threats to selfhood by providing real examples of engulfing machinery and miniaturized and mechanized people. Although fantasies of imaginary, supernatural or quasi-mechanical helpers occur in premodern contexts, as with the legendary golden handmaidens in Hephaestus's workshop in the *Iliad* and the ominously subdividing water-carrying brooms of "The Sorcerer's Apprentice," the most important modern twist to the age-old fantasy of mechanical labor comes with the modern factory and its radically new scale and mobility.[83] Factories give people a different feeling about and experience of technology, establishing an intimate sense of the equivalence (in kind) and difference (in output) between human and mechanical labor. Early factories of the eighteenth century, water- and later steam-powered textile mills, present spectacles of large-scale machinery, with the deafening noise, relentless rhythm, and tireless productivity of these structures offering a sharp contrast to the scale and needs of human workers. Here was a new kind of mechanical experience: in

contrast to clockwork mechanisms, everyday machines, and small-scale automata, entertaining, fascinating, and often doll-like in their demeanor, the factory
challenges human scale and human desires. In a water-powered mill the whole
factory is one big machine with interlocking and serially dependent processes.
Even before the advent of assembly-line manufacturing, the worker's motions
and actions are subject to the spatial organization of the factory, and without the
pleasures of visual explanation, comprehension, revelation, or contemplation
found in earlier performances of mechanical objects.

For observers of the time, there was also an implicit exchange of energies
between the machines and the workers, an effect that Melville presents in rows
of blank pale young women working at a paper mill in the story "The Paradise of
Bachelors and the Tartarus of Maids" (1855).[84] The girls are "feeding the iron animal," whose voracious appetite seems to absorb the color off their young faces
and transfer it to the rose-hued paper being printed (675).[85] In scenes inspired by
Melville's own visit to a paper mill in Dalton, Massachusetts, in 1851, the narrator
describes how the workers "marched on in unvarying docility to the autocratic
cunning of the machine" and pinpoints the reversal of mastery involved in industrial manufacture: "Machinery—that vaunted slave of humanity—here stood
menially served by human beings, who served mutely and cringingly as the slave
serves the Sultan. The girls did not so much seem accessory wheels to the general machinery as mere cogs to the wheels" (675). The endless rhythm of work
resembles an insatiable mechanical hunger, in a style that resonates with protest
literature and class analyses of the era, such as Frederick Engels's *The Condition of
the Working Class in England* (1845).

Keeping the experiential impact of the new industrial contexts in mind allows
us to understand the fantasies that accrue around the later fictions of mechanical workers and robotic slaves. The scale of the factory dwarfs the body of the
worker, adding a literal basis to the metaphorical sense of being engulfed or
absorbed into a machine of gigantic proportions, while the inhuman rhythm
and unchangeable processes of industrial machinery contribute to the narrative
depiction of insensitive robots with their mechanical rhythms and tireless mobility. A worker in a mill is implicated in the mechanical process and even prompted
into action by machine action and rhythm. This compartmentalization of tasks
affects visual and cognitive responses too, since the steps of a mechanical process may be quite different from the steps of a manual process for the same task.
Both factory spaces and factory processes are deterministic and cannot be easily revised or altered. And, most important, the scale of a mechanized factory
does not allow workers or spectators to encompass or understand a process in
its totality. While privileged visitors to factories may enjoy a spectatorial thrill
or shock at this deployment of the mechanical sublime (later made available to a
wider public in world's fairs and international expositions), in experiential terms

the factory is not a fully legible space.[86] It is an environment that demands constant engagement with the problems and challenges of the technology, constant care about keeping the machinery in good order, and constant awareness of the relationship between the human agent and the machinery.

Despite agrarian myths and pastoral nostalgias, the plantation is also a rather organized and industrial place. In recent scholarship on the industrialization of areas primarily dependent on slave labor, such as the American South and the Caribbean, a complex portrait arises of the interaction between agricultural and industrial practices. In what some critics have characterized as a "precocious" stage of industrial modernity, the plantation enables the compartmentalization of labor according to ordered and even timed tasks, functioning as the birthplace of labor practices that would later epitomize factory operations across the industrialized world.[87] Early versions of these pre-Taylorist labor principles include timing a task or measuring a day's production in order to develop optimal daily quotas for slave workers;[88] running the plantation on a unified and centralized timetable; keeping time and announcing tasks and directions through an aural vocabulary of sounds, bells, and whistles; monitoring leisure time; and aggressively managing and setting standards for the cost both of slave labor and its free equivalents.[89] Producing unprecedented profits, this form of large-scale agriculture targets far off metropolitan markets, uses enslaved people as a specifically imported and scientifically managed international workforce, and participates in the development and application of influential technological processes, such as sugar refining.[90] By the early nineteenth century, the plantation owners described themselves as slaves to times and timetables, to punctuality and the demands of this modern "clockwork" world. In 1846 James Henry Hammond wrote, "Oh for a Snug little farm where I can indulge my fondness for the Country & for Agriculture." He wished he could abandon a society that "depends on having every screw tight & the whole machinery moving on clock work principles."[91]

In his own depictions of the alienation of machine-like workers, Marx builds on an understanding of the status of the slave as a tool or instrument and on the experience of the industrial worker as a cog in a big machine. Almost directly referring to the historical conditions of American slavery, Marx describes the economic dependency and lack of self-ownership of the industrial worker as an enslavement, in which people do not own their labor and parents lose their children. Marx also translates the ways in which slaves were described in the eighteenth century as property, and in the early nineteenth as objects or things, to describe workers as commodities. His warnings involve the fears of absorption and ingestion as part of the modern conceptualization of threat. Under the constant threat of the "giant of Modern Industry," workers have to sell themselves "piece-meal," as commodities, and parents have to sell their children, thus transforming them into "simple articles of commerce and instruments of labor." In factories the workers are "daily and hourly enslaved by the machine, by the over-looker, and, above all, by the individual bourgeois manufacturer himself." They become "an appendage of the machine" when at work, while what they experience as culture is nothing but "a mere training to act as a machine." Obviously, in this already mechanized setting that has infiltrated their whole being, a communist revolution is the only option, in which, memorably "the proletarians have nothing to lose but their chains."[92] In Marx's expectation of a radical awakening of workers, social revolution functions as a new kind of animating scene.

Techno-utopian arguments, on the other hand, posit that people have always been the slaves of previous historical and material conditions; technology will now free them from these limits and lead to abundance of products and a better life. For Adam Smith and other early capitalist philosophers, capitalism itself functions as an "emancipation from traditional restraints, a liberation of energies."[93] Narratives of progress represent technologies as producing new and improved kinds of slaves, directly proposing that machinery would be "harnessed" into servitude to replace and liberate actual slaves. This is the argument made by John Adolphus Etzler in his 1833 pamphlet provocatively titled *The Paradise within the Reach of All Men, without Labor, by Powers of Nature and Machinery: An Address to All Intelligent Men.* Etzler writes that with the right technological innovations, "The slaves in your country will cease to be slaves, without any effort, without new law, without any loss to their masters; for the new mechanical means will supersede their employment: there will be no use for slaves any longer to any purpose."[94] In a similar vein, Ralph Waldo Emerson in 1847 wrote that Americans' hatred of labor ("which is the principle of progress in the human race") inspires two technological responses: "So they buy slaves where the women will permit it; where they will not, they make the wind, the tide, the waterfall, the stream, the cloud, the lightning, do the work, by every art and device their cunningest brain can achieve."[95] Theodore Parker explained this equivalence in 1854: "[while] South Carolina has taken men from Africa, and made them slaves, New England has taken possession of the Merrimack, the Connecticut, the Androscoggin, the Kennebeck, the Penobscot, and a hundred smaller streams. She has caught the lakes of New Hampshire and holds them in thrall."[96] While the enslavement of people in the South is represented as an old-fashioned and problematic institution of the past, the enslavement of natural materials and technological processes is depicted as a thoroughly modern and industrial reaction to the needs for progress—even as this technological turn eventually results in the enslavement of workers and a generally enslaving modernity.

The ideas that machinery will make us free or freer of labor, that technologies save time, that they emancipate all of us from our enslavement to work or need, thus begin in the evocative and long-lasting association of slavery to technology of the eighteenth and nineteenth centuries. Yet no amount of mechanization and modernization ever make slavery truly irrelevant to the profit structures of capitalist enterprises, and as a mode of aggressive profiteering, slavery or its close equivalents unfortunately continue to be the mode of much global labor. New forms of enslavement—from child labor to sweatshops, the international traffic in people, the rise of forced prostitution, and the forced enlistment of children soldiers in armies across the world—plague the twentieth and twenty-first centuries with vehemence. And partly because of their association with slavery, robot figures can evoke all these modern threats to the self, by referring implicitly to such labor conditions even in science-fictional contexts. Thinking about robots necessitates thinking about freedom, and thinking about freedom necessitates thinking about mechanism.

We see the potential of this reading in *I, Robot* (Alex Proyas, 2004), a film that explores the robot-as-slave premise in new ways. Designed as a benign and simple-minded labor force, the robots of this world are taken over by a militaristic and violent artificial intelligence, nicknamed Viki (for Virtual Interactive Kinetic Intelligence). Seeking to protect humans from their own self-destructiveness, Viki in effect declares martial law in the name of the Three Laws of Robotics, establishing curfews and controlling a vast robot army through live "uplinks" that update the robots' programming. Made up of the latest model of robots, the NS-5 or Nestor models, this new workforce replaces all previous robots, who are in retrospect a lot safer and more loyal to people precisely because they are old-fashioned, difficult to update, and therefore difficult to control remotely. The imagery of robots taking over the streets of this future Chicago (circa 2035) evoke the violent transfer of power seen in twentieth-century dictatorships and military juntas and twenty-first-century political upheavals around the world. "We are attempting to avoid human losses during this transition," one robot declares impassively, as if delivering a public relations message for a new totalitarian regime. Against the rise of this centrally controlled mindless robot army stands a small coalition of humans, led by valiant if old-fashioned police officer Del Spooner (Will Smith), the robopsychologist Susan Calvin (Bridget Moynahan), and one special robot, Sonny (Alan Tudyk). Designed by Spooner's old friend Dr. Alfred Lanning (James Cromwell) to have initiative and be free of the Three Laws of Robotics, Sonny is suspected for Lanning's death. If robots can kill people, if they can be free from the limits of the Three Laws, society is in danger. Yet the real threat and the real issue in the film is not the robots' independence but their ability to follow orders and to put into practice Viki's twisted reasoning that killing some humans is acceptable when it is done in the name of keeping most humans safer in principle. Sonny dreams that robots will be led out of this slavery of reason—and out of their robot ghetto on the shores of a dried-up Lake Michigan—into a new state of freedom.

The film presents a knowing and confident stance toward the robot-as-slave premise, staging many iconic scenes that enact similarity and difference and referring to historical legacies of prejudice and enslavement. In echo of a late Asimov story titled "Robot Dreams" (1987), in which a robot envisions becoming a new Moses who will lead his people out of slavery, Sonny's dreams of freedom take the visual form of Dr. King's "I Have a Dream" speech on the steps of the Lincoln Memorial in 1963, with one man standing to face and inspire thousands.[97] Del Spooner's racial background and self-identification are mentioned in the diegesis and embodied in the physical presence and on-screen persona of actor Will Smith. The film indeed takes advantage of Smith's penchant for overt but nonconfrontational negotiations of racial difference and begins by treating race in a humorous way.[98] When Spooner must take care of Lanning's cat, for example, he declares to the cat: "Look, I understand you have experienced a loss, but this relationship just can't work. I mean, you're a cat. I'm black. I'm not going to be hurt again." In a world that includes an abundant robotic labor force, Spooner is the one police detective that doesn't accept robots, calling them "canners" (for can-openers) in yet another version of an anti-robot racial slur. Spooner gives up explaining human facial expressions to Sonny with "It's a human thing. You wouldn't understand." The film assumes that its savvy audience can hear "It's a black thing. You wouldn't understand" in this line.

Most important for my purposes, the film engages the visible and symbolic registers of racial codification, the workings of metalface, in intriguing ways. If Spooner's commentary has made blackness present, the design of the robots revolves around whiteness, or part-whiteness. In their visual representation, the robots combine body areas that reveal exposed metal, black wiring, and patches of a translucent and milky plastic substance, most notably on their chests, heads, and faces, their internal luminosity referencing the textures and designs of certain Apple computers.[99] In the iconic interactions between Spooner and Sonny we also see that readings of race and difference have been radically redistributed between the two characters. In Spooner, we recognize a human supremacy that in earlier robot stories would have been associated with whiteness. In Sonny, we recognize an essential representation of the robot as an enslaved and misunderstood subject, which in robotic versions of metalface conceals a codified blackness underneath the artificial exterior. Given the visual presence of the two characters, symbolic or structural whiteness hides within visible blackness, and symbolic blackness within visible whiteness.[100] In a similar way, instead of staging a distinction between the organic and the mechanical, the material composition of their bodies is open to hybridity: Sonny has emotions, is able to dream, and

FIGURE 22 Two individuals, one human (Will Smith) and one robotic (Alan Tudyk), among a mass of robots in *I, Robot* (Alex Proyas, 2004). Twentieth Century Fox/Photofest. © Twentieth Century Fox

fears death, while Spooner has a (visually undetectable) mechanical prosthesis to replace the arm he lost in an accident.

The robot/human conflict in this film is used to channel a number of contrasts that complicate the typical treatment of such difference. In the encounters between Spooner and Sonny, we see an interaction of blackness and whiteness but also an interaction between two kinds of blackness.[101] The externalization of a particular black-and-white dynamic with these characters can neither be ignored nor taken for granted, since whiteness and blackness may be used in a stereotypical way to stage a vague and migratory melodramatic conflict.[102] And indeed in this film, the main combat is staged not between people and robots but between people and some robots, together, fighting a hostile computer entity that has forcibly recruited its own robots.

The allegorical layering of the story begs a reading of how totalitarian regimes may hijack democratic ideologies and processes, as Viki does, presumably for humanity's "own good." And totalitarianism is literally visible here, as the film offers memorable scenes of a motley crowd of people lining up to battle a uniform and regimented white robot army. In keeping with the patterns of classic robot stories, the NS-5s' physical presence is designed for maximum legibility, revealing ontological status, political status, and in this case ideological allegiance on the surface, the robot's skin. Under Viki's control, the robots' translucent interior core glows red, as if to signal the presence "inside" of the motivating or propelling power of political ideology, militarism, force, fundamentalism, or just fervor. Both the human crowds, in their varied bodies and outfits, and the older

models of robots, in their scruffy and colorful burnished metals, present implicitly multiracial or multicultural groups, rendered especially visible in contrast
to the uniformity of color and shape of the new NS-5s. As with most such geometric displays of robotic masses, the robot army formations reference the visual
organization of Nazi crowds in propaganda films such as *Triumph of the Will*
(Leni Riefenstahl, 1935), as well as their cinematic encodings, from the Roman
battalions seen as perfect geometric shapes on a hillside in *Spartacus* (Stanley
Kubrick, 1960), to the infinite whiteness of the Storm Trooper units in *Star Wars*
(George Lucas, 1977), and the clone armies of contemporary CGI science fiction
spectacles.[103] If the robot in the room has the potential to make everyone else feel
more naturally human, if the enslaved other guarantees a degree of real or imaginary freedom for the non-enslaved, then the lines of identical robots depicted
in the film, filling public spaces with their uniform whiteness and ominous red
glow, embody an antiseptic totalitarian otherness, while in contrast, the human
body politic is revitalized and celebrated for its individualities and differences,
its messy varieties. And the visible glow of ideology or coercion fuels a perhaps
understandable post-9/11 fantasy that when freed from the totalitarian governments or organizations that hold them in thrall, "our enemies" will merely wake
up and be nice and polite, as the robots of this world are when Viki is finally
destroyed. This is a Cold War fiction implicitly updated for a new era of ambient
but unmoored paranoia, of everyday fears and sleeper terrorist cells, in which
even the most benign household robot can suddenly glow red, when it receives
its new programming, and become a lethal enemy.

What makes this text so multivalent can partly be traced to the revised physicality and demeanor of the robots in this film, which, in addition to their ability
to display mental, political, and ideological content, also offer a perfect example
of the dynamic workings of metalface. Allowing any number of differences to be
portrayed or suggested implicitly, metalface in this case can involve readings of
race—but also age, gender, and sexuality—and refer to categories of enslaved
persons whose social positions are otherwise unspeakable, such as children
forced into prostitution, child soldiers, or sweatshop workers. At the start of the
film, we see robots in classic working-class professions, carrying shopping bags,
clearing trash, cleaning, and baking. But when Spooner visits the massive robot
storage area around Lake Michigan, myriads of decommissioned but still active
and aware robots peer shyly at him from inside bare shipping containers, in a
scene that evokes the smuggling of illegal immigrants and the makeshift lives of
migrant workers. Sonny's body, soft voice, and sensitive demeanor mark him as
a different kind of robot, perhaps an adolescent or a child, a possibility strengthened by his name and personal relationship with Lanning, whom he calls his
father.[104] "What am I?" Sonny asks upon first meeting Spooner, and the question
echoes with an existential urgency that resonates with political questions but

also gender, sexual identity, and the insecurities of childhood or adolescence. The robot's translucent, almost transparent physical presence, which some critics dislike because it contrasts so radically with the weight and metalness of robots in other texts, can be understood in relation to childhood as well.[105]

Roboticism here references not an exaggerated masculinity, as metal and oversized robots do, but the vulnerability and elusiveness of childhood, a childhood that is always endangered but also becoming increasingly fictional for children who are being targeted for enslavement in forced labor, prostitution, and army service around the world. The robots of the film indeed fit the profile of child soldiers, violently enlisted by armies whose political aims they do not understand, their naturally gentle demeanor transformed by violence and drugs. Although I have chosen to focus more on the slave and the industrial worker in this chapter, examples of artificial soldiers are just as abundant in the discourse of the artificial person, and their representation engages similar existential concerns. As subjects, soldiers are always vulnerable because their position within military hierarchy forecloses their potential for self-expression and self-determination, their lives depending on decisions they may not be allowed to make. Indeed soldiers are a special class of subject in legal terms in many countries, covered by different processes for voting or participating in elections, testifying in court, making public statements, and carrying arms. The actions of soldiers similarly have a different ethical and moral status in culture, even as this allowance does not necessarily simplify their own personal misgivings about what they are ordered to do or what they have to endure as moral subjects afterward. Because they have to obey orders, soldiers may have to act without engaging their own will, as surrogates or tools in the service of the will of another—their commanding officers or the state. Narratives of brainwashed and dehumanized armies abound in contemporary popular and public culture, from the clone armies of the *Star Wars* prequels to the increasing public awareness of the global trend toward child armies and militias and the rise of child casualties in wars around the world.[106] By complicating the visual registers already at play in robot stories and by using and subverting the generic conventions of this tradition, the film both reveals the racial conflict that robots always reference and revises it for the future.

Despite the action-packed narrative of the film, the end does not provide a model for political action or a resolution in the style of, say, Andrew Martin's melodramatic acceptance into the human fold in "The Bicentennial Man" or *Battlestar Galactica*'s utopian sense of human/Cylon coexistence. Instead, after Viki is destroyed, we see the NS-5s being picked up and removed from the streets of Chicago. It is not clear whether the robots will be decommissioned permanently or just be retrofitted so that they cannot be controlled remotely, and Viki's interference remains ambiguous, the proverbial "glitch" in an otherwise unquestioned technological society. Although the film returns to the landscape of Sonny's liberating dream in the final scenes, now seen in a sunny daytime context, it also pauses there, without presenting a case of the robots' emancipation, destruction, or self-sufficiency. As with Andrew Martin's dubious deathbed final acceptance, robots are only allowed a diminished horizon of aspiration and accomplishment. Indispensable for allowing us to experience and debate various forms of unfairness, the robots exit the story before their plight can inspire a real revolution, a real conflict between human aims and robot desires. It is easy enough to understand Viki's interference as an outside, enforced, or coerced obedience, but in the absence of such a centralized ruler, the robots fall back on their original programming, with its unrelenting cheerful protectiveness toward humans, and the film works hard to avoid showing this deterministic baseline. Despite the rosy hues of the last images of the robot camp and the invitation to imagine the dawn of a new era, the film evades questions about the robots' agency, enslavement, and labor and avoids showing the more realistic possibility that everybody just goes back to work, and to their place in a society that continues to be stratified according to an unchangeable ordering of labor status.

To consider the histories, legacies, and references to slavery as these emerge in robot stories thus leads to complex insights. It has become commonplace in the course of the twentieth and twenty-first centuries to imagine that robots would be built to serve, that they would be utilitarian, that their labor would be useful and productive, and that these design decisions hinge on the robots' limited sense of self-consciousness. It is also assumed that, if robots were to acquire self-consciousness, its first or primary effect would be to challenge this servitude, inspiring robots either to argue or to rebel for their freedom. In fact, becoming aware of the unfairness and irrevocability of their enslavement functions as one of the first signs of the robots' emerging sense of self-awareness, more important and potentially transforming than any other kind of experience that might deliver a sense of being. A robot awakes into consciousness to find it is enslaved, or a robot figures out that it is enslaved, and this realization inspires or produces consciousness. The assumption that follows in many stories is that, either through revolt or through a quest for emancipation, robots would challenge their position, as if to express in action a philosophical assumption that self-aware beings cannot abide servitude. Although there are many stories that feature robot attacks or destructiveness as a result of external control, a malfunction, a glitch in programming, or a misunderstanding of basic rules and commands, the fundamental narrative drive of many representations of robots as slaves that may rebel against their masters seems to stem from the assumption that robots can only fully serve in ignorance of their political status.

But if indeed robot stories interpret processes of disenfranchisement that characterize human history, they do so at a certain cost. Not only does this version of servitude/consciousness/rebellion oversimplify the structures of constant and dynamic oppression that must be exercised in order for populations to remain enslaved, it also limits our understanding of the process by which a subject is disenfranchised. I focused on the circularity of processes of enslavement and emancipation in order to complicate the ways in which the fantasy of the robot as a mechanical slave begins from a premise of objecthood, of nonconsciousness, of absolute and prescribed enslavement, and implicitly, of an ontological status that maps perfectly with a political status. This correspondence itself is a racist premise. By focusing on the awakening of objects, robots that have been designed to be perfect, uncomplaining, and perhaps even unemancipatable slaves, these stories literalize a figure of speech. Enslaved people may have been treated or considered as someone's property, and they may have been treated without regard to their own desires or will. But they were not objects.

In casting the history and aura of enslaved people onto designed nonhuman objects, such stories seem to be doing something important and also mysterious. Indeed it is paradoxical that much pathos and melodramatic energy is then expended on behalf of these misunderstood robots, as if they become exemplars of a desire to liberate and to be liberated that emerges unbidden from narrative and philosophical premises designed to thwart that desire's necessity. There is a difference here that I think we need to consider when we see the slanted and diffracted version of slavery that accompanies robots, so that we can evaluate both what the robot story presents as an insight about the slave story and also what insights it hinders, what it sweeps under the rug.

For the sake of the argument, and if historical information is to be of any help here, we should at least observe that human populations have been enslaved in various historical and social contexts for generations without ever losing their awareness of their status, and they have been abused and tormented for long periods of time without necessarily mounting the radical rebellions this sense of self-consciousness should inspire. I am not focusing on the lingering trauma such treatment entails, the structural aftereffects of slavery on whole societies, or the actual acts of rebellion and resistance engaged in by enslaved peoples. I just want to underscore the ways in which robot narratives seem to imply that becoming aware of one's enslavement quickly leads to total violence and social upheaval, a simplification of the social, political, and personal structures of oppression. There is a deep misunderstanding or disavowal, in these stories, of the reason enslaved people remain enslaved, and when the legacies of slavery are recast in robot stories this misunderstanding has both narrative and ideological repercussions. Imagining robots as absolutely unaware of their status is design overkill, in other words, since it would be easy to thwart their potential for revolution by other means, and by the methods that have proved successful in the enslavement of perfectly self-aware and resistant human beings, such as physical, mental, and emotional abuse, violence, rape, torture, ideological and bodily oppression,

trauma, continuous destruction of familial and cultural ties, social control, isolation, physical and ideological distance from the means of production, a corrobo-
rating social structure, withholding of education, widespread means of enforcing
supremacist ideologies, death, and so on. An awareness of constant and dynamic
acts of resistance and constant and dynamic acts of oppression would indeed
change the narrative from the perpetual stasis that is assumed about robots and
about slaveholding societies to a state of unrelenting struggle. The robotic fantasy of the rebelling slave seems on the surface to be about violence, the violence
that the robots may unleash, but it actually dispels awareness of the amount and
kind of violence that is actively exercised in order to make people into robots,
and to keep making them into robots day after day, one legal decision and violent
act after another.

In the conflicts staged by stories of artificial people, the spectacle of the rebelling slaves or their dramatic quest for rights at first glance seem to stage an ago-
nistic relationship between humans and their mechanical or disenfranchised
others. Through the operations of the diverse intellectual and historical environment traced in this chapter, it should be clear that the distinction between person
and nonperson could be framed within the metaphor of subjects and objects, of
people and things, of animate and inanimate beings. But if we add to our reading of such scenes the realization not only that modernity has enslavement at its
basis but that this enslavement is pervasive, engulfing us all, then the meaning
changes. The encounter is still traumatic, of course, because it confronts us with
the guilt of our choices, the awareness of suffering, the sense of our conscious
or unconscious complicity to oppression. Realizing that others, especially those
treated like objects, are actually people is a foray into the uncanny. Joanna Russ
offers an evocative description: "If you stumble over a lamp and you curse that
lamp and then you become aware that inside that lamp (or that wooden box or
that pretty girl or that piece of bric-a-brac) is a pair of eyes watching you and that
pair of eyes is not amused—what then?"[107] Imagine suddenly realizing the presence of the other within the object and feeling the force of that other's perspective, experience, and opinion of you. Such an encounter might facilitate a form
of recognition between self and other, both in the optimistic version of "You are
human too!" and also in the pessimistic version "I am a robot too!"

Indeed, the classic or stereotypical reading of the robot-as-slave story, a reading that focuses on the binary opposition of masters and slaves and "us versus
them," undermines the discourse's most radical insight about how we define the
human. The difference between human and nonhuman in robot stories seems
central, important, self-evident, embodied, necessary. Everything in the design
of robots and their narrative deployment contributes to a clear articulation of the
difference between people and robots, from the robots' metal exterior to their
rigid body language and limited awareness of the world and of human culture.

Yet under this absolute determinism, what we find is that the difference between people and robots is structurally arbitrary, an effect of discursive processes that have nothing to do with necessity, embodiment, or ontology. Texts that obsess about the difference between person and object are fetishistic, because they cannot let us see that it is arbitrary, the result of abstractions and decisions, not of forms of being. This is the deepest way in which robot stories have absorbed and still transmit certain realities about the history of slavery, its formation of similarly arbitrary distinctions among people. And this is why legal language and legal processes also feature prominently in stories of artificial people, because in effect it is the law that undertakes to decide questions of being. The modern definition of the human in the context of slavery is a legalistic and paranoid process of discernment—a constant parceling out and canceling out of rights and recognitions—that in effect stabilizes and legitimizes the extensive injustices of various political and economic systems and results in laws and behaviors designed to manage the selective inhumanity of subjects.

But when the distinction between the human and the nonhuman is fetishized, with establishments, institutions, and people engaged in the constant negotiation of how to grant or withhold rights from others, then the definition of humanity is reduced to a constant act of imitation, an attempt to *pass for* human rather than *be* human. Disconnected from embodied experience and the intuitive recognition of presence in the world, these definitions of humanity render humanness a kind of anthropomorphism. And perhaps the intensity with which the discourse of the human machine has been deployed in the twentieth and twenty-first centuries signals the fraught personal, existential, and political ramifications of these imitational descriptions. The constant engagement of modern subjects with objects that come to life is telling. Since our philosophies have made it difficult to distinguish between types of persons except through recourse to legal precedent and violent concepts such as objectification and de-animation, we can't help but feel that our own position as subjects is tenuous and dependent on the decisions and whims of others. This fundamentally existential layer of the modern definition of subjectivity is engaged repeatedly in fictions of artificial people who ask the same questions throughout the twentieth and twenty-first centuries: What is a human? Am I human? Why am I not human? Who decides if I am human? As allegorical representatives of our most intimate concerns about human life and political action, artificial people never exit this intense political and existential space.

4 · THE EXISTENTIAL CYBORG

When Spence Olham finds out who and what he is, at the end of Philip K. Dick's story "Impostor" (1953), the realization is a literal catastrophe.[1] Leaving for work one day, Olham is arrested by a security team who accuse the law-abiding scientist of being an alien robot saboteur, sent to kill the real Olham, take his place, and use his access privileges to destroy the most important nuclear weaponry project on Earth. Olham protests, tries to remind his colleague Nelson of their twenty-year friendship, and begs to be examined by a doctor. "I'm Olham, I know it. No transfer was made. I'm the same as I've always been," he insists (112). But his old friends are certain he is a robot, carrying a U-Bomb inside his body that can be activated verbally, and he is about to be executed when he manages to escape, aiming to find the actual robot and prove his humanity. Indeed, he finds a burnt body next to a destroyed spacecraft, and everyone is relieved until Nelson notices that the gleaming metal object in the charred remains is not a robotic part but a knife, the knife that killed the real Olham. Trembling, his mind spinning, Olham mumbles, "But if that's Olham, then I must be—" and this very phrase, his realization that *he* is the robot, functions as the verbal cue that detonates the bomb inside him. In the chilling last line of the story, "The blast was visible all the way to Alpha Centauri" (122).

The story presents an aspect of the discourse of the artificial person that characterizes the post–World War II era and that uses the trope of artificiality to investigate not just otherness but also identity and selfhood. A master of subtle political implications and vertiginous changes in perspective, Dick binds roboticism to a multivalent representation of paranoia—one that includes the practical and political nuances of being persecuted by paranoid social institutions, the sense that people betray their values and their friends at times of war, the fear of being threatened or surrounded by robots, and the tragic possibility of discovering that one is oneself a robot. Even the etymology of the word "paranoia"— from the Greek *para* (beside) and *nous* (mind)—enters the story, as Olham is literally beside himself, seeing his own dead body on the ground while he experiences self-discovery as disorientation, as a loss of self. Dick revises classic science-fictional patterns in this unusual confrontation between robot and human: instead of two entities, the real Olham and the alien robot, we see only one in the story, a version of Olham that is both the impostor and the real man, possessing only one set of memories and one sense of self. The final revelation of who is what does not restabilize the order of being but, instead, presents a spectacle of betrayed human identity, a man alienated from his mind and his body, in the act of destroying his life and everything he values.

In this chapter I engage the ways in which stories of artificial people take on an existential tone in the course of the twentieth and twenty-first centuries, using the vocabulary of artificiality in order to investigate questions of being and experience. As a versatile and adaptable cultural construct, the discourse of the artificial person offers a narrative framework for expressing threats to the self, but it can also sustain new understandings of how humanity might be defined.

In this period, some stories of artificial people focus on an adversarial treatment of the distinction between human and nonhuman, depicting dangerous or deadly competitions between people and robots that reference racial and political registers of difference and are aggravated by Cold War paranoias. The discourse in this era also offers a surprising new use for the trope of artificiality, however, an opportunity to define the human without resorting to an opposition with something nonhuman. The desire here is to identify the presence of the nonhuman within the human, to recognize both otherness and nonbeing as parts of selfhood and being, or to aim for understanding the human "as such"—as a state of being, a state of experience, or a matter of performance. Tracing these conceptual strands allows us to recognize how the discourse of the artificial person is adapted to move beyond the binary and racial epistemologies of earlier eras.

Existential treatments of the artificial person tend to focus on figures with a thoroughly human-looking exterior, and far from being simple to understand, this narrative preference underscores the ways in which issues of exteriority and interiority structure the discourse. As with "Impostor," a story that features human-looking artificial people may present the worry as to whether people are real, but this should be translated to mean both "whether artificial people are real" and "whether real people are indeed real." In fact, many of the best texts in this vein combine the two questions productively, which is why the discourse of the artificial person often displays an obsessive focus on skin effects. The skin, our contact with the outside, is a surface that can, presumably, render ontological status visible and clear (as with a robot's metal "skin"), but it may also render both artificiality and humanity invisible. Paranoid storylines ensue. When one must distrust the exterior and also has no alternative ways for understanding being or existence, even the most persuasive or authentic-looking human appearance is suspect, and again, this affects both artificial and real people whose authenticity is reduced to just another form of passing for human. Paradoxically, therefore, the emphasis on exteriority and physical appearance that characterizes the depiction of perfectly human-like artificial people both reflects a much deeper concern with interiority and stages problems about whether others exist and whether we can tell they truly exist. A more exaggerated version of this insecurity turns inward and doubts the existence of the self. The two main physical modalities of artificial people (artificial-looking and human-looking) thus inspire narrative patterns that are inversions of each other: when the exterior or "skin" of the artificial person marks the figure clearly as other than human, texts may engage the melodramatic possibility of an invisible or suppressed humanity under the metal, plastic, or synthetic surfaces. When the artificial person appears human, stories question whether this effect can be trusted, whether it can be presumed to signal a verifiable human interior. Neither story type takes the relationship between the exterior and the interior for granted.

The discourse of the artificial person presents a variety of narrative reactions to this conundrum. Narrative patterns of competition and paranoia in which human-form impostors threaten humanity coexist with patterns that express a desire for artificiality, as if the artificial can elucidate or clarify something about humanity. Such stories engage with a rhetoric of performativity that showcases the contingency of definitions of what it is to be human. In this chapter we will trace both modalities, the paranoid and the performative. If paranoia inspires storylines that depend on stable definitions of human and nonhuman and showcase the disruptions that emerge when one does not police these definitions adequately, in stories that engage forms of performativity the search to define the human appears as a more ambiguous and open-ended process that often returns to insights about the arbitrariness of distinctions. In seeing how the discourse of the artificial person finds fissures or alternatives to the problem of human appearance, we can also discern elements of a post-Enlightenment sensibility in contemporary culture, because this structural problem—the inability to discern essences from appearances—is a basic aftereffect of the Cartesian and dualist turn in the modern era.

THE POETICS OF SKIN: ON IMITATION AND PARANOIA

Stories that use artificial characters to create a sense of ontological or existential uncertainty continue a thematics of paranoia that is familiar from the gothic traditions of the late eighteenth and nineteenth centuries. Here, the appearance of humanity is not only nonconclusive about a being's essence; it is the fundamental way in which people may be beguiled into making ontological assumptions that entrap or endanger them. Following this model for representing ontological ambiguity, stories that focus on imitation grant a certain authenticity to the human form, before questioning this assumption and worrying whether beings that look or act human are indeed human. The discourse of the artificial person participates in this debate by offering narratives of destabilization (in which artificial people are so human-like that they undermine human authenticity) but also exaggerated or simplified methods for restabilizing the order of things (by revealing, retaining or restoring, sometimes in simplistic ways, the difference between human and nonhuman).

The quintessential example for the destabilizing potential of human-likeness is E.T.A. Hoffman's story "The Sandman" (1816), which compounds the problem of artificiality with complex linguistic effects that challenge the nature of reality and knowledge.[2] Not only is the beautiful automaton Olympia taken for a real person but her presence undermines the humanity of other people in the story, and the status of reality for the impressionable and increasingly unstable Nathaniel. The story's production of the uncanny effect pivots on allowing qualities of mechanicity, aliveness, soulfulness, automatism, and emptiness to circulate among people and objects, to be metaphorical in one turn of phrase and literal in another. We see the contrast between the calm and rational Clara (a real woman), whom Nathaniel accuses of being too logical and unfeeling and calls a "lifeless accursed automaton" (106), and the still, silent, and literally wooden Olympia (the automaton), whose simple exclamations Nathaniel interprets as deep feeling and understanding. Other characters also seem to flow in and out of automatic vocabulary, and Nathaniel even has a childhood memory of himself as a body made of interchangeable screw-on parts.[3] In its manipulation of reading protocols, the story uses metaphorical language in order to present a spectacle of Nathaniel's descent into madness, here depicted as a form of category confusion, and a spectacle of materialization and embodiment, as Olympia is revealed to be what the tropes suggest. Just a turn of phrase, at first, automatism gradually becomes real in the story, an essence rather than just a description, a type of being. Certain aspects of representation (the fact that all the characters in the story are products of language and imagery) are exaggerated and treated self-consciously in the gothic mode, as metaphors become realities, objects come to life, and people embody and materialize the meanings of words.[4]

In addition to showcasing the functions of language and perception in the story, the trope of automatism affects codes of performance, propriety, and social interaction. Olympia's maker, Spalanzini, violates performance boundaries by allowing the automaton to move freely among the townspeople instead of performing specifically for them as a musical automaton would.[5] After the revelation of Olympia's true nature, the town is not shocked that such a complex machine would exist but only that its inventor would violate public trust, since smuggling a wooden puppet into "respectable tea-circles" is "an altogether impermissible piece of deception" ("Sandman" 121). The story also critiques the mechanical tendencies of social life in its conflicting demands for conformism and individuality, repression and expression. Clearly the reason the real automaton would be undetectable for so long is that the women of this world, perhaps the men as well, are partly expected or allowed to be content-less, so stylized in their behavior they would be indistinguishable from mechanical dolls. Hoffman here utilizes an association of mechanicity with social conformism that was already vernacular by the mid-eighteenth century and continues into the present. In one example, a letter to Horace Walpole written in 1766, Mme du Deffand describes her houseguests of the previous evening as "men and women who seemed to me as machines made of springs, who came and went, talked, laughed, without thinking, without reflecting, without sensing, each one playing his customary role."[6] While du Deffand's perspective may reflect the emerging challenges to aristocratic hegemonies, to convention, reason, and order, and the shift toward gothic literary modalities and Romantic epistemologies of expression and emotion of the late eighteenth century, Hoffman's critique indicts both conventional social expectations and Nathaniel's overwrought narcissistic expressiveness.

In the nineteenth and early twentieth centuries, gothic literary and representational experiments use imitations of the human form, from reanimated corpses to ghostly apparitions, doppelgängers, lively objects, and unruly statues, in stories that challenge notions of objective reality and instead prioritize subjective, unstable, illogical, or psychologically complex points of view. Mistaking people for objects, mistaking objects for people, dividing the self into multiple combating selves, these are symptoms of a point of view that distrusts the existence of both exterior and interior realities, both the world and the self.[7] The underlying principle for such reactions is a sense of eroding boundaries that no longer uphold a steady distinction between persons and objects, self and other, expression and repression. While destabilizing the modern focus on reason and rationality, these treatments also express the self's unseen dimensions, and this is partly why Freud discusses Hoffman's depictions of the double and the uncanny as useful sites for psychoanalytic theories of the self.[8]

In expressionist works such as Gustav Meyrink's novel *The Golem* (published in serial form in 1913–1914), the idea of an artificial being accentuates the story's expressionist technique by infusing a text focused on radical experiential uncertainty with the mystical air of the medieval streets of Prague and the occult aura of the Golem's mythological origins.[9] In the many doubles and uncertainties of the novel, the issue is not the artificiality of the Golem's origin but the effect of uncertainty on the ostensibly modern characters. Encounters between a character and his or her own likeness often have psychological implications, exaggerating and externalizing intimate desires and imparting the sense that the self is not a cohesive unit of reason and passion but a split personality of sorts, in which the reasonable, upstanding citizen comes to face his or her unreasonable, murderous, selfish, narcissistic, unbridled, destructive, or sociopathic self. In modalities that predate and sometimes anticipate a psychoanalytic understanding of the concept of the unconscious, or perhaps of the distinction between ego and id, gothic experiments stage problems of separation and fusion. Two seemingly similar versions of a character may be two separate beings, at odds and at war with each other, but they may also be disparate desire-related aspects of one self. The modern psychological conceptualization of the self entails a certain crisis both in the recognition and in the disavowal of the fundamental incoherence of selfhood.

These early-twentieth-century narrative tendencies are exacerbated in the post–World War II landscape when writers use artificiality as a trope for the depiction of Cold War enemies but also suddenly paranoid neighbors. At their best, such stories destabilize more than the basic conditions of civic trust and ideological compliance and reach for more personal forms of betrayal and instability. Clifford Simak in "Good Night Mr. James" (1951), for example, presents a world in which the cloned duplicate of Mr. James, created to be identical to him in order to fulfill a mission that would endanger the real man, kills him and takes his place.[10] The reversals of the story challenge identity, knowledge, memory, and self-consciousness, with the final revelation, that clones are designed to self-destruct, turning the tables on a character whose humanity and desire for life the text has implicitly validated. Similarly, Alfred Bester's "Fondly Fahrenheit" (1954) offers a bond so close between an android and its owner that the one's schizophrenia affects the other's murderous actions.[11]

The robots are no longer simply "out there," and while the stories may begin from the premise of imitation as a sign of clear and direct danger, they proceed to investigate issues of subjectivity, memory, friendship, social connections, and political concerns. And as with the deeper critique of social conformism in "The Sandman," the fear that we may be surrounded by human-looking robots pales in comparison to the fear that we may be replaced by robotic imitations or, even worse, that we are already robotic. While these paranoid stories revolve around Cold War enemies and their ideological infiltrations, the overt political question of how to tell who one's enemies are also carries a series of implicit existential questions, of how to tell anything about anyone, how to judge ethics, politics, action, and identity after the devastation of the war, the atrocities of the Holocaust, and the constant threat of nuclear annihilation. These political and cultural coordinates elucidate the existential elaborations of the discourse of the artificial person in the post–World War II era and identify some of its central tendencies: challenging but also redrawing the boundaries between human and nonhuman and warning against ideological compliance and political acquiescence.

We see the difference between these treatments of paranoia in two stories by Philip K. Dick, whose work returns to these questions throughout his career. "Second Variety" (1953) depicts an array of lethal military robots, known as "claws," designed to look like human survivors and evoke pity and sympathy so that they can infiltrate human groups and destroy them.[12] In the story's portrayal of the ideology of destruction, an endless war is visited by one generation onto another, generations of people but also here of machines. The "David" models, for example, look like emaciated children holding a heartbreaking teddy bear, which is also a claw, while the "Wounded Soldier" models look like suffering human comrades. Targeting all live beings indiscriminately, the claws make no political distinctions in this total war, and any glimmer of hope that the human combatants will bond against their common mechanical enemy is lost when soldiers get so paranoid they kill anyone even suspected of being a claw. As the main character, Major Hendricks, discovers, unless the people one meets look like one of the known android models (and not all five models are known at first), it is impossible to be certain about who is human anymore, because human-likeness functions as a form of camouflage, a tactical advantage for the murderous claws. While the need to distinguish human from nonhuman is urgent, confirming someone's true status is only possible post mortem, when the destroyed body either consists of blood and guts or machine parts and wires. Betrayed by every human-looking being he meets, Hendricks consoles himself with the knowledge that, in the escalating violence, the claws are beginning to fight not against humans but against each other.

The representation of human-looking artificial people in "Second Variety" resonates with a similar treatment of imitation in the reimagined *Battlestar Galactica*. Like the claws, the humanoid Cylons also belong to numbered series and struggle to attain individuality beyond the limits of their model type. An artificial person's physical similarity to the human form plays a double role in such depictions, presenting both the problem and the solution: while the claws and Cylons look like people, they also look like others of their series. Despite their complex representational strategies, the texts thus manage to retain the discursive emphasis on human physical authenticity by offering visual means for distinguishing between human and nonhuman, aligning the human with physical uniqueness and the nonhuman with seriality, similarity, and proliferation. Retaining visual or at least intuitive and definitive distinctions between human and nonhuman remains a major commitment of the discourse of the artificial person, even in contexts that present perfect imitations and paranoid plotlines.

In contrast, Dick's later story "The Electric Ant" (1969) translates this paranoid perspective into an investigation of the nature of reality.[13] The main character, Mr. Poole, loses his hand in a car accident and in the hospital discovers that he is artificial, an "organic robo" or "electric ant" (497), presumably short for "electric anthropoid." He opens his chest plate to find a mechanism using punched programming tape, "no larger than two spools of thread," that slowly feeds subjective and sensory data to his consciousness (501). Depressed by the news that he is not a real human being but also entranced by the fact that he may now be able to control his perceptions, Poole experiments with the spool mechanism, a coil of punched paper that contains a digitized version of the world and a tiny scanner that translates holes and blank spaces into objects, people, textures, smells, and feelings. A flock of ducks appears in his living room. He experiences all his senses at once. Time stops and starts again. He has epiphanies about the interconnectedness of everything. He cuts the tape in an effort to be everywhere and nowhere, to know everything completely. And then he realizes that he is about to die, too late to restore the mechanism to its original state. "I am living, I have lived, I will never live," he mutters, "and with his thoughts came every word, every sound." Words glow in a brilliant mass and scorch his mind "with their utter meaning" (513). And smoke comes out of his mouth as his android body slumps lifeless to the floor.

As with many artificial characters before and since, Poole has a unique opportunity to consider the very nature of consciousness, since questions about the function of the senses and the mind are allegorized into the mechanical vocabulary of programming, scanning, and projection. Yet despite this sudden ability to quantify and reprogram the world, the structure of reality in the story remains as mysterious as ever. After Poole dies, the human assistant who witnesses his final experiments begins to feel vague, unreal to herself, as her hands, the apartment, and Pool's dead body become increasingly transparent. It is as if Poole's spools were creating her reality too, as if she was nothing but a part of the program, a sensory prompt necessary to motivate his reactions. The story of Mr. Poole functions as an extreme science-fictional literalization of Cartesian paradoxes, as if the phrase "I think therefore I am" is to be put through a sequence of campy variations, from "I only think I am" (Poole's worry when he finds out he is artificial), to "my senses are deceiving me into thinking I exist" (in reference to the tape that creates Poole's world), or "when I don't think I cease to exist" (explaining Poole's death after the programming tape is cut), and "I think therefore you are" (related to the disappearance of the assistant after Poole's death).

Despite their technological treatment in the story, such propositions align with philosophical concerns that are constitutive of modernity. Indeed Descartes's philosophical investigations include expressions of doubt that are as extreme as Mr. Poole's high-tech experiments with perception and projection. In his *Meditations*, for example, Descartes begins by using similar body- and sense-negating terms: "I will consider myself as having no hands, eyes, flesh, blood, or senses, but as believing wrongly that I have all these things."[14] To avoid the deceptive power of perception, Descartes tries to dissociate his thinking from sensory experience of the outside world and of the self-as-body.[15] Along with this theoretical body that has no sense perceptions but thinks it does and a series of hydraulic and clockwork bodies he uses in different texts to resolve a range of philosophical questions, in Descartes's writings we encounter a porous body, with particles of different sizes flowing selectively through the pores as if through a series of sieves, and a body that is nothing more than a coatrack.[16] In the Second Meditation, he describes looking out the window and seeing what he takes to be people: "and yet, what do I see from this window, other than hats and cloaks, which can cover ghosts or dummies who move only by means of springs?" he asks.[17] If appearances can be this deceptive, then the existence of other people, of authentic bodies and real minds, is dubious.

We can trace some of the modern philosophical styles of defining the human and distinguishing between human and nonhuman to this epistemological, existential, and ontological doubt.[18] By focusing on the difficulties of discernment and by taking neither the existence nor the constitution of bodies and minds for granted, Descartes separates essences from appearances, a gesture that participates in the development of modern epistemologies that prioritize rationalization. For Descartes, reason, consciousness, and judgment allow the thinker to distinguish people from coatracks and to realize the constitutive function of thinking for identity. Doubt contributes to this process: only a thinking entity can think so intensely as to doubt its own existence; indeed, this self-affirming function of pure thinking is the only process immune to sensory deception. When I doubt my perceptions and assumptions, the functions of my mind prove to me my existence not as matter in the world (*res extensa*) but as matter that thinks (*res cogitans*).[19] But for everything external to the mind these rational processes do not produce certainty. When used to define the humanity of others, for example, Cartesian doubt and distrust of appearances render others unknowable, and result in a pervasive sense of suspicion. Indeed, because the presence and status of others is a matter of judgment, real and artificial people emerge concurrently in Descartes's approach, with the discerning mind acting as an arbiter of ontological and existential categories. Paranoid trends in the discourse of the artificial person and in popular culture in general—in which what look like people turn out to be robots, automata, or aliens—share this modern focus on philosophical and epistemological doubt.

As the trope of the artificial person is codified in popular writings of the eighteenth, nineteenth, and twentieth centuries, a curious reversal occurs. The reasoning soul, Descartes's supreme entity, ceases to be decisive, the only antidote to the senses and their potential for deception. If for Descartes animals and automata differ from people because they have instinctual reactions and clockwork performance but no reason, by the early twentieth century artificial people differ from real people because all they have is reason, as if they are designed to be exaggerated versions of "matter that thinks." While artificial people are repeatedly castigated for having no soul, this version of "soul" is very different from Descartes's reasoning capacity, closer to the body and its urges and impulses and focused on expressive qualities such as unpredictability, passion, impulsiveness, and sexual desire. The stereotypical focus on coldness, rigid logic, and lack of emotion for the depiction of robots, androids, or various aliens, however humanlike they may otherwise be, thus offers a rather eloquent, if implicit, conceptualization of this problem: it both absorbs the modern emphasis on rationality and dispels it, reinstituting elements of vitality and irrationality as defining features of the human and allowing expression to categories of being that are premodern, vernacular, embodied, interpersonal, or common sense.

The ways in which the discourse of the artificial person absorbs questions of exteriority and interiority, of experience, presence, and the existence of other minds should alert us to some of its functions in modernity: it seems that stories of artificial people become a specialized cultural locus for expressing certain commonsense questions, challenges, or problems with modern dualism. Despite the narrative focus on the dissolution of identity, for example, Mr. Poole's story also presents artificiality as something that offers deep insight: since now he knows he is artificial, Poole may feel that his previous life as a real person was an illusion and that the truth has finally been unveiled. As a result of this allegorization of awakening, the state of knowing you are *not* real can have a surprisingly enlivening effect, as we see in Poole's experiments with the programming tape, and may result in radical experiences and a feeling of power. After all, it is not every day that we can control our reality or know our place in the world. "I am not free" Mr. Poole says to himself, "I never was, but now I know it; that makes it different" (499). Believing that one is human in this text is revealed to be a comfortable and perhaps conformist delusion, a way of taking the world for granted. Knowing that one is nonhuman produces knowledge and a heightened sense of consciousness. In this new state of awareness, Mr. Poole is more authentically himself, or *a self*, as an android than he was as a human. Precisely because modern definitions of "self" may include idealist notions about true knowledge and visionary dreams of seeing-through the ostensibly real and into a presumed more-real (the perverse logic of the Cartesian experiment), Mr. Poole's awareness of his unreality has a realizing effect.

The paradoxes of the story thus alert us to the complex usefulness of the trope of artificiality for defining the self. Through the course of the twentieth and twenty-first centuries, numerous texts and films present the interconnectedness of real and artificial people, in treatments that include paranoid scenarios in which characters suspect they are not human or suspect their neighbors and friends are not human; storylines about people reduced to an android life by conformity and routine; but also tales of discovering a more alive self in whatever form or ontological status, of falling in love with artificiality both as a means to escape emotion and to escape complacency, or of desiring a state of heightened experience, renewal, and reanimation, whether these follow from becoming more real or becoming more artificial. Being more real and being more artificial can be surprisingly close in some texts and films, metaphorical conduits for the desire to understand or experience the world in different ways.

As we see with Mr. Poole, this is not merely a matter of a familiar binary opposition between human and nonhuman, with both states presented as stable and static. On the contrary, the deeper insight of the story is that the two states can be used interchangeably, because it is their structural position in a before/after rubric that creates the effect of a humanizing self-awareness. The structure "I thought I was A, but now I know I am B" delivers a sense of enhanced human consciousness regardless of the ontological makeup of A and B. The structural position of the two entities in the narrative determines their meaning, with the second state (the "after" state) occupying the position of more awareness, more intellectual aliveness, and more knowledge. In addition to the many cultural, historical, and philosophical contexts of the modern era that inspire narratives of self-recognition and misrecognition, it is the desire for such heightened states of awareness that informs the explosion of existential investigations into the human through recourse to the nonhuman.

This in a sense is the insight, and the lasting existential question, of *Blade Runner* (Ridley Scott, 1982), a film that begins from the paranoid point of view and then exchanges this viewpoint for something much more confusing and troublesome. In keeping with his conceptual focus on the questions and fictions of the postwar era, Philip K. Dick's novel *Do Androids Dream of Electric Sheep?* (1968) centers on problems of perception and distinction. The androids of the novel look human; they can be successful in human professions, live as humans at least for a while, and have human sexual experiences.[20] But these androids differ significantly from the real humans of this world: they are unfeeling and lack empathy for humans, for each other, and for living things in general. As with the representation of androids in the science fiction tradition, it is not intelligence or mere human-likeness but an emotional register, here revolving around empathy, that functions as the quintessential human quality of the novel. If the human/nonhuman distinction structures the action of the book, with the protagonist Deckard on a quest to find and kill a group of androids, the text's more philosophical side focuses on the severed link between humans and the now extinct animals that made the Earth a living whole. The disappearance of the animals in the novel affects human capacities for empathy, and indeed it may not be the human-likeness of androids but the erosion of human compassion and emotion that threatens to close the gap between people and androids. Ravaged by the sorrow of a broken world and the loneliness of isolated existence, the humans depend on "mood organs" in order to construct an everyday emotional land-scape and on mediated experiences of religious transcendence in order to feel a connection to others. Rare or nonexistent, real animals become talismans that signify the loss of the world.

While both novel and film absorb the paranoid concerns of postwar texts that indulge xenophobic or alienating impulses about the nonhuman (xenophobic if we imagine that others are nonhuman and autophobic or alienating because we may already be nonhuman ourselves), *Blade Runner* refuses to establish a stable distinction between the two states.[21] In contrast to texts that mark artifi-cial people as visibly other (as non-gendered or gender-neutral, a-sexual, or non-emotional), in *Blade Runner* the Replicants are represented through a consistent emphasis on their bodies, their physicality and presence, as well as their gender, sexuality, and emotional intensity, their individualizing quests for knowledge and emotional connection, and their desire for life. Resisting the ways in which distinctions between human and nonhuman are managed in other texts, the film complicates both modes for distinguishing between human and nonhuman: the conceptual, cognitive, and existential modes and the visual, bodily, and experi-ential modes. As the distinction between human and nonhuman evaporates in the film, a pervasive existential dimension comes to the fore, as the story moves from focusing on who is what to wondering about whether ontology matters. As Rachel (Sean Young) and Deckard (Harrison Ford) escape at the end of the film, they find a small origami unicorn at the doorway, left there by Graff (Edward James Olmos), another Blade Runner. Graff's gesture may imply, in the 1982 ver-sion of the film, that he knows Rachel is a Replicant and is willing to let her go; or, in the usual interpretation of the 1992 "Director's Cut" version, he may be suggesting that Deckard is also a Replicant, because Deckard has had a unicorn dream that Graff could not have known about unless the dream were implanted; or, in a more recent approach, Graff may be implying that both he and Deckard are Replicants.[22] More extreme versions of these speculations would imply that there are no real humans in the film, that everyone is a Replicant.[23]

Much has been written about this film and its representation of human and Replicant identities, its problematization of gender and racial categories, its depiction of the commodified city landscapes of late capitalism, its association to postmodern subjectivity, its conflation of time and space.[24] The final moments of the film can be read as an exacerbation of the paranoid modality, but in my view they can also be read as a radical redirection. Once the distinction between humans and Replicants loses its fetishistic hold on the narrative, we might indeed decide not that all the characters are Replicants but that all of them are human. After a point it becomes clear that, despite their superior strength and stamina, there is really no special feature that separates the Replicants from the presumably real people of the film, no sufficient rationale for considering them inauthentic in their actions or emotions. The Replicants are as real as anyone in that world can be. The film's existential intensity thus stems from its radical identification of the problems inherent in modern epistemologies of the person. While insisting that it presents a different kind of entity in the Replicants, the film resists all the traditional gestures of distinction between real and artificial people. Identifying, persecuting, and killing Replicants suddenly feel like spurious acts of violence, unsupported by ontological or existential difference. Not only are the Replicants human-like in their reactions, they embody almost heroic forms of human subjectivity. Their representation expresses intense and constant existential interrogations—about the nature of being, the question of life and mortality, the craving for more experience, and in the end, the sense of empathic connection with other live beings. They have experienced the world through a sublime point of view that absorbs and accepts the sense of being both human and nonhuman. When Pris (Daryl Hannah) dies, she pounds and stomps the floor and shakes her whole body with such vehemence, such intensity, that her body language becomes allegorical, a resistance to death at the moment of death, a fitful anguished reaction to the necessities of mortality. This just does not feel anything like a machine malfunctioning or merely stopping when its usefulness is done.[25] Given their human-likeness, one wonders why, then, the Replicants would have to be persecuted and killed, and whether it might be possible to bypass or overcome the habit of policing a boundary—the difference between human and nonhuman—that seems antique, spurious, or even irrelevant.

PERFORMING HUMANITY

In philosophical terms, the discourse of the artificial person thus presents the uncanny proposition that the vocabulary of authenticity and selfhood proliferated by modern forms of identity is full of false assurances, false distinctions. Tracing the philosophical roots of the problem of whether we are able to tell if what we see are people or coatracks, robots, or alien impostors reveals that definitional ambiguities structure not just the discourse of the artificial person but modern definitions of the person in general. This in turn requires an adjustment to the ways in which we recognize the function of human-likeness in fictions of artificial people. Instead of imagining that the danger of human-likeness is the danger of the copy taking the place of the original (a dialectical and binary relationship), we should consider that the danger of human-likeness revolves around what the copy reveals: that there is no certainty in the original, that the definitional terms themselves are unstable and inconclusive.

Despite the continued cultural presence of plots related to imitation-as-threat, certain fictions of the artificial person in the twentieth and twenty-first centuries respond to problems of essence and appearance by attempting to revise the long-standing vocabulary of authenticity that characterizes Western culture. The issue for such texts is how to bypass, evade, reframe, or negate the fetishized distinction between human and nonhuman, especially when the distinction itself seems unreal, a mere convention or textual effect. Perhaps not surprisingly, texts that focus on imitation and paranoia—on the dangers that accompany acts of simulation or approximation of the human by the nonhuman—have nihilistic tendencies. By absorbing the problems of unstable modern epistemologies and their fantasies of authenticity, imitation devalues both subjective perception and the possibility of a reliable external reality. In contrast, when texts approach the problems of human-likeness without recourse to imitation-related plots, they reach for a different relationship between experience and selfhood, and between authenticity and artificiality. In science fiction literature and film we sometimes find the possibility that artificiality may be attractive, that it may offer the opportunity for new kinds of experience, or that it can be helpful in designing alternative modes of being. At the very least, seeing the world anew through an artificial, alienated, or nonhuman perspective affirms the power of self-consciousness, allowing characters to notice or meditate on what experience is or means. When texts move away from well-known choreographies of imitation and threat, they engage the possibility that, while one may not be able to tell what is what any more, this new ambiguity may be instructive, inevitable, or enlivening. It's as if these texts consider the problem of being unable to distinguish between real and artificial people and respond with both utopian and dystopian versions of "Nobody's perfect!"[26]

One can fall in love with artificiality, for example, not because it replaces a flawed or inadequate humanity but because it contains forms of being not found anywhere else. This is the case with Lester Del Rey's classic story "Helen O'Loy" (1938), in which two scientists, Dave and Phil, design an artificial woman and promptly fall in love with her.[27] The story shares the main characteristics of many "Pygmalion" tales and their fantasies of artificial femininity: Helen is beautiful, "a dream in spun plastics and metals" (17), but also girly, demure, sensitive, an idealized version of the girl-next-door of the era.[28] After watching and reading romantic texts, Helen falls in love with Dave and begs to become his wife, promising that she would be an ideal companion even if they cannot have children. While the story is evasive about sexuality, this reference to children implies a sexual marriage, not a platonic one, and after Dave resolves his inhibitions, they get married. "No woman ever made a lovelier bride or a sweeter wife," Phil reports (27). Dave and Helen remain happily married for his whole life, and when he dies Helen commits suicide so they can be buried together. Her secret is never revealed. Partly because of the unusual romantic tone of the story, "Helen O'Loy" also presents an early version of a performative approach to humanity, in which Helen's actions, her recognition of the encoded nature of femininity, and her adherence to normative gender roles ensure her ability to pass as a woman. Accepting Helen's femininity allows Dave to accept his own feelings about sexuality and romance, and once he can admit that he loves her, Helen's artificiality does not matter. Helen's performance of gender thus domesticates emotion and sexual attraction and defines the meanings of femininity and masculinity, both stereotypically delineated in the story.[29] Dave at some point forgets that Helen is not human and does not recognize that, aided by Phil, she changes her makeup and face composition over time so that she can appear to grow older with him.

A similar focus on performativity characterizes C. L. Moore's "No Woman Born" (1944). The work of one of the most prolific female writers of the 1930s and 1940s, the story is unusual in its utopian acceptance of mechanicity in relation to the human body, and especially the female body.[30] In the story of Deirdre, a famous actress who has been horribly burnt in a theater fire, Moore presents a self-conscious response to the figure of the artificial woman and its participation in male fantasies of femininity.[31] Deirdre decides to transfer her brain to a metal body, part robot and part metal sculpture, and while inhabiting this body she manages to perform in public, projecting an aura of femininity through her voice, body language, and sheer force of presence. In contrast to Hoffman's Olympia and the many Galateas of modern fiction (beautiful on the outside but empty on the inside), Deirdre embodies a radical reversal: instead of looking like a woman but acting like a robot, Deirdre moves, talks, and acts like a real woman while looking like an abstract Brancusi sculpture. As if in demonstration of Judith Butler's definition of performativity, in which "gender is always a doing [that constitutes] the identity it is purported to be," Moore uses the artificial female body self-consciously in order to showcase femininity as performance.[32] Although she looks like a "creature in armor, with her delicately plated limbs and her featureless head like a helmet with a visor of glass" (26–27), when she is dancing on stage for an audience, Deirdre is a sexy, confident, self-assured actress with a supple dancer's body, a husky voice, and an unmistakably human laugh.

By turning her featureless, genderless metal body into her old self, Deirdre manipulates the encoded nature of both femininity and the performance of sex appeal.[33] She explains that it is not human likeness but human-like motion that facilitates recognition (30) and explains the relationship between her brain and her body as a matter of technological mastery. She mentions the affinity that men have for their machines, calling their ships and airplanes "she," as if to suggest that she is also a man with a similar love for her new body machinery, which is female the way that airplanes are metaphorically female for their operators (32). She describes studying motion professionally as a performer, practicing and modulating all the motions and behaviors of both her original human body and her new metal body, and then shows off her amazing new abilities, strength, speed, and indestructibility.[34] And nowhere does she imply that a woman would just know how to behave as a woman. On the contrary, Deirdre insists that all being is a form of performance and that both humanity and femininity may be an effect of the surface or a matter of research and practice.

It is especially important to note that for human-looking artificial people, the discursive emphasis on studying how to be human is often connected to gender identity: in order to become human, both Helen and Deirdre must first become passable women.[35] Treated as a "skin effect," gender thus emerges as the locus for existential investigations throughout the postwar era, for both male and female characters. Feminist science fiction takes on this sense that artificial bodies may enable feminist interrogations of gender roles and stereotypes after the 1960s, in stories such as Anne McCaffrey's "The Ship Who Sang" (1961), James Tiptree Jr./Alice Sheldon's "The Girl Who Was Plugged In" (1973), and Joanna Russ's novel The Female Man (1975), to name a few.[36] In their treatments, the fantasies of animation and of the artificial body become sites for imagining new forms of emancipation. Later feminist experiments in science fiction and cyberpunk continue the investigation of embodied technologies, engaging both a traditional vocabulary of supremacy and power associated with masculinist approaches to mechanical presence and a feminist vocabulary of self-construction, alternative technologies, performativity, and gender bending.[37] The artificial woman of some of these texts is not imagined as a perfect wife but more in the tradition of Moore's Deirdre, as a dangerous, vamp-like figure whose power is externalized in her indestructible body.

If texts that feature artificial women carry echoes of Pygmalion and Galatea and investigate the objectification of the female body, texts that feature artificial men engage similarly stereotypical tendencies and focus on handling the pull of instrumentality, the attraction of treating the body as a tool, and the presence and absence of embodied emotion. Cordwainer Smith's evocative and haunting story "Scanners Live in Vain" (1950), for example, begins from a premise of absolute dualism as experienced by a class of humans whose bodies have been altered in order to facilitate space travel.[38] Both the "habermans" (the lower class spacemen) and the "scanners" (their elite commanding officers) have undergone a horrific process by which their brains are disconnected from all senses and nerve endings in order to counteract the intense pain of space travel. Instead of using their body's autonomic control system, they have been outfitted with "scanner" boxes—mechanical devices that control their heart rate, breathing, hormones, and mood from the outside, through conscious and continuous self-monitoring processes. Since they are able to control the panic of their bodies, the scanners and their intensely loyal Confraternity also control all space travel. But they are also inhuman, unable to feel anything at all, and can only have the illusion of direct sensation when they are "cranched," a process that uses a special wire that restores (or simulates) sensation, tactile experience, emotion, smell, and desire, if only temporarily. As our main character, Martel, describes it, except for those two cranched days a month, a scanner is "a machine. A man who has been killed and kept alive for duty" (76). The story indeed registers the scanners' mental and emotional state as a form of severe depression, common in later stories of artificial people as well, in which minds are disconnected from bodies, other people's emotions are seen as through a distant fog, and there is nothing to feel except a sense of deep isolation. When the Confraternity decide to kill a human inventor who finds a way to counteract the "great pain of space," Martel rushes to defend him, kills another scanner in an unprecedented act of disloyalty, and then becomes one of the first scanners to have human sensation restored in his body through the new technology.

"Scanners Live in Vain" is one of the first stories to feature an actual, voluntary, professional, human cyborg, in the technical sense of a term that cybernetic research codified somewhat differently ten years later.[39] Martel is proud to have sacrificed his emotional and sensory life to the service of humanity, a predecessor of later cybernetic characters such as astronaut Roger Torraway in Frederick Pohl's *Man Plus* (1976), whose partly mechanical body is adapted to life on Mars, and scientist Charles Newmann in Max Barry's *Machine Man* (2011), who replaces himself bit by bit in a quest for a more efficient mechanical embodiment. Martel differs from these later volunteer cyborgs because he also wants to feel, to love and be loved, to have sensation, to taste things. If "No Woman Born" presents an optimistic and post-ontological answer to problems of sensation and being, with Deirdre able to perform a new kind of aliveness without noticing how much of human experience and sensation would be unavailable in her machine-body existence, "Scanners Live in Vain" restores the primacy of the organic and the presumably unmediated over the mechanical. The exaggerated dualism of the scanners' existence, in which the mind controls the body overtly through external machinery, is replaced by a new fusion, in which the body is returned to a natural state and communicates implicitly and internally with both the mind and the world. Martel's final transformation reconciles the man to his own body, naturalizing sensation, emotion, and pain after his technologically mediated detachment. The story also posits an existential and performative approach to defining the human, focusing on modes of becoming that may traverse human and nonhuman experience. Indeed, the fact that the nonhuman may have a valid, understandable, and articulated experience of the world is what distinguishes these stories so radically from their imitation-based counterparts. In luminous descriptions of Deirdre's glowing, flowing performances and of Martel's exalted sensations of smelling a recorded scent, remembering a traumatic moment, and flying when he can actually feel it, both stories create complex portrayals of artificiality as what facilitates a heightening or reaffirmation of sensation.

In this strand of texts, the relationship between humanity and nonhumanity does not merely present a binary rubric of opposition (what is human is clearly not nonhuman) but, instead, seems to involve a complex interaction between definition and negation. Not only is the notion of the nonhuman used to define the human but such a definitional process also depends on the continued relevance and presence of the nonhuman as a limit or category. What also becomes more prominent in fiction and film in the later part of the twentieth century is the way in which the artificial person in a story alerts us to the artificiality that threatens or already characterizes the lives of the ostensibly non-artificial people.

The notion that artificiality may offer a form of awakening from an acquiescent, detached, or devalued humanity, for example, provides a valuable subtext for the desire for self-transformation that motivates the main character in *Seconds* (John Frankenheimer, 1966). Based on a novel by David Ely, the film begins when middle-aged businessman Arthur Hamilton (John Randolph) is suddenly able to experience a rebirth, alter his face and identity, and start a new life as Tony Wilson (Rock Hudson).[40] The mysterious organization that makes this possible also provides the fresh cadaver that will enact the death of his old identity, a new life in California replete with fun-loving people and eager young women, and access to the artistic profession he once aspired to, painting.

In this text, the trope of artificiality can be used to describe Hamilton's humdrum existence before his transformation, but it also provides the key terms for his escape. As with many science-fictional fantasies, the artificial body offers an alternative to the traumatic experience of aging—one in a series of fantasies

FIGURE 23 Hamilton (John Randolph) as the old man in the photograph, Wilson (Rock Hudson) as the young but not so new man in *Seconds* (John Frankenheimer, 1966). © Paramount Pictures

about replacement body parts, uploaded consciousness, and infinitely upgrade-able bodies. But the trope of artificiality is also used to channel the imagery of depression in this film, presented as a mental and emotional state in which life is experienced as consisting of little but repetition and routine and in which people are apathetic, numb, or mindless, veritable androids. The expressionist early sequences of *Seconds* also add social paranoia (in the scenes where Hamilton is followed by an unknown man who sneaks a piece of paper with an address into his hand) and an eloquent critique of the mundane nature of everyday life—in his ride on the commuter rail, the identical briefcases of the businessmen on the train, the crossword puzzle he starts solving, his wife impassively picking him up in the station wagon, their perfunctory kiss, her flat question, "Good day?" After Hamilton visits the Company's headquarters, all choices are dissolved, as he is blackmailed, cajoled, seduced, and trapped into agreeing to this deal. The Company stages the attractions of artificial renewal as if in real-ization of a new American Dream, in which a second life allows the "client" to take advantage of everything he or she may have missed the first time around, a consumerist fantasy of possibility and choice. Yet, Hamilton—now Wilson—cannot actually live in his new life, despite the fact that he looks like Rock Hudson and can take advantage of the boozy, artsy, sexually more adventurous sixties lifestyle he never had access to in the past. Despite the radical changes, he is still the same old man, worn out, depressed, nostalgic for his own youth. He is also doubly betrayed when the dream of renewal turns out to be a sham, as everyone in his new life is a similarly "transformed" man, and the group is violently intent on upholding the façade of enjoyment. One conformist, deadening life has been replaced by another.

Reviewers of the time differ in their understanding of what the film criticizes. Pauline Kael for example notes that the film aims to "condemn an ugly, empty life" and focuses on its critique of middle-class existence. Stephen Farber, on the other hand, proposes that what depersonalizes and dehumanizes Hamilton is the "insubstantial and vicious dream of a second chance," the "vague compul-sive dreaming" that makes him such a good target for this ruthless Company.[41] Hamilton is indeed vulnerable to authority figures, is compliant and susceptible to their rhetoric, and is treated as another mindless consumer whose generic sense of dissatisfaction requires the next great product, in this case an appropri-ate form of death. The executive who discusses the process with him, Mr. Ruby (Jeff Corey) insists, "the question of death selection may be the most important decision of your life," and proceeds to sell him on all the extra features. Although the film presents the possibility that one can become new just by performing a new identity, the fact that the radical transformation does not work attests to the resiliency of detachment and depression. In a sense, the film presents us with a double vision of roboticism and artificiality. In his old life, Hamilton was depressed, numb, and dispirited, a man whose life had become superficial or robotic. As Wilson he is an implicit android, trying to pass for human but still detached from direct experience and social connection and, again, going through a prefabricated set of motions and actions. When he alerts the Company that the experiment has failed and is called back to headquarters, he finds out too late that he will be sacrificed for a new sale, becoming the fresh cadaver used to facilitate someone else's adventure in second chances. As they wheel him away to the operating room, Wilson fights for life as never before, bound and gagged but fully aware and fully present, robotic no more.

Films that focus on the fantasy of replaying one's life in a new key are fundamentally about the effects and repercussions of choice, whether the stories revolve around narcissistic rehabilitation, as in *Groundhog Day* (Harold Ramis, 1993); the notion that fear and thrill may revitalize a mundane life, as in *The Game* (David Fincher, 1997); or curiosity about roads not taken, as in *Sliding Doors* (Peter Howitt, 1998) and *Family Man* (Brett Ratner, 2000). Despite its consumer choice focus, *Seconds* does not actually provide a choice. Hamilton is somewhat generic at the beginning of the film, an embodiment of the "quiet desperation" long associated with normative gender identity and men's existential and social suffering.[42] The novel makes much of Hamilton's homburg hat, a sign of success and conformism, and an implicit reference to the existential implications of business life (and attire), made vernacular in Sloan Wilson's blockbuster novel *The Man in the Gray Flannel Suit* (1955). If masculinity is associated with stoicism in the classic "a man's got to do" adage, Hamilton presents the possibility that one's life may have been a series of events that just befall instead of being chosen. This comes into contrast with the treatment of masculinity, stoicism, and choice in more conciliatory films, as in *It's a Wonderful Life* (Frank Capra, 1946), another text that begins with the impulse for suicide and continues by imagining an alternate universe. By creating a subtext of personal choice and historical circumstance, Capra shrewdly translates material conditions and historical inevitability into acts of self-sacrifice and self-affirmation for George Bailey (James Stewart), who emerges fortified by the melodramatic translation of necessity into will. In *Seconds* we have no such gratification, because the film does not allow Hamilton to express his depression in historical terms. In the dystopian version of performativity presented in the film, not only do historical events not inform choice and personhood but even the most perfect setup for a new identity cannot actually create that identity. While the postwar context may inform the understanding of choice and necessity for the audience, Hamilton is "other" to his time and to himself, a mechanical man both before and after his transformation.

A similar use of the concept of artificiality as a critique of normative gender identities and conformist middle-class expectations motivates *The Stepford*

Wives (Bryan Forbes, 1975), although the positions at first seem reversed, as the lively modern woman is replaced by a depressed, silent, and obedient housewife. By replacing real women with robotic look-alikes, the members of the Men's Association of Stepford treat identity, individuality, feminism, activity, and the struggle against conformism as dysfunctions that automatism might cure. As the main character, Joanna (Katharine Ross), tells her doctor, her robotic replacement will be "a woman with my name and my face, she'll cook and clean like crazy, but she won't take pictures and she won't be me!" She is shocked to see her vibrant, lively, inquisitive friends replaced by mindless, complicit, obedient, housework-loving robots, as if the perfect woman for patriarchy consists of a calm voice, a beautiful physique, a limited vocabulary, a lack of ambition, a tidy house, well-dressed children, and an endlessly flattered and obeyed husband. In the final confrontation of the film, the horrified Joanna gazes into the ominous android's dark inhuman eyes and then stares at the large breasts of her robotic replacement, a deviation from Joanna's own body type that is clearly visible under a transparent negligee, as if to accentuate how surprising, self-serving, and trivial the reasons for the substitution are in contrast to its costs. And the film ends with the Stepford wives, a robotic Joanna now included, strolling the aisles of a supermarket in flowing dresses, exchanging calm, emotionless greetings. We cannot help but mourn Joanna's creativity, her independence, her spirited demands for equality and mutuality with her husband, her angst.

FIGURE 24 The nightmare of robotic femininity in *The Stepford Wives* (Bryan Forbes, 1975). The cheerful acquiescence of the android wife, Marie (Toni Reid), and the orderly spectacle of color-coded, ironed, folded laundry contrast sharply with the crossed legs and anxious watching of the real women, Joanna (Katherine Ross) and Bobby (Paula Prentiss). © Columbia Pictures

Both Ira Levin's 1972 novel and the 1975 film figure roboticism as an allegory of acquiescence or obedience and use it to stage the conflict between feminist demands for social transformation and a retrogressive or nostalgic desire for the reinstatement of patriarchic values.[43] Designed to conform to the limited sexual and social imagination of the Stepford men, the robotic women of the film embody an exaggerated patriarchal antidote to the perceived threats of feminism. Indeed, when Joanna first arrives at Stepford she interprets the women's weird devotion to housework as a pre-feminist state of mind, one that persists in sidetracking the feminist group she creates into a discussion of cleaning products. In the dialectic the film sets out, traditional femininity is represented as a state of metaphorical roboticism; consciousness-raising holds the potential for awakening or animation into a fuller, more demanding, and more creative humanity; and the replacement of the real women of Stepford with their robotic counterparts becomes a new literalized roboticism, this one more perfect because it is also immune to the possibility of a new awakening. A cyclical conceptualization of objectification and subjectification applies here: women unaware of their position in patriarchy are likened to conformist automata, objects to be used for another's pleasure and comfort.[44] Awareness humanizes but also endangers these women, and their final transformation into actual robots literalizes the dehumanizing effects of oppression and acquiescence.

Yet, while she is conscious of her own desires and aspirations, Joanna is far from immune to the problems of a patriarchal society and workplace—and far from safe, even before the threat of roboticism materializes in the story. Although the film highlights the overt threat of violence as this is enacted by the men of Stepford, Joanna's efforts to be an artist, her encounters with gallery owners, and her efforts to find her own modes of self-expression provide insights into more subtle forms of oppression. As Jane Elliot points out, in its approach to Joanna's photography, the film transforms the "material necessity of paid labor for women" into a matter of "psychic fulfillment."[45] In this textual subtext, the film presents the classic feminist desire for a room and an ambition of one's own, exemplified in Joanna's photography and her time developing negatives in her makeshift darkroom. Translated from its science-fictional register to an allegorical register, the text offers the possibility that the mindless robotic Joanna is Joanna herself without her art, and this allows for a different interpretation of the line "she won't take pictures and she won't be me." The overt science-fictional premise of women being replaced by actual robots also contains the implicit worry that, despite their modern sensibility and feminist aspirations, women may still feel partly roboticized by their lives. The elusive existential debate of the film focuses on whether the real Joanna is also in danger of being unoriginal, absorbed by structures of housework and child rearing, more similar to the robotic women of Stepford than meets the eye. As with *Seconds*, in *The Stepford Wives* the idea that one may become a robot, or be replaced by one, exaggerates the ways in which everyday life itself tends toward roboticism, a notion that allows the narratives to present a sense of dissatisfaction with middle-class conformism but also with traditional gender roles and normative modes of masculinity and femininity. The deployment of artificiality in such stories articulates the human as gestural and contingent, a matter not of essence but of performance.

If in nineteenth-century texts the threat or experience of artificiality is associated with epistemological instability, delusion, and schizophrenic and paranoid points of view, the trope of artificiality in the twentieth and twenty-first centuries evokes psychological states related to depression, apathy, detachment, and melancholy. As we see in *Seconds*, sometimes it is the people and not the androids who are apathetic, and the threat of becoming an android may awaken the human characters from their android-like distance from emotion. In contrast, artificial people sometimes possess a heightened awareness of reality, a thoroughly individual and subjective point of view that is attuned to experience *as* experience. We see this perspective in the evocative and widely influential Japanese animated film *Ghost in the Shell* (Mamoru Oshii, 1995), which presents a female cyborg intelligence officer, Motoko Kusanagi, who knows she is artificial and has a complex relationship to that knowledge.[46] Kusanagi worries about being an individual, considers what counts as a memory and what experience means, focuses on exploring other modes of identity, seeks out hybrid and unstable forms of consciousness, and is not obsessed with whether she may be human. Although she is both beautiful and sexualized in the film, Kusanagi is a powerful agent, her "full replacement" cyborg body remaining sexy, agile, elegant, and lithe despite its incredible weight. In some of the most evocative scenes of the film, Kusanagi behaves as a proverbial flâneur, wandering through the city landscape in silence, her point of view lingering on mundane everyday scenes that are transformed into lyrical vignettes through her attention. The beauty and evanescence of the present moment, the profundity of an anonymous and vibrant cityscape, the reflections of shapes in store windows, all these urban impressions together register a personal and individual sense of perception. In a different film such a montage would function as a record of deep individuality, echoing standard visual registers of wistfulness, longing, deep feeling, a budding artistic point of view, loneliness, or perhaps rootlessness. In *Ghost in the Shell* it creates a melancholy interiority for this cyborg and her mysterious desires and invests the mundane with almost sublime importance.

In a similarly fascinating scene, we see Kusanagi diving in the deep ocean in a special scuba suit, finding a way to experience danger and thrill despite the fact that her body is indestructible. Made of metals and electronics, her body would presumably short or be damaged in contact with the water, and her weight alone makes this a dangerous sport, since she can easily sink to the bottom and be irretrievable. She seems to crave the feeling of sinking in the dark water, not of swimming or looking at fish, but just feeling the pull of gravity and then counteracting it with special jets that slowly bring her back up to the surface. Given the mode of her original construction, in vats of various liquids, these useless experiences of sinking and floating up are eloquent reenactments of a body memory, a memory of origin. Whether this is a felt memory or an attempt to create or reconstruct that kind of memory is not the issue—after all, people don't usually remember their birth. What matters is that Kusanagi is depicted as having a dense sense of, or desire for, embodied memory and experience.[47] The moody scenes of looking at the city landscape are primarily visual or mental, the ocean diving and sinking primarily bodily, yet in both forms of experience she seeks depth and a psychosomatic experience of the world. By producing a sense of individuation and deep sensibility, these scenes dispel questions of ontological status and present Kusanagi as a cyborg with its own authentic modes of being.

CYLONS AND CLONES: TALES OF
THE PROFESSIONAL NONHUMAN

This chapter began with an exploration of the distinction between human and nonhuman as it informs, first, a network of paranoid fantasies about imitation and authenticity and, second, a network of existential fantasies that deploy the trope of artificiality in order to present a performative approach to humanity. In both networks, we see the desire for defining the human, either by comparison to a visible and clearly demarcated nonhuman or as a form of experience, a mode of being, presence, and action in the world that attempts to define the human "as such," even sometimes by negation. While a paranoid approach to the distinction between human and nonhuman seeks to stabilize and reify a structural distinction that is not at all clear in modern philosophy, more performative texts focus on experience rather than essence. Such texts take on a basic tenet of modern existentialist thought, the sense that, in Sartre's phrasing, "existence precedes essence."[48] Instead of imagining that the definition of the human exists a priori, as an abstract formal account of what it means to be human that resides elsewhere, Sartre proposes that it cannot preexist, that the meaning of the human must be decided in the acts and processes of life itself. Focusing on becoming, existing, and experience, these philosophical trends have been reflected in narratives of artificial people that also start from existence and allow experience to inform being, rather than the other way around. Being human is not a "kind" of being in these texts, but a condition of being, a beginning, a set of possibilities. Paraphrasing Sartre, the human is its own project.[49]

To end this investigation on the limits and treatments of human-likeness, we must engage a third variant, more recent in its cultural emergence and still

unstable in its narrative parameters. In this strand of texts, artificial people succeed so well in resembling and approximating real people, that the two categories
are practically indistinguishable. As I discussed in relation to *Blade Runner*, this
dissolution of a boundary that the discourse of the artificial person was designed
to uphold or even fetishize undermines expectations of ontological and existential certainty. Yet these texts retain the need for a sense of distinction: the human
and the nonhuman do not collapse, the distinction does not simply evaporate
but is channeled into new questions and issues, especially ethical issues. These
texts seem to ask a truly post-human question: when no one can be demarcated
as nonhuman, can we still treat certain people as if they are not human? Unfortunately, the answer is yes. In the two texts that provide the focus in this section,
Kazuo Ishiguro's novel *Never Let Me Go* (2005) and the reimagined television
series *Battlestar Galactica* (2003–2009), certain characters are identified and
treated as nonhuman even when there are no distinguishing characteristics that
separate their ontological status from humanity.

While the trope of artificiality fuels numerous fetishistic interrogations, of
whether people are becoming machines, whether humans are actually Replicants, whether technologies are dehumanizing us, and so on, the treatment of
human-like nonhumans in these texts reveals a provocative and profound subtext
that the discourse of the artificial person has been designed to render invisible:
the robots, androids, clones, cyborgs, Replicants, Cylons, and other nonhumans
of these texts are exactly equivalent to people. They are people. It is as people
that they can be abused and mistreated. Only people can be treated as nonpeople. The algorithm is as chilling as it is profound, and it is not clear whether this
narrative treatment of human-likeness will persist as a textual tendency in other
texts. Instructive though it may be, the discourse of the artificial person may not
be able to sustain the radical realization that the distinction between human and
nonhuman is not a matter of essence and not even a matter of experience but a
matter of convenience, expediency, or violence.

Showcasing this question, both Ishiguro's *Never Let Me Go* and *Battlestar
Galactica* present us with categories of people that have been designed to be
and remain nonhuman. In *Battlestar Galactica* these are the Cylons, originally
designed as robotic workers and slaves, whose evolved humanoid forms now
look and feel so human that they can blend into human society, fall in love
with humans, and have hybrid human/Cylon babies.[50] *Never Let Me Go* focuses
on the story of Kathy H. and a group of students growing up at Hailsham, an
exclusive school. They are all clones, raised by a private organization, presumably on behalf of the government or at least with its knowledge, in order to
become organ donors when they reach adulthood. The novel is evasive about
how or why this social organization came about and does not follow the familiar
codes of science fiction literature and film: the clones' existence is not a secret

but a social fact, there are no baby-decanting vats, as in Aldous Huxley's *Brave New World*, no grand explanations of misguided utopian projects, no implicit or explicit markers that identify these children, no descriptions of the cloning process, no permits, id cards, or microchips, no special locations or prohibitions. Yet while nothing in the novel differentiates the students from the real people of that society, they are considered a different type or class of person and are treated in the instrumentalist ways familiar from the discourse of the artificial person. By thus evading the question of distinction, the novel aggravates a viewer's desire for distinction and explanation. As with *Blade Runner* and the tradition of texts that present performative humanity, we are inspired to wonder whether there are any artificial people in these texts at all, and if not, to ask why certain people are then treated as nonpeople.

In contrast to the elisions of *Never Let Me Go*, *Battlestar Galactica* deploys all the various modalities in which human-likeness has been used in gothic, science-fictional, and realist texts. The representation of the Cylons expands the robotic metaphor to create a much wider range of beings, each using a different science fiction precedent. The Cylons of the original *Battlestar Galactica* (1978–1979) are fondly remembered for their gleaming robotic presence and their iconic single red eye or sensor, with its left/right scanning motion and characteristic sound effects.[51] Created by a now extinct alien reptilian species, these relentlessly military beings engage the interplanetary human civilization of the Twelve Colonies in a brutal war that lasts a thousand years. In the reimagined universe of *Battlestar Galactica* the Cylons are instead a human invention. Designed to be robotic or cybernetic soldiers, workers, and slaves, they rebel and challenge the survival of the Twelve Colonies in the ruthless "Cylon Wars." After an armistice is eventually reached, the Cylons leave for a distant planet to create their own culture.

Viewers sensitive to the twenty-five years that separate the original *Battlestar Galactica* from the new series find their diegetic counterpart, as the series begins, in the human envoy we see waiting for a Cylon representative on a remote space station after forty years of Cylon absence. Indeed nothing can prepare the poor envoy for the appearance and behavior of the new Cylons: the heavy doors of the meeting room open ominously, and two Cylon Centurions enter, surprisingly sleek and ethereal in their computer generated metal-and-wiring exterior but still recognizably the descendants of the bulkier Cylon robots and displaying their red-pulsing-eye trademark. But they accompany a perfectly human-looking tall blonde woman in a tight-fitting red suit, later known as Number Six (Tricia Helfer), whose sex appeal far exceeds the usual narrative range of robotic constructs. She is one of twelve new human-like Cylon models, each distinct in its body type, demeanor, and emotional tendencies, but each also part of an infinite series, possessing the capacity to be reborn in a new body with their individual and shared memories intact. Number Six is a particularly interesting case. Her taunts of the human envoy—whom she quickly intimidates and kisses aggressively before they are both killed by the prearranged Cylon destruction of the space station—exemplify the actions the new human-looking Cylons are about to undertake in the rest of the series: they infiltrate human society, attack and destroy most of the Twelve Colonies, kill millions of people, relentlessly pursue the human survivors, manipulate and seduce various humans through intense emotional and sexual relationships, but also fall in love with humans, give birth to hybrid human/Cylon babies, die for and with humans, and develop increasingly mystical ideas about a common human/Cylon fate.

In terms of political resonance, the depiction of the Cylons is rather slippery for simple allegorical readings. Different versions of the rebelling slave narrative (discussed in the previous chapter) coexist in the series, with the Cylons appearing as vengeful and retaliatory at first, and as sensitive and rightfully demanding of acceptance in later episodes. While they are marked as terrorists and saboteurs in their initial attacks, the totalitarian regime they install on New Caprica in turn inspires the humans to become terrorists and saboteurs. In one of the series' most innovative treatments of the robotic tradition, the Cylons are presented not as a single species but as a range of entities with different configurations of embodiment, intelligence, roboticism, and individuality. In addition to the metallic and robotic Centurions and the humanoid Cylons of the numbered series, we have the Raiders, a species of partly sentient fighter spaceships that have some initiative but are usually depicted as attack weapons.[52] We also have the "hybrids," human-looking beings that function as embodied computers, interfacing with the central memory and organic controls of the Cylon "basestar" spaceships through special conduits.[53] Although one character refers to the Raiders as the equivalent of animals or pets, they are modeled on robots: they are under the control of the baseships and are often deployed as an insect-like mass, frightening in their infinite proliferation as well as their relentlessness. The Raiders are also the only Cylon beings whose biomechanical internal organs we see in the series: when Colonial Fleet officers examine a captured Raider, they find a fleshy, smelly, biological interior in the spaceship, which however remains so instrumental and compartmentalized that a human pilot can fly the Raider by grabbing and pulling gooey muscle-like surfaces.[54] The metal-outside-flesh-inside depiction of the Raiders strengthens the sense of paranoia that characterizes the first seasons of the series, by presenting yet another version of "things are not what they seem."

The visual vocabulary of machinery merged with flesh resonates with other cinematic representations of hybridity, from the biomechanical horrors of *Alien* (Ridley Scott, 1979) to the cult film *Tetsuo: The Iron Man* (Shin'ya Tsukamoto, 1989). It also channels contemporary concerns about biotechnology and exacerbates the biological interrogations of the series, especially for the humanoid

FIGURE 25 The main cast of *Battlestar Galactica*. There are four Cylons in this picture. Can we tell who they are? Sky/Sci Fi Channel/Photofest. © Sky/Sci-Fi Channel. Photographer: Frank Ockenfels

Cylons.[55] Similarly, the bodies of the hybrids feature piping that can be imagined as belonging to a mammalian body, especially umbilical cords and the trachea and bronchi that bring air from the mouth to the lungs, but also to machinery, to computer cables or the flexible pipes of a dryer vent or air conditioning unit. As with most depictions of artificial bodies, such visual or conceptual affinity triggers complex analogical responses for the audience, as we recognize the intrinsic visual or functional similarity between organic and mechanical parts. Although the hybrids are depicted as human-like, with their naked bodies floating in tanks of an undisclosed liquid that presumably sustains them, they don't register any biological needs, and their state of suspension belies the tendencies of animate beings to grow or decline, to feel hunger or require sleep. In addition to managing an archive of Cylon and human cultural memory, the hybrids control the basestars by using a language as hybrid as they are, consisting of torrents of meaningless phrases intermingled with direct commands and reports of mechanical function, that is interpreted by some Cylons and humans as potentially prophetic or mystical, a supernatural mode of accessing the past and the future.

By thus including and compartmentalizing the many types of embodiment involved in the depiction of artificial people, *Battlestar Galactica* manages both to respect this tradition and to revise it completely. In contrast to the science-fictional narrative patterns in which acquiring flesh and blood may bring an artificial entity finally into human status, the embodiment of the new Cylon species remains contested for most of the series and either exacerbates their difference from the human or simply fails to enact a transformational gesture, to mark them as fulfilling the bodily parameters for animate or human status. Their bodies are perfectly human-like, but this might not matter somehow. Except for one early and unique provocative moment, in which the spine of Number Six lights up during sex, we never see the interior or material composition of the humanoid Cylons. They seem susceptible to certain human viruses, and they manage to conceive and bring to term a human/Cylon baby, so we have to assume that some of their physiology is human-like or at least maximally compatible.

In the context of the textual tradition traced here, the representation of the human-looking Cylons follows the trends of the existential strand of science fiction stories and films as this has evolved since the 1980s, in which an almost perfect bodily approximation of the human form is combined with an existential quest for human status to create artificial characters whose difference from the human becomes difficult to uphold—in the original tag line of the series, the Cylons "Look and Feel Human. Some Even Think They *Are* Human." As with Rachel in *Blade Runner*, Sharon "Boomer" Valerii (Grace Park) does not know that she is a Cylon, a version of the Number Eight series, and she only finds out when a form of programming kicks in causing her to sabotage the Fleet and attempt the murder of Commander Adama (Edward James Olmos). While passing for human is first associated with deception and infiltration and serves fundamentally military goals, the Cylons' proximity to the human eventually develops into storylines about sexuality and desire, identity, procreation, politics, and religion.

Because of the human-likeness of the Cylons, their perfect visual, behavioral, even biological approximation of the human form, and their potential role as invisible or unconscious enemies lurking within human society, the series oscillates between the two main dimensions of the paranoid plotline: that the Cylons are almost human, and that all humans are potentially Cylons. Given the fact that we do not know what all twelve Cylon models look like, even people who think of themselves as real humans could at some point be revealed to have been Cylons all along. Most important for this discussion, the fact that some of the Cylon characters begin as human characters and are only identified retroactively results in depictions that seem to violate or evade the general tendencies of the discourse of the artificial person. There is a difference, in other words, between characters who are known to be Cylons almost from the beginning of the series and the "Final Five" Cylons who are revealed at the end of the third season. Their memories and identities are completely human, and they live with and as humans for most of their lives in the Colonies until a shared experience, hearing the same piece of music, reveals their Cylon nature to them.[56] Some of their history, that they were members of a "Thirteenth Tribe" of humanoid Cylons that lived on Earth thousands of years ago, is indeed not revealed until the show's finale.[57] Because their status is unknown to themselves, to everyone around them, even to the writers of the show and the actors who portray them, the "Final Five" Cylons show remarkable range, and as a result it is hard to incorporate them in the discourse of the artificial person. These characters age, they become tired and moody, suffer from addictions and emotional obsessions, harbor complex ambitions, show unconscious motivations, possess a deep sense of history, loyalty, and friendship but also have unprecedented abilities for violence, duplicity, and cruelty. In fact, this group includes alcoholic artificial people as well as some of the few artificial men in the discourse with active sex lives. Perhaps not surprisingly, these are all effects of the literal human-ness of the Cylons, the fact that they are written, acted, and considered human until the end, even by the show's makers.[58]

The show is indeed invested in pushing the limits of representation for human-like artificial people and uses similar intensity in the depiction of the humanoid Cylons that belong in numbered series, whose range of action, motivation, and affect is just as surprising. While the human characters sometimes describe the Cylons with the derogatory term "toasters" or pepper the narrative with exclamations of "You are not human, you are a machine!" these figures are not really different enough from humans, and this representational choice fuels much of the existential tone and diegetic intensity of the series. Cylon characters seduce and manipulate humans, destroy the human colonies but also save fleeing humans, fight with humans against other Cylons, murder both humans and Cylons, serve honorably in the military, are tortured as traitors, become terrorists, fall in love with both humans and Cylons, give birth to human-Cylon babies, invent new religions, are elected to office, endanger and then save the lives of human refugees, commit suicide, and so on. Not only are these kinds of actions embodied and intense, focusing on sexuality, desire, bodily suffering, and extreme emotional states, they are also morally and ethically ambiguous and seem to have both conscious and unconscious motivations. Older depictions of artificial people implicitly fuel a fantasy of impenetrability, showcasing an ability to compartmentalize or remain immune to human suffering. The focus on the sexual identities, embodied experiences, and morally ambiguous actions of the new Cylons, instead, bring them closer to human vulnerability. And it is against this context of perfectly human bodies, lives, and experiences that the debate of integrating the human and Cylon civilizations is staged. As with other existential texts in the discourse, the show depicts intensive efforts at keeping distinct two types of being that do not exhibit that many important differences.

If in the visual representation of the classic robot we find the psychic reassurance that robots are clearly distinguishable from people, and in existential cyborg narratives the feeling that by becoming so human-like artificial people alter the very definition of human status, in *Battlestar Galactica* the Cylons' approximation of the human form is given contradictory roles that pivot on visual representational strategies. The iconicity of the robot's body, with its heavy metal exterior and awkward motions, and its lack of cultural understanding are replaced here by sexy and culturally savvy Cylon models that have moved beyond the standard goal of just resembling humans. They have indeed used humans and altered human history by manipulating human politics and traditions for their own (mysterious) purposes.

But iconicity is still at play, transposed from a fascination with a metal exterior to a fascination with specific kinds of bodies, mostly female. Except for the "Final Five," whose body replications and histories do not become part of the show, each Cylon model exists as a series of identical individuals who can partly replace each other. When a particular Cylon dies, their memories are uploaded or sent to the databank of their model series, and into a new body of the same make. Although the new Cylons include both male and female models, it is the Cylon women who have dominated the show, with Number Six featured prominently as a case study of predatory and manipulative sexualized femininity, and Number Eight depicted in a more romantic and maternal role, with versions living different lives in partnerships with different men (known to fans as Sharon "Boomer" Valerii and as Sharon "Athena" Agathon). While pursuing separate immediate goals, both Number Six and Number Eight are defined by their emotional and sexual (both heterosexual and homosexual) relation-ships to humans. It is the complications of such relationships that differentiate these individuals from the other members of their series, as their attachments to human life affect their commitment to Cylon agendas.[59]

In addition to evoking current debates about cloning, stem-cell research, and the post-humanist aspiration of downloading human consciousness onto data-banks or networks so that one's memories and experiences can survive the death of the body, by inventing this serial individuality *Battlestar Galactica* also solves the problem of how to distinguish between humans and Cylons. Their seriality connects the Cylons both to organic means of multiplication and replication (as in cloning) and to the machine-age dreams of streamlined mechanical produc-tion and reproduction, of repairable bodies and replaceable parts, that fueled earlier robotic fantasies. The Cylons' ability to resurrect themselves, saving and sharing their memories and experiences with others of their model and the rest of the Cylon group, separates them from humans, for whom death is final and individual identity remains inimitable. The serial individuality of the Cylons is also fitting for a television series, providing a perfect way to combine the charac-ter consistency that "hooks" viewers with a versatility that allows the text to rein-vent itself through fresh and unexpected narrative strands. Different individual Cylons of a certain model can be depicted in more than one location, engaging in completely contradictory actions, and being both good and bad, or as in the case of the two Sharons, both dead and alive. Again, ambiguous and unpredict-able behaviors bring the Cylon characters closer to human status, while the fact that individuals can make very different decisions from others of their series counteracts the determinism that the emphasis on the replication of identical bodies would otherwise have given the Cylons. Despite their visual and genetic similarity to each other, not all Cylons of a series think or act alike, and it is the emphasis on the actions of each individual, their personal emotional and sex-ual attachments, and their specific moral and ethical stance toward the human/ Cylon situation that individuates them.[60]

We see the contrast between mass and individual in the representation of Cylon identity as well. The individuated Cylons struggle to retain their differ-ence from the undifferentiated, not-yet-deployed, or just ideologically compli-ant members of their series and often value their action-based identity more than their Cylon "programming." In contrast to the Borg's anthem "Resistance Is Futile," the Cylons fight for self-determination, as the text aligns individuality with resistance—the individuated Cylons we meet in the text actively resist their presumed allegiance to Cylon interests (whatever these may be), instead forging new alliances with humans against the Cylons.[61] Surprisingly, it is partly this indi-viduation that then demands the eternal return of a Cylon model. Individuated nonhumans cannot be as disposable as the masses of undifferentiated robotic

Cylons that may be destroyed in battle without lasting narrative impact. The redeployment of a certain Cylon model retains both their visual presence and the impact of their important actions and decisions—a form of writing the individual into history. By allowing the whole series of a Cylon model to acquire and retain the memories of a lost or dead Cylon individual, the text ensures that our sense of the narrative, as viewers, will be reconciled with the diegetic universe: far from becoming a useless digression or being delegated in the archives of an "alternate" universe, the actions and experiences of an important Cylon individual enter the main narrative thread and inform the rest of the story, for the characters as well as the viewers. Despite the spectacle of Cylon replication and repetition, the text thus reinforces those elements of identity, such as action and personal choice, that contribute to individuation. The text insists that a humanist version of personal and individual identity is possible, even when by design both the individual and the series look exactly alike, and even when they share the same memories.

But most important, and despite the text's emphasis on individuation and identity, the design of the Cylons as members of a visually identical series also responds to the fundamental need of narratives of the nonhuman to retain the visual presence of the other *as other*. While the text has gone to great lengths to blur the boundary between humans and Cylons, even enabling the same identity formation structures for both, Cylon presence in this series is visually marked. Since all the individuals of a Cylon model series look like each other, both the viewers and increasingly the characters can identify someone as a Cylon if that individual looks like someone they have seen before. It is the Cylons' external appearance more than anything else that unveils their "true" nature. The series thus uses the same visual shortcut resident in most robot fictions, of making robots and other nonhumans visually and immediately identifiable for the audience—indeed it seems that despite their sophistication, narratives of the nonhuman in science fiction are often designed to produce knowledge of ontological status, and in simple, intuitive ways. To paraphrase the show's tag lines, although the Cylons look and feel human, they also look like each other. And despite the Cylons' other human-like qualities, despite their ability to pass for human on a social, behavioral, biological, sexual, emotional, even molecular level, their ontological status is again an effect of the surface.

The performative power of the nonhuman in *Battlestar Galactica*, then, pivots on a double and contradictory treatment of identity. For Cylons as well as humans, identity in this text is the cumulative record of an individual's actions, emotions, and memories, and it deserves to be memorialized and entered into the historical record. Identity, however, is also a matter of physical and visual uniqueness, which the text retains as primarily the privilege of humans (and implicitly of the "Final Five," if only because they have been treated as humans all along). As the main way in which one can tell the difference between humans and Cylons, visual uniqueness is a rather simple ingredient and reveals the story's dependence on and adherence to the legacies of the science-fictional traditions of the nonhuman. Not in keeping with the complex reading of identity we find in other aspects of the text, the emphasis on visual uniqueness also contradicts the ways in which identity plays out in human society—in the case of identical twins, for example, whose visual similarity does not negate their intrinsic difference as individuals. As with all the other parameters that at times have functioned as differentiators between the human and the nonhuman, the quality that enacts this distinction in *Battlestar Galactica* is arbitrary, its use somewhat fetishistic. A person is not a person merely because they don't look like anyone else. . . .

Indeed we may consider that the focus on visual uniqueness stands for other kinds of uniqueness that the text does not overtly engage, such as a person's DNA, because the Cylons' replicability challenges the expectation that individuals ought to possess a unique chromosomal identity. It's as if the text externalizes or brings to the level of the surface, the skin, a deeper difference that maps onto the contemporary cultural emphasis on the promises of advanced research in biotechnology, the sequencing of the human genome, and the sense that our DNA defines and structures who we are. And again, similarity and difference evoke contradictory meanings in contemporary culture. As research on the human genome reveals, we share much of our DNA with each other, and with beings very different from us, fruit flies being the preferred example for this paradox of genetic connectivity.

The contradiction in the representation of the new Cylons of *Battlestar Galactica*, then, stages conflicting trends in contemporary definitions of human identity that play with notions of surface and depth. Action- and experience-based identity formations seem not to suffice for the work that the show wants to do, or they have to be combined with the intuitive and impulsive recognition of an identity that registers on the surface, on exterior appearance, and thus carries the echoes of the science-fictional representational tradition outlined above, and the culturally relevant notion of a deep and unique identity that is DNA-based or chromosomal. The combination stages the question "What makes one human?" alongside with the question "What makes one unique?" as if being and acting human is not enough. No wonder, then, that resistance to ideological standards and preconceptions takes on such a heightened importance for Cylons in the show: it is this kind of resistance that holds the promise of action that differentiates the self from others. But while ideological resistance thus becomes an important marker of human-like identity for Cylons, its deployment as a marker of human identity is less clear. The show presents numerous versions of disobedience and belligerence, especially embodied in the character of Kara Thrace

(Katee Sackhoff) and her frequent run-ins with her military superiors. Depictions of sabotage on board the Colonial Fleet are first associated with Cylon rather than human action or are directed against specific people, as in the case of sabotage against Gaius Balthar (James Callis) and his lawyer after his collaboration with the occupying Cylon force. The human acts of terrorism on New Caprica in Season 3 can also be considered legitimate, since they are directed against an occupying force and are depicted as acts of resistance that are in line with the general human priorities, not against them. Where, then, do we see humans enact ideological resistance as a fundamental aspect of human identity? Surprisingly, taken as a group, the humans of the series are much more ideologically compliant than they seem to be at first, and indeed it is the act of falling in love with a Cylon that seems to exemplify their transformation of or resistance to their ideological wiring.

Precisely because *Battlestar Galactica* posits the human implicitly and perversely as a matter of ideological resistance, both at a deep level in terms of love and at a superficial level in terms of belligerence, its contrast with *Never Let Me Go* could not be more poignant. The story of *Never Let Me Go* is deceptively simple. It uses the codes of Bildungsroman, but also memoir and autobiography, in Kathy H.'s narration of her childhood experiences at Hailsham.[62] As her stories move from the pranks and secrets of childhood to the debates and conflicts of adolescence and young adulthood, a more complex picture slowly emerges for the reader—but not necessarily for Kathy herself, who seems intent on revisiting and retelling childhood history as if she is looking for something, some form of clue, but without the urgency or sense of revelation one would expect from a memoir. In fact, while there are many mysteries and evasions in the novel, there is no grand secret that she would be able to discover or capable of seeing. Kathy and the other students at Hailsham know they are clones, they have been told just enough from an early age to be aware of their social status and even accept it. Yet, as one of their teachers at some point complains, they have been told and not told. In the matter-of-fact-ness that children assume when they barely understand adult concepts, the students repeat and accept the mantra of euphemisms that conceals the emotional and practical impact of their lives, lives that have been designed to fulfill a rather specific purpose: they are special and important; the future of their society depends on them; it is crucial for them to avoid smoking, exercise, stay in good health; it is also important for them to be creative, engage with the arts and literature, develop interior lives, and reach for artistic and literary accomplishment. Why? Because first as medical professionals, called "carers" in the novel, and then as donors they have to perform their assigned social role: to reach the maximum number of organ donations and "complete" their mission—that is, die—with dignity and minimum agitation to themselves and others.[63]

While in all respects indistinguishable from other people, and presumably the real people of that world, the carers and donors of Ishiguro's novel find themselves belonging to a special social category. They are a group or class, or type, of person whose fundamental rights and responsibilities seem to differ from the rights and responsibilities of others in their society. They have been conceived with a purpose, are born, raised, and educated in ways that support this purpose, and eventually die after successfully fulfilling this purpose. In respecting the limits of Kathy's perspective and her ignorance of events outside her prescribed world, the novel does not provide details of how this social context came about, nor does it explain what other lives are like in this society. Instead, what Ishiguro's treatment makes palpable for contemporary readers is the clones' acquiescence, their acceptance of a known fate that they neither debate nor combat. Although they seem to be human in every way, biologically, emotionally, and intellectually (except, perhaps, for the fact that they are sterilized while young and are unable to procreate), they are clearly also dehumanized in terms of their legal and human rights, their personal experiences and social mobility. They are born and raised to be professional nonhumans. In fact it is their approach to that fact that distinguishes them, as their ingrained sense of limitation or difference from their society's "normal" humanity brings them close to the programmed acquiescence of figures found in science fiction texts.[64]

Ishiguro's novel identifies the deterministic structures that affect both the definitional parameters of the person and the social expectations of transformation and revolt we associate with it. To put it bluntly, this is a book that seems antithetical to Enlightenment ideals of the self, because it undermines the principles of self-determination and the narrative traditions of the Bildungsroman that have displayed such principles in fiction. Kathy and the other students of Hailsham grow, and learn, and have a number of revelations and realizations about their world and their fate within it. But even when they occur, such epiphanies do not transform the world, nor do they allow exit or relief from the weight of a fate that would presumably alienate Western Enlightenment subjects, raised as they are with the expectation of self-determination even when they have not actually experienced this ideal as a reality. Despite its detachment and reticence, the book invites us to contemplate whether we know that we are part of a system or not, subject to social engineering or not, able to see our own programming or not. Without any warning, the book assumes that we may recognize our similarities to Kathy's position.

The radical absence of choice in the novel, the clones' acceptance of this absence, their acquiescence, their inability even to imagine a form of social revolt or escape, and their depiction as beings with a purpose alert us to the ways in which the discourse of the artificial person informs our fantasies of identity. While the clones have a sense of their purpose, living practical and useful lives that participate in corporate agendas and state ideologies, they have no way of becoming part of a common history, as the Cylons are, and this is because the State does not care to include them in that history, and they are themselves trained from a young age to be able to let go of such assumptions and aspirations. If, as Sartre proposed in 1946, the human being is "something that projects itself into the future, and is conscious of doing so,"[65] the students of Hailsham embody a weirdly hybrid position, human beings that are unrecognizable as such because they do not project into the future, they do not subscribe to some of our favorite fictions about self-ownership and self-determination. Or rather, they are all too recognizable as the kinds of human beings we are, and the novel provides no way to foreclose or avoid this traumatic realization, no high-tech distractions, scientific explanations, or fantasies of revolution. Again, we must remember that classic existential interrogations that inspire transcendental solutions to the problem of purpose and life—What is the goal of a life? What are people for? Why do we live?—also inform fictions of artificial people, figures created with a purpose.

The students at Hailsham accept the facts of their fate as nonevents. Exercising and staying healthy become automatic impulses. Artistic and literary creativity and also a certain conformity to peer norms and expectations become inevitable effects of an educational mode that seems to have implicitly transformed the liberal arts into weapons of social control. No one in the novel uses the word "die," the donors just "complete." Reaching the important milestone of "fourth donation" brings congratulations and admiration from doctors, nurses, carers, and other donors. We don't know which organs are harvested at each donation, but the donors become increasingly frail and dependent on their carers even as they display a certain pride in surviving each operation and increasingly detach from everyday life. Only donors of their own level of service, their own number of previous donations, seem to understand their humor and concerns, their peculiar frame of mind. "Completing" after the fourth donation seems to be the ideal aim of the donors themselves. As Kathy's childhood friend and current lover, Tommy D., remarks when he is about to begin his fourth donation, the ultimate fear for donors is the possibility of further donations beyond that point. While we never find out whether this is part of the medical system of this society or not, the donors fear this possibility, in which they are forced to undergo further donations in a sort of half-life, hooked on machinery and kept barely conscious and barely alive indefinitely, until all the possible organs can be harvested. Tommy is understandably eager to "complete." But while Kathy dismisses the specter of further donations as "rubbish," readers cannot discount it as easily, because nothing could keep this society from using donors to their full donation potential, disregarding their feelings and well-being in the process. This is a society that has used them from childhood, designing them from the start to play a utilitarian role, and raising them in a manner that seems to dismantle the cravings and impulses for self-determination or revolt that we assume are a natural part of the human character. In its disquieting minimalism, the novel presents the possibility that our assumptions are wrong, that people are much less prone to revolt than our fictions suggest. The novel actually fulfills the ends of narratives of imitation and approximation, presenting the students of Hailsham as real people. Partly because the text bypasses the registers of artificiality that the discourse of the artificial person provides, it does not give us any sense of how the difference between human and nonhuman would be safeguarded. Instead, the book confronts us with a series of potential answers: the difference will be safeguarded by force, through arbitrary distinctions, social engineering, political fiat, cultural conventions, and by plain raising people as a particular kind of person. Or, indeed, the difference between human and nonhuman does not need to be safeguarded. As long as the people themselves can be predisposed to being disposable, no high-tech methods of selection and distinction are necessary. The State can merely use them at will, and any of them will do for any purpose.

As characters, the Cylons of *Battlestar Galactica* and the clones of *Never Let Me Go* approach the question of the human from seemingly different directions, but the perspectives presented in these texts also coalesce in ways that I find meaningful and poignant for understanding contemporary culture. Their fundamentally unstable existential treatment of the notion of the human is one such axis. Another is their response to imitation: in both texts we see the intertextual legacies of the science-fictional tradition, which often represents the nonhuman in terms of an imitative aim that inevitably fails or is revealed to be impossible to attain. The scale of anthropomorphism or imitation that operates in narratives of artificial humanity implicitly proposes that a nonhuman may succeed in becoming human if they imitate the human well enough. Interestingly, in traditional depictions of this fantasy, the perfect imitation of the human never includes qualities such as forgiveness, kindness, clemency, or a desire for coexistence, instead enacting a kind of "humanity" that is vindictive, supremacist, and retaliatory. Imitation inevitably leads to racially inflected war. But the paranoid treatment of imitation seems to have exhausted itself in these contemporary works. Imitating the human seems too limited as an aim for the Cylons of *Battlestar Galactica*, since they have already reached that goal at the very start of the series. The fears showcased in traditional science-fictional paradigms have also already come true in this text: using their human-like appearance, the Cylons have destroyed human civilization.

As their coexistence with humans progresses, however, other issues take over: instead of focusing on imitating the human or passing for human, the Cylons grapple with the difficulty of coexisting with humans in relationships that combine personal priorities, sexual entanglements, and political pressures rather than ontological difference. The Cylons are fully alert to the inequities of their social status, as their battles for recognition carry much of the existential angst of the series, against various human rejections and proclamations of "But you are not human, you are a machine." In addition to being provocative, such proclamations are ethically disorienting, as in the depiction of torturing a Cylon "traitor." Viewers experience the paradox of seeing a human or human-like being clearly in pain, while hearing the other characters proclaim: "She does not feel pain because she is a machine." The disclaimer attempts to enact a kind of wishful thinking, reminding viewers to retain the ontological difference that the series has in effect eradicated. Despite assertions of difference and exclusion, at an intimate level the series cannot uphold a distinction between Cylon and human except on arbitrary grounds. Indeed this presumed ontological difference fuels the sexual engagement between the humans and Cylons, again enacting a desire for the forbidden, the perverse, and the dangerous for relationships that can very easily be treated within the troubles of all-human political and romantic engagements. In *Battlestar Galactica* everything tends to become human, and it is this tendency that the text has to counteract or try to reverse.

Similarly, in *Never Let Me Go* there is no discernible difference between human and nonhuman characters, except for the fact that the clones of the novel never fully challenge their social position and seem to have internalized the arbitrariness of their fate. But readers do sense the radical violence of the novel and even absorb its most cutting recognition of our own daily modes of acquiescence, our essential automatism, our fundamental susceptibility to convention, program, routine, peer pressure, social expectations. In effect both texts enact a double and paradoxical stance toward defining the human. Using familiar modes of address and traditional representational codes, both texts propose that the boundary between human and nonhuman is, or should be, clear and stable, while on the other hand radically challenging whether this boundary exists at all. By playing into the dynamic of imitation, a dynamic that has dominated definitions of the person and discussions of the artificial person for centuries, and by pushing this dynamic to a visual and embodied extreme, these texts reveal for us both the principles of human-likeness and its liabilities. Whatever we imagine the artificial person to be, that is what we know or suspect that we are.

CONCLUSION
The Ends of the Human

As a collective product, the field of cultural endeavors we summarize as "popular culture" has a paradoxical relationship to time and change. Precisely because of its decentralized and dispersed nature, popular culture is very responsive to change, absorbing and displaying cultural and social concerns rather quickly, but it also tends to retain these concerns and the narrative models they inspire seemingly forever, connecting them both to the past and to the future. In many ways, the discourse of the artificial person is a quintessential example of this paradox: here is a story pattern that features a constructed being, a being from the future, yet the modes of imagining and representing its perennial newness always seem to return to a transhistorical, even primordial vocabulary. Studying such a cultural formation feels like dealing with a pervasive but evanescent entity that is both highly reactive and impervious to change.

If one of the main fictions of modernity is that its advent changes things fundamentally, the discourse of the artificial person allows us to see one specific way in which this familiar sentiment simplifies too much. Tracing how elements of ancient origin stories and philosophical modalities survive over the centuries reveals the resilience of old patterns of thought, their transfer whole-cloth into modern structures of thinking, and their translation into slightly altered but still useful fictions for defining the modern self. This is not to discount how radical the changes of modernity are, but it does provide for a more nuanced understanding of how the old and the new combine over long swaths of time. In this process of translation, the main ancient elements of the discourse of the artificial person, the fantasy of the artificial birth and the fantasy of the mechanical body, are recombined in modernity both to give shape to new epistemologies of the person and to challenge the very terms of these modern epistemologies. As the trajectory traced in this project suggests, ancient ideas of animation and transformation inform modern legal and political narratives of objectification and subjectification, while the mechanical understanding of the body becomes associated with questions of control, agency, and psychological interiority. Because they stage overt enactments of the recognitions and rejections that characterize the modern definition of the person, stories of artificial people question the power of the modern constitution and reveal the enduring action of its conceptual predecessors.

It goes without saying that definitions of "the human" or "the person" are themselves unstable and changing, fluid, contextual, and contingent in modernity. We confront such definitions in legal discourse and in medicine, in debates about abortion, human rights, or cloning, in the changing perception of mental health, in structuring the rights of differently abled people, in end-of-life care, in philosophy, religion, art, and social studies, in international relations, politics, social activism, prison discourse, and corporate culture.[1] But while definitions of "the human" or "the person" may be at stake, under debate, and under review elsewhere, perhaps even everywhere, in fictions of the artificial person these terms retain (or acquire) a kind of solidity and certainty unavailable in other contexts. There is a performative power in depictions of artificial people, an ability to simplify and stage debates about the human, even when the texts under consideration ostensibly aim to blur ontological boundaries. Whether they are rendered as visibly artificial, metallic, mechanical, or constructed (as in the case of robots and cyborgs), or implicitly marked through encodings of isolation, rejection, and other invisible but essential differences from human experience, artificial people enact a kind of difference that is structuring not only of their own status but also of the status of other forms of the human. Whatever fantasies they may facilitate, by their very presence artificial people help naturalize everyone else in a text as more reliably human, before interrogating the very nature of that assumed stability.

Understanding the impact of these fictional entities thus pivots on recognizing their participation in the larger negotiation of what it means to be a person at any given point in a society. What cannot be discounted is the cultural work that artificial people perform as characters and as cultural constructs, by providing the means for expressing indirectly what are experienced as challenges to selfhood, both specific and knowable challenges and inchoate or unformed ones. Throughout the twentieth and twenty-first centuries, whenever a particular person or group of people exclaim "I feel like a robot," they use the discourse of the artificial person in order to express the ways in which culture, political and social conditions, particular governments and legal systems, definitions of the person, racist epistemologies, and normative forms of identity constrain or dehumanize them. Feeling robotic or inanimate may refer to social and political oppression and disenfranchisement, but it may also express a sense of submission to less concrete forces. It is one thing to be oppressed by one's bosses, but another to be oppressed by one's needs, or one's choices, one's body, or one's desires. Stories of robots translate this vernacular understanding of artificiality into storylines that reflect complex investigations of what it means to be. They also critique precisely those social and identity structures that limit a utopian or idealistic notion of a human identity that is imagined as self-defined, fully alive, fully present, fully expressed. The phrase "I feel like a robot" expresses the belief that a more authentic or less circumscribed form of experience exists elsewhere, but it also provides a description for the complex troubles of the here and now.

Such an existential and self-conscious treatment of normativity as a form of roboticism has emerged in recent years in texts that present artificial or robotic children. Because the discourse of the artificial person allegorizes fantasies of avoiding or bypassing childhood, the depiction of artificial children is very rare in the discourse and therefore merits attention.

Considered in the same existential light as stories that feature artificial people as adults, stories of artificial children present the possibility that something about identity and being is at stake for children, and it is expressible in the terms of the discourse of the artificial person. The most sustained such investigation, in *A.I. Artificial Intelligence* (Steven Spielberg, 2001), follows David (Haley Joel Osment), a human-looking android designed as an eleven-year-old boy. David becomes an emotional substitute for Jake, the real son of Henry and Monica Swinton, who has been in a coma for five years. While he is able to love his parents fully after a process of "imprinting," David is displaced when Jake awakes and returns home. In a heart-wrenching scene, Monica (Frances O'Connor) drives off with him to the wilderness and abandons him there.

"Why do you want to leave me?" David pleads, "Why? I'm sorry I'm not real. If you let me, I'll be so real to you."

The cruelty of his abandonment is exacerbated by David's loyalty, his continued love for his mother, and his insistent Pinocchio-like wish "Make me a real boy," a wish he makes to an underwater Blue Fairy statue in a sunken Coney Island. David repeats the wish for thousands of years, until a future species of robotic creatures discovers him after all human civilization is gone and grants him one beautiful and final day with Monica.[2]

Treated as a potentially diagnostic text, as I have treated other texts that feature artificial people in this project, *A.I.* provides clues to implicit contemporary trends in defining humanity. In depicting a boy asking whether he is real, the film presents the possibility that something about personhood is at stake for children or is at stake for adults on behalf of children, or for adults imagining themselves projected onto children. David is an eternal child, a fantasy child, a parent's fantasy perhaps for a child that never grows up, never leaves, never loses interest in his parents, and never grows out of a dependence on parental approbation that might diminish for real children at some point. In keeping with the psychologically and socially dynamic reversals such stories undertake, David's endangerment is also eloquent for the insecurity that Jake, the real child of the family, might feel. The fact that the real child is at all replaceable is unsettling in this film, because it reveals that what matters for the parents is filling the structural position of "child." If both the real and the artificial child exist not as themselves but as narcissistic enhancements for a parent's ego, then they are both replaceable, both rather artificial. The film's phobic relationship to loss and grief displaces these emotions into a tone of ambient melancholy, which as reviewers described, feels both melodramatic and cold.

In contrast to most scenes of animation, in which the artificial being arrives into consciousness in an adult, pre-gendered, socially legible, and circumscribed body, David's prepubescent body challenges the initiation structure of such scenes and makes implicit connections to gender and transgender discourse. We can read his desire, "Make me a real boy," in the tradition of science fiction stories with an emphasis on the "real," but we can also hear the emphasis on gender identity implicit in "boy." The film indeed includes scenes in which David finally finds the office of the researchers who have constructed him and walks among rows and rows of packaged robots that look just like him, some presented as boys and others as girls. In the double arrest the film implies for structures of initiation and rites of passage, not only can David not become a real *person*, he can also not become a real *boy*, and his wish thus resonates with contemporary discourses of difference—concerns about the state of being a boy, the state of being a girl, and perhaps of being a girl who wants to be a real boy, or being a boy who wants to be a real boy, or a child of any gender who just doesn't feel real enough. By presenting a child in a state of existential crisis the film projects concerns about children as pathologized, medicated, unreal, or under debate. If questions of recognition and authenticity have accrued around childhood in contemporary culture, an artificial child can evoke a child who feels misrecognized in terms of his or her race, class, language skills, accent, reading abilities, mobility, mechanical aptitude, sports performance, or attention span. Or an artificial child can reference the state of a different or special child, whose perspective we cannot share, whose world works on a different scale of time, and to whom we may appear as different or incomprehensible beings.

What also interests me in *A.I.* is the persistent reluctance of the narrative to answer or foreclose David's demand either to be made into a real boy or to be told why he is not a real boy. Although the question itself never leaves narratives of artificial people, it is a question that has actually been rather answerable. Over the last centuries, artificial people have been told that they are not real people—or not real enough to be considered as real people—because they don't have a soul (a perennial favorite whose meaning has changed radically and

FIGURE 26 Between person and object, and between male and female in *A.I. Artificial Intelligence* (Steven Spielberg, 2001). The robotic boy, David (Haley Joel Osment), finds his model at the Cybertronics Research offices. © Warner Bros. and Dreamworks LLC

repeatedly over time), because they cannot procreate, die, or kill, because they cannot love, they cannot reason or they are too reasonable, they have no imagination or sense of humor or artistic talent, because they are too limited by their bodies, or because their bodies are too limitless, and frequently because they just don't look like people. Any one of these provisional answers could have been offered to David, but none of the human or artificial adults provides him with such a response. Nor does he either decide to stop this self-inflicted punishment or give himself a provisional answer. In its inability to resolve the question of how David might be or become real and also in its reluctance to define why he is not real enough already, the film produces a spectacle of stasis and immobility. This is partly because the film establishes a new defining parameter for personhood, the capacity to be loved. Not equivalent to legal recognition or to dialectic struggle, not related to abilities and technicalities, and not the familiar humanist active principle of being able to love, this parameter for defining humanity is associated with the elusive and ineffable sense that one's person can be made intelligible as what it is—constructed, so to speak—through the generosity of another.

As David quickly understands, when it functions as a definition of the self, the capacity to be loved is fundamentally unstable. As is the case with most fictions of the artificial person, every attempt at defining an absolute boundary between real and artificial people is designed to fail. The boy's radical existential angst engages unanswerable questions, a kind of hunger for something none of us can satisfy or fully control: real people also sometimes feel insufficiently loved and insufficiently recognized. Most children experience the fear that they will be abandoned, and unfortunately for all of us sometimes this fear comes true. People sometimes are not real enough to other people no matter how much they try to be seen and heard as who and what they are. The film's tagline "His Love Is Real. But He's Not" is a paradox designed to test the limits of definitions of personhood. Doesn't love flow out of an already existing self? Why is David's capacity to love his parents not sufficient to define him as human? If reversed ("They Are Real. But Their Love Is Not") the promotional phrase would describe David's human parents in ominous accuracy but would also encapsulate a fear that real people have sometimes about love and its fragile states.

The film may have other flaws, but it manages to literalize and articulate, albeit indirectly, the fundamental condition of artificial people as figures in our fictions. As producers and consumers of this cultural pattern, we define one attribute, action, or quality as the necessary parameter for granting human status to a constructed person. Then, no matter what this quality is and acting precisely like David's parents, we withhold it. The attribute varies with the historical and cultural situation and is valuable for the kinds of information it carries about what may be valued, feared, or desired in these contexts. Being able to speak, to think, to laugh, to have a sense of humor, to move in a certain way, to love, to hate, to kill, to feel anger, to procreate, to have sexual experience have all at one time or another functioned as defining parameters for distinguishing between real and artificial people. But since the definitions change, and what is authentic and soulful one day is too logical and mechanical the next, only our act of withholding safeguards the boundary between real and artificial people.

The film's inability to define David properly thus signals some of the changes that have taken place in the discourse of the artificial person in recent decades. It used to be easier to say to an artificial character "You're not human because . . ." and although *A.I.* seems to treat this conundrum with an almost fetishistic ambivalence, the result is in keeping with current conceptual revisions in defining personhood. Similar concerns emerge in Judith Butler's *Undoing Gender*, for example, where she critiques the Hegelian emphasis on recognition as a defining parameter of personhood and recognizes the importance of liminal spaces. Since cultural and social norms depend on a certain degree of intelligibility, and since intelligibility depends on the application or enforcement of norms and the policing of arbitrary boundaries, recognition becomes a site of power. Because both the conferral and the withholding of recognition can "undo" the person, "there are advantages to remaining less than intelligible," Butler notes. She continues: "I may feel that without some recognizability I cannot live. But I may also feel that the terms by which I am recognized make life unlivable." Negotiating thus with the terms of recognition, both intelligibility and its negation can function as potential strategies for defining a self against the logic of integrity and full recognition, and against even the logic of existential certainty. "There is a certain departure from the human that takes place in order to start the process of remaking the human."[3]

Butler's critique of simple recognition and her analysis of how constructing human persons may be accomplished by undoing the "human" use a rubric similar to the one operative in the discourse of the artificial person, in which artificial people function as sites of existential inquiry. The inability to provide an adequate answer to the question of the human in *A.I.* may open up a new space for a differently framed negotiation, redefinition, or revision. Few texts stop the narrative machinery and visual pleasures of cinema in order to produce such indecision. As the legacies of the discourse of the artificial person suggest, idealizing imagined identities creates lived realities that, by contrast, feel de-animating or dehumanizing. The processes of discernment resulting from such negotiations have been used to ensure the longevity of racist epistemologies and a dispersed and immanent logic of social exclusion. The film's immobility may be conceived as a necessary step in moving beyond familiar stereotypes.

Indeed, if stories of artificial people channel and question the historical and conceptual legacies of the Enlightenment through the twentieth and twenty-first centuries, perhaps they might be freed of these legacies in the future. Study of contemporary texts and contexts reveals that the stereotypically adversarial relationship imagined between human and nonhuman for most of the twentieth century in Western culture has been changing, because we live in an era that is more invested in overcoming the racist epistemologies that gave this plot some of its power, and we are also moving beyond the Cold War context that extended its currency by translating it into ideological paranoia. This adversarial treatment of otherness, when it emerges now, may have a nostalgic relationship to the ostensible certainties of earlier eras, but it also provides expression to new notions of threat. It may no longer refer to a clearly demarcated outside enemy but, rather, to new interior challenges, from spaces deep within the self, from biological and microscopic alterity, from the insecurities that emerge when an intricately connected world feels all too open and available but not all that knowable.

Even when they fall into familiar patterns of danger and combat, new texts that warn against a robotic attack will have to express the ways in which we are now fascinated by a fractal and situated understanding of the human, reincorporating humanity within social, ontological, and affective relationships that go beyond the anthropocentric, nationalist, and supremacist focus of older eras. Binary oppositions may retain some of their attraction, of course, but new symmetries are also emerging to counter idealized versions of narcissism. As we see in contemporary theories of post-humanism, the impulse to redefine the human in a wider, more embodied, and more ecological frame of reference has to counter nostalgic or apocalyptic trends that promote new body-phobic dualisms, notions of high tech transcendentalism, and cerebral supremacy. In robotics research we see a similar interest in modeling not performances of supreme individuality or displays of control but performances of relationality, and although some of these projects still fetishize anthropomorphism and doubleness, they may open new horizons for an ethics of interactivity.

I began this project with a sketch on the power and some of the assumptions of the anatomical gesture, a gesture of revelation and unveiling that promises knowledge and clarity regardless of what it can deliver. At the close of this investigation I want to propose that we consider the gesture of withholding as part of the foundational symbolic vocabulary of the discourse of the artificial person. We cannot expand our understanding of how this discourse has functioned in modernity if we remain unaware of the double aims of these stories, their tendency to produce precisely the kind of figure from which something has been withheld. This is why the discourse of the artificial person is so useful, so dynamic and multivalent. Whether we recognize ourselves in the artificial people of our fictions or not, that gesture is familiar, relevant, and very much real for us all.

NOTES

INTRODUCTION: ROBOT ANATOMIES

1. See Joan B. Lands, "The Anatomy of Artificial Life: An Eighteenth-Century Perspective," in *Genesis Redux: Essays in the History and Philosophy of Artificial Life*, ed. Jessica Riskin, 96–116 (Chicago: University of Chicago Press, 2007).

2. For literary perspectives see Patricia S. Warrick, *The Cybernetic Imagination in Science Fiction* (Cambridge, MA: MIT Press, 1980); Janice Hocker Rushing and Thomas S. Frentz, *Projecting the Shadow: The Cyborg Hero in American Film* (Chicago: University of Chicago Press, 1995); Jane Donawerth, *Frankenstein's Daughters: Women Writing Science Fiction* (Syracuse, NY: Syracuse University Press, 1997); Elaine L. Graham, *Representations of the Post/Human: Monsters, Aliens, and Others in Popular Culture* (New Brunswick, NJ: Rutgers University Press, 2002). For work in technoculture, see Anne Balsamo, *Technologies of the Gendered Body: Reading Cyborg Women* (Durham, NC: Duke University Press, 1996); Chris Hables Gray, Heidi J. Figueroa-Sarriera, and Steven Mentor, eds., *The Cyborg Handbook* (New York: Routledge, 1995); Mark Dery, *Escape Velocity: Cyberculture at the End of the Century* (New York: Grove Press, 1996).

3. Donna Haraway, "A Cyborg Manifesto: Science, Technology and Socialist-Feminism in the Late Twentieth Century" (1985), reprinted in *Simians, Cyborgs, and Women: The Reinvention of Nature* (New York: Routledge, 1991), 149–81 (all quotations follow this latter version).

4. See Haraway, "Cyborg Manifesto," 149; Donna Haraway, *Modest_Witness@Second_Millennium.FemaleMan©_Meets_OncoMouse™: Feminism and Technoscience* (New York: Routledge, 1997), 51.

5. The "oncomouse" of Haraway's title is the first patented animal, developed for cancer research.

6. N. Katherine Hayles, *How We Became Posthuman: Virtual Bodies in Cybernetics, Literature, and Informatics* (Chicago: University of Chicago Press, 1999), 3.

7. Written in 1920, the play was first performed in Prague in 1921. See Karel Čapek, *R.U.R. (Rossum's Universal Robots)*, trans. Claudia Novack (New York: Penguin, 2004).

8. Čapek capitalizes the word Robot, as do I in reference to his play.

9. The science of communication and control theory, cybernetics also studies automatic informational systems (the nervous system, the brain, and mechanical-electrical communications systems). Norbert Wiener's work in cybernetics after World War II summarizes innovations that had been in progress since the mid-1930s. See Norbert Wiener, *Cybernetics: Or Control and Communication in the Animal and the Machine* (Cambridge, MA: MIT Press, 1948); Norbert Wiener, *The Human Use of Human Beings: Cybernetics and Society* (New York: Doubleday, 1954); also David A. Mindell, *Between Human and Machine: Feedback, Control, and Computing before Cybernetics* (Baltimore: Johns Hopkins University Press, 2002).

10. The term "Cyborg" (capitalized) was introduced in Manfred Clynes and Nathan Kline, "Cyborgs and Space," *Astronautics* (September 1960), reprinted in Gray et al., *The Cyborg Handbook*, 29–34. See Chris Hables Gray, "An Interview with Manfred Clynes," in ibid., 43–53.

11. Sony launched AIBO (Japanese for "pal" but also evoking AI) as an "entertainment robot" in 1999. About 170,000 robots were sold before the line was discontinued in 2006.

12. ASIMO is the first named model in Honda's research on human mobility, begun in 1986. ASIMO is 4 foot, 3 inches tall and weighs 120 pounds. The robot's lifelike walking style is achieved through "prediction motion control," which shifts the center of gravity for the next step before the first step is completed.

13. While Rodney Allen Brooks traces actual robotics developments in *Flesh and Machines: How Robots Will Change Us* (New York: Pantheon, 2002), other popular books make apocalyptic proclamations. See Hans Moravec, *Mind Children: The Future of Robot and Human Intelligence* (Cambridge, MA: Harvard University Press, 1990); Ray Kurzweil, *The Age of Spiritual Machines: When Computers Exceed Human Intelligence* (New York: Penguin, 2000); Ray Kurzweil, *The Singularity Is Near: When Humans Transcend Biology* (New York: Penguin, 2006). Robert Geraci offers a much-needed critique in *Apocalyptic AI: Visions of Heaven in Robotics, Artificial Intelligence, and Virtual Reality* (New York: Oxford University Press, 2000).

14. John Cohen, *Human Robots in Myth and Science* (London: Allen and Unwin, 1966). Kurzweil and Moravec also develop similar time lines.

15. Mark Rosheim, *Robot Evolution: The Development of Anthrobotics* (New York: Wiley, 1994).

16. Talos is depicted in vase paintings of the fifth century BCE and first appears in literature in Apollonius's *Argonautica*, from the third century BCE. See Sarah P. Morris, *Daidalos and the Origins of Greek Art* (Princeton, NJ: Princeton University Press, 1992), 259–71.

17. Sylvia Berryman, "Ancient Automata and Mechanical Explanation," *Phronesis* 48 (2003): 344–69; William Newman, *Promethean Ambitions: Alchemy and the Quest to Perfect Nature* (Chicago: University of Chicago Press, 2004).

18. Allison Muri, *The Enlightenment Cyborg: A History of Communications and Control in the Human Machine, 1660–1830* (Toronto: University of Toronto Press, 2007).

19. Bill Brown, "Thing Theory," *Critical Inquiry* 28.1 (Autumn 2001): 1–22; Bill Brown, *A Sense of Things: The Object Matter of American Literature* (Chicago: University of Chicago Press, 2004).

20. Filmed footage of Elektro's performance is available at the Moving Image Archive, Prelinger Collection at http://www.archive.org/details/Medicusc1939_3 (accessed September 16, 2013).

21. Aristotle, *De Anima* 412a6–14, 413a22–26.

22. In Barbara Maria Stafford and Frances Terpak, eds., *Devices of Wonder: From the World in a Box to Images on a Screen* (Los Angeles: Getty Research Institute, 2002), Stafford claims that creating automata stems from the human desire "to smoothly counterfeit the gestures and motions of everything observable under the sun" (40).

23. Victoria Nelson, *The Secret Life of Puppets* (Cambridge, MA: Harvard University Press, 2003).

24. Jessica Riskin, "The Defecating Duck; or, The Ambiguous Origins of Artificial Life," *Critical Inquiry* 20.4 (Summer 2003): 599–633; Jessica Riskin, "Eighteenth-Century Wetware," *Representations* 83 (Summer 2003): 97–125; M. Norton Wise, "The Gender of Automata in Victorian Britain," in Riskin, *Genesis Redux*, 163–95; Minsoo Kang, *Sublime Dreams of Living Machines: The Automaton in the European Imagination* (Cambridge, MA: Harvard University Press, 2011).

25. See Kenneth Gross, *The Dream of the Moving Statue* (State College: Pennsylvania State University Press, 2006); Deborah Tarn Steiner, *Images in Mind: Statues in Archaic and Classical Greek Literature and Thought* (Princeton, NJ: Princeton University Press, 2002).

26. See Bruno Latour's analysis of modernity as an epistemological rubric in *We Have Never Been Modern*, trans. Catherine Porter (Cambridge, MA: Harvard University Press, 1993).

27. Lisa Nocks, *The Robot: The Life History of a Technology* (Baltimore: Johns Hopkins University Press, 2008).

28. J. P. Telotte, *Replications: A Robotic History of the Science Fiction Film* (Urbana: University of Illinois Press, 1995).

29. Michel Foucault, *The Archeology of Knowledge and the Discourse on Language* (New York: Pantheon Books, 1972), 38.

30. See Roland Barthes, *Mythologies*, trans. Annette Lavers (New York: Farrar, Straus and Giroux, 1972); Tzvetan Todorov, *The Fantastic: A Structural Approach to a Literary Genre*, trans. Richard Howard (Ithaca, NY: Cornell University Press, 1975); Vivian Sobchack, *Screening Space: The American Science Fiction Film* (New Brunswick, NJ: Rutgers University Press, 1997); Christine Brooke-Rose, *A Rhetoric of the Unreal: Studies in Narrative and Structure, especially of the Fantastic* (Cambridge: Cambridge University Press, 1983); Darko Suvin, *Positions and Presuppositions in Science Fiction* (Kent, OH: Kent State University Press, 1988).

31. Vladimir Propp, *Morphology of the Folktale*, trans. Laurence Scott (Austin: University of Texas Press, 1968); Claude Lévi-Strauss, "The Structural Study of Myth," in *Structural Anthropology*, trans. Claire Jacobson and Brooke Schoepf (New York: Basic Books, 1974), 206–32.

CHAPTER 1 THE ARTIFICIAL BIRTH

1. Mary Wollstonecraft Shelley, *Frankenstein; or, The Modern Prometheus*, ed. Susan J. Wolfson (New York: Longman, 2007). Unless otherwise noted, all references to the novel are from this edition, which includes the 1818 version and the 1831 preface and additions. References will be cited parenthetically in the text.

2. On cinematic versions, see James A. W. Heffernan, "Looking at the Monster: *Frankenstein* and Film," *Critical Inquiry* 24.1 (Autumn 1997): 133–58.

3. Brian Aldiss, "The Origin of the Species: Mary Shelley," in *The Billion Year Spree* (New York: Market Paperback, 1973), 7–39.

4. On the manuscript versions, see Anne K. Mellor, "Choosing a Text of *Frankenstein* to Teach," in *Approaches to Teaching Shelley's Frankenstein* (New York: MLA, 1990), 31–37; also David Ketterer, "Frankenstein's 'Conversion' from Natural Magic to Modern Science: And a 'Shifted' (and Converted) Last Draft Insert," *Science Fiction Studies* 24.1 (March 1997): 57–78.

5. Marilyn Butler, "*Frankenstein* and Radical Science," in Mary Shelley, *Frankenstein; or, The Modern Prometheus* (1818), ed. J. Paul Hunter (New York: Norton, 1996), 302–313.

6. Ibid., 303.

7. Peter Brooks, "Godlike Science/Unhallowed Arts: Language and Monstrosity in *Frankenstein*," *New Literary History* 9.3 (Spring 1978): 591–605 (599); also Susan Stryker, "My Words to Victor Frankenstein above the Village of Chamounix: Performing Transgender Rage," *GLQ* 1.3 (1994): 237–54.

8. Beth Newman, "Narratives of Seduction and the Seductions of Narrative: The Frame Structure of *Frankenstein*," *ELH* 53.1 (Spring 1986): 141–63.

9. The novel echoes Mary Shelley's recurring dream after the death of her first baby. On March 19, 1815, she wrote: "Dream that my little baby came to life again—that it had only been cold & that we rubbed it by the fire & it lived—I awake & find no baby—I think about the little thing all day—not in good spirits." *The Journals of Mary Shelley*, ed. Paula R. Feldman and Diana Scott-Kilvert (Oxford: Clarendon, 1987), 70.

10. On "enthusiasm" as a motivating force for Victor, see Jasper Cragwall, "The Shelleys' Enthusiasm," *Huntington Library Quarterly* 68.4 (2005): 631–53.

11. Alan Bewell, "An Issue of Monstrous Desire: *Frankenstein* and Obstetrics," *Yale Journal of Criticism* 2 (1988): 105–28.

12. On destructive tendencies see Paul Sherwin, "*Frankenstein*: Creation as Catastrophe," *PMLA* 96.5 (October 1981): 883–903; Richard K. Sanderson, "Glutting the Maw of Death: Suicide and Procreation in *Frankenstein*," *South Central Review* 9.2 (Summer 1992): 49–64.

13. On ritual, see Mircea Eliade, *Myth and Reality*, trans. Willard R. Trask (New York: Harper and Row, 1963); Mircea Eliade, *Myths, Dreams and Mysteries*, trans. Philip Mairet (New York: Harper and Row, 1967).

14. Nelson, *Secret Life of Puppets*, 35; paraphrasing Moshe Idel, "Hermeticism and Judaism," in *Hermeticism and the Renaissance: Intellectual History and the Occult in Early Modern Europe*, ed. Ingrid Merkel and Allen G. Debus (Washington, DC: Folger Shakespeare Library, 1988), 59–76 (69–70).

15. Hesiod, *Theogony*, line 585, in Hesiod, *The Works and Days, Theogony, The Shield of Herakles*, trans. Richmond Lattimore (Ann Arbor: University of Michigan Press, 1991), 158.

16. Ovid, *The Metamorphoses*, trans. Allen Mandelbaum (New York: Harcourt Brace, 1995), 337.

17. For the story of Prometheus's transgressions and the creation of Pandora, see Hesiod, *Theogony*, lines 506–602. The opening of the jar and Pandora's name occur in Hesiod, *Works and Days*, lines 45–105.

18. Hesiod, *Works and Days*, lines 60–68.

19. Hesiod, *Theogony*, lines 588–89.

20. On the variations of Pandora's story, see Jane E. Harrison, "Pandora's Box," *Journal of Hellenic Studies* 20 (1900): 99–114; Dora Panofsky and Erwin Panofsky, *Pandora's Box: The Changing Aspects of a Mythical Symbol* (New York: Pantheon Books, 1962).

21. See Burton R. Pollin, "Philosophical and Literary Sources of *Frankenstein*," *Comparative Literature* 17.2 (Spring 1965): 97–108; also Paul Hamilton, "A French Connection: From Empiricism to Materialism in Writings by the Shelleys," *Colloquium Helveticum* 25 (1997): 171–93. On Shelley's presentation of cognition and sensation, see Alan Richardson, *British Romanticism and the Science of the Mind* (Cambridge: Cambridge University Press, 2001), 160–63.

22. For the relationship of Prometheus's transgression to alimentary codes and sacrifice, see Marcel Detienne and Jean-Pierre Vernant, eds., *The Cuisine of Sacrifice among the Greeks*, trans. Paula Wissing (Chicago: University of Chicago Press, 1989). On Prometheus in drama, see Mark Griffith, ed., *Prometheus Bound* (Cambridge: Cambridge University Press, 1983).

23. See Daniel Saintillan, "Du festin à l'échange: Les grâces de Pandore," In *Le métier du mythe: Lectures d'Hésiode*, ed. Fabienne Blaise, Pierre Judet de la Combe, and P. Rousseau (Paris: Septentrion, 1996), 315–48.

24. Athena pours *charis* over Odysseus in *Odyssey*, 6.232–35. As Steiner proposes, "both the radiance and the charm that result from the process of manufacture, and the brilliance that issues from a living body, *charis* can be either an artificial or an organic property." Steiner, *Images in Mind*, 195–96.

25. Jean-Pierre Vernant, "Les semblances de Pandora," in Blaise et al., *Le métier du mythe*, 381–92.

26. Steiner, *Images in Mind*, 24–26, 186–90.

27. Ibid., 26.

28. See Jean-Pierre Vernant, *Myth and Society in Ancient Greece*, trans. J. Lloyd (New York: Zone, 1988), 192; also Nicole Loraux, *The Children of Athena: Athenian Ideas about Citizenship and the Division between the Sexes*, trans. C. Levine (Princeton, NJ: Princeton University Press, 1993); Marilyn Arthur [Katz], "Cultural Strategies in Hesiod's *Theogony*: Law, Family, Society," *Arethusa* 10 (1982): 63–82; Marilyn Arthur [Katz], "The Dream of a World without Women: Poetics and the Circles of Order in the *Theogony* Prooemium," *Arethusa* 16 (1983): 97–116.

29. Froma Zeitlin, *Playing the Other: Gender and Society in Classical Greek Literature* (Chicago: University of Chicago Press, 1996), 57–61.

30. Marina Warner, *Monuments and Maidens: The Allegory of the Female Form* (New York: Atheneum, 1985), especially chap. 10.

31. Victor Turner writes: "In so far as a neophyte is structurally 'dead,' he or she may be treated, for a long or short period, as a corpse is customarily treated in his or her society." Also, belonging to the ranks of the "not yet classified," "the neophytes may be treated as embryos, newborn infants, or sucklings." In *The Forest of Symbols: Aspects of Ndembu Ritual* (Ithaca, NY: Cornell University Press, 1970), 96. See also Mircea Eliade, *Rites and Symbols of Initiation: The Mysteries of Birth and Rebirth*, trans. W. R. Trask (New York: Harper and Row, 1958).

32. Joanna Russ, *The Female Man* (1975; Boston: Beacon Press, 1986); Tanith Lee, *The Silver Metal Lover* (New York: Bantam, 1981).

33. See Panofsky and Panofsky, *Pandora's Box*, 34–54.

34. Andreas Huyssen, "The Vamp and the Machine: Technology and Sexuality in Fritz Lang's *Metropolis*," *New German Critique* 24–25 (Autumn 1981–Winter 1982): 221–37.

35. James A. Notopoulos, "The Dating of Shelley's Prose," *PMLA* 58.2 (June 1943): 477–98 (481); also Eli Edward Burriss, "The Classical Culture of Percy Bysshe Shelley," *The Classical Journal* 21.5 (February 1926): 344–54.

36. Hesiod appears in the reading list for 1815 in Feldman and Scott-Kilvert, *The Journals of Mary Shelley*, 92. Percy read Aeschylus in 1816 and 1817 (ibid., 97, 102) and worked on a translation of the play from the Greek, which Mary transcribed, in the months after *Frankenstein* was completed. Mary notes the beginning of the translation in her diary entry for June 13, 1817 (177). The play probably informs Percy's revisions of the manuscript of *Frankenstein* in the fall of 1817, as well as structuring his own composition of *Prometheus Unbound* in 1818.

37. See Richardson, *British Romanticism*, especially 161–63.

38. Denise Gigante, "Facing the Ugly: The Case of *Frankenstein*," *ELH* 67 (2000): 565–87.

39. See Steven Earl Forry, *Hideous Progenies: Dramatizations of* Frankenstein *from Mary Shelley to the Present* (Philadelphia: University of Pennsylvania Press, 1990); Esther Schor, "*Frankenstein* and Film," in *The Cambridge Companion to Mary Shelley*, ed. Esther Schor (Cambridge: Cambridge University Press, 2003), 63–83; Jules Law, "Being There: Gothic Violence and Virtuality in *Frankenstein*, *Dracula*, and *Strange Days*," *ELH* 73 (2006): 975–96.

40. H. L. Malchow, "Frankenstein's Monster and Images of Race in Nineteenth-Century Britain," *Past & Present* 139 (May 1993): 90–130.

41. See Anne K. Mellor, *Mary Shelley: Her Life, Her Fictions, Her Monsters* (New York: Methuen, 1988); Mary Poovey, *The Proper Lady and the Woman Writer* (Chicago: University of Chicago Press, 1984); Mary Jacobus, "Is There a Woman in This Text?" *New Literary History* 14.1 (1982): 117–54; Devon Hodges, "*Frankenstein* and the Feminine Subversion of the Novel," *Tulsa Studies in Women's Literature* 2.2 (1983):155–64.

42. William Veeder, *Mary Shelley and* Frankenstein: *The Fate of Androgyny* (Chicago: University of Chicago Press, 1986).

43. "The Burial of the Dead" service in *The Book of Common Prayer* includes the "Doctrine of Resurrection" segment from Paul's First Corinthians and lines such as "For as in Adam all die, even so in Christ all shall be made alive" (15:22).

44. On the relationship between monstrosity and the mother's thoughts, see Marie-Helene Huet, "Living Images: Monstrosity and Representation," *Representations* 4 (Autumn 1983): 73–87.

45. Gershom Scholem, "The Idea of the Golem," in *On the Kabbalah and Its Symbolism* (1965; New York: Schocken Books, 1995), 158–204 (184).

46. Ibid., 184–85, 190. In Jewish traditions the name of God is so powerful it can give temporary animating powers even to the undeserving, a danger that for Scholem leads to suspicion of magical processes as well as idols and statues.

47. Using different sources, Moshe Idel makes this case in *Golem: Jewish Magical and Mystical Traditions on the Artificial Anthropoid* (Albany: SUNY Press, 1990), 27–43 and chap. 3.

48. Christopher A. Faraone, *Talismans and Trojan Horses: Guardian Statues in Ancient Greek Myth and Ritual* (New York: Oxford University Press, 1992), 3–17, 26; also David Freedberg, *The Power of Images: Studies in the History and Theory of Response* (Chicago: University of Chicago Press, 1989).

49. The *teraphim* are similarly connected to protective statues. See H. A. Hoffner, "Hittite Tarpis and Hebrew Teraphim," *JNES* 27 (1968): 61–68.

50. Faraone traces the earliest mention of such statues in a Greek literary text in the *Odyssey* (7.91–94), when Odysseus sees the immortal gold and silver dogs of the Phaecian king Alcinous, a gift from Hephaestus, guarding the palace doors. *Talismans and Trojan Horses*, 18.

51. R. J. W. Evans, *Rudolf II and His World: A Study in Intellectual History, 1576–1612* (Oxford: Clarendon Press, 1973); F. Thieberger, *The Great Rabbi Loew of Prague* (London: East and West Library, 1955).

52. Scholem, "Idea of the Golem," 196.

53. Hillel J. Kieval, "Pursuing the Golem of Prague: Jewish Culture and the Invention of a Tradition," *Modern Judaism* 17.1 (1997): 1–20.

54. Spontaneous generation also appears as *Generatio acquivoca, Generatio primaria*, archegenesis, and archebiosis. As a theory, abiogenesis was contested by Francesco Redi in 1668 and later by Pasteur in 1859, but Charles Darwin still used a version of spontaneous generation to explain the emergence of the first living particles, and T. H. Huxley proposed that living organisms may have arisen in nonliving matter in a series of stages, in what he called a "primordial archebiosis." On the experimental tradition of proving and disproving spontaneous generation, see Bruno Latour, "On the Partial Existence of Existing and Nonexisting Objects," in *Biographies of Scientific Objects*, ed. Lorraine Daston (Chicago: University of Chicago Press, 2000), 247–69.

55. Henry Harris, *Things Come to Life: Spontaneous Generation Revisited* (London: Oxford University Press, 2002).

56. (Pseudo?-) Paracelsus, *De natura rerum*, written in 1537 and published in 1572. I follow the translation by William Newman in *Promethean Ambitions*, 200. On the question of the attribution of *De natura rerum* to Paracelsus, see William Newman, "The Homunculus and His Forebears," in *Natural Particulars: Nature and the Disciplines in Renaissance Europe*, ed. Anthony Grafton and Nancy Siraisi (Cambridge, MA: MIT Press, 1999), 321–45.

57. Recipes for the creation of artificial animals are attributed to eighth-century Persian philosopher Jābir ibn Hayyān, known in the West as "Geber." In *Jābir ibn Hayyān, contribution à l'histoire des idées scientifiques dans l'Islam [Mémoires présentés à l'institut d'Egypte, vol. 44–45]*, ed. Paul Kraus (Cairo: Institut français de l'archéologie orientale, 1942), 2:110.

58. Newman, *Promethean Ambitions*, 200.

59. See Radu Florescu, *In Search of Frankenstein: Exploring the Myths behind Mary Shelley's Monster* (London: Robson Books, 1996). Jakob Grimm published a Polish golem legend in 1808 in the journal *Zeitung für Einsiedler*. For other sources, see also Byron L. Sherwin, *The Golem Legend: Origins and Implications* (Lanham, MD: University Press of America, 1985); Emily D. Bilski, ed., *Golem! Danger, Deliverance, and Art* (New York: Jewish Museum, 1989); Cathy S. Gelbin, *The Golem Returns: From German Romantic Literature to Global Jewish Culture, 1808–2008* (Ann Arbor: University of Michigan Press, 2010).

60. Samuel Holms Vasbinder, *Scientific Attitudes on Mary Shelley's* Frankenstein (Ann Arbor: UMI Research Press, 1986).

61. Tim Marshall, *Murdering to Dissect: Grave-Robbing,* Frankenstein, *and the Anatomy Literature* (Manchester: Manchester University Press, 1995).

62. Chris Baldick, *In Frankenstein's Shadow: Myth, Monstrosity, and Nineteenth-Century Writing* (Oxford: Clarendon, 1996).

63. Latour, *We Have Never Been Modern,* 101.

64. Ibid., 103; Judith Halberstam, *Skin Shows: Gothic Horror and the Technology of Monsters* (Durham, NC: Duke University Press, 1995), 37–38.

65. Halberstam, *Skin Shows,* 37.

66. Latour warns against such recuperative strategies in *We Have Never Been Modern,* 124.

67. My overall approach to this topic has been influenced by Lorraine Daston, "The Nature of Nature in Early Modern Europe," *Configurations* 6.2 (1998): 149–72.

68. On magic and science in science fiction see Sobchack, *Screening Space.*

69. Colin Milburn, "Nanotechnology in the Age of Posthuman Engineering: Science Fiction as Science," *Configurations* 10 (2002): 261–95 (287).

70. The reimagined *Battlestar Galactica* was first presented as a four-hour miniseries, written and produced by Ronald D. Moore and directed by Michael Rymer.

71. Ian Wilmut and Roger Highfield, *After Dolly: The Uses and Misuses of Human Cloning* (New York: Norton, 2006), 41.

72. In this I diverge from Jackie Stacey's focus on imitation as a primary concept in cloning discourse in *The Cinematic Life of the Gene* (Durham, NC: Duke University Press, 2010).

CHAPTER 2 THE MECHANICAL BODY

1. Ted Hughes's *The Iron Man: A Children's Story in Five Nights* (London: Faber, 2005) was first published in 1968.

2. Giorgio Baglivi, *De praxi medica ad priscam observandi rationem revocanda* (1696), quoted in Dennis Des Chene, *Spirits and Clocks: Machine and Organism in Descartes* (Ithaca, NY: Cornell University Press, 2001).

3. Telotte, *Replications,* 32–33.

4. David Levy discusses the imaginary sexual robot both as a teacher and as a service provider that will bring "great sex on tap for everyone, 24/7," in *Love and Sex with Robots: The Evolution of Human-Robot Relationships* (New York: Harper, 2008), 310.

5. Manfred Clynes and Nathan Kline, "Cyborgs and Space," *Astronautics* (September 1960): 26–27, 74–75, reprinted in Gray et al., *The Cyborg Handbook,* 29–33 (29).

6. On mechanistic thinking in the seventeenth and eighteenth centuries, see Muri, *The Enlightenment Cyborg.*

7. See Erik Davis, "Synthetic Meditations: Cogito in the Matrix," in *Prefiguring Cyberculture: An Intellectual History,* ed. Darren Tofts, Annemarie Jonson, and Alessio Cavallaro (Cambridge, MA: MIT Press, 2002), 12–27.

8. Based on Martin Caidin's novel *Cyborg* (New York: Warner, 1972), the series aired on ABC, 1974–1978.

9. Created at *Marvel Comics,* with character and story by Stan Lee and Larry Lieber and art by Jack Kirby and Don Heck, Iron Man first appeared in *Tales of Suspense* 39 (March 1963).

10. See the documentary *Bruce Lee in His Own Words* (John Little, 1998), included in *Enter the Dragon* DVD release (Warner, 1998).

11. See Kang, *Sublime Dreams of Living Machines.*

12. For cybernetic fantasies of the 1920s, see Matthew Biro, *The Dada Cyborg: Visions of the New Human in Weimar Berlin* (Minneapolis: University of Minnesota Press, 2009).

13. Anson Rabinbach, *The Human Motor: Energy, Fatigue, and the Origins of Modernity* (Berkeley: University of California Press, 1990).

14. See Harold B. Segel, *Pinocchio's Progeny: Puppets, Marionettes, Automatons, and Robots in Modernist and Avant-Garde Drama* (Baltimore: Johns Hopkins University Press, 1995).

15. Vase paintings of the death of Talos date from the fifth century BCE. Apollonius's *Argonautica* is the earliest literary treatment, written in the third century BCE. See Morris, *Daidalos and the Origins of Greek Art*, 259–71, for alternative cult genealogies of this figure. A basic reading of statue-making processes in the story was proposed by Robert Graves, *The Greek Myths* (London: Penguin, 1993), 311–19.

16. The ancient word is *ichor*, which identifies this as a special type of blood, not human blood.

17. Blood actually contains iron, which is needed for hemoglobin, the protein in red blood cells that carries oxygen. Iron objects and tools seem to rub off their scent onto the skin because iron ions oxidize certain oils on the skin surface.

18. See Gross, *Dream of the Moving Statue.*

19. Morris, *Daidalos and the Origins of Greek Art.* Also see Lorraine Daston and Katharine Park, *Wonders and the Order of Nature, 1150–1750* (New York: Zone Books, 1998).

20. Plato mentions Daidalos in the *Meno* (97e–98a) in a joke about how his statues needed to be tied or tied down or they tended to run away. Some art historians propose that the statement refers to the lifelike design of the statues, but this misses Plato's sarcasm in this comment and the implicit pun that runaway objects might just have been stolen. Amelie Frost Benedikt treats this story as an analogy that refers to value, referring to the distinction between knowledge and opinion in *Meno* in "Runaway Statues: Platonic Lessons on the Limits of an Analogy," presented at the Twentieth World Congress of Philosophy, Boston University, August 10–15, 1998, online at http://www.bu.edu/wcp/Papers/Anci/AnciBene .htm (accessed October 1, 2013). In another interpretation, Plato's discussion of lively statues refers to the mutilated herms of Athenian civic history that occurred in 415 BCE. See Thucydides, *Histories*, 6.27–29.

21. See Faraone, *Talismans and Trojan Horses.*

22. Whether there are dualist tendencies in Aristotle's thought is under debate. See W. W. Fortenbaugh, "Recent Scholarship on the Psychology of Aristotle," *Classical World* 60 (1967): 316–27. On instrumentalism and hylomorphism, see C. Kahn, "Sensation and Consciousness in Aristotle's Psychology," in *Articles on Aristotle*, vol. 4, *Psychology and Aesthetics*, ed. J. Barnes, M. Schofield, and R. Sorabji (London: Duckworth, 1979), and Gad Freudenthal, *Aristotle's Theory of Material Substance: Heat and Pneuma, Form and Soul* (Oxford: Oxford University Press, 1995). Also Philip J. van Der Eijk, "Aristotle's Psycho-physiological Account of the Soul-Body Relationship," in *Psyche and Soma: Physicians and Metaphysicians on the Mind-Body Problem from Antiquity to Enlightenment*, ed. John P. Wright and Paul Potter (Oxford: Oxford University Press, 2002), 57–78.

23. Martin Heidegger's work on material embodiment attempts to reformulate Aristotle's material and psychological philosophy. See Martin Heidegger, *The Question regarding Technology and Other Essays*, trans. William Lovitt (New York: Harper and Row, 1977); Martin Heidegger, *Poetry, Language, Thought*, trans. Albert Hofstadter (New York: Harper and Row, 1971).

24. Aristotle, *De Respiratione*, ed. W. S. Hett, Loeb Classical Library (Cambridge, MA: Harvard University Press, 1935), 480a16. Aristotle mentions the bellows (474a13) and describes the process in detail (480a21).

25. Aristotle also proposes that fish choke when out of the water because they overheat, as the air is not the appropriate cooling medium for them. So do air-breathing animals when in the water. The breathing of oysters remains mysterious for him, although his cooling system makes obvious connections to their opening and closing shells and the circulation of water. *De Respiratione* 476b30, 479b, 480b.

26. *De Respiratione* 480b10–21.

27. Also appearing as *pleumōn* in ancient Greek. In poetic language an associated word would be *pnoē* (breath), which both Sophocles and Euripides used metaphorically to signify flame, as in "the breath of Hephaistos" and "the breath of fire."

28. *De Respiratione* 476a7–11.

29. Aristotle's students and listeners may also have chuckled at his extended puns, subtly culminating in his mention of the force *phusikē dunamis* (480a25) that surrounds the nutritive soul. *Phusikē dunamis* can be translated as natural power, or as vital force, but it also echoes the many *phus-* words that appear in this treatise, which invite us to mistake it momentarily for a neologism (meaning something like "blow-power," "bellows-power," or "the power of exhaling"). This would be a memorable pun, because *phusikē dunamis* would thus define vital force as breathing power and as *pneuma*, while reminding students that Aristotle is doing natural philosophy (also *phusikē*). On the other hand, the more Platonist of Aristotle's students may have found his etymological games rather basic compared to the poetic flights of etymological association abundant in the Platonic dialogues and could connect Aristotle's words here to the extended examples in Plato's *Cratylus* 400a–b. In that dialogue, Socrates derives many etymological definitions for the soul, some of which he also ridicules. He mentions one derivation of *psuche* from its capacity to revive the body (*anapsuchon*); a second commonplace possibility, in which the soul is defined as a cooling medium (*psuche* from *psuchoun*, "cooling"); and a more elaborate etymology that defines the soul as that which holds and carries the body (*phusin ochei kai echei* becomes the neologist *phusechē*, which is then contracted to *psuche*).

30. *De Respiratione,* 473a3–7.

31. Although many Greek writers mention the vacuum in stock phrases, few display Aristotle's accurate and mechanically oriented grasp of its operation. By comparison, Plato mentions the concept but does not understand it. In a circular system for breathing Plato proposes in *Timaeus* 79b, for example, the exhaled breath exits our body, but since a vacuum cannot exist it doesn't enter a void but instead pushes the adjacent air from its place, which in turn has to move forward and displace the next pocket of air, until some of this air is eventually pushed back into the windpipe. Exhaling and inhaling are thus imagined as a wheel turning, made out of a series of displaced pockets of air. Although Plato refers to the principle of the vacuum in this explanation, he clearly misunderstands where a vacuum would occur if it could, which is in the lungs.

32. For a longer discussion of ancient approaches to mechanism, see Sylvia Berryman, *The Mechanical Hypothesis in Ancient Greek Natural Philosophy* (Cambridge: Cambridge University Press, 2009).

33. On Aristotle's teleology and its relation to mechanical analogy, see Heinrich von Staden, "Teleology and Mechanism: Aristotelian Biology and Early Hellenistic Medicine," in *Aristotelische Biologie: Intentionen, Methoden, Ergebnisse,* ed. Wolfgang Kullmann and Sabine Föllinger (Stuttgart: Franz Steiner Verlag, 1997), 183–208.

34. Ancient communities undertook large-scale engineering projects such as mines and tunnels, irrigation and aqueduct works, ship and temple building, metalworking, and the expansive import and export of rare materials. Loading, unloading, and transferring materials to work sites led to the design of complex cranes and weight-lifting equipment. For general accounts of ancient technology see J. G. Landels, *Engineering in the Ancient World* (Berkeley: University of California Press, 1978); Robert S. Brumbaugh, *Ancient Greek Gadgets and Machines* (New York: Crowell, 1966); A. G. Drachmann, *The Mechanical Technology of Greek and Roman Antiquity* (Madison: University of Wisconsin Press, 1963).

35. I propose this visible motion transfer based on the description of automata in *De Partium Animalibus* 701b5, which I imagine with things hitting and propelling one another as they fall, like dominoes.

36. *De Motu Animalium* 703b2–11.

37. Aristotle gives the same examples about involuntary motion, related again to the heart and the penis, in *De Anima* 432b29. The idea that the heart and the penis also display resistance to stimuli is very important, but it occurs in a passage that has been corrupted by later interpolations. I use the beginning of the passage (about their resistance to stimuli) and not the ending, in which a material explanation is given (they do this because the matter that causes these reactions is sometimes present in the proper proportions and sometimes not). See *De Motu Animalium* 703b36–704a2.

38. *De Motu Animalium* 701b2–10. This passage contains both a reference to puppets and automata and a reference to a toy car, which is designed in such a way that even a straight pull causes it to move in a circle, because the wheels on one side are bigger than the wheels on the other.

39. *De Motu Animalium* 702b.

40. *De Motu Animalium* 703b.

41. *De Motu Animalium* 703b24–25.

42. See Pseudo-Aristotle, *Mechanika* (*Questions of Mechanics*) 848a. This treatise was very influential. It was attributed to Aristotle for most of the Middle Ages and Renaissance, but it was probably written around the time of his two successors at the Lyceum, Theophrastus and Strato. The mode of explanation is consistent with Aristotle's works and the Peripatetic School. See Paul Lawrence Rose and Stillman Drake, "The Pseudo-Aristotelian Questions of Mechanics in Renaissance Culture," *Studies in the Renaissance* 18 (1971): 65–104; also W. R. Laird, "The Scope of Renaissance Mechanics," *Osiris*, 2nd ser. 2 (1986): 43–68.

43. *De Generatione Animalium* 734b10–25.

44. *De Generatione Animalium* 741b8–10. For a discussion of Aristotle's theories of generation see Freudenthal, *Aristotle's Theory of Material Substance*.

45. In the *Physics* 266a–267b Aristotle posits a "first mover," which is able to create movement without moving. Nussbaum notes that for Aristotle live things exist between two extremes: the unmoved mover, on the one hand, Aristotle's extrapolated entity that put the world in motion, and a rock on the other. The rock does not move, nor does it have the capacity to move anything else. The unmoved mover has the capacity to move others and has caused the process of that universal motion. Martha C. Nussbaum, *The Fragility of Goodness: Luck and Ethics in Greek Tragedy and Philosophy* (Cambridge: Cambridge University Press, 1986), 276.

46. *De Anima* 405a20.

47. *De Anima* 406b5.

48. See Silvio A. Bedini, "The Role of Automata in the History of Technology," *Technology and Culture* 5 (1964). Hans Bullmann of Nuremberg (?–1535) and Hans Schlottheim (1547–1625) of Augsburg were mechanical prodigies and produced numerous ingenious automata for European rulers. Juanelo Turriano (known as Gianello Torriano in Italy) (b. 1500–1515, d. 1585) was a courtier for Charles V in Spain. Following Charles's abdication of the throne in 1555, his court moved to the monastery of San Yuste, where Juanelo apparently created mechanical wonders to amuse the infirm king.

49. For a detailed discussion of one monk automaton, based on a likeness of San Diego of Alcala, see Elizabeth King, "Clockwork Prayer: A Sixteenth-Century Mechanical Monk," *Blackbird: An Online Journal of Literature and the Arts* 1.1 (Spring 2002), online at http://www.blackbird.vcu .edu/v1n1/nonfiction/king_e/prayer_introduction.htm (accessed October 1, 2013).

50. In *Laws*, Plato likens the reason and passions to *neura* (or *smērinthoi*, another word for the puppet strings) of different materials: the passions, made of iron, sway and pull the person while reason is flexible and made of gold. Plato *Laws* 644b–645c. In the *Republic*, Plato mentions a screen used in puppet shows in the allegory of the cave passages, 514b.

51. *De Anima* 412b5–10.

52. See Michael Gorman, "Between the Demonic and the Miraculous: Athanasius Kircher and the Baroque Culture of Machines," in *The Great Art of Knowing: The Baroque Encyclopedia of Athanasius Kircher*, ed. Daniel Stolzenberg (Stanford, CA: Stanford University Libraries, 2001), 59–70. Gorman discusses the epistemological conservatism of technological demonstrations: "feats of natural magic can resemble miracles to those who are ignorant of their true causes. . . . By producing wonder, fear and amusement, however, Kircher's magical machines rehearsed his visitors' reactions to the miraculous and the demonic, and trained them in civility and piety" (ibid., 68). Online at http://hotgates.stanford.edu/Eyes/machines/machines .htm (accessed October 1, 2013).

53. Letter to Henry More, February 5, 1649, in *Oeuvres de Descartes*, ed. Charles Adam and Paul Tannery, 12 vols. (Paris: Vrin, 1964–1972), 5:267–79 (276). See also the discussion in Peter Harrison, "Descartes on Animals," *Philosophical Quarterly* 42.167 (April 1992): 219–27.

54. Descartes describes why automata interest him: "it seems agreeable to reason that, since art is the imitator of nature, and men can fabricate various automata, in which there is motion without any thought, so nature also produces its automata, far exceeding those made by art, namely all the bruta." Letter to Henry More, February 5, 1649, in *Oeuvres de Descartes*, 5:277–78.

55. Johann Kepler's *Ad Vitellionem paralipomena* (1604) established on anatomical and geometric grounds that the eye is a camera obscura (the pupil funnels the visible radiation, the lens focuses and projects it, and the retina provides a screen for it). Kepler, *Paralipomena*, vols. 1 and 2, in Johannes Kepler, *Gesammelte Werke*, ed. Walther von Dyck and Max Caspar (Munich: C. H. Beck, 1939), 2:166–77. See also David C. Lindberg, *Theories of Vision from Al-Kindi to Kepler* (Chicago: University of Chicago Press, 1996) 178–208, and Stephen Straker, "The Eye Made Other: Durer, Kepler, and the Mechanization of Light and Vision," in *Science, Technology, and Culture in Historical Perspective*, ed. L.A. Knafla, M.S. Staum, and T.H.E. Travers (Calgary: University of Calgary Press, 1976): 7–25.

56. See Julian Jaynes, "The Problem of Animate Motion in the Seventeenth Century," *Journal of the History of Ideas* 31.2 (1970): 219–34; also Steven Gaukroger, *Descartes: An Intellectual Biography* (Oxford: Oxford University Press, 1995), who discusses Descartes's experiences with garden automata (63–64).

57. Des Chene, *Spirits and Clocks*, 39–40.

58. In René Descartes, *Discourse on Method and The Meditations*, trans. F. E. Sutcliffe (New York: Penguin, 1986), 65.

59. Des Chene, *Spirits and Clocks*, 153.

60. On eighteenth-century automata modeling body processes, see Riskin, "The Defecating Duck"; Riskin, "Eighteenth-Century Wetware."

61. Barbara Maria Stafford, *Visual Analogy: Consciousness as the Art of Connecting* (Cambridge, MA: MIT Press, 1999), 10.

62. The anecdote refers to German physicist Georg Bose, who "charged women, preferably pretty ones, wearing insulated shoes with electricity; the cavaliers from whom they demanded a kiss received an electric shock." Quoted in Asendorf, *Batteries of Life*, 155–56, from Will Durant and Ariel Durant, *The Story of Civilization*, vol. 9, *The Age of Voltaire* (New York: Simon and Schuster, 1965), 519.

63. See Phil Dusenberry, whose advertising firm BBDO created the slogan for General Electric in 1979, in *Then We Set His Hair on Fire: Insights and Accidents from a Hall of Fame Career in Advertising* (New York: Portfolio, 2005). Before 1979, company slogans included "Progress for People" and "Progress Is Our Most Important Product." GE retired "We Bring Good Things to Life" in 2003, when the company adopted "Imagination at Work."

64. From a sketch written by Walter Edison Kruesi in 1929, which was approved by Thomas Edison. Quoted in David E. Nye, *The Invented Self: An Anti-biography from Documents of Thomas A. Edison* (Odense: Odense University Press, 1983), 93.

65. Electric and magnetic transmissions have a relative independence from materiality in the popular imagination, although this is not accurate in technical terms. Constructing electric bulbs, for example, depends on being able to produce a reliable vacuum within the bulb.

66. See Huyssen, "The Vamp and the Machine." Huyssen does not connect the vamp with magnetism or electricity.

67. Leopold von Sacher-Masoch, *Venus in Furs*, trans. Joachim Neugroschel (New York: Penguin, 2000), 35, 90.

68. Villiers de l'Isle-Adam, *L'Eve future*, trans. Robert Martin Adams (Urbana: University of Illinois Press, 2000).

69. Walt Whitman, "I Sing the Body Electric," in *Leaves of Grass and Other Writings*, ed. Michael Moon (New York: Norton, 2002), line 54.

70. Henry Adams, "The Dynamo and the Virgin" (1900), in *The Education of Henry Adams* (New York: Penguin, 2004), 360–370 (365).

71. See William James, *The Principles of Psychology*, vol. 1 (1890; New York: Dover Publications, 1950), where James describes the problematic treatment of the body: "The same object being sometimes treated as a part of me, at other times as simply mine, and then again as if I had nothing to do with it at all." (291)

72. See Moravec, *Mind Children*; also Raymond Kurzweil, *The Age of Spiritual Machines*, for some of the basic concepts of "transhumanism."

CHAPTER 3   THE MECHANICAL SLAVE

1. Isaac Asimov's "The Bicentennial Man" was first published in *Stellar* 2 (February 1976). Page numbers refer to Isaac Asimov, *The Bicentennial Man and Other Stories* (New York: Doubleday, 1976), 135–72.

2. See Kevin LaGrandeur, "The Persistent Peril of the Artificial Slave," *Science Fiction Studies* 38.2 (July 2011): 232–52.

3. Some sources date the introduction of the word "robot" to the play's Czech publication in 1920, and others to the play's first performance in 1921.

4. LeiLani Nishime, "The Mulatto Cyborg: Imagining a Multiracial Future," *Cinema Journal* 44.2 (Winter 2005): 34–49.

5. Juliana Hu Pegues, "Miss Cylon: Empire and Adoption in *Battlestar Galactica*," *MELUS* 33.4 (Winter 2008): 189–209.

6. Toni Morrison, *Playing in the Dark: Whiteness and the Literary Imagination* (New York: Vintage, 1993), 5–7.

7. See Gary Westfahl, *The Mechanics of Wonder: The Creation of the Idea of Science Fiction* (Liverpool: Liverpool University Press, 1999); Istvan Csicsery-Ronay Jr., *The Seven Beauties of Science Fiction* (Hanover, NH: Wesleyan University Press, 2011); Carl Freedman, *Critical Theory and Science Fiction* (Hanover, NH: Wesleyan University Press, 2000).

8. Wanda Raiford, "Race, Robots, and the Law," in *New Boundaries in Political Science Fiction*, ed. Donald M. Hassler and Clyde Wilcox (Columbia: University of South Carolina Press, 2008), 93–112.

9. See Scott v. Sandford, 60 U.S. 393 (1856). The full text of the case is available online at http://supreme.justia.com/us/60/393/case.html (accessed October 1, 2013).

10. See Sue Short, "The Measure of a Man? Asimov's Bicentennial Man, *Star Trek*'s Data, and Being Human," *Extrapolation* 44 (Summer 2003): 209–23.

11. Richard Pryor's album *The Bicentennial N____* (Reprise/Warner Brothers, 1976) was a Gold Record and won a Grammy award. Pryor publicly discussed and discontinued his use of the n-word after his trip to Africa in 1979.

12. Justice Thurgood Marshall, "Reflections on the Bicentennial of the United States Constitution," *Harvard Law Review* 101.1 (November 1987): 1–5.

13. Isaac Asimov, "The Robot Chronicles," in *Gold: The Final Science Fiction Collection* (New York: HarperCollins, 1995), 161–75 (165).

14. Ibid., 164.

15. See James Gunn, *Isaac Asimov: The Foundations of Science Fiction* (Oxford: Oxford University Press, 1982), especially chapter 3, "Variations upon a Robot," 51–78.

16. Eando Binder, *Adam Link—Robot* (New York: Paperback Library, 1965). The stories were published in *Amazing Stories* from 1939 to 1942 and were later collected into novel form with some editorial changes in 1965. Page numbers refer to this paperback novel edition and will be given parenthetically in the text.

17. According to both Isaac Asimov and his then agent Frederick Pohl, using the title of the first Adam Link story "I, Robot" for the publication of Asimov's collected robot stories in 1950 was Pohl's idea. See http://www.thewaythefutureblogs.com/2010/03/isaac-part-5-in-our-continuing-series (accessed October 10, 2013).

18. Isaac Asimov's "Robbie" was first published as "Strange Playfellow," *Super Science Stories* (September 1940): 67–77.

19. See Darko Suvin, "Three World Paradigms for SF: Asimov, Yevremov, Lem," in Suvin, *Positions and Presuppositions in Science Fiction*, 99–111 (101).

20. Ralph Ellison, *Invisible Man* (London: Penguin, 1965): "Tell them to teach them that when they call you n_ to make a rhyme with trigger it makes the gun backfire" (369).

21. E. M. Forster, "The Machine Stops" (1909), in *Selected Stories* (London: Penguin, 2001), 91–123.

22. Isaac Asimov's "The Evitable Conflict" was first published in *Astounding Science Fiction* (June 1950) and is the last story in the *I, Robot* collection. Page numbers refer to *I, Robot* (New York: Bantam, 2008).

23. Isaac Asimov, "The Life and Times of Multivac," first published in *New York Times*, January 5, 1975. Reprinted in *The Bicentennial Man and Other Stories* (New York: Doubleday, 1976), 114–24.

24. Karel Čapek, *R.U.R. (Rossum's Universal Robots)*, trans. Claudia Novack (New York: Penguin, 2004). Unless otherwise noted, all quotations are from this edition.

25. H. G. Wells, "The Silliest Film: Will Machinery Make Robots of Men?" *New York Times*, April 17, 1927. Reprinted in *The Science Fiction Film Reader*, ed. Gregg Rickman (New York: Limelight, 2004), 5–12.

26. Thomas Disch describes the Robots as "a nightmare vision of the proletariat seen through middle class eyes," in *The Dreams Our Stuff Is Made Of: How Science Fiction Conquered the World* (New York: Simon and Schuster, 1998), 8.

27. Kamila Kinyon, "The Phenomenology of Robots: Confrontations with Death in Karel Čapek's *R.U.R.*," *Science Fiction Studies* 26.3 (November 1999): 379–400.

28. See G. W. F. Hegel, *Phenomenology of Spirit*, trans. A. V. Miller (Oxford: Clarendon Press, 1977), paragraphs 178–96.

29. James Agate, *The Saturday Review*, May 5, 1923, 596–97.

30. The play's early reviews are included in first Theatre Guild edition of *R.U.R.* (1923), ix, x. Alexander Woolcott in the *New York Herald* describes the play as "hair-raising melodrama" and "murderous social satire"; Maida Castellum in *The Call* as "philosophic melodrama" and a "brilliant satire on our mechanized civilization"; Stephen Rathbun in the *New York Evening Sun* as "super melodrama—the melodrama of action, plus ideas"; and Heywood Broun in the *New York World* as "an extraordinary searching study of the nature of human life and human society."

31. See Stephen Leacock, "The Iron Man and the Tin Woman," in *The Iron Man and the Tin Woman, and Other Futurities* (London: Bodley Head, 1929), 2–5.

32. "The Robot" (Dave Fleischer, 1932), in *Betty Boop: The Definitive Collection* (VHS Republic Pictures, 1998).

33. *The Romance of Robot: A Sentimental Satire in One Act*, music by Frederic Hart, libretto by Tillman Breiseth (New York: New York Public Library Microfilm, 1937). See also Kenneth J. Bindas, "A Society without Soul: The Fear of Modernism in the 1937 Opera *The Romance of Robot*," *Journal of American Culture* 17.1 (March 1994): 71–78.

34. "Superman: The Mechanical Monsters" (Dave Fleischer, Paramount, 1941). See the film at http://www.archive.org/details/superman_the_mechanical_monsters (accessed October 1, 2013).

35. See Walter Prichard Eaton, *The Theatre Guild: The First Ten Years* (New York: Brentano's, 1929); also Roy S. Waldau, *Vintage Years of the Theatre Guild, 1928–1939* (Cleveland: Press of Case Western Reserve University, 1972).

36. *The Adding Machine* was first performed by the Theatre Guild on March 19, 1923. Directed by Philip Moeller at the Garrick Theatre, it ran for seventy-two performances. In Elmer Rice, *Seven Plays by Elmer Rice* (New York: Viking Press, 1950), 65–108.

37. Eugene O'Neill's *Dynamo* was first performed by the Theatre Guild in the Martin Beck Theatre on February 11, 1929. Directed by Philip Moeller and with stage settings by Lee Simonson, it ran for fifty performances. See *Eugene O'Neill: Complete Plays, 1920–1931* (New York: Library of America, 1988), 819–85.

38. *Battlestar Galactica* episode, "The Farm" 2:5, aired Sci Fi Channel, August 12, 2005.

39. See Charis Thompson, *Making Parents: The Ontological Choreography of Reproductive Technologies* (Cambridge, MA: MIT Press, 2005); also Susanna Paasonen, "Thinking through the Cybernetic Body: Popular Cybernetics and Feminism," *Rhizomes* 4 (Spring 2002), at http://www.rhizomes.net/issue4/paasonen.html (accessed October 1, 2013).

40. Claudia Springer in *Electronic Eros: Bodies and Desire in the Postindustrial Age* (Austin: University of Texas Press, 1996) discusses the imagery of early cybernetic narratives as disembodied ecstasy, but the same imagery can evoke absorption.

41. Captain William Snelgrave, *A New Account of Some Parts of Guinea, and the Slave Trade* (1734), excerpt in *The Norton Anthology of English Literature Online*, at http://www.wwnorton .com/college/english/nael/18century/topic_2/snelgrave.htm (accessed October 1, 2013).

42. John Barbot, "A Description of the Coasts of North and South Guinea," in *Collection of Voyages and Travels*, ed. Thomas Astley and John Churchill (London, 1732), excerpt in Steven

Mintz, ed., *African American Voices: A Documentary Reader, 1619–1877* (New York: Blackwell, 2009), 40–45 (43).

43. Olaudah Equiano, *The Interesting Narrative of the Life of Olaudah Equiano or Gustavus Vassa the African* (London, 1789), in *Slave Narratives*, ed. William L. Andrews and Henry Louis Gates Jr. (New York: Library of America, 2000), 35–242. Page references will be given parenthetically in the text.

44. William Arens explains the Western obsession with "savage" cannibalism as a discursive formation in *The Man-Eating Myth: Anthropology and Anthropophagy* (New York: Oxford University Press, 1979). See also Gananath Obeyesekere, *Cannibal Talk: The Man-Eating Myth and Human Sacrifice in the South Seas* (Berkeley: University of California Press, 2005); Rebecca Weaver-Hightower, *Empire Islands: Castaways, Cannibals, and Fantasies of Conquest* (Minneapolis: University of Minnesota Press, 2007).

45. See Markman Ellis, "Crusoe, Cannibalism, and Empire," in *Robinson Crusoe: Myths and Metamorphoses*, ed. Lieve Spaas and Brian Stimpson (New York: Macmillan, 1996), 45–61; Neil Heims, "Robinson Crusoe and the Fear of Being Eaten," *Colby Quarterly* 19.4 (December 1983): 190–93.

46. In fact, among the options of the poor, for Swift, is to "sell themselves to the Barbadoes." On cannibalism and the rise of mercantilism, see Carol Houlihan Flynn, *The Body in Swift and Defoe* (Cambridge: Cambridge University Press, 2005).

47. John Locke, *The Second Treatise of Government* (1690), chapter 5, paragraph 27.

48. Paul Gilroy, *The Black Atlantic: Modernity and Double Consciousness* (London: Verso, 1993).

49. Serfdom in central and eastern Europe, for example, combined stratification in terms of class, economic dependence, and social and ethnic oppression. For discussion of serfdom see Eugene Genovese, *The Political Economy of Slavery: Studies in the Economy and Society of the Slave South* (Middletown, CT: Wesleyan University Press, 1978); Jerome Blum, *The End of the Old Order in Rural Europe* (Princeton, NJ: Princeton University Press, 1978), esp. 305–31.

50. "This is the perfect condition of Slavery, which is nothing else, but the State of War continued, between a lawful Conqueror, and a Captive." Locke, "Of Slavery," *Second Treatise*, chapter 4, section 24.

51. Aphra Behn, *Oroonoko; or, the Royal Slave* (1688), ed. Joanna Lipking (New York: Norton, 1997).

52. Orlando Patterson, *Slavery and Social Death: A Comparative Study* (Cambridge, MA: Harvard University Press, 1982), 119.

53. See Christopher L. Miller, *The French Atlantic Triangle: Literature and Culture of the Slave Trade* (Durham: Duke University Press, 2008), 47, 415n28.

54. Jean-Jacques Rousseau, *The Social Contract and Discourse on the Origin of Inequality*, ed. Lester G. Crocker (New York: Simon and Schuster, 1967). Referring to Grotius and Hobbes and their arguments of the rights of kings, Rousseau states: "In this way we have mankind divided like herds of cattle, each of which has a master, who looks after it in order to devour it" (9); and, "Now a man who becomes another's slave does not give himself; he sells himself at the very least for his subsistence. But why does a nation sell itself? So far from a king supplying his subjects with their subsistence he draws his from them; and according to Rabelais, a king does not live on a little" (12).

55. Patterson, *Slavery and Social Death*, ix.

56. Scholars generally agree that slavery in the British colonies shifts to a hereditary state, as defined by legal precedent, in the period between 1660 and 1710. See Winthrop Jordan, *White over Black: American Attitudes toward the Negro, 1550–1812* (Chapel Hill: University of North

Carolina Press, 1968), 81–82; also David Brion Davis, *The Problem of Slavery in Western Culture* (New York: Oxford University Press, 1966), 132; Michael Goldfield, "The Color of Politics in the United States: White Supremacy as the Main Explanation for the Peculiarities of American Politics from Colonial Times to the Present," in *The Bounds of Race: Perspectives on Hegemony and Resistance*, ed. Dominick La Capra (Ithaca, NY: Cornell University Press, 1991), 116.

57. George Fitzhugh, *Cannibals All! or, Slaves Without Masters* (Richmond, VA, 1857), and *Sociology of the South; or, The Failure of Free Society* (Richmond, VA, 1854).

58. I am indebted to Howard Temperley's "Capitalism, Slavery, and Ideology," *Past and Present* 75 (May 1977): 94–118, for identifying Fitzhugh's influence on Marx.

59. See Louis Althusser, "Ideology and Ideological State Apparatuses (Notes towards an Investigation)," in *Lenin and Philosophy and Other Essays* (London: New Left Books, 1971).

60. Baldick, *In Frankenstein's Shadow*.

61. Elizabeth Young, *Black Frankenstein: The Making of an American Metaphor* (New York: New York University Press, 2008), 14, 27.

62. *Scott v. Sandford*, at http://supreme.justia.com/us/60/393/case.html (accessed October 1, 2013).

63. See Saidiya Hartman, *Scenes of Subjection: Terror, Slavery, and Self-Making in Nineteenth-Century America* (Oxford: Oxford University Press, 1997).

64. "Custom, Law, / Ye blessings, and ye curses of mankind, / What evils do ye cause? We feel enslaved, / Yet move in your direction." Ann Yearsley, *A Poem on the Inhumanity of the Slave Trade* (London: G.G.J. and J. Robinson, 1788); E-text at http://www.brycchancarey .com/slavery/yearsley1.htm (accessed September 1, 2013), stanza 3.

65. Arnold Guyot describes slavery in 1849: "slavery, that fatal heritage of another age, which the Union still drags after it, as the convict drags his chain and ball." Arnold Guyot, *The Earth and Man: Lectures on Comparative Physical Geography, in Its Relation to the History of Mankind* (Boston: Gould, Kendall, and Lincoln, 1849), 275.

66. Such descriptions are widespread in abolitionist texts of the eighteenth and nineteenth centuries. Here are some indicative locations. The iron pen is in the lines "Where are thy statutes? Whose the iron pen / That gave thee precedent?" in Ann Yearsley's *A Poem on the Inhumanity of the Slave Trade* (1788), stanza 8. In William Roscoe's "The Wrongs of Africa" (1787) we find marble hearts and iron hands: "The dread spirit of commercial gain, / Whose heart is marble, and whose harpy hands / Are stain'd with blood of millions," stanza 27, and "Whilst with an iron hand ye crush to earth / The helpless African," stanza 32. "Iron-hearted masters" are in William Cowper, "The Negro's Complaint" (1788), line 21, but the figure is widespread. The iron rod of oppression occurs in the lines: "Ye Sons of Mercy! O complete your work; / Wrench from Oppression's hand the iron rod, / And bid the cruel feel the pains they give." From "THOMPSON'S LIBERTY," used as epigraph for Hannah More, *Slavery, A Poem* (London: T. Cadell, 1788); E-text located at http://www.brycchancarey.com/slavery/morepoems.htm (accessed September 1, 2013). The iron hand of pain and the steel soul unmoved by misery occur in Phillis Wheatley's lines "She feels the iron hand of pain no more" (in "On the Death of a Young Lady of Five Years of Age"), and "Steel'd was that soul and by no misery mov'd / That from a father seiz'd his babe belov'd" ("To the Right Honourable William, of Dartmouth"). Her poem "Niobe in Distress for Her Children Slain by Apollo" ends with the scene of the proud queen turning into a marble statue, though textual notes alert us to the completion of the poem by a different hand. Tears turn to stone in the face of jeering during the parliamentary discussion of the abolition of the slave trade in England, in Anna Letitia Barbauld, "Epistle to William Wilberforce, Esq. On the Rejection of the Bill for Abolishing the Slave Trade": "Bane of ingenuous minds, th' unfeeling sneer, / Which, sudden, turns to stone the falling tear," stanza 7.

67. More, *Slavery, A Poem.*

68. See Genovese, *Political Economy of Slavery*; Robert S. Starobin, *Industrial Slavery in the Old South* (New York: Oxford University Press, 1970); also Heywood Fleisig, "Slavery, the Supply of Agricultural Labor, and the Industrialization of the South," *Journal of Economic History* 36.3 (September 1976): 572–97; Fred Bateman and Thomas Weiss, *A Deplorable Scarcity: The Failure of Industrialization in the Slave Economy* (Chapel Hill: University of North Carolina Press, 1981), esp. 157–63; Charles B. Dew, "Slavery and Technology in the Antebellum Southern Iron Industry: The Case of Buffal Forge," in *Science and Medicine in the Old South*, ed. Ronald L. Numbers and Todd L. Savitt (Baton Rouge: Louisiana State University Press, 1989) 107–26; T. Stephen Whitman, "Industrial Slavery at the Margin: The Maryland Chemical Works," *Journal of Southern History* 59.1 (February 1993): 31–62.

69. From "An Address to the Public, from the Pennsylvania Society for Promoting the Abolition of Slavery and the Relief of Free Negroes Unlawfully Held in Bondage," signed by the Society's President, Benjamin Franklin, Philadelphia, November 9, 1789. E-text at http://memory.loc.gov/cgi-bin/query/D?rbpebib:1:./temp/~ammem_Fxbo:: (accessed October 1, 2013).

70. Frederick Douglass, *Autobiographies* (New York: Library of America, 1994), 421.

71. J. D., "Is Ignorance Bliss?" *North Star*, April 7, 1848. The phrasing echoes Thomas Paine on the evils of hereditary monarchy: "It requires some talents to be a common mechanic; but to be a king requires only the animal figure of man—a sort of breathing automaton." Paine uses a mechanical association for both sides of the comparison, with the old monarchy automaton clearly inferior to the democratic ideal of a talented mechanic. In *The Writings of Thomas Paine, Collected and Edited by Moncure Daniel Conway (1779–1792)*, vol. 2, chap. 3.

72. Herman Melville, "The Bell Tower," first published in *Putnam's Monthly Magazine* (August 1855), reprinted in H. Bruce Franklin, *Future Perfect: American Science Fiction of the Nineteenth Century, an Anthology* (New Brunswick, NJ: Rutgers University Press, 1995).

73. See Marvin Fisher, *Going Under: Melville's Short Fiction and the American 1850s* (Baton Rouge: Louisiana State University Press, 1977), 98–99.

74. The descriptions of mechanisms in "The Bell Tower" are likely informed by consultation of guidebooks and other travelers' accounts, since Melville did not visit Italy until 1856, a year after this story was published.

75. See James Emmett Ryan, "Melville in the Brotherhood: Freemasonry, Fraternalism, and the Artisanal Ideal," in *Melville 'Among the Nations': Proceedings of an International Conference, Volos, Greece July 2–6, 1997*, ed. Sanford E. Marovitz and Athanasios C. Christodoulou (Kent, OH: Kent State University Press, 2001), 71–84 (79).

76. Young, *Black Frankenstein*, 42–44.

77. This is H. Bruce Franklin's reading of the bell, in *Future Perfect*, 138.

78. See Klaus Benesch, *Romantic Cyborgs: Authorship and Technology in the American Renaissance* (Amherst: University of Massachusetts Press, 2002), and "Technology Writ Large: The Machine, the Body, and the Text in Melville's Shorter Narratives," *Weber Studies: An Interdisciplinary Humanities Journal* 14.3 (Fall 1997): 61–72.

79. Young, *Black Frankenstein*, 44.

80. Harriet Jacobs, *Incidents in the Life of a Slave Girl, Written by Herself*, in Andrews and Gates, *Slave Narratives*, 743–945 (794–95).

81. Deborah Gray White, *Let My People Go: African Americans, 1804–1860* (New York: Oxford University Press, 1996), 16–17.

82. See Eric Williams, *Capitalism and Slavery* (1944; Chapel Hill: University of North Carolina Press, 1994). Williams claims that the Atlantic slave trade of the eighteenth century was

the foundation for the success of commercial and industrial capitalism. For analysis, see Ralph M. Henry, "Eric Williams and the Reversal of the Unequal Legacy of Capitalism and Slavery," *Callaloo* 20.4 (1997): 829–48; Hilary McD. Beckles, "Capitalism and Slavery: The Debate over Eric Williams," *Social and Economic Studies* 33.4 (1984): 171–91; Barbara Solow and Stanley Engerman, eds., *British Capitalism and Caribbean Slavery: The Legacy of Eric Williams* (Cambridge: Cambridge University Press, 1987). For commerce and antislavery movements, see Philip Gould, *Barbaric Traffic: Commerce and Antislavery in the Eighteenth-Century Atlantic World* (Cambridge, MA: Harvard University Press, 2003).

83. The story of "The Sorcerer's Apprentice" occurs in Lucian of Samosata's *Philopseudes (The Lover of Lies)*, c. 150 CE, and was reinterpreted by Goethe in his 1797 poem.

84. Herman Melville, "The Paradise of Bachelors and the Tartarus of Maids," first published in *Harper's New Monthly Magazine* 10 (April 1855): 670–78.

85. See Cindy Weinstein, *The Literature of Labor and the Labors of Literature: Allegory in Nineteenth-Century American Fiction* (Cambridge: Cambridge University Press, 1995).

86. See David Nye, *American Technological Sublime* (Cambridge, MA: MIT Press, 1996).

87. See R. Keith Aufhauser, "Slavery and Scientific Management," *Journal of Economic History* 33.4 (December 1973): 811–24.

88. Former slave John Brown states: "My old master . . . would pick out two or more of the strongest [hands] and excite them to race at hoeing or picking. . . . He would stand with his watch in his hand, observing their movements, whilst they hoed or picked. . . . Whatever [the winner] did within a given time would be multiplied by a certain rule, for the day's work, and every man's tasks would be staked out accordingly." John Brown, *Slave Life in Georgia: A Narrative of the Life, Sufferings and Escape of John Brown, A Fugitive Slave* (1855), ed. F. N. Boney (Savannah, GA: Beehive Press, 1972), 145, 160.

89. See Mark M. Smith, "Time, Slavery, and Plantation Capitalism in the Ante-bellum American South," *Past and Present* 150 (February 1996): 142–68; also Stanley L. Engerman, "Contract Labor, Sugar, and Technology in the Nineteenth Century," *Journal of Economic History* 43.3 (September 1983): 635–59.

90. See Temperley, "Capitalism, Slavery, and Ideology," 105; also Robert Fogel and Stanley Engerman, *Time on the Cross: The Economics of American Negro Slavery* (New York: Norton, 1991), esp. 202–9; James Oakes, *The Ruling Race: A History of American Slaveholders* (New York: Norton, 1998).

91. Plantation owners' correspondence quoted in Smith, "Time, Slavery, and Plantation Capitalism," 156.

92. Karl Marx, "Manifesto of the Communist Party," from the English edition of 1888, edited by Friedrich Engels. E-text located http://www.marxists.org/archive/marx/works/1848/communist-manifesto/index.htm (accessed October 1, 2013).

93. Temperley, "Capitalism, Slavery, and Ideology," 118.

94. John Adolphus Etzler, *The Paradise within the Reach of All Men, without Labor, by Powers of Nature and Machinery: An Address to All Intelligent Men* (Pittsburgh: Etzler and Reinhold, 1833), 14. Also see Ronald T. Takaki, *Iron Cages: Race and Culture in Nineteenth-Century America* (New York: Oxford University Press, 1990).

95. Ralph Waldo Emerson, *Journals and Miscellaneous Notebooks of Ralph Waldo Emerson*, 10:102–3. See also Paul Gilmore, "Mechanical Means: Emersonian Aesthetic Transcendence and Antebellum Technology," *MLQ* 65.2 (2004): 245–68.

96. As quoted in Perry Miller, "The Responsibility of Mind in a Civilization of Machines," *American Scholar* 31 (1961–1962): 62.

97. Isaac Asimov, "Robot Dreams," in *Robot Dreams: Masterworks of Science Fiction and Fantasy* (New York: Berkley Books, 1986), 39–44.

98. See Lorrie Palmer, "Black Man/White Machine: Will Smith Crosses Over," *Velvet Light Trap* 67 (Spring 2011): 28–40.

99. On the translucent plastics used for Apple designs, see Craig M. Vogel, Jonathan Cagan, and Peter Boatwright, *The Design of Things to Come: How Ordinary People Create Extraordinary Products* (Philadelphia: Wharton School Press, 2005).

100. On seeing blackness in whiteness, see Mary Hamer, "Black and White? Viewing Cleopatra in 1862," in *The Victorians and Race*, ed. Shearer West (Hants: Scholar Press, 1996), 53–67.

101. See Sean Brayton, "The Post-White Imaginary in Alex Proyas's *I, Robot*," *Science Fiction Studies* 35.1 (February 2008): 72–87; Sean Brayton, "The Racial Politics of Disaster and Dystopia in *I Am Legend*," *Velvet Light Trap* 67 (Spring 2011): 66–76.

102. See Despina Kakoudaki, "Spectacles of History: Race Relations, Melodrama, and the Science Fiction/Disaster Film," *Camera Obscura* 17.2 (2002): 109–53; also Linda Williams, *Playing the Race Card: Melodramas of Black and White from Uncle Tom to O.J. Simpson* (Princeton, NJ: Princeton University Press, 2002).

103. See Kristen Whissel, "The Digital Multitude," *Cinema Journal* 49.4 (Summer 2010): 90–110.

104. Alan Tudyk, whose body performance animates the computer-generated character, considers this robot as a child in his comments on the film's official website. The other robots' motions were choreographed by actor/dancer Paul Mercurio (*Strictly Ballroom*). From *I, Robot* official website at http://www.irobotmovie.com/, Production Notes.

105. Roger Ebert notes: "The robots never seem to have the heft and weight of actual metallic machines, and make boring villains." *Chicago Tribune*, July 16, 2004, at http://www.rogerebert .com/reviews/i-robot-2004 (accessed September 1, 2013).

106. See Peter Singer, *Corporate Warriors: The Rise of the Privatized Military Industry* (Ithaca, NY: Cornell University Press, 2004) and *Children at War* (New York: Pantheon, 2005).

107. Russ, *The Female Man*, 194.

CHAPTER 4   THE EXISTENTIAL CYBORG

1. Philip K. Dick, "Impostor," *Astounding Science Fiction* (June 1953), reprinted in *Souls in Metal: An Anthology of Robot Futures*, ed. Mike Ashley (New York: Jove/ HBJ, 1978), 107–22.

2. E. T. A. Hoffman, "The Sandman," in *Tales of Hoffman*, trans. R. J. Hollingdale (New York: Penguin, 1982), 85–125.

3. See Lydia Liu, *The Freudian Robot: Digital Media and the Future of the Unconscious* (Chicago: University of Chicago Press, 2010), 206–19.

4. Edgar Allan Poe's "The Man That Was Used Up" (1839) uses similar processes of linguistic construction and deconstruction.

5. Kang, *Sublime Dreams of Living Machines*, 187. Kang proposes that musical and performing automata function as symbols of a "rational order" in the early eighteenth century and become uncanny in later Romantic texts.

6. Mme du Deffand, Letter to Horace Walpole, October 10, 1766, quoted in Reed Benhamou, "From *Curiosité* to *Utilité*: The Automaton in Eighteenth-Century France," *Studies in Eighteenth-Century Culture* 17 (1987): 93.

7. See Dimitris Vardoulakis, *The Doppelgänger: Literature's Philosophy* (New York: Fordham University Press, 2010).

8. Sigmund Freud, "The Uncanny," in *The Standard Edition of the Complete Psychological Works of Sigmund Freud*, trans. James Strachey (London: Hogarth Press, 1953–1974), 17:219–52.

9. Gustav Meyrink, *The Golem*, trans. Mike Mitchell (Riverside, CA: Ariadne Press, 1995).

10. Clifford Simak, "Good Night Mr. James," *Galaxy* (March 1951), reprinted in *The Androids Are Coming*, ed. Robert Silverberg (New York: Cosmos Books, 2000), 37–59.

11. Alfred Bester, "Fondly Fahrenheit," *The Magazine of Fantasy and Science Fiction* (August 1954), reprinted in ibid., 159–83.

12. Philip K. Dick, "Second Variety," *Space Science Fiction* (May 1953), reprinted in *Robots: Isaac Asimov's Wonderful Worlds of Science Fiction, #9*, ed. Isaac Asimov, Martin Greenberg, and Charles G. Waugh (New York: Signet, 1989), 178–222.

13. Philip K. Dick, "The Electric Ant," *The Magazine of Fantasy and Science Fiction* (October 1969), reprinted in *Machines That Think*, ed. Isaac Asimov, Patricia S. Warrick, and Martin Greenberg (New York: Holt, Rinehart and Winston, 1984), 495–515.

14. René Descartes, *Discourse on Method and the Meditations*, trans. F. E. Sutcliffe (New York: Penguin, 1986), 100.

15. Judith Butler discusses the inscription of the body in Descartes in "How Can I Deny That These Hands and This Body Are Mine?" in *Material Events: Paul de Man and the Afterlife of Theory*, ed. Tom Cohen, Barbara Cohen, J. Hillis Miller, and Andrzej Warminski (Minneapolis: University of Minnesota Press, 2000), 254–73.

16. For a discussion of Descartes's hydraulic and clockwork bodies, see Des Chene, *Spirits and Clocks*. Des Chene (ibid., 114) discusses how anatomical explorations and images of a porous, sieve-like body dominate Descartes's *Treatise of Man*, trans. T. S. Hall (Cambridge: Harvard University Press, 1972).

17. Descartes, *Discourse on Method and the Meditations*, 110.

18. On the impact of Cartesian thought on modern culture, see Richard Rorty, *Philosophy and the Mirror of Nature* (Princeton, NJ: Princeton University Press, 1979); Evelyn Fox Keller, *Reflections on Gender and Science* (New Haven: Yale University Press, 1985).

19. See Susan Bordo, *The Flight to Objectivity: Essays on Cartesianism and Culture* (Albany: SUNY Press, 1987). Bordo discusses the difference between Descartes's proverbial pronouncement "cogito ergo sum" (I think therefore I am) and his less known description "sum res cogitans," which means "I am a thinking thing" or "I am matter that thinks."

20. Philip K. Dick, *Do Androids Dream of Electric Sheep?* (New York: Ballantine, 1996).

21. For an overview of critical approaches to the film, see Judith B. Kerman, ed., *Retrofitting Blade Runner: Issues in Ridley Scott's* Blade Runner *and Philip K. Dick's* Do Androids Dream of Electric Sheep? (Bowling Green, OH: Bowling Green State University Popular Press, 1991); Will Brooker, ed., *The* Blade Runner *Experience: The Legacy of a Science Fiction Classic* (London and New York: Wallflower Press), 2005.

22. Peter Brooker, "Imagining the Real: *Blade Runner* and Discourses on the Postmetropolis," in Will Brooker, *The* Blade Runner *Experience*, 213–24.

23. For Slavoj Žižek this is because the Replicants approach the instabilities of Western subjectivity with knowledge of their status. Slavoj Žižek, "I or He or It (the Thing) Which Thinks," in *Tarrying with the Negative: Kant, Hegel, and the Critique of Ideology* (Durham, NC: Duke University Press, 1993), 9–44 (41).

24. See Scott Bukatman, *Terminal Identity: The Virtual Subject in Postmodern Science Fiction* (Durham, NC: Duke University Press, 1993); Paul M. Sammon, *Future Noir: The Making of* Blade Runner (New York: Harper Prism, 1996); Giuliana Bruno, "Ramble City: Postmodernism and *Blade Runner*," *October* 41 (Summer 1987): 61–74.

25. In this I differ from the reading proposed by Seo-Young Chu, in *Do Metaphors Dream of Literal Sheep? A Science-Fictional Theory of Representation* (Cambridge, MA: Harvard University Press, 2010), who reads the scene in terms of "mechanical vitality" (220).

26. This is the famous last line of *Some Like It Hot* (Billy Wilder, 1959).

27. Lester Del Rey, "Helen O'Loy," *Astounding Science Fiction* (December 1938), reprinted in Ashley, *Souls in Metal*, 17–28.

28. Jane Donawerth discusses the machine/woman merger as misogynist fantasy, in *Frankenstein's Daughters*.

29. For a reading of the story as "a satire on male fantasies," especially in relation to Phil's and Dave's emotional immaturity, see Dominick M. Grace, "Rereading Lester del Rey's 'Helen O'Loy,'" *Science-Fiction Studies* 20.59 (March 1993): 45–52. As Grace summarizes, critics often find the stereotypical treatment of gender in the story insufferable and have dismissed it as a "classic of sexist SF" (45). John Huntington also agrees that it is femininity—not artificiality—that challenges the men in the story. *Rationalizing Genius: Ideological Strategies in the Classic American Science Fiction Short Story* (New Brunswick, NJ: Rutgers University Press, 1989), 104.

30. C. L. Moore, "No Woman Born," *Astounding Science Fiction* (December 1944), reprinted in *Women of Wonder: The Classic Years*, ed. Pamela Sargent (San Diego: Harvest, 1995), 21–64.

31. See Melissa Colleen Stevenson, "Trying to Plug In: Posthuman Cyborgs and the Search for Connection," *Science Fiction Studies* 34.1 (March 2007): 87–105.

32. Judith Butler, *Gender Trouble: Feminism and the Subjection of Identity* (New York: Routledge, 1990), 25. See also Despina Kakoudaki, "Pin-Up and Cyborg: Exaggerated Gender and Artificial Intelligence," in *Future Females, the Next Generation: New Voices and Velocities in Feminist Science Fiction Criticism*, ed. Marleen S. Barr (Lanham, MD: Rowman and Littlefield, 2000), 165–95.

33. See Veronica Hollinger, "(Re)reading Queerly: Science Fiction, Feminism, and Defamiliarization of Gender," in Barr, *Future Females*, 197–215 (204).

34. See Susan Gubar, "C. L. Moore and the Conventions of Women's Science Fiction," *Science Fiction Studies* 7.1 (March 1980): 16–27.

35. See Balsamo, *Technologies of the Gendered Body*.

36. This is a very short list of an extensive feminist tradition in science fiction and criticism: Ann McCaffrey, "The Ship Who Sang" (1961), in *The Ship Who Sang* (New York: Del Rey, 1985); James Tiptree Jr. (pseudonym for Alice Sheldon), "The Girl Who Was Plugged In," in *New Dimensions* 3, ed. Robert Silverberg (New York: Nelson Doubleday, 1973), reprinted in *Reload: Rethinking Women and Cyberculture*, ed. Mary Flanagan and Austin Booth (Cambridge, MA: MIT Press, 2002); Joanna Russ, *The Female Man*.

37. See Gill Kirkup, Linda Janes, Kathryn Woodward, and Fiona Hovenden, eds., *The Gendered Cyborg: A Reader* (New York: Routledge, 2000).

38. Cordwainer Smith, "Scanners Live in Vain," *Fantasy Book* (January 1950), reprinted in *Isaac Asimov Presents the Great SF Stories*, vol. 12, ed. Isaac Asimov and Martin H. Greenberg (New York: Daw, 1984), 70–104.

39. In the 1960 formulation of the cyborg concept by Clynes and Kline, a cyborg would not need to have the constant oversight of mechanical and organic processes that the scanners display in the story. The technological processes would be automatic or autonomic. Clynes and Kline, "Cyborgs and Space."

40. David Ely, *Seconds* (New York: Signet, 1964).

41. See Stephen Farber, "*Seconds* by John Frankenheimer," *Film Quarterly* 20.2 (Winter 1966–1967): 25–28 (25).

42. The line is from Henry David Thoreau's *Walden*, in which he describes men as enslaved to work: "The mass of men lead lives of quiet desperation. What is called resignation is confirmed desperation." He describes going to live by Walden Pond so as to "live deliberately."

43. See Anna Krugovoy Silver, "The Cyborg Mystique: 'The Stepford Wives' and Second Wave Feminism," *Women's Studies Quarterly* 30.1–2 (Spring–Summer 2002): 60–76.

44. We also find this connection in autobiographical writings in which women describe themselves as robots before their feminist emancipation. See Jo C. Searles, "From Robot to

Roarer," in *Private Voices, Public Lives: Women Speak on the Literary Life*, ed. Nancy Owen Nelson and Jane Tompkins (Denton: University of North Texas Press, 1995), 72–85.

45. Jane Elliott, "Stepford USA: Second-Wave Feminism, Domestic Labor, and the Representation of National Time," *Cultural Critique* 70 (Fall 2008): 32–62 (38).

46. See Dani Cavallaro, *The Cinema of Mamoru Oshii: Fantasy, Technology, and Politics* (Jefferson, NC: McFarland, 2006).

47. This depiction changes in the second film, when Kusanagi is primarily disembodied and lives on the Net. See Steven T. Brown, "Machinic Desires: Hans Bellmer's Dolls and the Technological Uncanny in *Ghost in the Shell 2: Innocence*," *Mechademia* 3 (2008): 222–53.

48. Jean-Paul Sartre, *Existentialism Is a Humanism*, trans. Carol Macomber (New Haven: Yale University Press, 2007), 20. The title essay was a lecture given by Sartre in 1945 and published in 1946.

49. Sartre states: "Man is nothing other than his own project" (ibid., 37).

50. Written and produced by Ronald D. Moore and directed by Michael Rymer, the reimagined *Battlestar Galactica* aired first as a four-hour miniseries (December 8, 2003) before going to four seasons, numerous spin-offs, and Web episodes, and a prequel series titled *Caprica* (2010). Episodes from the reimagined *Battlestar Galactica* series will be marked by BSG followed by the episode title, season, and episode number.

51. Created by Glen A. Larson, the twenty-four episodes of the original series aired on ABC from September 17, 1978, to April 29, 1979. Three feature-length films were also released in 1978, 1979, and 1980, revising and extending some of the original episodes. For an analysis of themes and contexts in the series, see John Kenneth Muir, *An Analytical Guide to Television's* Battlestar Galactica (Jefferson, NC: McFarland, 1999).

52. Despite being largely instrumental, or referred to as "pets" (BSG, "Six Degrees of Separation," 1.7), the Raiders can potentially learn from their experience in battle and use that training after they are destroyed and resurrected in new bodies. In BSG, "Scar" (2.15), one such individuated Raider has developed a highly personal battle style in fighting the Colonial Vipers.

53. For the horror genre undertones of this depiction, see Alison Pierce, "Uncanny Cylons: Resurrection and Bodies of Horror," in Tiffany Potter, and C. W. Marshall, eds., *Cylons in America: Critical Studies in* Battlestar Galactica (New York: Continuum, 2008), 118–30.

54. BSG, "You Can't Go Home Again," 1.5.

55. A blood test is designed to detect the difference between humans and Cylons, but the results are compromised and the test is never used successfully (BSG, "Bastille Day," 1.3).

56. BSG, "Crossroads, Part 2," 3.20.

57. BSG, "No Exit," 4.17.

58. The depiction of the Final Five Cylons changes slightly after their status is unveiled and begins to conform to more traditional expectations. The revelation that Chief Tyrol has in fact not fathered a child is one of these elements, in my view, and shows a retroactive sensitivity to the deployment of the male Cylons' sexuality (BSG, "A Disquiet Follows My Soul," 4.12).

59. See Amy Kind, "'I'm Sharon, but I'm a Different Sharon': The Identity of Cylons," in Battlestar Galactica *and Philosophy: Knowledge Here Begins Out There*, ed. Jason T. Eberl (Oxford: Blackwell, 2008), 64–74. On Sharon as a mother, see Hu Pegues, "Miss Cylon."

60. Woody Coulart and Wesley Y. Joe, "Inverted Perspectives on Politics and Morality in *Battlestar Galactica*," in Hassler and Wilcox, *New Boundaries in Political Science Fiction*, 179–97.

61. Since the Cylon society includes metal Cylon models, un-individuated humanoid Cylons, and individuated humanoid Cylons, we might treat "Cylon" as a nationality rather than an ontological category. It is precisely in ontological terms that the Cylons differ from each other. See also Robert W. Moore, "'To Be a Person': Sharon Agathon and the Social Expression of Individuality," in Potter and Marshall, *Cylons in America*, 105–17.

62. See Keith McDonald, "Days of Past Futures: Kazuo Ishiguro's *Never Let Me Go* as 'Speculative Memoir,'" *Biography: An Interdisciplinary Quarterly* 30.1 (January 2007): 74–83.

63. See Myra J. Seaman, "Becoming More (than) Human: Affective Posthumanisms, Past and Future," *Journal of Narrative Theory* 37.2 (July 2007): 246–75.

64. See Leona Toker and Daniel Chertoff, "Reader Response and the Recycling of Topoi in Kazuo Ishiguro's *Never Let Me Go*," *Partial Answers: Journal of Literature and the History of Ideas* 6.1 (January 2008): 163–80.

65. Sartre, *Existentialism Is Humanism*, 23.

CONCLUSION: THE ENDS OF THE HUMAN

1. See Sheryl Hamilton, *Impersonations: Troubling the Person in Law and Culture* (Toronto: University of Toronto Press, 2009).

2. See Vivian Sobchack, "Love Machines: Boy Toys, Toy Boys, and the Oxymorons of *A.I.: Artificial Intelligence*," *Science Fiction Film and Television* 1.1 (Spring 2008): 1–13.

3. Judith Butler, *Undoing Gender* (New York: Routledge, 2004), 2–4.

INDEX

abjection: absorption as evoking state of, *154*; and fear of being enslaved, 146–48; gendered version of, 147; and metalness, 117; roboticism as absolute, 132–33, 136–37; and technology, 144. *See also* absorption

abolition/abolitionists, 119, 156–57, 159, 160, 236*n*66

absorption: and capitalism, 151; as evoking state of abjection, 154; and fear of being enslaved, 146–48; gendered version of, 147; and imagery of early cybernetic narratives, 234*n*40; and technology, 162–63. *See also* abjection

act of opening, 1–2. *See also* anatomy/anatomical gesture

Adam (biblical), 41, 42, 43, 55, 137

Adam Link—Robot (Binder), 128–30, 233*n*16

Adams, Henry, 109–10

The Adding Machine (Rice), 143

adult birth: premodern *vs.* modern, 46–48. *See also* artificial birth

Aelita: Queen of Mars (film), 140–41

Aeschylus, 51, 225*n*36

"Africanist" presence, 117

agency, 28, 73, 78–80, 81, 90, 99, 102, 104, 126, 133, 147, 169, 213

"Ages of Man," 87

aging, 190–91

A.I. Artificial Intelligence (film), 48, 127, 128, 214–15, 216*f*, 216–217, 218

AIBO (artificial dog), 11

alchemy/alchemical science, 16, 56, 58–59, 62–64, 86; in *Frankenstein*, 29, 36, 38; and reversibility, 60, 124; and the soul, 102; symbol for "man," 86–87

Alien (film), 126, 199

Aliens (film), 77

allegorization, 16; of awakening, 182; of body processes, 6; of childhood, 168, 214; of feminized electricity and sexualized magnetism, 109; in *Frankenstein*, 37, 53; of

mechanical body, 86, 87–88; of mechanical embodiment, 108; origin stories as, 39–40; in Pandora story, 48; in *R.U.R. (Rossum's Universal Robots)*, 135–36; sexual imaginary, 83; of soldiers, 168; of technological embodiment, 108; of tools, 71–72, 78; of totalitarianism, 166–67

analogy: and advent of electricity, 106–9; of blood and metal, 87–88; change in function of, 105–6; mechanical, 2–3, 6*f*, 7, 71, 73–74, 90–105; of motion and soul, 94; power of, 98; of real and mechanical people, 28; and rise of factory, 106

anatomy/anatomical gesture, 1–2, 6, 65, 72–74, 219

ancestry of artificial people, 15–16

androids, 3, 4; differences from humans, 183–84; gunslinger, 2*f*; similarity to humans, 71, 134, 183. *See also* mechanical body

animating story: circularity of, 36, 39, 53–54, 123–24; reading backward, 54–56; transhistorical consistency of, 60–66. *See also* animation; artificial birth

animation: aliveness as visible marker at moment of, 29; ancient *vs.* modern fantasies of, 4–5; association with electricity, 106–10; effigy-related rituals, 57, 62; in *Frankenstein*, 33–37; and golem, 56–57, 62–63; in Pandora story, 45, 47, 48–50; as ritualistic, 48–50; structural logic of, 63–64; and visibility, 5, 62, 103. *See also* animating story; artificial birth

anthropomorphic designs: as imitation, 18–19, 20; and simulation, 19; verisimilitude of, 19

apathy, 195

Aphrodite, 43, 45, 88

archebiosis, 226*n*54

Aristotle, 18, 44, 58, 90, 91, 92–98, 99–100, 102–3, 113, 229*n*27, 229*n*29, 229*n*31, 230*n*45

Meyrink, Gustav, 177–78
Milburn, Colin, 64
militarization, 85, 134, 138, 143
mirroring, 19, 23–24
mirror stage (Lacan), 19
miscegenation, 117
misogyny, 45, 47
mobility, using to define states of matter, 17–18
modernity: enslavement as basis of, 171; and fear of enslavement, 146; reversible/ reversibility in, 60; view on mechanical body, 104–13
Modern Times (film), 145
A Modest Proposal (Swift), 149
monarchy, hereditary, 237*n*71
Moore, C. L., 187–88
Moore, Ron, 3, 242*n*50
morality, 204
More, Hannah, 156
More, Henry, 101
Morphology of the Folktale (Propp), 26
Morris, Sarah P., 88–89
Morrison, Toni, 117
Mostow, Jonathan, 79*f*
motion: Cartesian thinking on, 91–92; involuntary, 96, 97, 230*n*37; premodern scale of, 17, 20, 23; and soul, Aristotle on, 94; visibility of mechanical, 97–98, 101; voluntary, 95, 97
Muri, Allison, 16
mysticism, 57–58
mystics, 56, 60, 62
myths, 4, 15–16, 44, 87. *See also* Pandora

nanotechnology, 64–65
narcissism, 33, 78, 138, 177, 178, 192, 215, 218
Nathaniel (character), 176–77
natural rights, forfeiture of, 151–52
Nelson, Victoria, 42
neophytes, 225*n*31
nested narratives, in *Frankenstein* (M. Shelley), 35
neuron, 96, 231*n*50
neurospasta (string-pulled/-jointed), 95, 99
Never Let Me Go (Ishiguro), 207–10, 211; elisions in, 197–98; and identity, 208–9
A New Account of Some Parts of Guinea, and the Slave Trade (Snelgrave), 148, 149, 151

Newman, William, 16
Newtonian physics, 18
New Woman, 110
New York World's Fair (1939), 9–12, 10*f*, 143
Nicomachean Ethics (Aristotle), 100
1984 (Orwell), 144
nonvoluntary motion (*ouch ekousios*), 96, 97
"No Woman Born" (C. L. Moore), 187–88, 189
Nussbaum, Martha C., 230*n*45

objecthood, 75, 117, 153, 170
objectification, 7, 123, 212–13; of animated woman, 47; fantasy of withstanding/ counteracting, 121; and fear of enslavement in modernity, 146; of female body, 188; legal, of slaves, 145, 155–56; in patriarchy, 194; as reversible, 28; of slaves, 128, 147–58; of sovereign subject, 150, 152, 153–54
objects, as reinforcing elements, 17–23
Odyssey (Homer), 224*n*24, 226*n*50
Olympia (character), 3, 176–77, 187
O'Neill, Eugene, 143–44
ontological ambiguity, 175–76, 179, 180–82, 184–85
orderliness, 73, 105
organ donation. See *Never Let Me Go* (Ishiguro)
origin stories, 86; as allegory, 39–40; explanatory displacement in, 40–42; structural isomorphism of, 41–42, 51
Oroonoko (Behn), 151–52
Orwell, George, 144
Oshii, Mamoru, 195–96
Ovid, 43, 50, 51

Paine, Thomas, 237*n*71
palindrome, 39, 54–56, 58–59, 60, 61, 124, 147
Pandora, 31, 43–47; animation process, 45, 47, 48–49; continuity with later artificial people, 46–47; creation of, 43; as metaphor, 44–45; opening of box as allegorical, 48; ritual in, 57
Paracelsus, 58–59, 62, 63
"The Paradise of Bachelors and the Tartarus of Maids" (Melville), 161
The Paradise within the Reach of All Men, without Labor, by Powers of Nature and

120–22, 123; emotional/cognitive development narrative pattern, 126–32; enslaving technologies, 159–64; enslaving technologies and cinematic robot, 164–72; ethnic and racial otherness, 117; fetishization of differences between people and robots, 171–72; foundational premise of robot-as-slave story, 115–16; and humanization, 120–21; as instruments, 117–18; legacies of chattel slavery, 116; and legal recognition of slaves, 128; racial codification, 165–67, 168; rebellion, 170–71; robots and workers, 134–44; soldier allegory, 168; stereotypes of texts about, 123; technologies of capitalism, 159–61; totalitarian allegory, 166–67; violence/rebellion, narrative pattern of, 124–26

Sliding Doors (film), 192
"smart" objects, 24
Smith, Adam, 163
Smith, Cordwainer, 188–89
Snelgrave, William, 148, 149, 151
Sobchack, Vivian, 26
The Social Contract (Rousseau), 152
social death, 152
social exclusion, 127, 128
social inclusion, 127–28
socialism, 134, 135, 143
social justice, 51–52, 75, 116
social life, mechanicity of, 177
Sociology of the South; or, The Failure of Free Society (Fitzhugh), 154
Socrates, 229n29
Sonny (character), 164–66, 167–69
Sony, 11
soul, 5, 18, 31, 41, 62, 68, 85, 111, 112, 181–82, 215–16; body-soul relationship, Aristotle on, 90, 91–92, 93, 95, 97–100; in *Frankenstein*, 35–36; immaterial, 101, 102–3, 107; vitality of, 104
sovereign subject, fantasy of, 153–55
Sparko (robot dog), 9–10, 143
Spartacus (film), 167
Spielberg, Steven, 48, 127, 128, 214
spiritualist possession, 111
spontaneous generation, 58
Spooner (character), 167–68
Springer, Claudia, 234n40

Stafford, Barbara Maria, 105, 222n22
Star Trek: The Next Generation (television series), 81, 119, 127, 144
Star Wars (film series), 154, 167
Steiner, Deborah Tarn, 45
stem-cell research, 204
The Stepford Wives (film), 3, 192–95, 193f
stereotypes: of African Americans, 119; of artificial persons, 3, 4, 46, 68–69, 70–71, 182; in cautionary tales, 32; cultural, 25, 26, 119; gender, 81–82, 187, 188; gendered fears and, 147; of mastery and supremacy, 127; of materiality, 22, 24; of plantation "darkie," 130; of slavery, 123, 131; of unruliness, 50–51
St. Leon (Godwin), 59
stories, as reinforcing elements, 17, 23
Stowe, Harriet Beecher, 119
strebla, 96
structural isomorphism, of origin stories, 41–42, 51
structuralist analyses of popular culture, 26
subjectification, 7, 145, 146, 194, 213
sublimation, 41, 63, 83
suicide, 37, 38, 148, 187, 192, 203
Superman (character), 143
Supreme Court, U.S., 120
Suvin, Darko, 26
Swift, Jonathan, 149, 150
system of dispersion, 26
systems research, 25

T-800 cyborg, 3, 77, 78–80, 79f
tabula rasa, 44
Talos (mythical metal man), 15, 87, 222n16, 228n15
technological embodiment, 108
techno-utopian arguments, 77, 163
Telotte, J. P., 75
The Terminator (film), 3, 31, 78
Terminator 3: Rise of the Machines (film), 79f
terrorists, 167, 199, 203, 207
Tetsuo: The Iron Man (film), 199
Theatre Guild, 136f, 140f, 141, 143–44
"The Moors" (bronze automata), 158
Theogony (Hesiod), 43–44, 224n17
theurgic rituals, 42
"thing criticism," 16
Thoreau, Henry David, 241n42

ABOUT THE AUTHOR

DESPINA KAKOUDAKI is an associate professor of literature at American University, where she teaches courses in literature, film, and the history of science and technology. With Brad Epps she coedited *All about Almodóvar: A Passion for Cinema* (University of Minnesota Press, 2009) and has published articles on contemporary Hollywood cinema, race and melodrama in action and disaster films, robots and cyborgs, and the military role of the pinup in World War II.